# *Bay View,*

# An American Idea

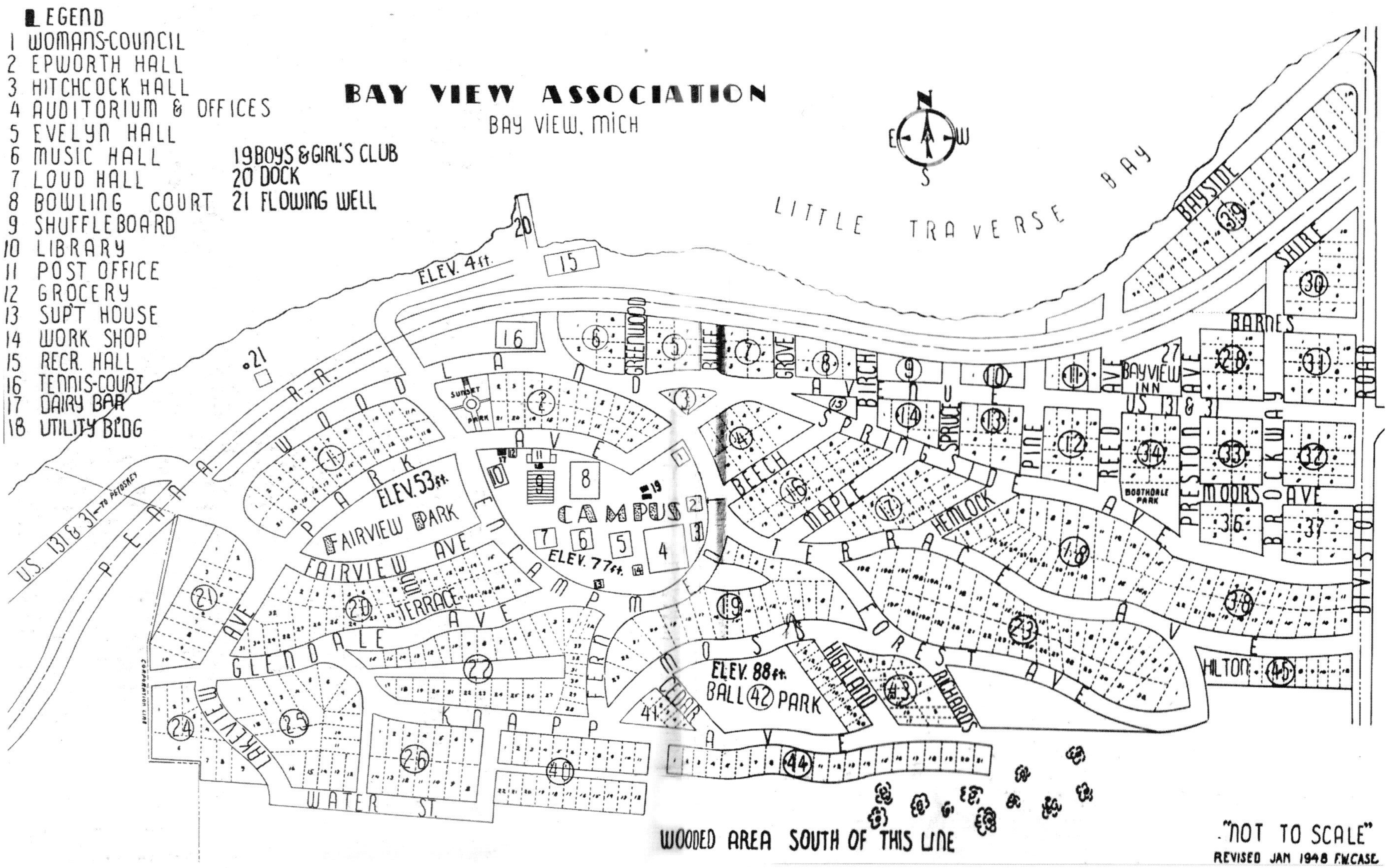
BAY VIEW ASSOCIATION
BAY VIEW, MICH
LEGEND
1 WOMANS-COUNCIL
2 EPWORTH HALL
3 HITCHCOCK HALL
4 AUDITORIUM & OFFICES
5 EVELYN HALL
6 MUSIC HALL
7 LOUD HALL
8 BOWLING COURT
9 SHUFFLEBOARD
10 LIBRARY
11 POST OFFICE
12 GROCERY
13 SUP'T HOUSE
14 WORK SHOP
15 RECR. HALL
16 TENNIS-COURT
17 DAIRY BAR
18 UTILITY BLDG
19 BOYS & GIRL'S CLUB
20 DOCK
21 FLOWING WELL
N
E
W
S
LITTLE TRAVERSE BAY
ELEV. 4 ft.
ELEV. 53 ft.
ELEV. 77 ft.
ELEV. 88 ft.
CAMPUS
FAIRVIEW PARK
BALL 42 PARK
BAYVIEW INN
BOOTHDALE PARK
SUNSET PARK
US 131 & 31
US 131 & 31 — TO PETOSKEY
BAYSIDE
SHIRE
BARNES
ROAD
DIVISION
BROCKWAY
AVE
MOORS
PRESTON
REED
PINE
SPRUCE
BIRCH
GROVE
BLUFF
GREENWOOD
BEECH
MAPLE
HEMLOCK
HILTON
RICHARDS
HIGHLAND
CEDAR
FERN
TERRACE
FAIRVIEW AVE
GLENDALE
LAKEVIEW
WATER ST.
KNAPP
PARK
WOODLAND
FOREST AVE
ENCAMPMENT
SPRING
PEARL
R.R.
CORPORATION LINE
WOODED AREA SOUTH OF THIS LINE
"NOT TO SCALE"
REVISED JAN 1948 F.W.CASE

# Bay View,
# AN AMERICAN IDEA

BY
MARY JANE DOERR

FOREWARD BY
DR. PHILIP P. MASON

The Priscilla Press
Allegan Forcst, Michigan
2010

**Cover image by Robert Cleveland.**

**Layout and design of text and cover by**
**Deborah M. Neumann.**

**Please direct any questions or comments concerning this publications to:**
**Mary Jane Doerr**
**mjdoerr@sbcglobal.net**
**MaryJaneDoerr/Facebook**

**ISBN: 978-1-886167-31-5**

# Table of Contents

# Foreword

Chautauqua, an adult education movement, began on the shores of Chautauqua Lake near Jamestown, New York, in 1874 and soon spread to all parts of the United States especially into semi-rural areas. In the beginning, it was closely associated with the Methodist Church and other religious organizations and the programs emphasized Christian instruction and preaching. Later, secular subjects became more popular and summer assemblies were established, featuring lectures by nationally known authorities on current affairs, politics, prison reform, child labor and women's suffrage. Music was an important aspect of Chautauquas, presenting performances by orchestras, bands, opera and theater troupes and singing groups. In order to accommodate large audiences, some areas built permanent facilities, while other locations erected large temporary tents that could be moved from place to place for summer programs.

The popularity of Chautaquas and their impact on rural America and on American cultural history has captured the attention of many historians and writers. Hundreds of journal articles and newspaper feature stories, as well as popular and scholarly books, have been written and published on the subject. The founding Chautauqua program in New York has received the most widespread attention by these writers, though other local Chautauqua assemblies have been studied as well.

Michigan also had Chautauqua assemblies and camp meetings located throughout the state. The most prominent one was located in Bay View, near Petoskey, in the north western part of the Lower Peninsula. It was founded in 1875 as a camp meeting site, sponsored by the Methodist Church, but it soon expanded its scope to include a summer assembly program that featured nationally known celebrities who spoke on such popular topics as women's suffrage, prison reform, child labor and current social and political affairs.

As the Bay View program became more recognized, it attracted an increasing number of members and participants from all parts of Michigan and other mid-western states. The Bay View Musical Festival started in 1886 has operated continuously since that time. A summer university program, accredited by the University of Michigan, was established in 1888 and correspondence courses started in 1893, along with the publication of *The Bay View Magazine.*

Until now, no comprehensive history of the Bay View Chautauqua has been written. Mary Jane Doerr has filled this void with an exhaustively researched and well-written study, *Bay View, An American Idea*. She utilized the Bay View Archives, collected and founded by the author's mother, Jane Doerr, and researched other local, state and national archival and library institutions to locate relevant material. To supplement the published and archival sources, Mary Jane Doerr and others conducted a series of oral history interviews with individuals and families that had been involved in the Bay View Chautauqua Assembly. She gives special attention also to a study of the history of the community, its hotels, summer cottages, conference facilities and the development of Bay View as a resort center.

For students who are interested in American culture, as well as the operation of the Bay View Chautauqua Assembly, the author has brought together detailed information on a variety of topics. She describes the contributions and challenges facing some of its leaders, namely, John Hall, Bishop Raymond Wade, Dr. Hugh Kennedy and Dr. Wesley Hager, and devotes special attention to the nationally known celebrities who gave lectures, musical performances and religious presentations. She provides biographical information on many of the several hundred speakers who addressed the assemblies between 1885 and 2009. Typical of the women speakers, for example, were Jane Addams, Maud Ballington Booth, Mary Livermore, Margaret Sangster, Dr. Anna Howard Shaw, Lucinda Hinsdale Stone, and Frances Willard, all respected leaders of the women's suffrage movement.

The Bay View Chautauqua Assembly also attracted other distinguished national figures, and the book's appendix gives a detailed list of the preachers, political leaders, authors, social reformers and educators who came to speak. William Jennings Bryan, for example, was often a featured assembly lecturer. Booker T. Washington, Jacob Riis, Russell Conwell, Carl Sandburg, Stanley Kresge, Bruce Catton and Lorado Taft attracted large audiences at their presentations. The musical performers were also popular with the assembly members, among whom were the Fisk Jubilee Singers, the Detroit Symphony Orchestra, the Dixie Jubilee Singers, African Boys Choir, Williams' Jubilee Singers, Gladys Swarthout, Ossip Gabrilovitsch and James Melton.

Doerr gave special attention to the Blanshard brothers, Brand and Paul. They lived at a family cottage in Bay View and from 1909-1914 covered news events for the *Daily Resorter* relating to the community, the assembly, its speakers and their topics. They met with and interviewed featured speakers, who during these years included William Jennings Bryan, Helen Keller, Dr. John Harvey Kellogg, Grace Hemingway and nationally known reformers such as the Reverend Charles Stelzle, Charles Zublin and Dr. William Sadler. According to Rufus Blanshard,

Paul's youngest son whom Ms. Doerr interviewed in 2000, his father and uncle were deeply influenced by their experiences at Bay View, and their contacts with many of the speakers. Brand Blanshard, who became a distinguished philosopher at Yale, and Paul, a well respected writer, editor and reformer, left a magnificent account of life in Bay View during their tenure there.

This *"American Idea"* is a valuable addition to the literature on the Chautauqua movement in the United States. It serves as a model and inspiration for other local communities to follow when describing their own Chautauqua associations. Mary Jane Doerr is to be commended for her endeavors.

Philip P. Mason
*Distinguished Professor of History Emeritus*
WAYNE STATE UNIVERSITY
Detroit, Michigan

***Local papers estimated the ferries carried up to 75,000 customers a month.*** *(Author's Collection)*

# Acknowledgements

Growing up in Bay View during the 1950s and 1960s when many of the old Victorian cottages were vacant even during the summer months, I had an enduring sense of the mystery of a silent past. That same curiosity led my mother, Jane Park Doerr, to establish the Bay View Archives which resulted in many national and state awards being conferred upon her.

Many experts have assisted me with this project. On the Internet, I "met" Jane and Rufus Blanshard. Rufus was the son of the "Great Unitarian" Paul Blanshard and the nephew of American philosopher (Percy) Brand Blanshard who both helped document Bay View history during the early twentieth century. Jane, a copy editor, and Rufus clearly understood the need for this history and enthusiastically supported it. David Glick, retired senior administrator of the Edison Institute in Dearborn (Henry Ford Museum and Greenfield Village now called The Henry Ford), provided focused criticism. Glick lives in the Chautauqua community of Lakeside, Ohio, and has authored articles on the Chautauqua movement. Arts and Crafts historian and Bay View resident, Dr. Beverly Brandt, professor at Arizona State University, provided expertise on the manuscript and much appreciated advice and management of the publishing process, having just published her own book *The Craftsman and the Critic*. Despite her own busy schedule, Dr. Brandt was very supportive in meeting with my publishers Larry and Priscilla Massie.

Much of the research was done at the State of Michigan Library. Suzanne Ternan made countless trips to Lansing with me to photocopy newspaper articles and made available her historical research and photographs of Evelyn Hall. Michigan native and longtime Bay View resident, Liza Lee Collins, volunteered years of her time as a professional journalist, editor and librarian with much needed insight and invaluable help. Her husband Richard Adams provided wonderful assistant with the computer programming for the manuscript.

Through many long summers of extensive research, the staff of the Petoskey Public Library – former director Rex Miller and his staff Barbara Cook, Mary Sue Prantera, Drew Cherven and John Alberts - provided endless assistance. At the Auburn Hills Library of Oakland Community College, the late librarian Joyce Zurel found rare books from libraries all over the country. Dennis Souter provided technical advice on research tools. At Jackson's Ella Sharp Museum, archivist Jim Zuleski supplied information on Samuel Oliver Knapp, Mary T. Lathrap and the

First United Methodist Church of Jackson. Author and librarian M. Christine Byron aided me at the Grand Rapids Public Library with materials on The Woman's Christian Temperance Union.

Michigan's State Historic Preservation Officer Brian D. Conway and his staff made available records concerning the Bay View landmark designation. Former State Historic Preservation Officer and author Kathryn Eckert shared information about the landmark effort and architect W.E.N. Hunter. Benjamin Levy, former director of the Landmark Program at the National Park Service, supported this project authoring letters and offering suggestions. Lynne Francis of the American Institute of Architects Michigan supplied information and photographs concerning Hunter.

I wish to thank: Biruta Adul for locating the Simons Communion Service in Riga, Latvia; Barbara Asbury for information on Bay View's Morning Council; Dr. and Mrs. James Beard for reviewing the manuscript; Marcia Busyn for providing a brochure on Harbor Point and Irma T. Jones; Jo Ellyn Clarey for consultation on the Michigan's women's movement and review of the manuscript; Brian Collins for his continuous encouragement and help with historical pictures; John Maxwell Doerr for critique of the manuscript; Mark Drinkall and Kathy Duquette for research material at the University of Michigan Bentley Historical Library; Robert Hamilton and Mike McCleer for information about Hunter churches; the late Lowell Kosloskey for expertise on Emmet County records, documents and genealogical sources; Lois Larsen Miller for knowledge of the Bay View Theatre Arts Department; Kathy Palmer for documentation on the Methodist Episcopal Church of Traverse City; Nancy Rajala for information on John Manley Hall; Peter Sims for review of the chapter on music; Julie Stivers for her brochure on Charles Fallass; the late Gertrude Solms for early history of the Bay View Association and Panhellenic; Ruth Tomkinson for facts about the Bay View Campus Club; Doris VandenBelt for updated history of the Bay View Woman's Council; and former Michigan State Archivist Geneva Wiskemann for review of the manuscript.

Candace Eaton Fitzsimons, foresighted former director of the Little Traverse Historical Society supported the project from the beginning. The entire board, past and present, of the Little Traverse Historical Society has been a source of constant inspiration with their dedication to the history of Emmet County. Zelda Gilman contributed to research of the early newspaper stories.

Finally, I want to thank Ken Winter, long time editor of the Petoskey *News-Review* and my editor Babette Stenuis Stolz for supporting me as a special writer. My thirty years of interviews for articles for that newspaper plus the newspaper's past publications dating back to 1874 formed the basis for this story.

Lastly, this book would never have been published without the assistance of Dr. P. Philip Mason, longtime member of the board of Wayne State University Press, former director of the Walter P. Reuther Library at Wayne State University, author of many books on history, and professor of history at Wayne State University. From his first reading of the manuscript to its publication, he was a constant advocate.

Many people have played an important part in Bay View's history. While some are readily known and honored for their efforts, the accomplishments of others have disappeared in the exhaustive annals of lost history. To all, recognized and unrecognized, I offer my heartfelt gratitude.

# Introduction

One lovely summer evening my niece gave me a book *Saving the Summer Cottage*. This "hot" new read gives points on how families can save their treasured heritage, the family cottage, even when siblings marry, have children, and the family outgrows the dwelling. I had read *The Big House*, another book about a generational home, where family members deal with financial concerns, property taxes, and societal changes that forbid the confluence of family traditions and contemporary living. Also, I have witnessed firsthand how families can be split by arguments over shared property.

Her point was obvious. "Don't sell our family cottage". Our family summer home is located in Bay View, Michigan. The community is a Chautauqua assembly and camp meeting with roots deep within our country's history. Somehow, the community has managed to survive the Depression and the destructive era between the world wars that lead to the death of the Chautauqua era, as well as the loathsome years of the 1950s and 60s when historic properties went unappreciated. My niece and her husband choose to raise their children in this summer community, and, in doing so, she feels their lives have been enriched in ways not otherwise possible.

This indefinable life-changing element found in these Chautauqua communities which literally impacted every American town after the Civil War until the Depression, tends to elude writers, sociologists, historians, scholars, everyone. Traditionally, writers have been turned off by communities such as Chautauqua in New York State as being "too" perfect. Sociologists have called them "white utopias" that marginalized Native Americans, blacks, Jews, Catholics, immigrants, the poor and all the less fortunate. Historians struggle with accounts of these places as local records are often inaccurate or nonexistent. Despite its problematic initial layer of records, scholars and doctoral candidates have now become intrigued with this American phenomenon and are drawing conclusions that could be ill founded.

"What is Bay View?" Reverend Dr. Wesley Hager, a former president of the Bay View Association, once asked. Answering his own question, he wrote: "Bay View is a prayer, a dream, a hope. Bay View is life at its very best, life that is rich and full and abundant and deep and always growing. Bay View exists in the hearts of the people who have enjoyed its surroundings, benefited from its culture, partaken of its activities, and profited from its rich religious heritage."[1] Working as a special writer for the Petoskey *News-Review* for over thirty years covering Bay View, has given me a wide knowledge of the community's mystique with its "inconvenient" history of skewed secondary sources and difficult to research primary sources, besides its myths and legends.

Historically, Bay View is an example of two strictly American phenomena: the camp meeting and the Chautauqua assembly. Both were national movements that swept across this grief-stricken country after the debilitating Civil War which author Robert H. Wiebe described in his book, *The Search for Order,* (1967) as a chaotic time. The country was moving from a predominantly agrarian society to an urban culture. Traditional values were tested in the decadence of urban communal areas and found wanting in the polluted, industrialized cities. Moral integrity was discarded in favor of the pragmatic Darwinian principle of the "survival of the fittest."

During this time, Bay View was established in 1875 as a camp meeting. Ten years later, a cultural Chautauqua assembly movement emerged in 1885 which immediately became a magnet for preachers, national celebrities and assembly-goers. The "Big Sunday" camp meetings were a local custom not found at the thousands of assemblies that speckled America's landscape. The three-pronged "Bay View System of Popular Education" included an assembly, university (1888) and correspondence course (1893) modeled after Chautauqua's education program. It attracted the middle-class to hear celebrated thinkers, take classes at the Summer University and subscribe to the Bay View Reading Circle and *Bay View Magazine* (1893-1922).

Pioneering the first university-level summer school in Michigan, the Bay View Summer University offered the only such program in northern Michigan until 1959. It gave area teachers an accessible opportunity to update their teaching credentials. In 1935, the Summer University was accredited by the University of Michigan, paving the way for general acceptance by colleges and universities nationwide. The Bay View Music Festival, begun in 1886 under the Summer University, is now the oldest continuously-operating summer music festival in the United States. The University's 300-piece Egyptian Collection is now a substantial part of the antiquities at the University of Michigan's Kelsey Museum of Archaeology.

As a watering place, Bay View was not an escape. It was a setting where audiences heard first hand of the tarnished facets of their Gilded Age. The assembly featured a potpourri of entertainment and lecturers on a wide variety of social causes and injustices. Economic socialist Richard T. Ely spoke out against the destruction of human values while, on the same platform, Reverend Russell H. Conwell preached the gospel of wealth. The all-black Fisk Jubilee Singers entertained, while international newspaper correspondent George Kennan lectured on the hardships faced by Russian peasants.

These cultural and religious activities took place in vintage Victorian buildings surrounded by almost 450 distinctively different summer homes and the Bay View woods. Untouched in nearly a century, the woods are now part of some of the oldest forestland left in Michigan and constitute one of the largest wooded tracts remaining in Emmet County. The entire Bay View grounds with its layout of parks, public areas, curving streets, preserved woods and rich Victorian architectural heritage is an antidote for urban sprawl. In recognition of its unique architecture, romantic physical design and historical significance, Bay View was listed on the State of Michigan Register of Historic Sites on June 5, 1957 and placed on the Register of National Historic Sites in 1972. In 1980, the Michigan Society of Architects designated Bay View one of Michigan's "50 Most Significant Structures." In 1987, the National Park Service made Bay View the first American Chautauqua assembly to be designated a National Historic Landmark. That designation represented a resurgence of interest in historic property in Michigan and was a culmination of the state's largest community landmark effort to date.

When I first began writing in the late 1970s for the local newspaper, I thought Bay View's history had been thoroughly investigated because of the number of books published on the subject. My first clue that some of Bay View's history was undiscovered, was when I found the enormous number of nationally significant women who appeared on the Bay View platform in the 1890s (nearly 200 in all), a fact that had literally been ignored or incorrectly reported in all accounts. In one history where the subject was addressed, the women's titles and affiliations were wrong. Women such as Reverend Dr. Anna Howard Shaw, Jennie June Croly, Frances Willard, and Mary Livermore, who played tremendous roles in our country's history, and women like Mary T. Lathrap and Anna Smeed Benjamin, who changed Michigan women's history, visited Bay View many times, addressing hundreds of women each time. To learn why these women considered this an important stop on their summer speaking schedules, I had to find original sources.

In doing so, I learned that under John M. Hall's leadership as the first director of the Bay View Assembly, the women's movement was so active in Bay View that, in the 1890s, it was considered the regional summer headquarters of the Woman's Christian Temperance Union (WCTU). The locally-based Woman's Council was the motivating force behind the establishment of the Michigan Federation of Women's Clubs. Decades before women had any opportunity for a higher education, the correspondence course, the Bay View Reading Circle and *Bay View Magazine,* reached over 125,000 readers nationally and were adopted as the educational program of over 1000 women's clubs across America.

In interviews for the newspaper, I discovered more missing history. From a meeting with a relative of Ernest Hemingway, Sterling Sanford, I discovered not only more about the Hemingway family and their close relationship to Bay View, but also about the Blanshard brothers, Paul and Brand. In reading Paul's books, I found that it was from his experience as a writer for the local paper and his years in Petoskey with its essentially two school systems that lead him to challenge the country's trend toward support of Catholic schools in his controversial 1949 best seller, *American Freedom and Catholic Power*.

From Homer Larsen, I heard of the prejudice against blacks in the 1930s, nothing surprising. Countee Cullen was a guest of Larsen's both times the great poet appeared on the Bay View platform. That fact led me immediately to the next question where had the Fisk Jubilee Singers, the Dixie Jubilee Singers, the Virginia Jubilee Singers, the Williams' Jubilee Singers, the African Boy Choir, Booker T. Washington, the Jewish rabbis and the Native Americans stayed when they came? Some speculate that the Williams' Jubilee Singers in 1914 stayed at the Petoskey's "black hotel" and only sang the spirituals for their white audiences. Both ideas are obviously wrong since the black couple, Mr. and Mrs. Paine, didn't open their hotel and nightclub on Michigan Street in Petoskey until the 1920s or possibly later, according to Al Gruler. Also, the original Fisk Jubilee Singers, who appeared four times in Bay View before World War I, were sons and daughters of slaves and introduced the world to "spirituals" achieving great acclaim in the epitome of the music world, Germany. I have to assume they were proud of their heritage. In the Bay View Archives, there is a picture taken at the Bay View beach of several fasionable ladies surrounding a handsome young black man, apparently proud of their association with a celebrity on the Bay View Assembly stage.

Other events in Emmet County led me to further question commonly held beliefs. There was the educated black family, the Morgans, who came out of slavery and settled in northern Michigan to become successful brick manufacturers and helped found and plat Boyne City. As for the Native Americans, there were the wonderful accounts of how the Odawa sailors always won the statewide Harbor Springs regattas in the 1890s. Each year, they registered for the races, competed with some of our country's wealthiest industrial families and always came in first due to their superior seamanship. Then, I found a letter from a daughter of a Bay View founder telling of her father's friendship with Chief Petoskey. It was Petoskey's granddaughter who played the organ for the camp meetings wearing her bright red dress. The letter writer told how her two brothers' first language was Odawa - not English. From other accounts, I found out about Odawa-speaking Bay View campers such as Mrs. Ralph Connable who was fluent in Odawa. The conclusion was obvious - there must have been much interaction between the Odawas and the Methodists to enable the Methodist newcomers to become fluent in the Odawa language.

Further proof of the interactivity came from EBay where I found a picture of Chief Petoskey seated on the Speaker's Stand in the middle of the Bay View campground. In one of Frances Willard's books, there was a story about Chief Petoskey. Furthermore, Chief Andrew Blackbird of Harbor Springs was featured on the 1887 Chautauqua assembly. Obviously, my research was leading away from commonly held beliefs of the marginalization of the blacks and the Odawas in the early days. What happened? What caused the change between the time of Chief Petoskey and Countee Cullen? Besides these inconsistencies, I discovered fun loving, rather indulgent religious attitudes permeating early newspaper accounts of the camp meetings and assembly events belying the traditional accounts of religious severity.

Then, I faced my biggest challenge. My research showed a large body of published information about the Bay View Association to be inaccurate, which meant I had to find reliable primary sources, prove the mistakes and document the factual information before making any attempt at a discussion of the relevancy of the topic to the country's history or that of the state of Michigan. Not only was the first layer of documentation difficult to find, as it was spread all over the country, there was an entire layer of published material which included many inaccurate assumptions based on erroneous conclusions. My purpose then for writing this book was to investigate Bay View's history and evaluate its impact based on research from as many primary sources as possible. For me, this was an absolute necessity so that publications now coming out can be based in fact. I decided upon chronological organization for clarity sake combining that approach within the subject areas.

In the first chapter, I address the possible reasons why volumes of people from all parts of the world came to Petoskey during the late 1800s. One of those early visitors was Samuel O. Knapp, a leader in the copper rush in the Upper Peninsula. I credit him with convincing members of both synods of the Michigan Methodist Episcopal Church to form a Michigan campground in Petoskey. I make the case that Knapp, as an amateur horticulturalist, laid Bay View out in the Romantic style of landscape design, a major reason for its survival over a century and a quarter and its designation as a National Historic Landmark. In chapter two, I orient Bay View as part of the national camp meeting craze, which actually dates back to the Revolutionary War but was wildly embraced after the Civil War. I credit Reverend Fayette L. Thompson for much of the success of the camp meeting. In the third chapter, I introduce John Manley Hall, the first and foremost director of Bay View's Chautauqua Assembly, and his leadership in developing a nationally known assembly. Although some histories center on other personalities, I make the case that it was Hall with his creativity, resourcefulness and inspiration who established all of the present-day Bay View programs and departments. I found his enormous ingenuity and open-mindedness brought in diverse talent including blacks, Native Americans, musicians, lecturers, thinkers, politicians of all convictions, and people from all points of view. I promote the concept that talent was selected on availability, significance and fees rather than a cohesive or planned agenda or ideology. The fourth chapter presents the scope of Hall's "Bay View idea" of self improvement as opposed to the Chautauqua ideal of a "vacation with a purpose." Two young men who grew up under Hall's educational program, Paul and Brand Blanshard, are discussed in chapter five. These two men who became international leaders in their respective fields exemplify how the popular ideas promoted in Bay View had major influence on our country's thought and philosophy. In chapter six, *Women in Council*, I address the here-to-forth unexplored and extensive Bay View women's movement, showing its importance. Some have proposed that this subject would be best addressed separately. However, the movement is historically based in the Chautauqua movement and is an integral part of the Bay View story. Alone, it would lose its significance. In chapter seven, I discuss why Bay View was not as seriously affected as other Chautauqua assemblies during the years between the wars, attributing it to the leadership of Dr. Hugh Kennedy. Although not a major figure in the nation-wide church or the movement, he accomplished what no one else could at any other Chautauqua. He maintained Bay View without debt or bankruptcy and showed surpluses in the budget and gave tax refunds to the cottagers during the depth of the Depression. In chapter eight, I show how Bay View was affected by events in Eastern Europe after World War II, attributing the continued existence of the community to an internationally-known bishop of the Methodist Church, Dr. Raymond J. Wade.

Recently, Chautauqua assemblies have been evaluated by four pillars of religion, education, recreation and culture. Chapter nine is about one of these pillars – recreation - and discusses reasons why this Bay View program is the largest and most successful among all the assemblies still in existence. In chapter ten, I consider the pillar of culture which since the 1940s, has centered on the Bay View Music Festival. Today, the Bay View Department of Performing Arts includes the festival and the Theatre Arts Department, and Bay View is one of only two Chautauquas that mounts its own productions, not relying on "road shows". I consider how this has come about despite continual financial crises, inconsistent leadership, continual reorganization and lack of fund raising or grants. Also, I address why this aspect of culture has remained prominent from 1945 until the 1990s. In chaper eleven, I tell about how Bay View provided northern Michigan's only college-level classes for nearly 70 years. In the final chapter twelve, I give an accounting of the controversy surrounding the preservation of Bay View's history and its physical attributes through the National Historic Landmark designation and a disputed highway project. A subsequent lawsuit over US-31 in 1988, which caused deep rifts within Emmet County, has since been cited by nearly 200 court cases throughout America.

Boosterism can be a pitfall when considering the history of a misunderstood place full of unsupported myths and historical inaccuracies. Giving a bus tour one day to a group of New Orleans tourists on their way to the Odawa Casino, I took them through Bay View, pointing out the summer home of Louisiana Governor Huey Long's family. The group was stunned. The tour leader told me that she had been through Bay View three times and never understood the place. When *Detroit Free Press* special writer Thomas BeVier covered the Bishop John Shelby Spong lectureship on July 23, 2004, he referred to Bay View as largely Republican and religiously conservative, implying that it was incongruous for the association to sponsor a preacher such as the "Episcopalian champion of gay and lesbian rights" on the assembly platform. His assumption couldn't have been less accurate.

Understanding and defining Chautauqua-like places, categorizing the movement into modern groupings such as education, culture, religion, and recreation, and avoiding boosterism denies the nature of the movement - freedom and individualism - and perhaps is not possible. I have hopefully achieved an historical explanation of this northern Michigan story while pointing out the shortcomings of the Bay View experience while dwelling on its contributions. Awhile ago, I asked my grandniece why she wanted to come to Bay View each summer and not go to camps near her home. She said: "Because here, I am free." In those few words lie the aspect of what may be the defining element of the Bay View idea, the Chautauqua ideal, the camp meeting and the reverence for our summer homes. This is a place where we find a sense of freedom from our complex world with its demands and restrictions.

The American philosopher Brand Blanshard and his brother Paul compared the philosophy of Bay View with its landscape in 1911. "The Bay View Idea is like the cascading terraces, ever upward."[2] The Bay View experience is not just a "vacation with a purpose," but one of self-improvement for those who understand the intent and gain from its significance.

This idea embodies the continual striving for personal betterment and is the philosophical basis for the programs of the Bay View Association: religious, educational, recreational and cultural. In this time of national concern and strife, it is as author David McCullough concluded in his 1993 address to New York's Chautauqua Assembly. This is indeed a time when all America needs "a watering place."[3]

— CHAPTER ONE —

# A Watering Place

Along the shores of Little Traverse Bay on the northwest coast of Michigan's Lower Peninsula when Woodrow Wilson was president, a young Bay View resident named Victor Blandford took regular walks to Petoskey's mineral well on the Bear River. Blandford was a rather shy individual with the inquisitive mind of a man who later invented the white-flame burner. On one of these walks he struck up a provocative conversation with a particularly discerning gentleman. Blandford was inspired by the nature of the conversation and mentioned it to a friend who informed him that he had been talking with the vice president of the United States Thomas R. Marshall.[1]

***Vice President Thomas R. Marshall (1913-1921) vacationed in Bay View and Petoskey starting in the 1890s until his death in 1925.*** *(Author's collection)*

Famous for his wit, Marshall was known for his story of two brothers. "One ran away to sea, the other was elected vice president, and nothing was ever heard of either of them again." He may have been a *persona non grata* in Washington, but in Petoskey he was not only a regular visitor but a celebrity. So, the next time Blandford saw his new friend, he asked Marshall why he hadn't identified himself. Marshall told Blandford that people acted differently toward him when they found out who he was. Blandford continued seeing Marshall daily, but their future conversations never had the spontaneity of the first encounter.

Given the turmoil in Washington during the Wilson years of the Great War and his estrangement from his aloof superior, Marshall was ill-prepared to assume the responsibilities of the presidency should Wilson die in office, a

***The Mineral Well in Petoskey.*** *(Author's Collection)*

real possibility at that time. World War I was raging in Europe and the president was gravely ill - a fact scrupulously hidden from the public by his wife and other government leaders. Some congressmen asked Marshall to step in but he refused. It is no wonder that he took long contemplative walks on the Petoskey beach during his annual summer interludes. Today, we can only ponder these times when, in an unlikely place like Bay View, anyone could interact with the nation's vice president to consider social, political, and economic issues. Such were the days of Chautauqua assemblies when people could freely mingle with the influential.

During the zenith of the Chautauqua assemblies, the number of visitors to Emmet County (where Bay View and Petoskey are situated) was staggering. In Bay View, two train stations and two sets of tracks serviced six suburban trains daily out of Chicago, Cincinnati and St. Louis, and numerous ones from the eastern part of Michigan. Every twenty minutes, local trains ran from Charlevoix to Harbor Springs. On the bay itself, local steamers operated between these communities while steamships such as the *Manitou* carried thousands of passengers between Chicago and Harbor Springs.

Emmet County opened up to travelers when the Grand Rapids and Indiana Railroad (GR&I) began passenger service to Petoskey in December of 1873. Two years later, Bay View was founded and held its first camp meeting in the summer of 1876. The camp meetings soon attracted anywhere from two to 5000 people and by the time the Bay View Assembly was inaugurated in 1886, housing was critical. In 1887, Assembly Superintendent John M. Hall made an appeal for all available rooms to be rented. The newspapers reinforced that plea stating that "resources of Bay View and Petoskey will be over-taxed next week to take care of the crowd."[2] The railroad companies had to expand service to Petoskey and Bay View beginning with the 1888 season.

By 1893 and 1894, the dilemma had worsened. All of the rooms at more than fifteen area hotels and the Bay View public buildings were booked, and the camp-ground association begged cottagers to take in roomers.[3] A dining hall was built in the 1890s to help handle the overflow. In 1895, another crisis erupted. There were 1000 more people on the grounds than the previous year, and rooms and food scarce. "The bakery has 300 or 400 loaves to sell daily. The demand is 600. The other 200 people must go without or go to Petoskey. ... It is nothing less than cruelty to bring people into an atmosphere so conducive to appetite, and when they ask for bread give them a stone."[4]

Association members heeded the pleas. Many cottages were built as multiple family rental units as cottage floor plans indicate. Over thirty-five rooming houses sprang up in addition to the village's five hotels - the Bay View House, the Hilton Hotel (now Crist Hall), the Howard House (now Stafford's Bay View Inn), the Southern Hotel (Block 17, Lot 1) and the Terrace Inn.

***Suburban Station and Trains, Petoskey, Michigan. Notice Cushman House in background.*** *(Author's Collection)*

Numerous additions were made to these hotels to keep up with demand. At the height of Bay View's popularity, all five hotels had overflow cottages nearby.

The population of Bay View in those early days far exceeded that of today. No official census was ever taken, so the best information comes from contemporary newspaper estimates. In 1901, the *Grand Rapids Evening Press* reported that more than 10,000 people made their summer home in Bay View. In 1906, the *Daily Resorter* reported a "conservative estimate of four or five thousand inhabitants." In 1911, the Bay View Post Office served over 5000 people. By 1917, the post office had four clerks and, the following year, it employed five clerks to handle the volume of business.[5]

How did it happen that so many people like Thomas R. Marshall were drawn to Bay View, Petoskey and its surrounding area? What lured people from all parts of the country and the world? Why were they willing to endure traveling by train, sometimes through forest fires where red-hot falling limbs threatened their safety? Why did they come to this hamlet where, by all reports, hotel accommodations and food were limited? What was the attraction that brought them to a place populated mainly by Odawas, wolves, and black bears?

Historian Theodore Morrison credited Bay View as being the first of an estimated 350 independent Chautauqua assemblies in America in his eloquent history *Chautauqua.* While the tribute is distinctive, like other assemblies Ocean Park, Maine; Ocean Grove, New Jersey; and Lakeside, Ohio, which all pre-date Chautauqua, New York, Bay View's roots are in the camp meeting movement that preceded the Chautauqua movement by a century. In the past, historians have credited the Cumberland Presbyterians with originating the camp meeting movement in western Kentucky very early in the nineteenth century. "It was the invention of the Concord Presbyterians, but the Methodists know a good thing when they see it, and quickly adopted this service. This is a great evangelizing force," the Reverend Dr. Daniel Steele of the Boston School of Theology told a Bay View audience on July 9, 1895, at Bay View's twentieth anniversary celebration.[6]

New evidence, however, in Kenneth Brown's research suggests that the camp meeting movement began much earlier in American history in North Carolina or possibly Georgia, giving credence to the idea that the movement was influenced by the plantation slaves who held their revival meetings in the forests and fields away from the eyes of the slave owners.[7] The movement may have affected the many Presbyterians preachers who ministered to the slaves prior to the Civil War. However, the emotionally-charged camp meetings apparently soon turned off the rationally-minded Presbyterians and it was the perfection-minded Methodists who seized on the idea as a way to evangelize the "unchurched," and revive their church spirit.

Methodism, which has been referred to as America's church, was growing rapidly in the nineteenth century. The

***The Cushman House in Petoskey where Vice President Marshall stayed each summer.*** *(Courtesy of Larry Massie)*

sect expanded from approximately 14,000 members at the end of the American Revolution to around 600,000 in 1833, fueled by the zealous leadership of its circuit riders. In about 1845, when the fervency cooled, the "Holiness Movement" sprang up among Methodists who were eager for a church-wide revival to match that of earlier days. After the interruption of the Civil War, places such as Ocean Grove were founded as Holiness camp meetings.

By that time, membership in the Methodist Episcopal Church had reached one million. At the end of the century, there were fifteen million citizens who belonged to some facet of the Methodist Episcopal Church in the US. Writer Alpha G. Kynett, in his 1895 article, "Bishops of the Methodist Episcopal Church," attributed this growth to the church's exceptional bishops. "Like the circuit riders, these men created fervor that symbolized the American spirit."[8] Their energy fueled revival meetings first on the East Coast and then across the country.

In the first decade after the Civil War, Michigan Methodists had been talking about a statewide campground – somewhere as "free as possible from the allurements to vice and folly usually found at watering places." This campground would be to the people of the Midwest what Martha's Vineyard and Ocean Grove were to those on the East Coast and what Lakeside was to those in Ohio.

Looking for a suitable site, during the summer of 1874 or 1875, Sam Knapp and his wife Sarah were in the little frontier village of Petoskey, which is Odawa for "place of the rising sun."[9] [10]The couple explored the sandstone cliffs and rocky beaches of Little Traverse Bay which the Native Americans called "the little crossing." Knapp preferred the bay's south shore, warmed at night by the land breezes and cooled during the day by Lake Michigan's prevailing northwest winds.

Knapp was also looking for unusual plant specimens for his conservatory in Jackson, Michigan, where a fine grapery and white cut-leaf weeping birches surrounded the couple's Francis Street home. Encircling those birches were western varieties of fruit trees. Nearby, Knapp had built several steam-heated greenhouses, each with specially-designed, mechanized equipment to provide the tropical climate for his Chinese sago palms, Japanese plums, rare Mexican plants and Australian tree ferns. Many said that Knapp's subtropical garden had the most beautiful plants and flowers and the largest variety of palm trees certainly in Michigan.

The Knapps were so taken with Petoskey that when their summer interlude ended, they purchased three lots on Lake Street. Heading south with plant specimens, rocks and fossils for their gardens and a vision to share with their minister the Reverend Joseph H. McCarty of Jackson's First Methodist Episcopal Church, they felt they had found the perfect site for a state camp meeting. On the cascading banks east of Petoskey there was an abundance of wood for summer homes, fresh spring water from a sizeable stream and cooling air-conditioning from Lake Michigan's winds. Best of all, the site featured what many east coast campsites had – a grove of trees that formed a natural amphitheater for camp meetings.

Knapp's career had been questionable before he joined Jackson's Methodist Episcopal Church. Born in Royalton, Vermont, in 1816, Knapp arrived in Michigan in about 1844 with letters from prominent Vermont citizens testifying to his skills and worth as a man.[11] He found work in Jackson introducing state prison inmates to the woolen manufacturing trade, setting up new machinery and superintending the Jackson Prison. In Michigan's UP in 1845,

***S. O. Knapp*** *(Courtesy of Larry Massie)*

***Mrs. Sarah Knapp*** *(Courtesy of Larry Massie)*

he led a party of four men, including two Ojibwas, to explore ancient mining pits along the Ontonagon River.[12]

Knapp became the agent for the Vulcan Mining Company in 1847 and returned to Ontonagon. That winter, he discovered a mass of copper ten feet long by three feet wide and two feet thick at an ancient Indian mining site. Historians now consider this event to be one of the most important discoveries in UP history. It was evidence of ancient miners, the Mascoutins, who predated the Ojibwa people as inhabitants of the area. Knapp and his colleagues removed ten wagonloads of ancient stone hammers and, using a rudely constructed sled and canoe, transported the six-ton copper mass to the Ontonagon River. The mass was then shipped to New York City. Knapp apparently accompanied it and met William Hickok, major stockholder of the Vulcan Mining Company, and told him about Ontonagon's possibilities. The company's other stockholders, of whom Knapp was one, told him to inquire in Detroit about the possibility of buying this UP site referred to by miners as "Old 98."

In Detroit, Knapp bought half of "98" with an option to buy the adjoining section after he had arrived in Ontonagon and determined which half would provide the greater return. Once in Ontonagon, in April of 1848, he notified the owners of Section 98 that the Vulcan Mining Company would take the north half. Since several minority stockholders objected to the purchase, Hickok and Knapp formed a new company, the Minesota Mining Company (spelled by them with one "n") in 1848 to manage the new location.

The remaining stockholders of the Vulcan Mining Company, in particular those who were also stockholders of the Baltimore Mining Company, were not included as stockholders in the new venture. The Minesota Mine turned out to be a real "gold mine" earning its nickname the "Mother of Mines." Between 1848 and 1870, it produced almost thirty-five million pounds of copper, making it the richest mine ever opened in the United States by size and yield. By 1865, the mine had paid dividends of $1.76 million on an initial investment of $366,000.[13] Knapp's discovery "spurred America's first great mineral boom, one that far exceeded in total dollar value the more famous California Gold Rush," according to State Archeologist John Halsey.[14]

Researchers have credited Knapp with the mine's high production. He supervised it from 1848 until about 1851, increasing the work force from twelve Cornish miners to 350 employees. He oversaw the mapping of the mine, providing ten shafts to allow for the greatest production of copper with the fewest employee hours. He supervised the building of the village that surrounded the shafts and oversaw production of crops of potatoes and turnips to furnish the community's food supply.

Some sources report that Knapp sold his holdings in 1851. Others give the year as 1856. Still other sources indicate he left as superintendent but kept his holdings. David J. Krause's review of the company records in his book, *The Making of a Mining District,* found that Knapp was no longer mentioned in the records after 1851. Whatever the case, Knapp was a wealthy man at the age of thirty-five in 1851 and probably used his earnings to purchase land in Jackson - a home and a forty-seven acre tract abutting the north side of the Jackson State Prison.

Given the enormous monetary returns and the manner in which the Minesota Mining Company stockholders gained the deed to Section 98 and formed the new company, two lawsuits ensued in the Michigan State Supreme Court. In his book *The Mining Ventures of this Ontonagon Country,* author James Jamison maintained that there was evidence of foul play, although the Michigan Supreme Court sided in 1871 with defendants Knapp and Hickok and other members of the Minesota Mining Company. Jamison referred to Knapp as "a man of absolute astuteness" whose business transactions were so questionable that he "cannot imagine Knapp ending his days as a hymn-singing flower grower" - referring, of course, to Knapp's later life in Bay View and Jackson. Writer Halsey referred to Knapp as engaging in "sharp business practices."

Whether he was a sharp businessman or an opportunist, Knapp's shrewdness was also recognized by geologist and author David J. Krause for different reasons. Given the uniqueness of native copper in the UP, not found anywhere else in the world in such pure and large masses, Krause credited Knapp and three others with recognizing the UP's rich copper phenomenon. They forged ahead in their mining efforts despite skepticism from the scientific community.

After returning to Jackson, Knapp entered community life. Despite his independent nature, he was a popular leader who was respected among his associates. In the UP, he was instrumental in establishing the village of Rockland. In Jackson, he used his wealth to help build the 1870 Jackson Methodist Episcopal Church. He was president of Jackson's board of education although he had no children. In Lansing, he was a member of the State Board of Agriculture and a longtime member of the State Pomological [fruit growing] Society. After the court settlements, he retired from the State Board of Agriculture and joined the camp meeting movement.

Arriving home from his summer interlude in Petoskey, Knapp contacted his minister, Reverend McCarty, who wrote to the officials of the GR&I on August 26, 1875 about a possible site for a Methodist camp meeting. An act of Congress had opened Emmet County to homesteaders and hundreds of people were flocking to the area. The GR&I was cutting fares and scrambling to find new markets for its recently instituted passenger service. The company offered the Methodists land near Bear Lake, so Reverend McCarty addressed the Detroit Annual Conference of the Methodist Episcopal Church on September 2, 1875, and the Michigan Annual Conference on September 10.

In one of its first joint efforts since the Civil War, the conferences formed a campground committee.[15] The Detroit Annual Conference appointed Dr. Elijah H. Pilcher, Seth Reed, Robert Bird and banker David Preston. The Michigan Annual Conference appointed Dr. Joseph H. McCarty, William H. Brockway and T. H. Jacokes, along with A. A. Knappen and L. M. Edmonds.[16]

The railroad impressed the joint committee by furnishing them with a "chair car" for a tour of various northern Michigan sites. On September 17, 1875, The *Emmet County Democrat* listed the group visiting Petoskey as Preston, Reed, Bird, McCarty and his wife, Knapp, Brockway, Barnes, Moore, and Hinman of the GR&I.[17] After the tour, the joint committee held its first official meeting on November 9, 1875, in McCarty's pastoral study at the Jackson church.

This meeting formed the organizational roots for the Michigan State Camp-ground Association of the Methodist Episcopal Church (MSCGA).[18] Reverend Dr. E. H. Pilcher was elected president; Reverend John M. Arnold, first vice president; Reverend William H. Brockway, second vice president; Reverend J. H. McCarty, secretary; and Detroit banker David Preston, treasurer. They adopted the articles of incorporation and by-laws written by President Pilcher, who was also a lawyer and medical doctor besides a Methodist minister.

Next on the agenda was the decision on a site. In addition to the GR&I offer of the Bear Lake (now Walloon Lake) property, there were other serious land proposals at Ludington, Clam Lake (Cadillac), Otsego Lake, Traverse City and Cheboygan. Judge Aaron Moors favored a site in Traverse City and Brockway argued for Ludington, a site proposed by the Flint and Père Marquette Railroad Company which eventually became Epworth Heights. At the next meeting - on January 20, 1876 - the group voted

***The dummy attached to Engine 22 was the local train service to the various resorts and towns. (1882).***
*(Courtesy of Charles Conn, Photograph from Alan McCune Collection)*

*The Howard House, now Stafford's Bay View Inn, was another of the five hotels in Bay View.* (Author's Collection)

stone quarry, situated at the corner of Howard and Rose streets. He convinced Rose, whom historian Harriet Kilborn called "the architect of Petoskey's future," of the financial and commercial merits of the campground. In a 1932 speech to the Petoskey Kiwanis Club, Hon. Charles J. Pailthorp, a young lawyer in 1875, recalled this time. "One day we woke up to the fact that there was something going on that we might be vividly interested in. We had not given it much attention . . . We discovered that a committee had been here looking up a location and that they had visited what is now Bay View and were very favorably impressed."[20]

with Knapp in favor of the area east of Petoskey, even though the site was not readily available. Odawa and Ojibwa Indians owned the land as a result of a July 31, 1855, treaty with the US government.

Knapp has been referred to as the "quiet promoter" of Bay View, but "quiet" is the wrong word. Since he left no personal diary or papers, there are few documents to verify the extent of his endeavors. Furthermore, this effective leader had no offspring to champion his accomplishments after his death. Certainly, regarding Bay View, he was anything but quiet. Sources flatly state that Bay View would never have been located near Petoskey had it not been for Knapp's judgment and persistence.[19] The trustees were aware of his reputation and respected him for his accomplishments in the UP, his leadership on the board of the Michigan Agricultural College and his obvious knowledge of resources needed to build a "city in the woods." They informed GR&I President William O. Hughart on February 8, 1876, that they "could not proceed until a proper title to the lands in question be secured."

Hughart summoned the public-minded Petoskey citizen Hiram O. Rose, owner of Petoskey's lime-

Petoskey was not as developed as Traverse City and citizens lacked the ready cash to buy the land. So the residents agreed to build railroad tracks from the village to the camp grounds in time for the camp meeting on August 2, 1876, and Hughart agreed that the railroad company would provide the cash to purchase the property. With the help of young Pailthorp, Rose raised approximately $3250 in pledges from Petoskey citizens to purchase the land from its Native American owners. Rose himself donated several plats from his holdings. Rose and W. G. Hinman of

*Somewhat unwieldy yet handsome, the Bay View House was begun in 1877 and added onto numerous times until the 1920s. The veranda offered visitors a spectacular view of Little Traverse Bay and the dining room boosted of serving 250 guests. It was often recognized as the finest hotel in northern Michigan. Tragically, it burned in 1929, one month before the stock market crash amid persistence rumors of arson. It was under insured for $50,000 and valued at $150,000. Consequently, owner George W. Childs, Jr. was never able to rebuild it.* (Author's Collection)

the GR&I land department hitched up a couple of ponies to a cutter and personally drove around the region to contact the Odawa and Ojibwa owners.[21] The property was deeded to GR&I agent John M. Matheany of Fort Wayne, Indiana, who then deeded it to the GR&I.

At their March 22 meeting, campground trustees instructed their officers to close the contract and sign all necessary papers. On May 25, 1876, a warranty deed for 316.18 acres, less the railroad right-of-way, was tendered to the GR&I at Hughart's Grand Rapids office. The MSCGA agreed to make $10,000 worth of improvements to the grounds within five years and conduct camp meetings for fifteen years. The association could elect at any time to pay the railroad $4000, and that sum would be accepted as fulfillment of the conditions of the contract.

Everyone benefited from the deal. The railroad found new customers for its new passenger service at a time when Michigan's lumber business was waning with the dwindling supply of virgin timber. Petoskey gained an economic advantage for its commercial establishments and employment opportunities for its citizens created by the tremendous influx of summer visitors. The Michigan Methodist Episcopal Church got its camp meeting site. Native Americans sold their land.

One glitch in the proceedings was overcome in the fall of 1876. The 316.18 acres purchased by the railroad did not include the shoreline, because the Native Americans who held title to those parcels were not living there at the time. "Everyone interested felt that the Camp Grounds would be so much more valuable with the shore line [sic]," wrote researcher Floy Irene Graham.[22] So, in the fall of 1876, Rose and Hinman again hitched up that cutter drawn by "those two fast Indian ponies" and drove as far north as Sault Ste. Marie and south as Traverse City to locate those who held title to the shoreline. Rose spoke Odawa and transacted the deals, and Pailthorp took care of the legal work. By 1877, the MSCGA included a beautiful shoreline, adding ten acres to the original purchase. For Rose's help in securing the transaction, the trustees offered him his pick of any lot on the grounds.[23]

In the spring of 1876, the religiously-centered board of trustees may have been unconcerned about beachfront property. So, with the warranty deed in progress, trustees Pilcher, Moors, Tracy, Reed and Knapp met in Petoskey May 2 and 3, for a walking tour of the property. They wanted to find the best location for the Speaker's

***The First Methodist Episcopal Church in Jackson, Michigan, was the site of the founding of the Michigan Camp-Grounds Association of the Methodist Episcopal Church on November 9, 1875. W.E.N. Hunter, the same Detroit architect who designed John M. Hall Auditorium, did a wrap around renovation of this church in 1921. However, the interior of the church was left intact and remains as it was originally built in 1870.***
*(Author's Collection)*

***The Terrace Inn was built by William and Josephine DeVol of Lebanon, Indiana, on the site of a former rooming house. It opened in 1911 as Bay View's newest and most modern hotel.*** *(Author's Collection)*

*The interior of the Terrace Inn was furnished with then stylish Arts and Crafts furniture and the hotel was considered Bay View's most modern hotel.* (Courtesy of Patty Rasmussen Rave)

not intersect in hard right angles, but wind among each other in fanciful curves and mazy [sic] circles. This arrangement first confuses the stranger and then charms him," architectural historian Dr. Ellen Weiss reported.[26] In Bay View those "fanciful curves" became avenues surrounding cascading terraces, hills and intermittent parks, allowing each block and lot the possibility of "a cottage with a view" of the water. One of Bay View's streets, Encampment Avenue, surrounded Tabernacle Park and the Speaker's Stand exactly the way campground cottages surround the grove of oaks and the preacher's stand at Oak Bluffs.

The Native American owners had cleared an area in Bay View now known as Fairview Park and had some lime works in progress on the first ridge overlooking Little Traverse Bay. The rest of the grounds were heavily wooded. Bay View's first caretaker, Benjamin F. Darling, remembered that the grounds were pretty much as "nature had left them" with some trees so

Stand for the upcoming meeting. By this time, McCarty had left for a new church assignment in Louisiana so President Pilcher selected the spot for the Speaker's Stand.[24]

None of the Bay View founders (that we know about) were Michigan-born. All had come west around the time of Michigan's statehood in 1837. While pioneers were moving into Michigan, Methodist minister and circuit rider Seth Reed returned east in 1864 to join the Providence Conference and find a healthier climate for his ailing wife. On Martha's Vineyard, her health improved in the pleasant seaside climate and the atmosphere of the Wesleyan Grove camp meetings. While Reed was living there, the Martha's Vineyard Camp-Meeting Association developed plans for a new subdivision called Oak Bluffs. In the center of the development was the camp meeting site, where a speaker's stand was erected in front of a grassy area of crudely constructed benches in a grove known as Tabernacle Park.

The atmosphere charmed Reed according to local papers which reported the influence of the East Coast campground on the selection committee who visited Petoskey in the fall of 1875. Reed told the local press, "While comparing this ground with the one at Martha's Vineyard, which is similar to what they propose to make this, they said that there were about 1500 buildings erected upon that grounds, and some of them were very elegant in their appointments, costing considerable sums, and the streets laid out very regular, and in a tasty manner."[25]

Apparently in Bay View those very regular Oak Bluffs streets turned into winding paths in a romantic plan more like the layout of Martha's Vineyard's Wesleyan Grove where, "The streets and avenues of the forest city do

*Judge Charles J. Pailthorp had just arrived in Petoskey as a young lawyer when he and H. O. Rose were notified by the Grand Rapids and Indiana Railroad of the Michigan Methodist Episcopal Church's interest in a campground near Petoskey. Pailthorp is pictured here with his son and grandson.* (Courtesy of Robert Pailthorp)

large they could not be felled with a five-and-a-half-foot saw.[27] Sixty lots were laid out that first summer all with a view of the bay. Nearly all were sold by the end of the year.

Inspiration for Bay View's romantic layout must have come from Knapp. DeLand's *History of Jackson County, Michigan* credited Knapp for the layout, an ingenious system that took advantage of the area's cascading ridges while limiting the effects of erosion from the sandy soil. Knapp worked with Petoskey resident John Keep to survey the property. Keep, a Civil War veteran, had taken up a homestead on Mitchell Street, four miles east of Petoskey. As a surveyor and civil engineer, he worked for the GR&I surveying the ground for the railroad between Grand Rapids and Petoskey. He also surveyed the State Road (Mitchell Street) in Petoskey. In contrast to Bay View, Petoskey was laid out on a grid plan with straight-line streets. Since Keep surveyed both, projects, Knapp evidently was the designer of Bay View's layout.

***The first GR&I Railroad station proved inadequate in size and was replaced in 1896 by a larger building. Notice the horse car on left.*** *(Peggy Child Smith Collection)*

Knapp's knowledge of botany would have made him aware of new ideas in vogue at the time – those of Frederick Law Olmsted, the 1859 planner of New York's Central Park. Witold Rybczynski's 1999 book about Olmsted, *A Clearing in the Distance*, pointed out how widespread Olmsted's influence was in America at that

***The numbers of tourists during the summer months was so high the Grand Rapids and Indian Railroad built this depot in 1896 to handle the passengers visiting Bay View. Note the two sets of tracks between the depot and Little Traverse Bay.*** *(Courtesy of the Little Traverse Historical Society)*

time and anyone with Knapp's background would have been very much aware of him.[28]

In her 1993 book *Buildings of Michigan*, historian and former Michigan State Preservation Officer Kathryn Bishop Eckert quoted Frederick Law Olmsted, Jr., in a 1915 letter. He stated that the Michigan State campus was "in some respects probably the very best example of the type of landscape characteristic of the American college campus of the nineteenth century." S. O. Knapp had been in charge of the second wave of building construction on the East Lansing campus (now Michigan State University) as chairman of the building committee between 1868 and 1874. In his 1908 account of the history of Michigan State University, Charles Garfield cited Knapp's extraordinary business sense:

> *Mr. S. O. Knapp, of Jackson, came upon the board when his practical knowledge of affairs was most needed in the erection of the second set of buildings and in the development of the campus. Unusual duties were placed upon the shoulders of Mr. Knapp because of his ability and his nearness to the College.*[29]

Michigan State archeologist and author John Halsey speculates that Knapp "would have taken a strong role in shaping the East Lansing campus, but there is little in the way of easily available primary documents to prove whether or not he did take a major hands-on role in campus gardens, greenhouses, arboretums, something that he took an intense personal interest in at his home."[30]

Unlike the much-admired Michigan State University campus layout, Knapp's Bay View's layout of numbered blocks and lots may have afforded everyone a lot with a view but it was not only confusing but drew unseemly comments about this ardent teetotaler. Some writers have insinuated that he and his committee must have been drunk when they mapped Bay View. Historian Clark Wheeler wrote, "One has the impression in studying the map that the block numbers were fired at random from a two dollar shot gun into the map."[31] He compared it to a Boston "calf path." *Daily Resorter* writer Paul B. Blanshard compared it with cemetery lots.

A century later, though, in 1987 that romantic design was the significant factor in Bay View's National Historic Landmark designation. Architectural historian Ellen Weiss mentioned in her essay for the 1986 landmark application the strong possibility of Olmsted's influence. Eckert speculated in her book that the "Bay View exercise in sinuously curved streets to intensify nature may have been important for subdivision planning in the twentieth century when Bay View became famous and much visited."[32] To S. O. Knapp then goes the credit for selecting the Bay View site, designing the grounds, and, during the uncertain days

***The Russet Inn was one of the most successful of the some thirty-five rooming houses located in Bay View, besides the five major hotels.*** *(Author's Collection)*

***Despite the rudimentary transportation facilities of the GR&I at that time, enthusiasm was high for these people going to Bay View for a July 4th picnic in the 1880s.*** *(Courtesy of the Little Traverse Historical Society)*

between 1878 and 1882, he took over as president when the fledgling association was struggling. As with his tenure at the Minesota Mine and Michigan Agricultural College, there are few documents revealing his astute management practices that typified his life. He died in 1883 just after stepping down as Bay View's third president.

Knapp did not live to enjoy the fruits of his labors or even witness the transfer of the deed. On October 22, 1890, the Bay View property was transferred from the GR&I to a newly-named Bay View Camp-ground Association of the Methodist Episcopal Church. Bay View was incorporated as a resort under an act authored by Bay View resident Hon. John W. Moore of Saginaw and introduced in the Michigan legislature by Judge Peeler of Bay View. Petoskey's H. O. Rose attributed Bay View as the first of many Emmet County resorts. "Bay View started all the resorts of this region for it was like a homesteader, when he secures a good farm others come, so when it was seen that the project was good others went into it.... Bay View would never have been located at this place had it not been for the efforts of S. O. Knapp."[33]

The trustees' decision, with the support of the Petoskey people, to side with Knapp on the site and its layout, despite complications has proved to be a wise one. In his *Forum on the Bay*, author Robert Carter credited Bay View's superb location and wonderful climate as reasons for its survival during a difficult twentieth century of two world wars, the Great Depression, the counterculture of the Vietnam era, and downturn in interest in historic properties. Knapp spearheaded the movement that started Bay View and created a watering place for more than a century of future gatherings in the grove.

— CHAPTER TWO —

# 'Twas a Very Big Sunday

The Reverend William Hadley Brockway regretted missing that spring walking tour of the new property in 1876. Impressed with Reverend McCarty's appeal for the Methodist camp meeting site, he had traveled to Petoskey with the joint committee on September 17, 1875, and made a similar junket to Ludington, Michigan, in October. Brockway liked the Ludington location better and cast the only vote against Petoskey.[1] When the votes were counted, however, he took the decision in "good spirit" and was placed on the "Titles and Ornamentation Committee" with Knapp.

It was an elegant name for a mundane job - clearing timber, grading roads, surveying the land, marking positions for the parks, and supervising the laying of wooden tracks between Petoskey and the campground. Brockway immediately took charge. He was accustomed to working with railroads having supervised the building of the Northern Central Michigan Railroad from Jonesville to Lansing in 1872 and 1873. In Petoskey, he organized volunteer laborers in laying the rails from the village to the future campsite.

When the wooden tracks were in place, delivering cut lumber to Bay View to construct cottages was easy. Bay View is downhill from Petoskey, so all they had to do was to give the rail cars a good shove. A large black mule then pulled the cars back to Petoskey for each new load of lumber or passengers. The wooden tracks were not strong enough for the large engines of the heavier coaches so Pullman cars were always left in Petoskey - except once. "One night the brakeman forgot to set the brakes on three of the Pullmans. The next morning they were gone. Sometime during the night the cars had coasted to Bay View. It took a team of mules to haul them back, one by one."[2]

On those flimsy wooden tracks, the lumber for the new Speaker's Stand was delivered. "Your grandfather worked hard at clearing the land," Martha Brockway Gale wrote to her nephew Bruce Brockway in a 1950 letter. "I can remember seeing him out supervising stump pulling in Fairview Park. As I remember some of the other men on the board, I think my father worked harder in the early days than any of them."[3]

Like Knapp, Brockway was a hardy woodsman whom the Native Americans affectionately called "Penabic"or "Iron Man." Other times they referred to him as the "Beaver," since he was always working. "He was blessed with the iron in his frame to endure the toils and perils of that inclement region of the north," another daughter, Mary Dickie, wrote of her father. Even so, he enjoyed dressing very well in Prince Albert style, tailor-made, black-broadcloth suits.

Those were strange tastes for a hardened circuit rider who spent ten years at Fort Brady in Sault Ste. Marie in the 1830s and 1840s. There were few roads in Michigan at that time and most of them were "corduroy" log paths that led through heavily wooded areas or across muddy swamps. During those ten years, Brockway traveled by canoe to Detroit church conferences several times. Eight times, he skirted the south shore of Lake Superior with his Ojibwa guide to visit Indian missions at Fond du Lac in northern Wisconsin and

*The Speaker's Stand or Secretary's Office (1876) and the Bay View Bookstore (1881) were two of the first buildings on the grounds.* (Author's Collection)

***Campers in 1876.*** *(Author's Collection)*

***The first camp meeting in 1876 in front of the Speaker's Stand.*** *(Author's Collection)*

Sandy Lake in northern Minnesota. In the winter, Brockway was forced to cover his mission area by snowshoe and dog team. While he was absent from Fort Brady for months at a time, his first wife Clarissa often took care of as many as fifteen orphaned Objiwa children in addition to the couple's own two sons.[4]

During his fifty-seven years in the Methodist Conference and his many assignments with the Indian missions, Brockway became fluent in the Odawa language. With so many Native American children living with his family, the language became his sons' first language. Years later, his daughter Martha remembered her father often speaking with Chief Petoskey at the camp meetings.[5]

Petoskey carpenter William Samuel Batt completed the Speaker's Stand in time for the first camp meeting.[6] The *Emmet County Democrat* reported that Reverend Dr. Elijah Pilcher preached the sermon on August 2nd to approximately 150 worshippers who sat on hastily-constructed wooden benches made out of tree stumps, situated around the Speaker's Stand. He delivered the opening address in the "dense forest of beech, maple, birch, and hemlock," the Reverend Dr. William H. Shier wrote in the 1925 Bay View history *Golden Jubilee*.[7] At the end of his sermon, Pilcher dedicated the grounds to the worship of "Almighty God." His message must have stirred the hearts of all who heard him because, by the following Sunday, between 2000 and 3000 attended the first Big Sunday service.

During the camp meeting week, thirteen men held the first annual meeting of the association on the hill behind what is now Vernor Hall. This group included President Pilcher; Reverend Robert Bird, minister of Petoskey's Methodist Episcopal Church; J. M. Arnold; Reverend Dr. W. H. Shier who later became the association's longest-serving president; W. A. Scripps; Knapp; Brockway; William Phelps; the Reverend D. F. Barnes from Adrian; D. Burnham Tracy of Grand Rapids; Judge A. P. Moors; R. N. McKaig; and Reverend Seth Reed. There was a "spirit of harmony that characterized the deliberations," Reverend Shier later wrote.

By the time he became connected with the campground movement, Pilcher, Bay View's first president, had already had an enormous effect on Michigan's educational system. He had helped found Albion College, the University of Michigan, and Michigan State University.[8] A medical doctor and a minister, he was a trained lawyer and wrote the articles of incorporation under which the new campground would operate legally. Anyone wishing to build a cottage had to first be approved for membership by the association and pay ten dollars in dues. Before a cottage could be sold, the prospective buyer had to be approved for membership in the same manner.

With a legal structure in place, like the biblical Paul who felt compelled to travel to Indo-Europe, the sixty-seven-year-old Pilcher accepted a Macedonian call from the beleaguered Canadian Methodist Episcopal Church,

***Campground life in the early days of the camp meetings.*** *(Author's Collection)*

and Brockway became president. Before his departure, Pilcher made his most enduring contribution. As he wrote in his 1885 autobiography, he suggested the name of Bay View. The suggestion was passed at the January 30, 1877 meeting. Since Seth Reed actually entered the motion, most historians have attributed the honor to him instead of Pilcher. On July 29, 1890, the name was officially changed from the Michigan Campground Association of the Methodist Episcopal Church to the Bay View Campground Association of the Methodist Episcopal Church.[9] Today, the only reminder of Pilcher's contributions to Bay View is a copy of his 1875 articles of incorporation in the Bay View Archives. Not even a street is named after him.

Having a street or what was then a muddy pathway named after him was nothing Pilcher probably cared about, but rough as the Bay View terrain was, the citizens of Petoskey were proud of their accomplishment in securing the camp meeting location near their village. Each day of the meeting, the crowds grew larger for what would be called locally "Big Sunday." The *Emmet County Democrat* in 1876 editorialized: "This is a great era in the history of Petoskey. We, as a town, have donated liberally towards securing the location of these grounds at this place, and now we see the result, our town filled to overflowing with strangers coming here to enjoy this delightful climate in the worship of God, and recreation from labor."[10]

The camp meeting resembled already-established east coast meetings in both style and philosophical concept. Describing typical camp meetings, Charles Edwin Jones wrote, "Usually camp regulations reiterated the prohibitions of the General Rules. They required attendance at services and outlawed alcoholic beverages, promiscuous courting and Sunday money transactions. To maintain nocturnal decorum, ministers patrolled the grounds. Religious services and devotional activities filled the waking hours."[11] His description might have been of Bay View whose trustees wrote: "…all the features of an old-fashioned camp-meeting [will] be retained. Several sermons each day, with prayer and conference meetings, having in view the conversion of sinners and the sanctification of believers. Come, with your tents and families, not for pleasure and recreation, but to worship the Lord in the beauty of holiness. Every convenience will be provided, good order maintained and everything banished from the grounds that tends to dissipate religious impressions or interfere with the work of the Spirit."[12]

With only campfires, lanterns and the northern Michigan twilight to brighten the night sky, campers let sunset and sunrise dictate their motto - "early to bed and early to rise." On weekdays, the Camp-Meeting Proper began at 6 a.m. with Prayer Meeting. That was followed by the "Normal Lesson" twice a day, four days a week;

***Dogs were often shot on the grounds, a policy that writer Paul Blanshard later vehemently opposed.*** *(Peggy Child Smith Collection)*

lectures at 10 a.m.; conversations in the afternoon; Bible readings at 5 p.m. or 7 p.m. (depending on the day); and more lectures at 8 p.m. On Tuesdays and Saturdays, participants finally had social hour at 8:30 p.m. Card playing, drinking (alcohol), smoking and dancing were forbidden.

Reverend and Mrs. H. D. Jordan of Albion fondly remembered the community spirit of the early days when prayer meetings began as soon as the tents were pitched. "Everyone started at once to do something for the Master as soon as they could and there was a lack of cut and dried programs for spiritual campaigns but every one [sic] worked where they saw an opportunity for work," the couple told the local papers years later."[13]

Mr. and Mrs. L. R. Damon attended that first camp meeting but stayed at Petoskey's Cushman House instead of tenting. Later in 1902, they recounted their memories to the *Daily Resorter*:

> *We used to come down to Bay View on democrat wagon or on an improvised horse car....This horse car was a funny contrivance....Rev. Mr. Tracy of Detroit had a passenger transportation "trust". He had built an open car which was drawn by a horse. The affair was rickety and ran off the track continually. Then all the passengers had to get off and put it back on.... In spite of the crude accommodations fully 3000 attended 'Big Sunday' the first year. Many came in wagons drawn by oxen.*[14]

The couple remained at the gathering place to build one of the earliest cottages in the dense overgrowth:

> *The woods were so thick that we could find only one of the stakes that marked out our lot. On that account we made a mistake and had to turn the cottage around when the street was put through. We moved into the cottage before the carpenters had finished their work, and were obliged to set up the cook stove outdoors. It was a very rainy season – rained nearly every day – and so my daughter and I took turns holding an umbrella while the other did the cooking. The woods were thick indeed. It took me an hour to go from where the station is now [west of the present tennis courts and north of Woodland Avenue] to the camp meeting grounds and two hours to make my way from the camp meeting grounds to the bay. One evening we started out to visit a neighbor and got lost within 150 feet of the house. For several seasons*

**Henry Balcom was a caretaker of Bay View grounds in the early days.** (*Author's Collection*)

*we went to Petoskey for the mail. In those days mail was carried from Charlevoix to Cheboygan by mounted Indian. He changed horses every ten miles. His regularity was remarkable. He used to gallop past the cottage almost exactly at midnight, night after night.*[15]

Mr. and Mrs. Benjamin F. Darling of Jackson also attended the first camp meeting. Darling, a contractor and builder, stayed on as Bay View's supervisor to build about one hundred of the first "wooden tents."[16] He and his wife lived in the single-walled Speaker's Stand during the long cold winter months. Darling, a Civil War veteran, was fascinated with the wild animals while his wife worried about the Native Americans. "There were lots of Indians, then ...and they were as afraid of me as I was of them. They used to go through the grounds on their trail and when they saw me, they would stop and gape in wonder: then they would gather up their blankets and speedily decamp....Bears were thick enough....We used to throw fish heads upon a nearby brush pile. During the night the bears came for their meal of fish. There was one particularly bold old fellow, who came out in broad daylight, took a reserved seat on the platform of the newly-built station, and after having viewed the depredations of man leisurely strolled off into the forest.[17] The local paper had a different take on the camp meeting scene. "Ladies who do but little work at home have cooked, washed, hoed and dug."[18]

***Mary Torrans Lathrap, Bay View's first woman speaker, preached at the first camp meeting in 1876, returned in 1877 and numerous times after that. She was on the building committee for the 1870 Jackson First Methodist Episcopal Church where Bay View was founded, was a founder of the national WCTU and president of the Michigan WCTU from 1882 until the early 1890s.*** *(Author's Collection)*

The second camp meeting was held during the week beginning July 31, 1877. It was preceded by a week-long Sunday School Congress under the leadership of the celebrated Reverend Dr. Jesse Lyman Hurlbut of New Jersey.[19] For the "camp-meeting proper" the Reverend Dr. John S. Bayliss of Indianapolis was one of the featured preachers and was considered impressive. The reverends Dr. Frank Beard, Dr. William H. Perrine and Bishop William Xavier Ninde were also on the program. Progressive in their ideas, the founders included a woman speaker at the first two camp meetings - Mary Torrans Lathrap from Knapp's hometown church, the Jackson Methodist Episcopal Church where Bay View was founded.[20]

For the third camp meeting, Ralph Connable of Petoskey made a special gift, a pulpit of tree stumps (in keeping with the twig furniture fad of the day) to be used by the preachers at the Speaker's Stand. "It is on rustic order, the stand being formed of a birch stump. There are three hemlock stumps whose roots are so intertwined and grown together that they are really one," local news account reported.[21] On July 31, 1878, Connable presented his gift as an "altar of thank offering" for having found a place where his "asthma was conquered." Proceeds derived from the pulpit were to go to the Petoskey Methodist Episcopal Church and receipts from the sale of pictures of the pulpit were to be used to build a chapel in Bay View.

The Connables, a family long associated with Ernest Hemingway, were very active in Bay View. They came to Petoskey from Jackson in the 1870s. Besides the Book and Stationary Store and being a partner in a produce business, Ralph owned the Connable Fish Company, the lake steamer *Clara Belle* and the tugboat *Parmalee.* At the corner of Michigan and Emmet streets in Petoskey, he built a house where the couple had twelve children - only four of whom lived to adulthood. Ralph Connable, an Albion graduate, built a cottage at Block 6, Lot 2 and, in 1896 he purchased the property at Block 20, Lot 16. In 1877, Connable put in Bay View's first waterworks system "to supply the grounds with an abundance of pure water."

Connable's wife, Mary Stanton Connable, was a remarkable woman. Fluent in five languages, she learned Odawa after settling in Petoskey. A noted musician, she had been Chicago's first woman church organist. In Petoskey, she organized an orchestra and she and her brother, N. P. Stanton, violin instructor at Albion College, gave concerts at the Methodist Episcopal Church. She was active in the Women's Foreign Missionary Society and, by 1900, she was playing the pump organ for Bay View camp meetings.

With the active interest of locals, the Sunday meetings were the highlight of the six-day gathering. Each

Saturday evening, Reverend Brockway took large chains and locked the Woodland Avenue gates so that only pedestrian worshipers could enter the open-air sanctuary. Rickety horse-drawn carts brought passengers to the gates for the exorbitant price of ten cents. Steamers *Van Raalto* and *Mary* brought people from around Little Traverse Bay; the *Clara Belle* brought those from Traverse City; and the *Wright, Faxton, Friant* and the GR&I brought hundreds from Charlevoix, East Jordan and Boyne City. At that time, the Bay View pier extended northwestward and farther into the bay than it does presently, but the lake level determined when boats could dock at the Bay View pier or needed to land in Petoskey or Harbor Springs. The "dummy" - a train that ran from Petoskey to the surrounding areas – brought several thousand people to the grounds.[22]

Estimates of the crowds vary from 1500 in the 1870s to between five and ten thousand by the 1890s. Weather was always a factor. A 1890 newspaper reported the railroad had taken in $175 in nickels on one really Big Sunday. "Large numbers of country people drove in to attend the services, and the park north of the hotel [The Bay View House] was well filled with a motley assortment of vehicles. Here and there all through the grounds were groups of people seated beneath the trees resting, visiting or partaking of picnic dinners,"[23] is how the newspaper described the day.

With such enormous crowds, "pocket picking" proved fruitful and parishioners were relieved sometimes not only of their sins but of their valuables as well. During the 1887 Big Sunday services, Samuel Phelps of Detroit lost his pocketbook with $90 in cash, his return train tickets and baggage receipts.

Sometimes, Big Sunday was a huge disappointment. In 1885, for example, the scheduled headliner, Bishop Willard Francis Mallalieu accepted an engagement at Ocean Grove instead. (What a slight!) The Reverend Dr. Lewis Fiske, president of Albion College and a cottager, substituted on short notice to disparaging newspaper reviews that his sermon was "beyond the level of his parishioners."

The Big Sunday schedule varied from the regular schedule and from year to year, but the 1891 schedule was typical. Beginning with a Love Feast at 8:30 a.m. which was a service of testimonies and praise typical of the camp meetings nationwide, the morning sermon followed at 10:30 a.m. at the Speaker's Stand, if the weather cooperated. This service was led by one of the local ministers. Picnic lunches followed - in the parks or dinner at one of the hotels or boarding houses for those lucky enough to get in. The 2:30 p.m. service featured the main speaker, a prominent minister, usually from out-of-state. Children's Hour followed at 4 p.m. The Bayside Service (sometimes called Vespers) was held at 6:30 p.m. at the beach. It attracted primarily young people and later became known as the Young People's Meeting. A 7:30 p.m. Song Service was held at the Speaker's Stand, accompanied by another sermon delivered by one of the local or visiting ministers.

A time for celebration arrived when the Michigan Camp-ground Association (Bay View) met conditions laid out in its original contract with the GR&I and ownership of the 326.18 acres (less the railroad right-of-way) was

***The wooden dock extended northwest out into Little Traverse Bay farther than today's dock to accomodate ferries.*** *(Courtesy Peggy Child Smith Collection)*

turned over to the association. In his 1890 *Bay View History,* President Dr. William H. Shier proudly wrote: "Some encampments and summer resorts have developed faster than Bay View but we do not happen to know of any one that has done so much and avoided an embarrassing debt."[24]

While the trustees had reason to be pleased, the *Daily Resorter* editor was not always thrilled with their frugality. He spouted off about Bay View's parsimoniousness, religious piety and excessive zeal:

> *There are certain narrow-minded small-souled individuals among the good people of Bay View who blame the publisher of the RESORTER because the Bay View Association does not see fit to avail itself of the advertising columns of the paper. These petty simpletons take all manner of ways to show their dislike of the paper, and exert all their feeble abilities to insure it.*
>
> *The climax of meanness and audacity was reached yesterday, when a big red-whiskered bully, with no more religion nor good breeding than a third-rate hamfatter, drove the RESORTER newsboys off the grounds, dragging one little fellow by the collar as though he were a jail-bird, and ordering them not to venture on the grounds again, Sunday or any other day.*
>
> *We of course do not blame the association for the unwarranted action of an individual, but we wish to say that some of the fossilized specimens of humanity who have been so anxious to be advertised will get all the notoriety they desire if the outrage is repeated.*[25]

Despite the lack of advertising in the local paper, Big Sunday was an enormous attraction because of the sheer spectacle of the event and the indistinguishable relationship between the Protestant church and American society in the nineteenth century. Deep in the dense forest of northern Michigan, it was great entertainment, and everyone wanted a part of the action. Socially and financially, it benefited one and all to promote the camp meeting. Petoskey businessmen, Native Americans, loggers, newspaper writers and editors, and nearby farmers all attended. Even GR&I President William O. Hughart was often on the grounds for Big Sunday. Monday morning newspapers usually included a full account of the preacher's comments along with biblical references and editorial opinions. O. L. Shepard asserted in his 1923 *History of Lakeside* that the influence of the camp meeting broke down denominational barriers and promoted a truly united spirit among camp-goers. From the very beginning, Bay View was ecumenical as noted in the *Daily Resorter* in 1892: "Although this is an [sic] Methodist Camp Meeting ground, it is not

***Chief Petoskey was a friend of Reverend William Brockway, a founder of the association, who was fluent in Odawa. Chief Petoskey is seen here in 1877 on the Speaker's Stand with Ralph Connable's rustic pulpit.*** *(Author's Collection)*

designed to be denominational, but all who wish can secure a lot and remain thereon during the session, of course, subject to the rules and regulations governing the Association. Lots have already been secured by Presbyterians, Baptists, Episcopalians, and other parties belonging to no denomination."[26]

Members of the local Odawa and Ojibwa tribes frequently attended the early camp meetings. Frances Willard told a story in *Woman and Temperance* about Chief Petoskey signing the pledge of temperance at the 1877 camp meeting. The old Indian leader pointed upward toward the sky, saying in Odawa, "I'll meet you beyond that sky, where we shall need no more moon or sun, for He will be the light thereof."[27] Chief Petoskey's granddaughter accompanied the singing on the pump organ for meetings.

When the Old Auditorium was built in 1887, Native Americans stopped attending. "When we held our meetings out under the trees there used to always be a large number of Indians [who] attended, but since we went into the auditorium they have ceased: they seem to have an antipathy to entering such a building. This is indeed a fact to be deplored and lamented," John M. Hall told the *Daily Resorter* five years later.[28]

Another issue to be deplored was the inconsistent treatment of African Americans. The assembly hosted blacks such as Booker T. Washington and singing groups such as the Fisk Jubilee Singers, the Williams Jubilee

***Hitchcock Hall.*** *(Author's Collection)*

Singers and the Dixie Jubilee Singers as well as many speakers who lectured on the "Negro problem." On Sundays, though, the great day of the camp meetings, the "Colored People's Church" met separately at Hitchcock Hall or Epworth Hall and was led by one of the local ministers.

As the popularity of the camp meeting grew, facilities of all kinds were needed in addition to the Old Auditorium, the Speaker's Stand, and the Old Chapel. Horace Hitchcock, a staunch Methodist from Royal Oak, Michigan, and a member of Detroit's Central Methodist Church, took over the Bay View Sunday school program in 1886. He soon realized how much a building on the grounds could do to promote the Sunday school movement statewide. He raised approximately $3000 from the Michigan Sunday School Congress and the Women's Missionary Society Bible studies. J. L. Hudson of Detroit, founder of Hudson's department stores, made a substantial donation of $100. From Buffalo, N.Y., came a telegram: "Congratulations on new hall. Chautauqua sends greetings. May we all aim higher, work harder, live more nobly, study more diligently, love more ardently, and serve humanity more faithfully. John H. Vincent."[29]

Hitchcock Hall was such a success that the campground association built Epworth Hall. For a cost of $2500, it was completed in the summer of 1891 and dedicated on July 23. Epworth League and the Bay View Summer University used it, but the building became the

***Epworth Hall.*** *(Author's Collection)*

property of the Bay View Camp-Ground Association. The *Daily Resorter* described the structure: "The commodious building contains on the ground floor two large parlors which may be opened together for an audience room, the matrons' rooms and library. On the two floors above are eighteen sleeping apartments. Around the north and west sides are wide porches which add to the beauty of the building and help to make it one of the handsomest on the grounds. The parlors are pleasantly located and attractive in appearance. On the wall hangs a picture of the famous Epworth rectory in England."[30]

For the most part, subjects addressed by preachers at the camp meetings were biblical and traditional, not political. The 1888 national controversy in the Methodist Episcopal Church, however, heated up alongside the campfires when Bishop Thomas Bowman explained the church's position regarding women delegates to the General Assembly. Frances Willard, who had appeared on the Bay View Assembly program the previous summer, and four other elected women delegates had been denied entrance to the Methodist Church General Assembly at the Metropolitan Opera House in New York City. At the assembly, Bishop Stephen Mason Merrill made an ill-considered comment, "There were just two classes who ought never to preach – fools and women." Not surprisingly, it touched off a national controversy.

Most speakers in Bay View vocalized opposition to the action taken by the national church, perhaps because women heavily outnumbered men on the grounds. Reverend Dr. Fiske, president of the co-educational Albion College and a Bay View resident, led a public discussion of the subject on July 25, 1888. The Reverend T. A. Smart thought that women had a natural right to attend the General Assembly. Reverends Jordan and Damon said the action of the General Assembly was dictated by prejudice. Agreeing with the action of the General Assembly was Reverend D. F. Barnes, a regular camp meeting preacher, a cottager, and a Bay View president and vice president. He opposed the admission of women to the General Assembly because the constitution of the national Methodist Church did not permit it.

This incident pointed out a chasm between traditionally-minded camp meeting-goers and the Bay View Assembly progressives. Shortly after the July 25 discussion, the Reverend Dr. Anna Howard Shaw spoke to the association. After first being denied ordination because of her gender, she was the first woman to be ordained in the Methodist Church. Assembly guests such as Willard and Shaw addressed issues facing the nation, and their appearances in Bay View forced religious leaders to deal with the issues.

Dancing became another divisive topic in 1896, a year after Jane Addams spoke on the Bay View platform about her approval of dancing at Chicago's Hull House. Bay View trustee Reverend A. J. Richards received complaints that young people were dancing in the assembly buildings. In letters to her nephew, Martha Brockway admitted that she and the daughter of Senator John Moon, a president of the association, frequently went dancing at Petoskey's Arlington Hotel. Reverend Richards winked at the complaints in his response. "I don't know of a single overstepping of the rules as far as I have seen. I am in perfect sympathy with the young people and their pleasures, and have seen no reason for the complaints that have been made."[31]

Smoking was not winked at, however. A *Daily Resorter* reporter was walking the grounds smoking when he was approached by a cottager. "'Young man if you smoke in these grounds you must swallow the smoke. Other people have rights.' Just think of the gall of it. You would think he owned the air. I went a short distance further, when, so help me, I ran into this sign: 'If you chew tobacco on these grounds you must spit in the lake.' That was worse than the other. The idea of any one [sic] having the nerve to make a cuspidor out of Lake Michigan."[32]

A disagreement with the famous lecturer Reverend Frank Gunsaulus resulted in a national controversy published in a major Chicago daily newspaper in 1889. Gunsaulus, a Chicago resident, was seen "promenading" on the Bay View grounds smoking a cigar. Frances Willard immediately commenced a Woman's Christian Temperance Union meeting at Loud Hall to address the issue since smoking was not allowed. Only the Bay View board of trustees had authority to regulate such matters, but no one believed that the board would take formal action, so the WCTU felt compelled to formulate a resolution. The *Petoskey City Record* chastised the WCTU for not following parliamentary procedure for which the WCTU members heralded themselves as experts.

Not only was the WCTU dissatisfied with the performance of their elected board, but so were other members who thought the general physical condition of the grounds had the appearance of a "backwoods hamlet" rather than the advertised healthy summer resort. They formed the Cottagers' Improvement Association to gain support for change. It was a grassroots effort to motivate the governing body to take action. The most pressing needs were an electrical system to light up the grounds and a water system to protect the cottages from fire. The Cottagers' Improvement Association decided to push for a five-dollar tax on each cottager to pay for these improvements. When the Old Chapel burned in December 1895, the insurance money was used to install a water system with a new well and a pump house on the west shore of the beach, upstream from the sewage system drain. Once this facility was operational, they realized there would be enough power generated by the boiler to install a Westinghouse lighting system throughout the grounds in 1896.

All of this came about not without bickering among the members. The board was aware of widespread dissatisfaction with its performance. At the 1895 annual association meeting, President Dr. Shier began the proceedings

***At the July 18, 1895, annual meeting the board of trustees were dismayed about the griping concerning their management. Judge Moore declared that "if anybody had anything to say the annual meeting was the proper place in which to say it… Moore paid a high compliment to the trustees, who work without compensation and whose summers are crowded with annoyances while the rest of the cottagers are having a good time."*** *(Courtesy of the Little Traverse Historical Society)*

by contrasting the unpleasant atmosphere with the early days of the camp-meetings when everything was perfectly harmonious. Trustee Judge Moore referred to the grumbling on the grounds about the delay in completing the waterworks, declaring that "if anyone had anything to say the annual meeting was the proper place in which to say it...." He complimented the trustees "who work without compensation and whose summers are crowded with annoyances while the rest of the cottagers are having a good time."[33]

Perhaps the rules were not as stringent as thought if the cottagers were having "a good time." Just as the Reverend Richards displayed a more equable attitude toward complaints about dancing, there must have been some tolerance underneath all the pomp and circumstance of WCTU prohibition, Victorian propriety, Methodist rigidity and Bay View frugality. Senator Moon's daughter was not only seen dancing at the Arlington Hotel, she was the hotel's bowling champion the summer her father was president of the association.

Bay View even had an unsupervised place for courting. Big Cedar, a 400-year-old tree in the Bay View woods, was known throughout the region as "Lover's Lane." The Bay View woods were also referred to as "Cupid's Nook," "Lover's Retreat" and "Amorous Acre." The X-rated nature of this subject in Victorian days means that these "love feasts" in the forest chapel were taboo and there are no sheepskin-bound volumes of the history or recollections of Cupid's Woodland Experiences, and nothing is mentioned in Bay View's sanctioned histories. The *Daily Resorter* ran humorous accounts of the "sighs" of young lovers being cut short when mundane chores needed attention, such as fetching drinking water from the upper streams of Mt. Pisgah.

Besides marital wannabes, camp meetings attracted popular leaders of the Methodist Episcopal movement. In addition to Chautauqua's Bishop John Hyle Vincent, some of the national church leaders who appeared regularly in Bay View in the early days were Bishop William X. Ninde, president of Garrett Biblical Institute; Bishop William Taylor, missionary from Africa; Bishop James M. Thoburn, pastor of the Metropolitan Church in Washington, DC; and Bishop Thomas Bowman, a powerful speaker and a nationally-respected Methodist leader who was Chaplain of the US Senate during the final days of the Civil War. During the years he visited Bay View, he was president and chancellor of DePauw University.

***Peter Valti was a valued employee knowing where all of the water pipes were located in the early days.***
*(Courtesy of the Ditto Family)*

***Big Cedar was a 400-year-old tree in the Bay View woods that went down in a thunderstorm in 1896. It was said to be so large it took six men to surround it at the base. Notice the man sitting in front of the tree. The trail near the tree was known locally as Lover's Lane.***
*(Courtesy of Little Traverse Historical Society)*

Bowman was extremely popular and much admired. Matilda Barclay, a Bay View resident from Detroit's Ferry Street raised $128 from ninety-one Bay View residents to purchase an oil portrait of Bowman. In 1888, portrait artist and charter member of the Detroit Art Association, William Brewster Conely, came to Bay View to tent in the woods. Serving in the Civil War, he sustained a bone infection from a wound that never healed. Permanently handicapped, he had to drain the wound daily for thirty-nine years until his death in 1911. Despite this hardship, he was a respected artist who made his living at his craft. The largely self-taught painter was known throughout Michigan as a portrait artist and, today, Conely's work is

***Margaret Custer Calhoun sought solace with Dr. William Shier and his family at their Bay View cottage after her husband and family were killed at the Battle of The Little Big Horn. She studied elocution at the Bay View Summer University, gave recitals at Petoskey's Arlington Hotel before touring the country, and later became the librarian for the state of Michigan.*** *(Courtesy of Monroe County Historical Commission Archives)*

represented at the Detroit Institute of Arts (DIA). While he tented in the Bay View woods, he painted an oil portrait of a Franciscan friar in Harbor Springs and one of Bishop Bowman.[34]

Another was of Dr. William Henry Shier. Although not a founder of the MCGA, Shier is closely associated with Bay View's early days of the camp meetings because of his vivid historical descriptions and his long service to the association. He joined the movement early in the spring of 1876 and built the third cottage on the grounds. After attending the first annual meeting of the association

***David Reed was a member of Bay View from 1877 until his death in 1906. His wife was Lydia Ann Reed. The couple's son Harry Armstrong Reed; Lydia's half brothers General George Custer, Tom Custer, and Boston Custer; Lydia's half sister Margaret's husband Captain Calhoun were all killed at the Battle of The Little Big Horn in 1876.*** *(Courtesy of Monroe County Historical Commission Archives)*

***Lydia Ann Reed***

in August 1876, he was elected to the board of trustees the following year.

During the next forty years, Shier served on the Bay View board as vice president, secretary and treasurer, and became the association's longest-serving president (1887 to 1907) to date. He guided the institution from infancy and constant debt to a firmly-established, nationally-recognized community where education, culture, recreation and religion thrived. Like the founders, Shier had been a Methodist circuit rider. Born in New Jersey in 1832, he moved to Michigan when he was thirteen and attended a Detroit business school. He then returned east to become secretary of the New Jersey Locomotive Machinery Company. In 1858, he married Henrietta Allaire Seelye and went to Texas to supervise the building of a railroad. At the outbreak of the Civil War, he and his ailing wife made their way through combat lines back to Michigan. In Detroit, he met Reverend Seth Reed and converted to Methodism. He became a minister and joined the soldiers on the front lines. After the war, Albion College awarded him a doctor of divinity degree and he served as resident pastor for some fifteen churches in southern Michigan, two of which were the Court Street Methodist Church in Flint and St. Paul's Methodist Church in Monroe.

Grandson Robert Shier described his grandfather as formal and austere: "I often heard my mother remark that he was always most patient with his grandchildren and that he was very charitable in his judgment of others; understanding and sympathetic with those who came to him with their difficulties."[35] One family who came to him in a time of great need arrived at the Petoskey railroad station on July 13, 1877. The Custer family from Monroe, Michigan, included Harry and May Custer; Margaret (Maggie) Custer Calhoun; Lydia Reed (Harry and Maggie's half-sister), her husband David Reed and their daughter; and Annie Yates and her three little children. Yates was Maggie and Libby Custer's close friend.

They all were still mourning the deaths of their relatives the previous year at the Battle of The Little Bighorn. Killed that day with General George Armstrong Custer were brothers Tom and civilians Boston (Harry, Lydia, and Maggie's brothers) and Harry Armstrong Reed (Lydia and David's only son); Captain Yates (Annie Yates' husband and father of her three children); and Captain Calhoun (Maggie's husband). Maggie, a young bride of three years, suffered a nervous breakdown after the massacre. At the Custers' Monroe home, Maggie's mother lay dying, never recovering from the shock.

***Local carpenters took pride in their individual designs for each wooden tent.*** *(Author's Collection)*

The trip to Bay View was particularly sad as the group was en route to Fort Leavenworth for the military funeral and burial of their loved ones. It had taken a year for General Sherman's army to get to the battlefield and retrive the bodies of the officers for transport to Kansas for military honors. General Custer's widow, Libby Bacon Custer, whose family routinely summered at Walloon Lake nearby, was not with the group. She was already on a train east accompanying her husband's body to West Point, where he was to be interred.

There are no known personal accounts of the family's time in Bay View or of their activities at the camp meeting, only that they stayed at the Cushman House in Petoskey before moving out to the Shier cottage and tenting on the Bay View grounds. The family sought solace through Dr. Shier[36] along with Bay View President Pilcher and Reverend Seth Reed who had served the Monroe Methodist Church as ministers and were close to the family. Reed had been General Custer's Sunday school teacher.

The family continued to summer in the area. David Reed and his wife Lydia were Bay View members from 1877 until his death in 1906. On August 11, 1886, Maggie gave a "recital" at Petoskey's Arlington Hotel. She had studied dramatic elocution with Edna Chaffee Noble, a lecturer on the Bay View Assembly platform in 1886 and 1890. Receiving favorable reviews from various newspapers, Maggie Custer toured America giving these "recitals." In 1891, she became the librarian for the state of Michigan. Two years later, she resumed her recital career. She later remarried but died of cancer in New York City after refusing treatment.

Another personality permeating the sketchy pages of Bay View's early history is the Reverend Fayette L. Thompson, who served as minister of the Petoskey Methodist Episcopal Church from 1892 through 1895. In 1895, he took over management of the Bay View Camp-Meeting. He ran it successfully with a budget of $250 which included assembling a hymnal, distributing advertisements, taking charge of young people's meetings and organizing the speakers. Thompson took a pulpit in Jackson, Michigan, after 1895 but preached regularly throughout the state. The *Big Rapids Current* called one of his sermon there "one of the most eloquent and forceful efforts ever addressed to the young people of our city." Thompson assumed management of the camp meeting in Davenport, Iowa, but returned to Bay View to run its camp meeting. He also served as Bay View's vice president for a year in 1901.

The *Daily Resorter* credited Thompson with much of the success of the camp meeting: "Other princely workers have been there, but during the past eight years the heaviest burdens had rested upon the shoulders of Fayette

***Families brought their children and house staff with them for several weeks during the warm July August days to enjoy both the camp meetings and the assembly offerings.*** *(Author's Collection)*

L. Thompson. It is he is who has largely determined the successful policy of the camp meeting and who has worked that policy out. He has taken the initiative in everything. He has worked hard through the winter months in preparing for the summer gathering.... Moreover, he has had a clear grasp of the situation. He realized that the camp meeting must be suited to existing conditions and it was this realization which led him to adopt the policy of uniting piety with brains. He was clear sighted enough years ago to foresee the trend of the day and more particularly of this resort, and to plan accordingly. Consequently the program has been so arranged as to challenge both intellect and emotion."[37]

That wide appeal of the meetings resulted in change. The tents quickly becoming wooden and permanent, and the "unchurched got churched". The spontaneous, fervent camp meetings in the woods that had so enthralled Native Americans and entertained northern Michigan loggers, evolved into moments of rest and relaxation for summer visitors. Campers began arriving early to enjoy quiet time in the grove. With improved housing, campers spent more time on the grounds. Soon, summer vacations became the major focus and the camp meetings faded into a secondary interest.

"So it has come to pass that the camp-meeting is less used as an evangelizing force on the frontiers and more of the nature of a vacation service. Our Lord and Master took a vacation when he was weary, and did good during his period of rest," the Reverend Dr. Daniel Steele of Boston told the Bay View congregation.[38] Recognizing the secular trend, he gave it doctrinal justification.

The arching grove of beech trees that formed a place of prayer for camp meeting-goers had become a bower of power for the Bay View Assembly which was formed in 1886. Within just a few years, the Bay View Assembly became the major focus of attention. "We believe in the camp meeting but we have the profound conviction that it, itself, even in its distinctive sphere depends to a high degree on the assembly," observed a writer in the *Daily Resorter* in 1889.

Some felt that the assembly had desecrated their "natural temple," the camp meeting, and a rivalry began within the Bay View management. Writer Dr. A. Douglas MacNaughton later alluded to this in his history of the Michigan Methodist Church, citing the charge among many Methodists that Bay View was primarily intended for entertainment purposes. In response to these charges, the camp meeting dates had been moved ahead to precede the assembly. But that action inadvertently led to the camp meeting serving as a warm-up act for the main show to follow. "The Bay View camp meeting has been eclipsed in importance, in the estimation of a great many, by the assembly and the university. But to the pioneers of the resort, who remember with pleasure the grand meetings held in the open air, in God's first temples, the native woods, there is nothing which can take the place of the camp meeting."[39]

It took another decade, but, after a successful run of more than thirty years, the camp meeting finally ended in 1908 due to a number of factors. The Bay View management was in disarray with no clear leadership. The faithful Thompson had resigned. Shier stepped down as president of Bay View, and the 1889 *Daily Resorter* prophesy came true. The camp meeting simply could not sustain the interest of the populace, and the final meeting was held July 7 through July 13, 1908. This phenomenon had come to the end of its time. The Lakeside camp meeting also ended that year.

Today the altar calls, the Amen Corner and the baptism of the Holy Spirit of the camp meeting days are gone. There is something eternal, however, about a group of Methodists singing the Chautauqua hymn "Day is Dying in the West," overlooking Petoskey which is Odawa for the "place of the rising sun." The Camp Meeting Proper came to an official end in 1908, but its traditions were carried on within the Bay View Assembly.

*It is more religious to laugh than to groan.*
*Anyone can groan, but it takes a David, a Paul,*
*or a modern heroine to laugh*
*in the midst of persecution.*

Reverend Thomas Dewitt Talmage, Bay View Camp Meeting, July 18, 1886

— CHAPTER THREE —

# By The Wayside

The camp meeting had been going about ten years when a tall distinguished-looking young man came to a meeting. Leaning up against a beech tree, he pondered the Big Sunday service scene. A bystander described how "he looked so intent, so absorbed, I wondered what was in his mind. I was soon to learn that he was meditating on a great possibility that rapidly grew into a definite plan".[1]

That great possibility forming in the thirty-five year old lawyer's mind was something only John Manley Hall could have imagined as he stood at the edge of the grove. In front of him, long-bearded officers of the debt-ridden association were seated on the Speaker's Stand. A loquacious preacher was giving a typically long-winded sermon. Chief Petoskey's granddaughter wearing a bright red velvet dress, played the little pump organ to accompany the singing of several thousand Victorian campers, backwoods loggers, local farmers, and Native Americans all dressed in their Sunday finery. Sitting on stones and pews rudely constructed of boards laid across tree stumps and sawhorses, the crowd's only protection from the weather's erratic moods was the beech grove's leafy umbrella. From a flimsy shanty, the men of the "amen corner" heartily expressed their approval of the speaker's remarks.

*John Manley Hall (circa 1910).*
*(Courtesy of David L. Bieber, great-grandson of John M. Hall)*

Encircling this natural amphitheater was the sandy Encampment Avenue separating the camp meeting from the cloth and wooden tents. Beyond the avenue, "tangle foot"[2] covered the ground and invariably tripped even the most careful walkers as they made their way from campsites to the grove. In this crude atmosphere, with its rudimentary water and sanitation facilities and lack of substantial structures, this visionary individual dreamed of a great assembly that would attract thousands from all parts of the country.

Hall was the only son of Rosana Blanchard and John P. Hall, early settlers of Macomb County, Michigan.[3] He spent his childhood on a farm in Mt. Clemens, growing up with a half-sister and two half-brothers from his father's first marriage. When he was sixteen, his father passed away, and he and his mother moved to Flint and joined the Court Street Methodist Episcopal Church. Nine years later Hall graduated from Albion College and moved to Detroit to study law with the Hon. Alfred Russell. He then returned to Flint to practice with the law firm of Hall & Brennan. In 1878, he married Mary M. Fox, daughter of David Fox, president of Flint's First National Bank. Fox was also a pioneer lumberman, former mayor of the town, and a founder of the Flint Wagon Works.[4] Sometime in the late 1880s, Hall and his wife adopted a daughter, Dorothy.

When the New York Chautauqua expanded its program in 1878 with an innovative educational reading program called the Chautauqua Literary and Scientific Circle (CLSC), within just six years, national membership totaled over 2000, with more than 130 circles in 110 cities. Hall managed the Michigan circles from his home on Church Street, holding meetings at Court Street Church. By1883, crowds became so large they had to be moved to the city's opera house. The circles were well known throughout the state, and Henry Ford met his wife Clara at a CSLC meeting.[5] Both Lewis Miller and John Heyl Vincent, co-founders of the Chautauqua Institutions and its correspondence course, quickly noticed Hall's success. In the 1889 issue of the *Chautauquan* they wrote: "It is said that although Michigan is one of the smallest States [sic] in population, it leads all others in Chautauqua work, in proportion to population, having nearly one-fifteenth of all the Chautauquans. This is in large measure due to the energy of Mr. John M. Hall of Flint, Michigan."[6]

Reverend William H. Shier, minister of the Flint church, admired the way the young entrepreneur promoted the circles. Shier shared his feelings with his good friend, Reverend Seth Reed, and the two ministers decided that Hall was the catalyst to revitalize the now stagnating growth of the MCGA. The Methodist campers had been relatively successful, but, by 1885, the trustees wanted further expansion. There were 131 cottages on the grounds and several public buildings, including a Speaker's Stand and a bookstore in Tabernacle Park, railroad depot, boathouse, chapel, crude dorm, dining room and primitive hotel. The trustees knew they needed to sell more lots and increase incentives to attend the camp meetings if they were going to eliminate the association's accumulated debt of $5000. Also, the Petoskey people were pressing Bay View officials to inaugurate a Chautauqua assembly. *Petoskey City Record* editor J. C. Bontecou editorialized that "Many Michigan people go to Chautauqua [New York] every year, solely because of the scientific and literary advantages afforded by that association. Were similar opportunities given at Bay View, they would spend their summers here where everything else is more favorable for a summer rest than at Chautauqua Association. [sic]"[7]

***Mary Hall (circa 1910).***
*(Courtesy of David L. Bieber, great-grandson of John M. Hall)*

Bay View planners made an unsuccessful attempt to establish a CLSC course but substituted their own course because it was cheaper. Editor Bontecou continued to pressure association officials:

> *With Bay View as the headquarters of Michigan Chautauquans the association would be able to reach out and find a point of contact with the intellectual life of almost every village in the state; for in every hamlet are to be found Chautauqua students.*[8]

By this time, the camp meeting included a Sunday School Congress, a ministerial union, missionary days and temperance days run by the WCTU. Plans to institute a CLSC reading program were scrapped in 1885 because of the red ink. That fall on October 29, 1885, at a Grand Rapids board meeting, Hall was elected superintendent of Bay View's new Chautauqua Educational Department and charged with organizing "a summer system of popular education." He proudly announced his election: "By the grace of Dr. J. H. Vincent, Superintendent of the Chautauqua Circle at large, and the action of the Board of Trustees of the Michigan Camp-ground Association, I have been honored with the superintendency [sic] of this department and of the Bay View Assembly."[9]

Chautauqua founders Miller and Vincent supported Hall's appointment because of his success with the Michigan CLSC. In subsequent years, Vincent visited the grounds several times to address CLSC graduates and quickly claimed Bay View to be the "most successful independent Chautauqua" in the country. No mention of the organizational structure was made in these initial business arrangements, but financial and managerial separation of the camp meeting association and the assembly program later caused a chasm within Bay View management and between Bay View and Chautauqua.

To a high-energy person like Hall, who often worked fourteen hours a day, Bay View was a challenge he relished. With no inkling of impending repercussions, Hall began plans for the inaugural season. He leased his own lot and made plans to build a cottage, *Wayside*, at Block 1, Lot 11.

Like Chautauqua, Hall's "Bay View idea" consisted of a three-part program eventually to be known as the Bay View System of Popular Education. It included the Bay View Assembly, the Summer University, and a correspondence course, The Bay View Reading Circle and *The Bay View Magazine,* for those wishing to continue their studies over the winter months. The assembly, begun in 1886, was followed by the Summer University officially in 1888 and the Bay View Reading Circle (BVRC) in 1893. To advise him on the assembly, Hall organized a board headed by Alexander Winchell, U-M geology professor and Michigan's second state geologist. A progressive, he had promoted Charles Darwin's history of evolution in a number of his books.

The first season went well. Hall erected a large tent (with "conveniences") in the middle of the grounds, which he called the Temple of the Scribes, as headquarters for press correspondents. He invited publishers from around the state. Musicians, entertainers and speakers provided a ten-day program of lectures, concerts, cooking lessons, travelogues and CLSC meetings, all with an indication of things hoped for - a summer university, museum, library and correspondence course.

While the assembly started out with Michigan talent, it soon became a place where people from all over the country connected with the cultural, educational and political climate of the day. By the second year, the assembly was expanded to include a ministers' institute directed by Reverend Alfred A. Wright of Boston, and a missionary congress led by Reverend Dr. Arthur T. Pierson of Philadelphia. The Detroit publishing firm of Phillips & Hunt ran a bookstore. Ida A. Harper of the Cleveland *Leader* painted an idyllic picture of the grounds in1887:

> *The assembly was opened last year as an experiment, and was so very successful that this year the grounds were leased from the Campmeeting [sic] Association and the assembly put on a permanent footing. The amphitheater, "hall in the grove," chapel, and all those buildings so dear to the heart of every true Chautauquan, are all handsome and substantial structures and the assembly is established on a sound financial basis. The hotels are filled to overflowing and all the cottage rooms are taken, many visitors having to go to Petoskey to sleep....*
>
> *The desire is very strong to linger awhile longer at Bay View. The air is so pure and delicious that it causes us to look with scorn upon any one [sic] who would ask "Is life worth living?" Every one of the three hundred pretty cottages perched upon the high terraces overlooking the lake, and all the people singing praises in the great amphitheater, and the scores of happy children playing upon the shore make eloquent reply.*[10]

New association members were frantically building "wooden tents" so they could enjoy the summer season. Season ticket sales by 1888 were over 1500, well above

***Chautauqua Cottage, now the Woman's Council, was built in 1887 for education classes and CLSC reading circle meetings.***
*(Courtesy of Little Traverse Historical Society)*

the previous year's total of 1100. By 1889, assembly receipts reached $3600, two hundred dollars over expenses and nearly $1000 over the previous year's take. A reporter for *Frank Leslie's Illustrated Newspaper* called Bay View the "Chautauqua of the Northwest… the very cream of the literary, oratorical, and musical world."[11]

During the fall and winter of 1886 and 1887, Hall raised approximately $1100 among Michigan Chautauquans to build a "home" for all Chautauquans and a wooden structure for the assembly lectures and programs. Chautauqua Cottage (now the Woman's Council Building) was designed by French-born Flint-based architect Francis Xavier Oliver (1826-1911) and built by the Petoskey firm of David and Peter Leonard Seibert. Oliver had designed a number of the original buildings in downtown Flint. He and the Seibert firm eventually built all the wooden structures on the Bay View campus with the exception of, possibly, Vernor Hall.

Chautauqua Cottage housed the CLSC meetings and various classes of the Bay View Summer University. Hall enthusiastically described this new building in the October 1887 *Bay View Assembly Herald*: "Everybody admired it, and Chautauquans were proud of it. Its exterior was as beautiful as tower and broad, sweeping verandas and artistic details could make it, while its interior was as handsome as inviting easy chairs, carpets, and draperies, pictures, models and Japanese decorations could make its spacious parlors."[12]

Not so beautiful was the Old Auditorium, which was as mundane as its name, although Hall glorified it in his advertising. With $500 from his Chautauqua funds, he had this $1200 wooden structure hastily constructed in time for his 1887 assembly program. "It will be nearly double the size of the building heretofore used and be one of the finest structures for the purpose to be found at any Assembly," he boasted, making no mention of the financial discrepancy.[13]

The camp meetings of the previous decade had had regional appeal, featuring Michigan speakers and ministers within the sect. In contrast, the assembly attracted nationally-known clergy on the Chautauqua circuit: the Reverend John DeWitt Miller (whom poet-author Carl Sandburg found impressive as assistant editor of the *Lyceumite* trade journal for the Chautauqua movement); the Reverend Russell H. Conwell, founder of Temple University; the Reverend Frank W. Gunsaulus, director of Chicago's Armour Institute of Technology; Reverend Jesse Lyman Hurlbut, author of popular Sunday school literature, who came for the first camp meeting in 1877 and returned in 1891, 1892 and 1915; Reverend A. J. F. Behrends, pastor of Brooklyn's Central Congregational Church; and Reverend S. Parkes Cadman, later president of the Federal Council of Churches.

Reverend Thomas Dewitt Talmage, a Presbyterian who had served as chaplain in the Union Army during the Civil War, had an audience of 2200 for his 1901 appearance. Widely known and respected, he was pastor of the First Presbyterian Church in Washington, DC between 1895 and 1899, when his sermons were printed in 3500 newspapers across the country. He was the keynote speaker at Graduation Day for the BVRC members.

The WCTU was already established in Petoskey when the Bay View Chautauqua Assembly was inaugurated in 1886. With strong support from local "white ribboners," Hall arranged for appearances by prohibitionist Frances Willard for 1887 and 1889.[14] She launched the WCTU Institutes and later served on the board of trustees of Hall's BVRC. Willard's association with Bay View led to a WCTU announcement that fall in *The Union Signal* that another new building was planned at Bay View: "R.G. Peters and his wife of Manistee, Michigan, have given $5,000 to be used in building for [sic] the W.C.T.U. headquarters of the Methodist Episcopal summer resort grounds at Bay View, Michigan."[15] Peters had just endowed a $50,000 building at Oberlin College and had been extremely generous with many needy organizations. Evelyn, his wife, was an active WCTU worker in her city and in Chicago. Nearly a year later, Hall appeared before the trustees of the MCGA to exhibit architect Oliver's plans for what would become the most celebrated building on the Bay View campus.

The year's delay was disastrous. In 1889, Peters' enormous business conglomerate, the R.G. Peters Salt and Lumber Company, one of the largest in the state, went into bankruptcy. The $4300 cost of Evelyn Hall was a debt that had to be paid through a loan taken out with a Petoskey

**Evelyn Peters** *(Courtesy of Bentley Historical Library, U of M)*

**The Fisk Jubilee Singers were so popular among audiences they appeared in Bay View in 1890, 1891, 1897, and in the present John M. Hall Auditorium in 1915. They were registered at the Bay View House.** *(Author's Collection)*

bank by the MCGA. Peters paid the interest until he recovered financially and could pay off the loan.[16] Despite complications, Evelyn Hall was dedicated on July 24, 1890, with many national and state WCTU officers attending. A suite of rooms was set aside for Willard, but her attention was focused internationally by 1890, and she never saw the building. Evelyn Peters became critically ill in 1890 and never saw it either.

Unlike other Chautauqua leaders, Hall had no preconceived philosophical agenda. Consequently, the Bay View talent in the 1890s included an assortment of lecturers, musicians, round table discussions, magicians, jugglers, readers and Bible lecturers. Bay View's Chicago booking agent, Harry Harrison of the Redpath Lyceum Bureau later described Bay View's assembly goers as more "interested in poets and poetry, art, literature and polite travelogues than evangelical orators and loud gospel."[17] Names common on the Bay View roster were journalist and social reformer Jacob Riis, Dr. John Harvey Kellogg, politicians William Jennings Bryan and John Worth Kern, prison reformer Maud Ballington Booth and educator Booker T. Washington. Other speakers included the president of the 1893 Chicago World's Fair, Hon. Thomas W. Palmer; foreign newspaper correspondent George Kennan; Michigan Senator Julius Caesar Burrows; U-M champion of academic freedom Moses Coit Tyler; and Cuban diplomat Gonzales de Quesada. Some of the speeches were covered in local newspapers. Regrettably, there are no copies of speeches such as that of ex-Indiana governor Will Cumback's talk on "The Model Husband," or the 1893 speech of Lee Merriwether on "Europe on Fifty Cents a Day", although his 1886 book, *A Tramp Trip,* documents the gist of his lecture.

The opening of the assembly was a festive occasion always free to the public and often featured musical entertainment such as local bands from Petoskey, Kalkaska or Alma. In 1890, the Fisk Jubilee Singers was the headliner. The troupe was the first black entertainment group to tour the US. By the time they appeared in Bay View, the fourteen vocalists had already toured Germany, then pinnacle of the music world. Among the nine singers who checked into Bay View's premier hotel, the Bay View House, was soprano Maggie L. Porter-Cole, one of the brave members on the group's first harrowing 1871 national tour.

The Fisk Jubilee Singers, whose purpose was to raise money for Fisk University, introduced the world to Negro spirituals. Featured in their Bay View concerts were their special arrangements of plantation melodies sung by their parents as slaves as well as their special arrangements of other folk tunes. Porter-Cole's version of the Swiss song "Flower of the Alps" was so well received by the audience of 1500 people that she followed it with an encore Scottish tune "If a Body Meet a Body Coming thro' the Rye." Other impressive singers with the troupe were tenor C. W. Payne and bass J. N. Caldwell. The Fisk Jubilee Singers returned to Bay View in 1891, 1897 and, again, in 1915 when three-year old Mildred Place Panney heard them and never forgot their beautiful singing and has loved music ever since.[18]

Jacob Riis's Bay View appearances usually followed the publication of a book. In1892, he was on a tour for his second book, *Children of the Poor*. A follow-up visit came in 1896 and another occurred on August 3-4, 1898, when the book, *Out of Mulberry Street,* was released. The main thrust of his lectures and stereopticon slide presentations was that it was the duty of the state to provide a healthy environment in which boys and girls could grow up. In his lectures, he told about children in New York being forced to forage through garbage for food. He gave details about his encounters as a police reporter on New York's Mulberry Street with children who worked from seven in the morning until eight at night for as little as one dollar a week.

Also on the program in 1890, 1891 and 1892 was the "Father of the Modern Health Food Industry," Dr. John Harvey Kellogg of the Michigan Battle Creek Sanitarium. This medical doctor was the leading proponent of preventive medicine and had been director of the famous sanitarium for fourteen years. His advice on biological living was decades ahead of his era, and his adamant stand against alcohol supported the WCTU's position. His wife, a devoted WCTU volunteer, also spoke at Bay View WCTU meetings and taught cooking in 1891 in the "large pavilian [sic] between the Tabernacle and Epworth House". Kellogg returned in 1910 to lead Bay View's Health Conference.

If Teddy Roosevelt's famous remark that Chautauqua "is the most American thing in America" was true then the most Chautauqua thing in the Chautauqua movement was William Jennings Bryan. Derogatorily dubbed the Chautauqua "savant" by critics, the "Great Commoner" made his living speaking at Chautauqua assemblies, garnering perhaps as much as $25,000 a summer at a time when the average American's annual wage was not even $500. Certainly, Bryan's great reputation as an eloquent speaker came from the Chautauqua throngs he inspired with such famous speeches as the "Cross of Gold" and the "Prince of Peace."

The popularity of Bryan's message with the common people was due to his unique blend of Christian morality and public responsibility. Bay View championed the "Great Commoner", inviting him to its platform no fewer than five times over three decades – from the early years when he served as a US Congressman through his three unsuccessful bids for the White House and the beginning of his challenge of evolutionists and modernists.

The first time Bryan came to Petoskey was August 25, 1891, when he was running for the US House of Representatives from his home state of Nebraska. He stayed at the Cushman House. He was scheduled to return in 1898, after running unsuccessfully on the "silver" platform as the Democratic presidential candidate, but was in Florida involved in protests of the Spanish American War. The following year, on August 3, 1899, he did appear on the Bay View platform as he was preparing for another White House bid. In his "silver-tongued" manner, he told more than 2000 people inside the Old Auditorium (and hundreds surrounding the hall) of his populist stand on the silver question, although the crowd was largely opposed to his position. "They talk about the silver sentiment being a disease, and say it is like whooping cough or the measles, it has to run its course…If I were going to describe it as a disease I would want to name it yellow fever. The old yellow fever killed the man who had the fever, but the new yellow fever kills the man who does not have the fever."[19]

He explained why he favored an income tax and why tariffs put the burden of taxation on those least able to pay, the poor. He foresaw the movement for independence in India and assessed British rule as unsuccessful, despite popular claims. The Commoner then took some time away from politics but, by 1905 he was back on the train touring the country. He came to Bay View again on August 1 to speak on "The Value of an Ideal."

In 1908, Bryan ran again for president, this time with Hoosier John Worth Kern as his running mate. Kern, a graduate of the University of Michigan, was related by marriage to another Hoosier, W. J. DeVol, who built and owned Bay View's Terrace Inn. During the presidential campaign of 1908, Kern rented The Florence Cottage (the same place where Hemingway later stayed) for his family for the summer and did so annually until 1912. Kern had been unsuccessful in his bid for governor of Indiana in 1900 and 1904 but was selected to complete the national ticket with Bryan at the Democratic convention in Denver in July, 1908. He "would make a strong man for second place," Mayor Dahlman of Omaha told the national press. Although the Bryan/Kern team lost the election in 1908, Kern was elected US Senator from Indiana.

On August 2, 1911, when William Jennings Bryan returned to Bay View, he was the guest of Senator and Mrs. Kern at The Florence Cottage. Indiana Governor Thomas R. Marshall, who was again summering in Petoskey at the Cushman House, introduced Bryan at the auditorium and joined Mrs. Kern, her son, and Bryan for dinner at the Bay View House after his speech. Two years later, Marshall became the US vice president and Bryan, secretary of state. Bryan appeared again on August 11, 1918 to speak about the war, the liquor question, women's suffrage, and man's relationship to his society, his government and his God. Bryan held the packed house spellbound for two hours.

Bryan's tremendous popularity in Emmet County is paradoxical. He was a member of the Presbyterian Church USA and actively involved in the fundamentalist movement which led him to become the prosecutor in the famous Scopes trial.[20] Most of the leading Bay View speakers at the time were socialists or modernists like most Chautauquans, and opposed religious fundamentalism.

Today, Bryan is depicted as a scientific ignoramus in many history textbooks and particularly in the play *Inherit the Wind*, while his detractors, the modernists, since witnessed how Hitler used their philosophy to justify the sterilization and murder of millions. Recent reassessments in various sources show Bryan to be a man far ahead of his time whose political proposals included direct primaries, women's suffrage, direct election of senators, no lame-duck Congress, tariff reduction, a graduated income tax, enforcement of the Sherman Anti-Trust Act, publication of campaign contributions, guaranteed bank deposits, the eight-hour work day, licensed corporations and conservation of resources. All these proposals have been enacted over the last century. Bryan was arguably the most forward-thinking of the "radicals" who appeared on the Bay View platform in the early days.

One casualty of the budget constraints and scheduling "snafus" came when Hall turned down the opportunity to engage Mark Twain for July 20, 1895. Foreign correspondent George Kennan was already contracted for that day. Major James Pond's diary documents that Hall told him that he didn't feel Twain would have a sufficient draw to attract an audience of 2000 to warrant engaging him. So Twain's manager Pond, "took the risk outside, and won." He booked the Petoskey Opera House which was filled to almost double its capacity with 750 people, about one-third of the capacity of the Bay View auditorium. George Kennan was in the audience to hear Twain.[21]

The Bay View Summer University, the second goal of John M. Hall's educational system, was the most ambitious. A university wasn't quite what founding fathers had in mind when they formed their camp meeting corporation in 1875, but education, as it supported religious beliefs and the betterment of all, was a goal. In the articles of incorporation drawn up by President Elijah Pilcher, the camp meeting institution was "to authorize Societies organized for intellectual and scientific culture, and for the promotion of the cause of religion and morality."[22] Consequently, when Hall embarked on this assembly venture, education and a "university" were easily accepted as part of everyone's long term vision.

As early as 1885, English professor M. Louise Jones discussed the possibilities with Hall. The following year, the nucleus of a "university" began with three or four instructors including Jones, Lansing School Superintendent Reverend David Howell, Professor Henry A. Mills and seventy-five students. Cooking, elocution, a Sunday school normal department, New Testament Greek, art classes, a teachers' institute, a ministers' institute, art, and music were the courses offered.

As it developed, the Summer University included an odd assortment of liberal arts and popular interest classes, religious instruction and a normal program. Professor Alexander Winchell of U-M became the Summer

***Williams Jennings Bryan came to Bay View four and possibly five times. In 1908 his running mate for vice president was John Worth Kern, the brother-in-law of William DeVol, the builder of the Terrace Inn.*** *(Author's Collection)*

*William J. DeVol and his wife Josephine had three daughters, Cordelia, Beatrice, and Virginia who were active in local activities. DeVol's sister was married to John Worth Kern, William Jennings Bryan's vice presidential running mater in 1908. Here the family enjoys downtime at their family cottage.* (Courtesy of Patricia Zetterberg)

University's first president. Matilda H. Ross of Grand Rapids, nationally known expert on kindergarten education, taught primary, normal, and kindergarten classes. State education superintendent David Howell conducted the teachers' institutes. Bertha Ward took care of the children's chorus. Professor E. E. Stephens of Flint conducted the assembly chorus. Alfred A. Wright taught Greek. Professor H. A. Mills taught art. Other offerings included cooking, history and philosophy. The most popular sessions were the teachers' institutes in the Normal Methods department.

The department of education and the teacher's institute in 1887 turned out to be Hall's greatest achievement. "The department was begun as an experiment, but its success together with the delight of the instructors over future prospects, and the earnest support given by the two hundred or more teachers at the Assembly have led the management to make it a permanent school," he reported in the *Assembly Herald* in October of 1887.

The success continued, and, in 1891, the *Daily Resorter* reported that fifty teachers from Emmet County attended the institute taught by college instructors and public school administrators from Michigan and other states. By 1894, attendance had grown to 800 teachers. *The Bay View Assembly Record* reported in 1895 that: "Bay View is fast becoming a summer Mecca for the school teachers of all the neighboring states, and it may be expected that before many years that name will bring into the minds of every ma'am in Michigan, Indiana and even Illinois recollection of five weeks' university work under trained specialists happily combined with a pleasant summer's outing."[23]

The education of five-year-olds was a progressive idea being actively embraced in Grand Rapids. Considered on the "cutting edge" of educational philosophy, the program was begun in 1887 by Matilda H. Ross of Syracuse, New York, and Grand Rapids. She took charge of the primary and normal classes using the kindergarten as a laboratory where pedagogy learned in the classroom could be demonstrated and practiced. In 1888, Ross had twelve assistants. In 1889, the *Daily Resorter* critiqued the theory: "The motion exercises, methods for securing attention, for drawing out answers, and teaching independent thought and developing the memory, are worthy of profound attention and imitation."[24]

At the National Educational Association meeting in 1890, Swedish teacher Meri Toppelius presented a new method of teaching woodworking to children to promote academic learning. The method, called Sloyd, was developed in her homeland. In 1891, she was hired to come to Bay View to teach in the teachers' institute and the kindergarten. She was so popular that enrollment reached nearly forty children, and many more were turned away. The *Daily Resorter* described her methods: "They make simple pieces, but their minds are trained to design. The constructive sense is awakened, the hands and eyes are developed, a sense of tastiness and form is aroused and physical exercise is united with all. A love for labor is not the least thing that is caused by training in Sloyd, in fact it is perhaps the greatest merit the system has."[25]

The success of the Summer University enabled Hall to convince one of Michigan's philanthropists, Henry Martyn Loud, an Oscoda lumberman, to join its board and give $3500 for a new building.[26] F.X. Oliver designed it, and the Petoskey firm of Seibert built it in time for the 1888 summer season. It was named Loud Hall after its funder.

In December of 1895, disaster struck. The rickety Old Chapel burned. The Bay View Association board of trustees took the insurance payment to offset the cost of a new Westinghouse lighting system to be installed on the grounds the following summer. Despite this, Hall went ahead with plans for a new Conservatory of Music to be built on the site and completed in time for the 1896 season. Though the cost is unknown, assembly supporters held benefits to raise funds for the new building.

The Summer University grew quickly, filling all available space in the campus public buildings including the new classrooms at Loud Hall. Initially, students came from three states – Michigan, Ohio and Indiana - but, by

1891, enrollment reached 350 students from twelve states. By 1892, there were some ninety courses offered, with forty-five instructors and 711 students. By 1894, total college enrollment peaked at 743 students, with the College of Liberal Arts and the School of Methods being the most successful. Student and faculty housing was provided in the dormitory space on the top floor of Loud Hall as well as single and double rooms at Epworth, Evelyn and Hitchcock halls, and Chautauqua Cottage.

As early as the 1890s, space was a major problem for the Summer University with all of its tangential programs. "This is the fifth session of the school and already every available room is rented for the entire term, lasting four weeks"[27], the *Daily Resorter* noted in 1891. The liberal arts school and the school of business were at Loud Hall, along with children's classes, the library and the kindergarten. Art and photography classes were conducted at Chautauqua Cottage, along with the CLSC discussion groups. Hitchcock Hall housed the Sunday school meetings and the Bible classes as well as a 300-artifact Bay View Egyptian collection.

Music classes were at the Conservatory of Music along with the cooking school. Dean David Howell complained to the *Daily Resorter* in 1891 about the teaching situation at the conservatory**.** "Often the tea-pot and frying pan came into conflict with the teacher's rod and the musician's keyboard and I agreeably assimilated intellectual food with samples of the new dishes with the culinary department"[28] To handle the overflow, a large tent was erected between Loud Hall and the Conservatory where John Harvey Kellogg's wife Ella taught her cooking classes.

During the first decade, the Summer School faculty included outstanding professors. In 1889, the *Daily Resorter* agreed: "It is a compliment to Mr. Hall that he should have secured workers of such ripe fitness as the Yale instructors in Hebrew and Biblical Greek, and as Professors King, Fall, Lodeman and Perry in their respective departments. We are impressed that it is here that Bay View has a high future before it. Let this spot be a summer university."[29]

Also on the faculty were Professor Wooster W. Beeman, head of the mathematics department at U-M; Dr. John M. Coulter of Lake Forest College and the University of Chicago; Dr. William A. Merrill of Indiana University; Professor Frederick S. Goodrich of Albion College; Dr. Richard G. Boone of Michigan State Normal College; Professor Frank M. Mills of Cornell University; Dr. William B. Shafer of Lehigh University; and Richard T. Ely of the University of Wisconsin.

Frances Willard recommended Dr. Richard T. Ely's book, *An Introduction to Political Economy* in her 1889 Bay View CLSC Round Table Discussions. She was highly praised for her selection and three years later Hall secured Ely to head the Bay View Summer University. When the economist came to Bay View, he was at the beginning of his long and distinguished career. During the 1880s, Ely had spent six summers at Chautauqua, New York, and supported the correspondence courses there. By 1892, however, his academic affiliation with Johns Hopkins University was severed in a philosophical dispute, and he moved west to become the director of the school of economics, political science and history at the University of Wisconsin. Devoted to the Methodist Church and the Chautauqua ideal, Ely continued his summer academic life at Bay View, bringing with him David Kinley (who joined him at the University of Wisconsin), and professors Herbert W. Magoun and Frank E. Millis, both from Johns Hopkins University.

Ely's lectures at the Old Auditorium and at Epworth and Evelyn halls included talks on "The Nature of Socialism," "The Strengths of Socialism," "The Weakness of Socialism," and the question "How can the good in socialism be incorporated into our social order?" These radical ideas regarding strikes and unions soon caused him difficulties in Madison in a famous case involving academic freedom. Unfortunately, Hall was not able to retain Ely, and he returned to Chautauqua to resume his summer teaching there.

Replacing him was Dr. John Merle Coulter, one of the foremost botanists in the country. Coulter was then president of Lake Forest University and a lecturer at the University of Chicago. Born in China in 1851 to a Presbyterian missionary couple, Coulter was a philosophica fit. Eugene Cittadino described Coulter as "…a kind of hero who belonged to the American Midwest of the late nineteenth century: a pioneering educator from a small town with a clear vision of the moral and intellectual responsibilities of colleges and universities, a vigorous natural leader and engaging speaker, a scientist who combined rugged field experiences with scholarship and laboratory work, and a deeply religious man committed to the reconciliation of science with Christianity."[30] Coulter stayed until 1896 when he assumed the first chairmanship of the University of Chicago's Department of Botany. His family continued to summer at their Harbor Point cottage –"on the other shore". Years later, he led a group of students who studied the dunes of Little Traverse Bay in conjunction with that university's study of the southern Lake Michigan dunes**.**

Another University of Wisconsin professor, Helen Campbell, spoke in Bay View in 1894 and recapped her experiences in the Wisconsin *State Journal*: "A season at Chautauqua allows your correspondent right of comparison, and the points in favor of Bay View are easily summed up…. As to the work of the many schools, nothing more admirable is being done anywhere, and in some points I am inclined to think Bay View leads. The natural methods prevails, and from languages up and through, to methods in teaching and the freshest and most vital work in the Art School, and in music,—all is stamped with the seal of executive power and trained ability of the highest."[31]

## AT DAY'S END

Is anybody happier because you passed
his way?
Does anyone remember that you spoke
to him today?
The day is almost over, and its toiling
time is through;
Is there anyone to utter now a kindly
word of you?
Can you say tonight, in parting with the
day that's slipping fast,
That helped a single brother of the
many that you passed?

Is a single heart rejoicing over what
you did or said;
Does the man whose hopes were fading,
now with courage look ahead?
Did you wast the day, or lose it? Was
it well or sorely spent?
Did you leave a trail of Kindness, or a
scar of discontent?
As you close your eyes in slumber, do
You think that God will say,
"You have earned one more tomorrow
by the work you did today"?

**--John Hall**

Mrs. Mary W. Ball of Grand Rapids gave a collection of European coins. Olivet College donated a section of a whale's spinal column in 1891. Bay View Museum curator Helen Guittard and Commission Chairwoman Anne Lewis wrote in *Bay View Beginnings, The First 25 Years, 1875-1900,* that the museum acquired in 1892 the skeleton of a mastodon weighing 1000 pounds discovcred by Charles Cummings. In a later account by Profcssor M. Louise Jones, Michigan Senator Thomas Palmer, who was president of the 1893 Columbian Exposition, gave the museum three hundred state government documents which she considered to be quite rare.

Also rare was a collection of some 300 Egyptian artifacts. Like most Victorians, the people of Bay View were fascinated by Egyptian history. They subscribed to the popular idea that knowledge of ancient Egypt would ultimately prove the Bible to be historically accurate. About the time Hall formed the Bay View Assembly, Dr. Camden Cobern was serving the Detroit Conference of the Methodist Episcopal Church. Apparently from 1883 until 1896 he was the minister of the Cass Avenue Methodist Church, then the Jefferson Avenue Methodist Church both in Detroit and, then at the Ann Arbor Methodist Church.

Cobern, who held his doctoral degree in philosophy from Allegheny College, went to Egypt in 1889-1890 to work at one of the excavation sites like many missionaries, ministers and lay people did at the end of the nineteenth century. Cobern worked with the great English Egyptologist, Sir Flinders Petrie, as he wrote in his article for *The Quarterly Statement of the Palestine Exploration Fund* in 1890. Although he was honorary secretary of the English-based group, there is no information about him at the present organization.

The first announcement of Hall's arrangements with Cobern was in 1890 in the *Bay View Assembly Herald.* "For several months, a special agent, Reverend C. M. Cobern, of Detroit, has been in Egypt making a collection of antiquities, which is now on the way. Every article has been bought under the eye of a specialist and selected for its historical interest. Dr. Cobern's enthusiasm as an Egyptologist gained many valued gifts to the museum. Miss Hattie M. Conner, a missionary, gave a much prized collection she was eight years in the making. Capt. J. P. Hodgson of New York, a companion with Dr. Cobern on the Nile, commissioned him to buy the finest mummy to

In addition to outstanding professors, universities include museums and libraries. As early as 1887, Hall initiated plans for both. A short teaser in July of the 1887 *Emmet County Democrat* is the first indication of his progress. "The museum on the camp grounds is under the management of the Methodist Work Concern of Chicago. You can't miss the tent." Not until several years later did the paper tell why it was such a must-see. "The museum has been under way for two years, and the collections of Chinese curiosities, birds, reptiles, shells, specimens of copper, agates and all sorts of curios indicates [sic] that the work has been in charge of efficient management. These are articles in a collection possessing historic value and others of great natural beauty. A collection of Michigan shells gathered and presented by Dr. Leach occupies a case in Loud Hall where the greater portions of the specimens are exhibited."[32]

Dr. Morgan Lewis Leach, a Methodist Civil War doctor from Traverse City, was Bay View's first curator and compiled many of the collections that formed the original Bay View Museum. The *Bay View Assembly Herald* reported that Leach assembled the collection of preserved animals (which included a passenger pigeon) and arranged for its display.[33] Other collections which he presented to Bay View in 1889 included 449 seashells and 500 botanical specimens.

There were minerals from the Upper Peninsula, Rocky Mountains, and Pacific Coast, and samples of copper and iron. Mrs. T. I. Dale from Grand Rapids gave some Mexican antiquities and natural history specimens from California. She and others from Grand Rapids are credited with donating eighteen pieces of Pueblo pottery from the Santa Fe area in 1891. This collection was transferred to Albion College in 1963 for safekeeping but was returned to Bay View in 1994 as part of the larger Bay View collection of Native American artifacts.

*Rev. Camden Coburn was commissioned, probably by John M. Hall, to assemble the Bay View Egyptian Collection in 1890 on his travels through Egypt. The 300-piece collection is at the Kelsey Museum of Archaeology at the University of Michigan where some thirty pieces are on display at the new William E. Upjohn Exhibit Wing.* (Author's Collection)

be found, and Ibrahim Abdel Samad, of Cairo, contributed many rare antiquities."[34]

The following year - in 1891 - Cobern made his first of many appearances on the Bay View program, bringing with him this valuable collection. His lecture centered on ancient monuments and, with an air of religious arrogance, he spoke of the dignity and strength of "primitive man." Most importantly, he spoke of his discovery in Egypt of the different postures assumed on Egyptian tombs and tablets of those who worshipped the gods as opposed to those who revered their ancestors: "In all the ancient and middle empires the posture of adoration is given only to the deities and never in a single instance to the ancestors. This is a far-reaching observation hitherto unobserved by scholars. Prof. P. LePage Renouf, the greatest Egyptologist in the world, said to Dr. Cobern that the Egyptian revelations completely annihilated Herbert Spencer's argument for ancestor worship drawn from the Egyptian monuments."[35]

Included in the collection were glass and marble beads, a range of materials from grave reliefs, mummy masks, figural canopic jars, amulets, funerary figurines, and mummies of a child, a cat and a bird. A description in the July 14, 1891, *Daily Resorter* includes Assyrian tablets from Nineveh and a celebrated temple stone. The collection was used as a teaching tool for classes in the Summer University. The BVRC published a special edition and reprint of Amelia B. Edwards' 1891 book, *Egypt and its Monuments*, to educate its readership.

Unfortunately, the much-prized collection arrived with some damage to the artifacts. Hall and Dr. Cobern secured the services of Messrs. A. F. Ruch & Sons, Petoskey "decorators" to repair and retouch some of the curiosities. Some of the mummies were "badly disfigured but are still in the ring" through the skillful touches and care of these artists. The collection was displayed at Hitchcock Hall with a 'good description of the antiquities.'"[36] In a later interview, U-M Egyptologist Dr. Louise Shier reported those "good descriptions" were in Sir Flinders Petrie's handwriting.

No record exists to document the cost of the collection. There was only a brief remark by M. Louise Jones that a Captain Hodgson commissioned Cobern and three other contributors. Dr. George Robinson of McCormick Theological Seminary alluded to the collection's value in 1902. "Your Oriental Museum can not [sic] now be duplicated for five thousand dollars, some exhibits not at all."

In 1894, Cobern preached in Ann Arbor on Egyptian history and then appeared in Bay View that same year and nearly every summer until 1915. He published several books on Egyptology. *Ancient Egypt in the Light of Modern Discovery* (1892) and *Recent Explorations in the Holy Land* (1916) are two of the best known. Cobern joined the Redpath Chautauqua circuit about 1908. The subjects of his lectures were "Personal Adventures among the Arabs," "Afternoons with Great Men," "The World Four Thousand Years Ago," "The Might and Mystery of Ancient Egypt," and "The Learning of the Ancients." The publicity materials sent out by the Redpath Agency in Chicago in 1908-09, state that Cobern made a second discovery in Egypt and was known as the man who discovered "bricks without straw" made by the Israelites while they were in Egyptian bondage. The materials indicate that this second discovery was made while he was visiting Sir Flinders Petrie.

Contemporary accounts claim Cobern was a compelling lecturer. Bishop Joseph F. Berry reported in the *Michigan Christian Advocate* that Dr. Cobern "produced a profound impression both by his address and sermons." Paul and Percy Blanshard in the *Daily Resorter* in 1909 stated that "He did not once descend in his addresses to ordinary quality." The *Bay View Magazine* indicated that Cobern's audiences grew daily when he was in Bay View.[37]

One young Bay View person influenced by Cobern and the Bay View Egyptian Collection was Dr. Louise A. Shier, granddaughter of Bay View's longest-serving president, Dr. William H. Shier. She received her doctorate in

Egyptology from the U-M and was a staff member of the Kelsey Museum of Archaeology for forty years, eventually becoming the museum's acting curator. On August 8, 1963, Shier became curator of the Bay View Museum. A week later, the Bay View board of trustees approved the permanent loan of the Bay View Egyptian Collection to the Kelsey Museum. Dr. Shier personally transported the collection to its new home. On June 22, 1971, the Bay View board of trustees accepted U-M's offer of $5000 to purchase 293 items in the Bay View Egyptian Collection.

"Many of the artifacts are of very high quality," wrote former Kelsey Museum curator Margaret Cool Root.[38] But, she added, "climate conditions and security were not adequate at the Bay View site and the materials could no longer be supported there in good conscience." Although the Kelsey Museum traded several scarabs to other institutions in 1987, the artifacts in the Bay View Egyptian Collection are displayed regularly at the museum, included in traveling exhibits, and the subject of museum publications including *The Gods of Egypt and Faces of Immortality*. During the summer of 2001, the four canopic jars, a mummy cloth fragment from the Persian Period (525-336 BC) and a winged scarab amulet from the same time period were part of the traveling exhibit, "Exploring Ancient Egypt," mounted by the Detroit Institute of Arts in collaboration with the University of Pennsylvania Museum of Archaeology and Anthropology, the Chicago Field Museum of Natural History, and the Kelsey Museum of Archaeology. From time to time, the Bay View Museum displays items that were not taken to Ann Arbor, along with 1890s-era newspaper articles about the collection.

As early as 1887, John M. Hall began a building fund for a library and museum building. The fund soon grew to $2000 with a list of about 130 donors including J. L. Hudson of Hudson's Department Stores. Permanent cases were purchased to display the items at Loud Hall in anticipation of the forthcoming new building. For unknown reasons, the building was not erected, perhaps because of deficits. In 1895, cottagers pledged between five dollars and twenty-five dollars each toward construction of a new building for the museum and library. An endowment plan was even set up for future donations and 150 cottagers pledged assistance. In 1902, the association appealed to Andrew Carnegie for a grant to build a combination library, museum and art gallery. Nothing came of that request, and the Egyptian Collection remained in Hitchcock Hall until it was moved in 1915 to the northwest wing of John M. Hall Auditorium rooms that were thought to have been intended by Hall to house the collection.

Like the Bay View Museum, the Bay View Library was conceived during the initial phase of the Summer University in 1888, with a loan of books from the Methodist Book Concern. Forming the nucleus of the collection, those one hundred volumes consisted of the works of Shakespeare, Longfellow, Hawthorne, and classic Welsh authors. Within the next few years, the collection increased to 1000 volumes on subjects pertaining to Summer University classes. During these initial years, the library was located in a room at Loud Hall and was open to the public for one hour three days a week. It boasted 2075 volumes with $200 in books added to the collection that summer, books which anyone could check out for a deposit of one dollar or a season charge of thirty-five cents. The efforts were applauded in the *Daily Resorter* in 1892: "Altogether, Bay View may be proud of her library. It is rapidly growing in size, and in the favor of the summer residents there is no doubt but its growth is still larger."[39]

In the first ten years of his tenure, Hall accomplished a building campaign of seven campus buildings in addition to his other responsibilities as superintendent of both the Bay View Assembly and Summer University. In 1889, *Daily Resorter* praised his industrious nature:

> *John M. Hall is the trichotomy [sic] of the Bay View assembly....He started the work as a past time [sic]. Last year, he wrote 7,000 letters, traveled 8,000 miles and worked fifteen hours a day. The expenditures were about $2,500 the first year. They were $3,800 last year. Mr. Hall edits, manages, publishes, and mails the Bay View Assembly Herald, the June edition of which was 100,000. For these three years, Mr. Hall was the assembly incarnate. He stood under all financial obligations, formulated all plans, and was mainly responsible for all our unique and famous specialties. The results have shown the wisdom of the camp ground trustees. The cottages have nearly trebled. The grounds have been beautified, enlarged and made famous, and the camp meetings themselves have become a means of great grace to multitudes who had never heard of Bay View or had never before thought to enjoy it.*[40]

Not everyone enjoyed the classes and lectures. Disruptive children and crying babies became a major irritation, and a stormy controversy erupted. In 1889 the *Daily Resorter* columnist was incensed by the prevailing negative attitude toward these little future assembly-goers:

> *The left-handed request uttered yesterday that mothers with children would leave the Auditorium is an innovation in Chautauqua ideas. Chautauqua was founded not least for tired mothers, whose favored children were college bred, and who did not wish to part intellectual company altogether with them, and it would balk the purposes of Chautauqua's best souls if it were made apparent that these mothers were unwelcome at these annual*

*gatherings of the Chautauqua clans. We have observed several persons, men, who have eyed the slightest turning of prattling of children as if it were an offense against heaven. We beg such to remember that there is a mother behind the child, and one observation of mothers is that they don't get too much of the literary side of life, even at the best, and to establish the canon that the best, the most refined entertainment at Bay View or any of its advantages is not for them, would be a shot at the heart of Bay View. The constituency of mothers who summer at Bay View cannot afford governesses. The applause which followed the announcement was a disgrace to Bay View.*[41]

Superintendent Hall came up with a solution. He combined the resources of the university with the needs of the assembly. The innovative kindergarten program was expanded to include the hours of the assembly.

Some accounts of the early days show more tolerance and a better spirit with special days on the program. In the 1890s, these included Children's Day, Christian Endeavor Day, Education Day, Epworth League Day, Farmers' Day, Federation Day, Grand Army of the Republic Day, Graduation Day, Harbor Springs Day, Hoosier Day, Missionary Day, National Day, Petoskey Day, Prohibition Day, Recognition Day, Recreation Day, University Day and WCTU Day. These celebratory days were all supported by parent organizations such as the Albion Alumni Association, Bay View Battalion, Bay View Evangelical Association, Bay View Improvement Association, Bay View Press Club, Bay View Reading Circle (BVRC), Bay View Foreign Missionary Circle, Bay View Women's Press Club, Boys' Congress, Chautauqua Literary and Scientific Circle (CLSC), Christian Endeavor, Epworth League, Farmers' Alliance, Grand Army of the Republic (GAR), Hay Fever Association, Illinois Club, Indiana Club, Michigan Federation of Women's Clubs, Photography Club, Southern Club, WCTU, Woman's Council, Women's Home Missionary Society of Bay View, Woodland Avenue Improvement Association, YMCA and

**The Kindergarten program was organized in the 1880s as part of the Summer University.** *(Author's Collection)*

YWCA. Each organization had a pin to represent membership which people proudly wore - such as white ribbons for the WCTU or a BVRC pin with "Mehr Licht" (German meaning "more light")". A *Daily Resorter* writer poked fun at it in 1894. "It is a poor sort of a 'critter' at Bay View that can't sport at least one banner or pin with a strange device, and some individuals look like a walking "ad" of some badge factory. But the custom leads sometimes to the forming of pleasant friendships, and promotes sociability, – and so, who wants to quarrel with it?"[42]

There was quarreling, though, within the ranks of the Bay View leadership over finances as well as other contentious issues. The rancor culminated in a changing of the guard. The only hint of a pending problem had come at a meeting of the Cottagers' Improvement Association in August of 1896 at Evelyn Hall. That was the first year the Assembly and the Summer University failed to produce the financial rewards to which the association had become accustomed. On August 18, the *Daily Resorter* reported: "Supt. J. M. Hall then took the floor and made some timely statements in regard to his relation to Bay View, in order to set at naught numerous reports which were being circulated. Mr. Hall's remarks were substantiated by several of the trustees who were present."[43] John Coulter announced some changes in the advertising policy and everyone thought that would correct the situation. It did not and Hall resigned two years later.

*Woman's [sic] clubs are today suppressing*
*selfish and superficial social customs.*
*They are God-sends to the women in the small villages*
*where the individual interests are narrow.*
*They break down the iron bars of narrow individualism.*
*They change the small ineffective "I" to the*
*large influential, useful "we".*

Mrs. Ada Iddings Gale, author,
Bay View Woman's Council, August, 1894. Evelyn Hall

— CHAPTER FOUR —

# The Bay View Idea

Horace Hitchcock of Royal Oak, Michigan, took over Hall's position for the 1899 season. It was a magnanimous act. Despite his generosity in raising funds for Hitchcock Hall, he was unpopular with the constituency. He received the fewest number of votes in his 1896 bid for the Bay View board of trustees. His personal situation at the time was complicated as his cottage at Block 17, Lot 7 was being rebuilt after a disastrous block fire.

Hitchcock had been a member of the Bay View assembly board since 1888, so he had an appreciation for the Bay View idea and devoted himself to the cause. An articulate lecturer, Hitchcock had one of the largest private collections of stereopticon views in the country - about 6000. His passionate faith, along with that of the more devout members of the association, strongly influenced the 1899 program. He changed Hall's very active, tightly scheduled program to a less structured format. There were fewer activities, and Sundays were reserved for religious activities announced with scriptural passages such as, "Ye shall keep my Sabbath and reverence my sanctuary." It was an earnest attempt to stop what researcher Robert Carter later called the "influence of the intellectual air pervading the institution" and return it to the reverent fervor of earlier days.

Judging from the program, activities weren't coordinated. Hall scheduled the Bay View Reading Circle at Evelyn Hall for a month each summer, but those activities were reduced in size and number and conflicted with assembly and camp meeting activities. On Sundays, there were often two vesper services, one in the afternoon at Evelyn Hall for reading circle members and another at dinnertime on the waterfront. Ralph Connable, the Petoskey businessman who had installed Bay View's first water system, was unhappy. In 1899, he wrote to one of Bishop Vincent's relatives: "My present idea is to have Petoskey insist on the old-fashioned Chautauqua program."[1]

Hall's departure at the end of the 1898 season may have been for family reasons. In March 1897, his niece, Carrie Skillman Sanford, died. Nine months later, her mother, Phebe Hall Skillman, who was Hall's half-sister, died. Then in September 1898, Hall's own mother, Roxana Blanchard Hall Richards, passed away. Carrie Sanford left a son, Sterling, from an unhappy marriage that had ended in divorce. Sterling was cared for by his grandmother Phebe until her death. At her funeral, Hall's half-brother agreed to raise Sterling if Hall would be the youngster's legal guardian.

Another possible explanation for Hall's departure was the official one. While he had been managing the Bay View Assembly and Summer University and organizing the construction of the campus buildings, Hall continued to run the CSLC at Chautauqua Cottage and throughout Michigan. After thirteen years, in 1893, he launched what became his most widely known accomplishment, the BVRC and *The Bay View Magazine,* his own correspondence course.

***The African Boy Choir was one of Horace Hitchock's featured entertainment in 1900.***
*(Author's Collection)*

Unlike the CSLC, which focused on various disciplines, Hall concentrated on yearly studies of specific countries - the religion, music, literature, history, culture, philosophy, politics, geography and economy. In a sixty-page magazine issued monthly, subscribers were introduced to each country with informative articles, reading lists of books for study, an outline of assignments, subjects for reading circle discussions, questions for members to answer and regular tests.

Test questions were difficult and required a thorough knowledge of the reading assignments. To aid the students with their assignments, the BVRC published textbooks so that the large numbers of members who lived in small towns without access to libraries could complete reading assignments. In the twenty-nine years of its existence, the BVRC published at least fifty-two books authored by respected experts.

In his biography of his uncle *John Heyl Vincent*, Leon Vincent attributes the popularity of the CLSC reading circles "to certain beguiling features." These "features," which were adopted by the Bay View course, included dividing the students into "classes" with class colors, flowers, mottoes and officers. At the end of four years, a graduation ceremony was organized at Bay View. These features created a college spirit among the students, appealing to the public's desire to belong and to be a part of a university atmosphere. Reviewing the magazine as part of a national study, Donna Ullrich, former journalism instructor at the University of Detroit-Mercy commented: "Bringing the world into the homes of its readers was the goal of *The Bay View Magazine* in 1893 when it began 29 years of not only educating but graduating its subscribers. The magazine published seven issues each year and continued the educational goals of the Summer University."[2] Furthering the university appeal, Hall included on his governing board President William Gay Ballantine of Oberlin College; President John M. Coulter of Lake Forest University and the University of Chicago; Kansas State Normal School English Professor M. Louise Jones; and *Harper's Bazaar* Editor Margaret E. Sangster. He later added World WCTU President Frances E. Willard; New York's Calvary Baptist Church Pastor Dr. R. S. MacArthur; *Christian Union* Editor Dr. Hamilton W. Mabie; and U-M graduate, Wellesley College President and University of Chicago Women's Dean Alice Freeman Palmer.

After four years of study, students reached their goal and were awarded diplomas. The first graduation ceremony, in 1897, was an elaborate affair called Processional Day. However, with the graduation of members came the question of how to retain them as subscribers. The solution was to expand the magazine by adding new courses of study.

The success of the BVRC was due in many respects to the demographics of American society. People in small towns, where the reading circles flourished, were anxious to expand their education but had little time or money to attend college and no access to libraries. Iowa, which also bragged of having the largest number of Tent Chautauquas, had the largest number of BVRC.[3] In 1894, circulation of the magazine was only 1500 but, by 1895, the number had doubled and, by 1896, the number was up to 6000. In 1897, Hall wrote in *The Bay View Magazine*: "There are moments when I feel elated. This is one of them. I have been thinking of the success of the Bay View Reading Circle. Today we have 7,000 students."[4]

In Bay View, meetings of the BVRC were held at Evelyn Hall, while the CLSC meetings continued at Chautauqua Cottage. Chautauqua, New York, ran an advertisement in *The Bay View Herald* in 1895 but ceased publishing information about Bay View in its magazine *The Chautauquan* after 1894. Finally, at the turn of the century, it ceased advertising in the Bay View Assembly Program. Dr. Theodore L. Flood, editor of *The Chautauquan*, did not consider the BVRC a formidable competitor. In a letter to an associate in 1897, he dismissed the notion of any competition as wishful thinking. "As to John Hall and his 7,000 members, I do not believe he has any such number enrolled. I sent an agent into that territory myself within nine months and his report was that John Hall's could not exist a great while."[5]

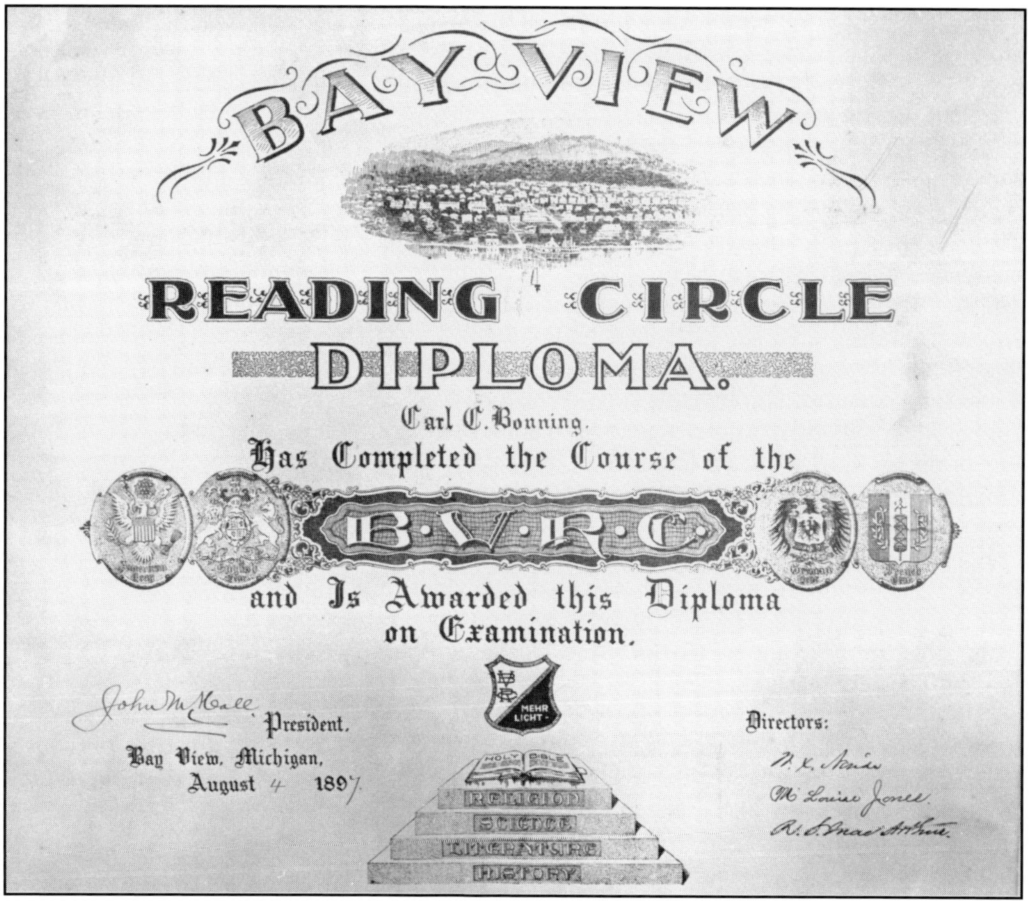


***Upon completion of the four year reading course, students received a diploma in an elaborate ceremony in Bay View.***
*(Author's Collection)*

Alfreda Irwin, late historian-in-residence at Chautauqua Institution, suggested in a 1984 interview that Vincent and Miller must have realized they could not contain the movement, but may have regretted the formation of the BVRC. From Leon Vincent's biography of his uncle, it seems that Vincent was preoccupied with other challenges. In 1888, Vincent was raised to the office of bishop of the Methodist Episcopal Church. During the 1890s, he was on the lecture circuit, traveling throughout Europe and the United States. In 1896, he became chaplain at Harvard University. That same year, he visited Bay View to install J. W. Duncan as the new director of Bay View's CLSC. He preached the baccalaureate sermon on University Sunday and gave the Recognition Day address for the CLSC graduates. The CLSC continued for some years, but without Hall's leadership the meetings soon ceased. Leon Vincent appeared regularly on the Bay View platform speaking about literature, often addressing the graduating classes of the BVRC.

The growth of the reading circle continued until 1914 when the membership peaked at 25,000 with a magazine circulation of 125,000 across fifteen states and the Hawaiian Islands territory. Nationally, one thousand women's clubs adopted it as their educational program. In towns like Lake Crystal, Minnesota; Jefferson, Iowa; and Paulding, Ohio, the BVRC thrived. However significant the numbers were, the BVRC membership never challenged the 700,000 membership figures of the CSLC. However, both courses contributed greatly to a national trend. By 1923, over two and one-half million Americans were enrolled in some kind of correspondence course.

During this entire time, Hall kept the price of *The Bay View Magazine* and the course at a level his members (which included young people, teachers and housewives) could afford. More importantly, the price was always below that of the CSLC. In 1893, a year's subscription to *The Bay View Magazine* cost fifty cents and the Reading Circle Course cost $2.50, including the textbook. Later, that price was raised to $1.50 for a year's subscription and $3.50 for the course. Through this correspondence course, Hall brought a world of knowledge to his readers at a very low profit for himself. In 1905, he wrote in *The Bay View Magazine*, "At present, the profit on each subscription is only 10c."[6]

Trips to Bay View were part of the attraction of the BVRC. The groups always stayed at Evelyn Hall where a reading room was stocked with major daily newspapers from all over the country. In 1896, the *Daily Resorter* noted: "The Circle headquarters in Evelyn hall [sic] are an attraction to visitors. Beautiful pictures of many circles, banners, and flags of the four nations studied - Germany, France, England, and the United States - adorn the walls, and besides there is a well supplied reading table and easy chairs. Circle members and friends are always at home there and the pleasant general secretary Miss Carrie B. Taylor is at her desk ready to do any favor or explain the circle plans."[7]

Hall and secretary Taylor planned social excursions for members during their time in northern Michigan. In 1896, one hundred members took a trip on the Chicago and West Michigan train to the clay banks at Bay Shore and enjoyed a picnic as guests of Mr. and Mrs. Homer Sly on their estate at Rocky Beach. For five years, BVRC members made trips to Beaver Island. There were get-togethers at Hall's Wayside Cottage and daily lectures at Evelyn Hall. There were parties and campus-wide receptions when all of the halls were decorated with Japanese lanterns and open to visitors. For several years, Professor Hill, superintendent of the Central Iowa Assembly in Humboldt, Iowa, escorted groups to Europe.

The demands of the Reading Circle and *Bay View Magazine* had become so great by 1898 that Hall felt he could no longer devote enough time to the Bay View Assembly and Summer University. For many years, this official reason - and a distinct change in Hall's lifestyle - supported rumors that Hall had profiteered from his *Bay View Magazine* venture at the expense of Bay View.[8] Whatever the reason for his departure, what had begun as Bay View's "winter work," the BVRC became Hall's personal business and was the focus of vicious attacks. Writer Paul B. Blanshard approached Hall in1914 about the reasons: "...when J. M. Hall has been urged to revive the reading club's summer work he has replied that this is his private business and when he comes to Bay View his private interests are left at home, lest some one [sic] may say he is using Bay View for personal gain....This policy may be a wise one, but many regret that our summer life loses by it. Mr. Hall's silence is carried so far that most people have no idea of the extent and usefulness of the Bay View reading club."[9]

When Hall arrived in Bay View in 1886 to begin an assembly program, there were 131 cottages on the grounds. In just two years, Hall's assembly program created such enthusiasm that by April 20, 1888, 402 lots had been leased. The 1894 program of lectures, music, culture, recreation and popular education received rave reviews in the local paper: "This year the attendance and receipts have increased over any previous year by 33 percent, and after paying all expenses on the basis of liberal contracts, will have a surplus in the treasury."[10]

By July 24 of the following year, the same newspaper quoted assembly cashier Henry D. Shier as saying that one-day ticket sales were over $2000. Out of such revenues, Hall was paid a yearly salary of $1000 from 1886 through 1898. The contract stated that any losses from Bay View Assembly would be subtracted from his salary. Aside from providing an assembly program with far-reaching appeal that he had probably been funding out of his own pocket, Hall had secured the construction of the association buildings. The obvious result was a substantial rise in the property value of the BVCGA.[11] In truth, Bay View had profited at Hall's expense.

Some association members did not see things that way. If the value of buildings erected by the assembly was not considered, and the tripling of membership was ignored, the assembly could be said to have created significant debt. Judge Clement Smith clarified the situation somewhat at the dedication of the new John M. Hall Auditorium in July 1915: "Financially, it [the assembly] was not prosperous, but it had built and owned five buildings on the grounds. These were Loud Hall, the Conservatory, Evelyn Hall, Hitchcock Hall, and Chautauqua Cottage, including the furniture and personal property therein, and covering the museum and the library. This property was and is valuable. The indebtedness of the Assembly was around $2,700.00."[12]

Hall's departure from Bay View also coincided with the illness and death of Mary Hall's father. In 1901, the couple rented *Wayside,* thinking they would be confined to Flint. David S. Fox died suddenly in June. After the funeral, the couple came to Bay View and checked into a room at Evelyn Hall so John could fulfill his duties as head of the BVRC.[13]

The extent of Mary Hall's inheritance from her father's estate is unclear. Fox had been one of the founders of the Flint Wagon Works, which was bought by Buick Motor Car Company in 1903. Later, William C. Durant became its general manager and in 1908 formed General Motors. David Fox's death, however, occurred prior to the formation of General Motors and Fox's second wife, Florence, inherited most of his estate.[14] The only evidence of Mary's inheritance comes from Hall's estate which included 1313 shares of General Motors stock while the assets of the BVRC and *Bay View Magazine* were only valued at seven percent of his total assets.[15] Mary's inheritance had apparently been put in Hall's name.

***Judge Clement Smith.*** *(Courtesy of the Solms Family)*

With the death of Fox, the Halls' lifestyle changed dramatically, making it look as if Hall had made enough money in the Bay View venture to improve his financial position. On July 9, 1902, Hall purchased land in a prestigious new suburb of Detroit to build a house where he could be near libraries and museums. The house at 165 Boston Boulevard (now 351 East Boston Boulevard) was in the residential neighborhood of Detroit's elite businessmen. His neighbors included J. L. Hudson, the Dodge Family, the Grinnell Brothers, Henry Holt of Holt Publishing, the Johnsons of the Johnson Milk Company, and Henry and Clara Ford. Later, Stanley Kresge (a member of the Metropolitan Methodist Church where Hall attended) and Detroit merchant Benjamin Siegel built houses nearby on West Boston Boulevard.

Hall's house cost $15,000 and had a third floor card room and a ballroom with a "sprung" floor made of half-moon shaped wooden springs.[16] Even in 1902, that feature was expensive and odd for a staunch Methodist who did not dance, smoke, drink or play cards. It was a common architectural feature though of the times and, since the rear section of the house could be locked separately from the family quarters in the front of the house, Hall probably used the third floor with its separate entrance and staircase as the editorial offices of the Bay View Reading Circle and *The Bay View Magazine*. Production could continue even when the family was out of town.

Another significant event occurred in Hall's life at that time. A fire destroyed the Seventh-Day Adventist *Review and Herald* Printing House in Battle Creek in 1902. This had been the printer for Dr. John Harvey Kellogg's Good Health Publishing Company. He had persuaded Hall to use his publishing house for the *Bay View Magazine*: "3,000 prints were lost. Not anything was saved," wrote Hall in *The Bay View Magazine* in February 1903.[17] From then until 1907 when he returned to an official position in Bay View life, Hall traveled extensively throughout the US and abroad, using these trips to gather new materials for his publications. He and his family went around the world, and from 1906 through 1907 he was in Great Britain.

Times were not so prosperous back in Bay View, although there were some highlights. After only one season, Hitchcock's assembly program also took on a decidedly eclectic appeal, with speakers, entertainers, musicians and ministers from all over the country. It was not unusual for the assembly to include southerners on the platform having entertained Gen. Robert E. Lee's confidant and former Georgia governor John Brown Gordon in 1894. However, the most significant event of the 1902 season was the appearance of General Robert E. Lee's nephew, Major General Fitzhugh Lee, on July 30. Before the major general spoke, Bay View President Shier introduced J. J. Robbins from Boyne Falls. Robbins had been captured by Lee's uncle in the Civil War and released on parole. Shier commented upon Bay View's liberality in listening to speakers of all political opinions and creeds. "Especially glad are we," said he, "to greet General Lee, who is a thorough American. There is hardly a chapter in our country's history upon which the name of 'Lee' is not indelibly stamped."[18] Michigan's Governor Aaron T. Bliss, whose nephew's family had a cottage at Block 16, Lot 3, made the official introductory remarks. Then the southern gentleman, the former governor of Virginia – stylishly dressed in a Prince Albert coat, white vest, black trousers and oxford shoes - spoke to a receptive crowd that honored him with the Chautauqua salute by waving white handkerchiefs.

The cordial fanfare Lee received was significant since Shier, four Bay View founders, and many local residents had served in the Union army. The Grand Army of the Republic (GAR) had a Bay View Battalion which had a reunion each summer. However, there was a sizable population in the Little Traverse Bay area of ex-Confederates. During his visit, Lee formed a social group called the Southern Club. Mrs. Henry Shier, sister-in-law of Bay View's President Shier, gave a dinner party for Lee and other southerners. It was held, however, on the "other shore" at the Harbor Point clubhouse – NOT in Bay View. Lee was chosen as the club's vice president. The club continued to meet annually until at least 1906, when they met at Bay View's Evelyn Hall.

Despite Lee's appearance, the 1902 summer did not end well. Just like Hall, Hitchcock faced financial worries: The *Daily Resorter* reported that: "Mr. Hitchcock has fire in his eye. He is determined that the debt must be paid, and that soon. Last Saturday morning the total indebtedness was $2800, the same evening $1200 of it had been accounted for. The assembly officers feel that with the debt cleared away the assembly would be in a condition of greater usefulness and would be able to keep out of debt from this time on."[19]

The debt was managed for the next season, but Horace Hitchcock died suddenly on August 28 at the end of the 1903 season in his room at Hitchcock Hall. The Bay View Board of Trustees turned to a professional manager, F. Gillum Cromer, a former superintendent of the public schools in Franklin, Ohio, to run the assembly and Summer University for the 1904 season. Cromer had been in Chautauqua and was familiar with the "mother" program. He had successfully organized the Miami Valley Chautauqua Association as president and general manager. In Bay View, he contracted an assortment of talent through booking agencies as Hitchcock had done, but featured no headliners. He did not have the finesse or the connection with the community that he apparently had with his own Chautauqua. Lack of organization in the Bay View leadership resulted in a fiasco, and he only stayed one season.

For 1905 and 1906, Thomas Gordon, Jr., a Bay View trustee from Howell, took over the planning with even less success. He programmed a Mexican instrumental trio, two Scottish singers, dramatic readers, missionaries, pastors, singers, stereopticon travelogues, impersonations and Oriental entertainers. Gordon was able to highlight his 1905 season with the return engagement of the ever-popular William Jennings Bryan.

By this time the assembly had become an overwhelming financial burden. Attendance had dropped at all meetings due to a number of unavoidable factors. The logging camps of the 1890s were gone as were the loggers who had enjoyed the diversions of the assembly. Native Americans so fascinated by the camp meetings of the early days and its Ojibwa and Odawa-speaking founders, began holding their own camp meetings at Wa-ga-na-ki-si or Cross Village and other locations. The popular Farmers' Day, which began in 1897 with the appearances of Mary A. Mayo of the Michigan Farmers' Institute, and Bay View resident J. L. Snyder, president of Michigan Agricultural College, was no longer a draw. Local farmers had neither the time, nor finances to attend the assembly. Another problem was that Bay View was not on a major Tent Chautauqua route.

When Bay View was founded, the western mineral range of the UP was flourishing, more heavily populated than northern Michigan and stronger financially with the booming mining industry. Bay View founders, several of whom were well-acquainted with the UP, apparently felt that Bay View's location on the railway and steamship routes between the more populated southern urban areas and the then-affluent UP was a particularly good one. Attendance figures ranged from between 5000 to 10,000. However impressive these numbers were, Bay View never

***John Hall's home in Detroit. The barn at the right was burned during the 1967 Detroit riots.***
*(Courtesy of David Bieber)*

***There were a number of Indian camp meetings in Emmet County. Here is a picture of the Shoh-She-ke-Shirk "Greensky" Indian Camp Meeting Grounds at Northport, Mich.*** *(Author's Collection)*

had the enormous attendance of eastern resorts such as Ocean Grove with its 12,000-seat auditorium. Bay View's Old Auditorium seated only 2500. Hall later alluded to this discrepancy in a letter written April 1, 1913, to Dr. James S. Montgomery, pastor of the Metropolitan Memorial Methodist Episcopal Church in Washington, DC: "You know the conditions at Bay View. We are not in the midst of a populous region, and not one-fifth of our attendance comes from within twenty-five miles of us; the result is, we never have the large audiences that other places have, and accordingly our revenue is reduced and in order to make both ends meet, we must use the utmost economy."[20]

Researcher Harry S. McClarran listed only ten Chautauqua assemblies in Michigan in contrast with Illinois which led the nation with thirty-three. In his list, Iowa followed with twenty-five and Ohio with twenty-four. Consequently, Bay View was isolated from the mainline of circuit routes where the Chautauqua assemblies were more numerous. However, instead of recognizing the situation, people in Bay View and Petoskey, including the editor of the *Daily Resorter* in 1906, blamed each other for the troubles:

> *It is a noticeable fact that the people of this city do not show as much consideration for the Bay View Assembly as they did in former years, and not so much as they should, if the Resorter is reliably informed.*
>
> *In the first place when Mr. Winston went about the stores and other places in his efforts to sell season tickets for the course of attractions that had been engaged for the summer he met with all sorts of rebuffs on all sides. No one would give any particular reason, but they (many of them) would not buy.*
>
> *As a result the attractions afforded were not so largely attended as they should have been - both because of their merit and for the purpose of continuing the right feeling between the resort and this city.*[21]

Bay View was the first of the many Emmet County resorts. The success of the camp meeting spurred the formation of other resort communities like Wequetonsing, Harbor Point, the Chicago Club, the Belvedere Club, Roaring Brook, Menonaqua, and others. When interest in the camp meetings faded, Bay View instituted the popular assembly that brought thousands more to northern Michigan annually. So, in 1906, with attendance declining there was a feeling of responsibility to continue the assembly to attract visitors to northern Michigan and boost the local economy. A *Daily Resorter* writer considered the possibility that the assembly program and camp meetings were no longer needed to bring tourists into the area – that people were being attracted by Emmet County's weather:

> *It is hard to tell if there was any real lessening of the population at the close of the assembly. The owner of the boarding house declares that for*

***Inside the Old Auditorium.*** *(Author's Collection)*

*two years there have been more at the tables the week following the close of the assembly than any other week of the year. This would indicate that the nature of the resort is changing. And that the attraction here is more and more the superb climate. If this be so the efforts of those directing affairs should be to make it develop to the fullest the opportunities for enjoying the climate and not to feel that the whole future of Bay View depends on the assembly program. Should this continue it would relieve some of those in charge of the program of some of their anxiety for they could cut down on the numbers of the program without fear of a deserted village the next years and could arrange differently without fear that the resort would go out, that Bay View was in her dotage and soon would her requiem be sung.*[22]

Viewing the situation with 20/20 hindsight and the knowledge that the assembly would soon be reinstated, we now know the major problem was not the fading interest of the people. It was in the leadership of the assembly and the programs. Hall and Hitchcock had something not easily duplicated. Being a good manager of an assembly program took more than just the ability to organize. It took a deep understanding of the community being served as well as national and international events. In 1923, writer Hugh A. Orchard summed up the qualities: "The successful manager must also, by all means, be a student of affairs. He must not only keep fully abreast of the times, but actually ahead of the times. He must have the faculty for sensing the trend of things; must possess a kind of prophetic vision of what will be apt and profitable in thought leadership a year or years in the future. To be so equipped he must of necessity be a constant reader, an argus-eyed observer, and a keen and accurate analyst of the heterogeneous thought, passions, and prejudices that daily utter the innermost life of the world."[23]

Judge Clement Smith reported in July of 1915 that "The years 1905, 1906, 1907 and 1908 were without an assembly but had some entertainment during the season." Other sources report that the assembly was canceled only in 1905 and 1906. The 1907 and 1908 minutes of the Bay View Evangelistic Association indicated that its meetings were moved out of Evelyn Hall to make room for the Ben Greet Players. Journalist C. Donald Call plugged the assembly in a 1908 column:

*Wake up, people, Bay View is not dead, though she may have been sleeping. This year the association presents a strong program of seventeen numbers. It was impossible to re-establish the as sembly this year, but the great demand of the people for something along that line has resulted in a four week's [sic] pro-*

*gram of delightful and useful lectures, concerts, and entertainments, given by the best talent obtainable in America. The course tickets are but two dollars. It is the duty of persons now to put up your little hammer, buy a ticket, and give your whole, hearty support to this great project, that next year the assembly and summer university may be with us as hereintofore[sic].*[24]

He described some of the entertainment in a later column on August 4:

> *Bay View people and people of the surrounding vicinity have been under the impression that the assembly program for this summer is not up to the standard. Hence they have not gone. No greater mistake could have been made, for last night proved this conclusively. The entertainment by Edwin Brush, of Chicago, was the cleverest piece of work of that nature ever done [sic] here. Not only were his tricks good, but an inexhaustible supply of puns kept the large crowd in continuous laughter. His illusions were illusions in the truest sense of the word. The Japanese ring trick and the Hindu basket trick were clever pieces of work. Many magicians have been at the Auditorium in former years but none have [sic] given the satisfaction that Edwin Brush ddi [sic] on Monday night.*[25]

A comparison of new membership fees sheds light on the assembly's importance to Bay View's total welfare. The association collected between $500 and $800 in new membership fees during 1905. In 1906, fees decreased to $500. In 1907 and 1908, when news got out that there would be no assembly, revenues dropped to a dismal $100. Even at this early date, the Bay View programs were interdependent. When the assembly folded at the end of the 1906 season, the camp meeting soon came to an end. Dr. Charles Swift, chairman of the Anatomy Department at the University of Chicago Rush Medical School, later described the situation: "The place was certainly in the doldrums. There was nothing much to do, excepting go down to the depot and see the trains come in and see the afternoon train go out. But when he [Hall] came back again he began to scout around to get another program started, which he did. All the members of the association helped out to an extent, and we got the association on its feet again, and it has been going ever since."[26]

It wasn't as easy as Swift made it sound. The 1907 season ended with the election of new trustees. The *Daily Resorter* reported that "The Bay View people will be glad to hear of the re-election of John M. Hall and Judge Clement Smith to the board of directors"[27] Realizing how dire the situation had become and how difficult it was to run a successful assembly, having tried it himself, newly elected President Thomas Gordon began making arrangements with Hall to return as manager of the assembly. Each cottager was encouraged to contribute ten dollars to support a new assembly. Hall personally called upon cottagers to persuade them to contribute. They secured 275 pledges, but 100 cottagers refused to cooperate. In January 1908, Hall wrote to Thomas Gordon that his request for ten dollars from each cottager had failed and, in a despondent tone, he ended the letter: "There will be no assembly this year, and that will end the matter."

It did not end the matter. Gordon persisted and on November 9, 1908, he signed a contract with Hall. The parties agreed to launch an assembly program costing between $2500 and $4000 each year for a period of ten years with cottage owners contributing $2000 each summer. If the amount received from the entertainment fell short of the expenses, then, according to the contract "Hall and Gordon agreed to make good to the association the full amount of the deficiency." Five hundred cottagers contributed $2000, but the ten dollar fee per cottage owner was considered an unpopular "tax" that the trustees did not enforce, and it was eventually repealed in 1918.

In 1909, that "tax" was the ticket to a new assembly program which brought the crowds back to Bay View along with more cost overruns and consternation. An explosion erupted that fall at a trustees' meeting in Saginaw when discussion turned to the assembly program. The benevolent Charles W. Fallass, Petoskey drugstore retailer and the longest-serving trustee on the Bay View board, wrote to Clement Smith on October 30: "Now it seems to me, that our dependence is on Mr. Hall - that there is no one to take his place - that if he withdraws his active support, it will mean a heavy blow to Bay View. I believe, indeed I know, that it is all unnecessary, that a little sympathetic appreciation from a majority of the board would keep Hall at work."[28]

Judge Clement Smith summed up his reaction to President Gordon in a letter on November 1: "It is my judgment that success at Bay View largely depends on the assembly. Personally, I do not need an assembly and am not supporting it for selfish reasons. I am supporting it because I believe it means a better and greater Bay View for the public generally. It is apparent from the support actually given that a large majority of the members of the association favor the assembly. It is also apparent from the attendance last summer that the people who came to Bay View and the northern resorts appreciate the benefit of our assembly."[29]

Vigilant regarding any possible debt, Gordon wrote back to Smith on November 8, 1909: "I went to Detroit the latter part of last week and had a long interview with Mr. Hall, the outcome of which was he agreed with me that the terms of the contracts should be kept, to the letter. These same things [were] said last year, so I have reasons to believe that they may be violated again, if we continue to operate the assembly, for I had promises last year that the expense would be held within the defined limits; and you know they were greatly over reached, and I now think it almost impossible for Hall to keep within the $4000 limit."[30]

Hall himself had a few comments about the board's attitude in a letter to Smith November 8, 1909: "I agree with you that if we are going to succeed at Bay View, we must all work together, and enthusiastically endorse everything to which we have committed ourselves. Bay View cannot stand long without the summer work as our people would find after a few years." A few trustees were suspicious of Hall. One board member wrote harshly in 1909, "I don't like Hall's methods of doing things." Another man wrote, "As for Hall I don't trust him." Hall was deeply mindful of this distrust and mentioned it in a letter to Gordon.[31]

Somehow, the differences were resolved and the Bay View Assembly and Summer University flourished for the next six years, bringing some of the most famous lecturers, educators, ministers, authors, speakers, singers and actors available on the circuit. Hall made every attempt to remain within the constraints of the budget while attracting the highest caliber talent. In the fall of 1910, he turned to the Chicago office of Redpath-Slayton Lyceum Bureau to book the Dunbar Quartette, Alton Packard, and the LeBrun Grand Opera for $500 for three days of concerts.

Letters in the Redpath correspondence files at the University of Iowa show that Hall tried to reduce Dr. F. W. Gunsaulus's fee from $400 to $200 because Gunsaulus had "a reason to wish to go to Bay View." It took over forty letters of correspondence with the Redpath office between October and May, and a personal letter to Gunsaulus, President of the Armour Institute of Technology, whose charity benefited "crippled children and neglected girls," to resolve the issue. When Redpath submitted the bill to Treasurer Shier, the fee was $360.

***Chalk talk artist Evelyn Bargelt was contracted in 1911 with Epworth Heights in Ludington.*** *(Author's Collection)*

Hall booked in conjunction with the Ludington Chautauqua, Epworth Heights, the next season. For a lump sum of $1690, the two Chautauquas contracted crayon-lecturer Evelyn Bargelt, humorist Strickland W. Gillilan, a men's singing group called The Hussars, the Russian Balalaika Orchestra, the great woman orator Leonora M. Lake, who authored Pennsylvania's state factory inspection law, and the Honorable George D. Alden.

Despite the cancellation of the camp meeting, religious commitment continued with Hall's scheduling of religious conferences. He booked some of the outstanding ministers in the country: Dr. James S. Montgomery, pastor of the Metropolitan Memorial Methodist Episcopal Church in Washington, DC. In a letter dated April 1, 1913, Hall attempted to book Montgomery privately, skipping the Redpath management fees. Montgomery wrote back: "May I say that my family already is looking forward to this summer at Bay View. No place on earth is to them as this beautiful spot on 'Little Traverse.'" Montgomery asked his Redpath managers to book him into Bay View in the summer of 1913 for a fee of $100 because Montgomery had relatives who owned the Bark Cottage at Block 6, Lot 2.[32]

While these names may be unfamiliar today, they were some of the most popular speakers on the Chautauqua Circuit at the time. Hall's contemporary, *Daily Resorter* writer Paul Blanshard, gave the best assessment of the assembly program:

> *Now just think a moment what you have received from the assembly and the 'man that hath no thanks within his soul is fit for treasons, strat-*

*agems and spoils.' There have been about twenty-nine entertainments and seventy-two lecturers and conferences to which your assembly ticket has given admittance. Do you know what that means? It means that you hear the best entertainments and best lecturers on the whole American platform, not for half a dollar apiece, but for an average expense of about two and ninety-seven hundredths cents. So it is with ample reason that we congratulate ourselves at the close of our assembly. Long live Bay View! Long live the men who have made it what it is! As long as John M. Hall and Thomas Gordon, Jr., remain where now they are, we will trust that in spite of the great success of Bay View's past, its future will be far greater and brighter still.*[33]

Sterling Sanford remembered how his uncle agonized over entertainer fees and cancellations. Hall scheduled Booker T. Washington for a second appearance in 1912 but told Sterling that Washington's fees were too high. Maud Ballington Booth's fee for her appearance July 31, 1914, was an affordable $150. Dr. Camden Cobern's fee was a reasonable $250. One can only imagine what Washington's fee was. Along with those constant fee fiascoes, Hall also endured disappointments when his famous guests canceled. Anti-Standard Oil muckraker Ida Tarbell was scheduled to speak in 1914 but canceled due to a death in the family. Congress was still in session July 27, 1914, when US Vice President Thomas R. Marshall was scheduled to speak.

As important as the intellectual, educational, cultural and religious events were to Hall, recreation and children's activities remained high priorities. Athleticism is not an attribute associated with the tall gangly Hall who was six foot four inches tall, but he must have loved children since he provided for them in summer school classes. During the winter of 1910, he planned a new building to be designed by the Detroit architect W.E.N. Hunter: "This year the new Recreation Hall, containing a large and completely equipped swimming pool, will make swimming one of the most attractive features of Bay View life."[34] The $13,000 building, which Hall donated, included a swimming pool for 200 bathers; stone floors; dressing, lounging and toilet rooms; and parlors arranged for children as well as adults. It even included a bowling alley. The association assumed ownership in 1912.

In the Summer University, Hall always hired a director of athletics, a Sloyd (Swedish method of woodworking) teacher, an arts and crafts professor, and a physical culture teacher to work with the children. In the 1890s, he planned annual Children's Day on the assembly program that attracted as many as 350 children. In 1909, he hired the Chautauqua circuit's nationally known-storyteller Grace Hemingway (Ernest's aunt) to lead a children's hour. In Chicago, she was known as "the story lady," frequenting slum schools where she told stories to underprivileged children. Dedicated to early education, she stated in her publicity materials that a "Chautauqua that neglects the children is missing much of the educational value of the Chautauqua institution."

***Sterling Sanford, grand nephew of John M. Hall, met his wife Marcelline Hemingway at Bay View. His memories of the early days when he spent summers with his great uncle John at Wayside were invaluable to this history.*** *(Courtesy of James Sanford)*

From August 2 to 9 that year, she entertained both children and adults in the common rooms at Epworth Hall every day at 9 a.m. Sterling Sanford remembered how good-looking and fascinating she was and how people flocked to her. Dressed in costumes native to the countries or historical periods, she told the stories of the "Land of Wooden Shoes," "Fables New and Old," "Japanese Stories," "Myth and Legends," "Stories of Knighthood," "Modern Stories," "Heroic Girls and Boys," and, for parents, she added "Returns We Should Expect from Children."

If Grace Hemingway expected any returns from her nephew Ernest, she was not disappointed. Except, according to Sanford, the senior Hemingways were embarrassed by their son's novels. Sanford recalled that when Ernest sent his father a copy of one of his books *In Our Time*, the older Hemingway wrapped it up and sent it back. "They were straitlaced Congregationalists who did not discuss such things," said Sanford.[35]

The Hemingway family first summered at Walloon Lake in 1898. Ernest, born in Oak Park, Illinois, in 1899, spent his childhood summers enjoying outdoor life at the Windemere Cottage. He, his sisters, his father Clarence and mother Grace Hall Hemingway (who was a cousin of John Hall) would board the lake steamer *Manitou* in Chicago. From Harbor Springs they would take a train down to Walloon Lake. During the summers, the family visited Bay View where Ernest's mother, a fine contralto who debuted at New York's Madison Square Garden with the Metropolitan Opera Company, enjoyed the music programs and later studied art.

Sanford, who later married Hemingway's sister Marcelline, enjoyed the dual privilege of seeing talented performers on the Old Auditorium stage and meeting them personally at his Uncle John's house. Sanford found the assembly program to be particularly outstanding the week of August 4, 1913, when Madame Ernestine Schumann-Heink and Helen Keller were both on the roster.

Schumann-Heink was the Pavarotti of her day. She was the first singer to break with the Metropolitan Opera and make a successful recital career. Her Bay View concert on August 8, 1910, in the Old Auditorium was sold out three days beforehand. Over 2100 attended. On that program was an accomplished twelve-year-old pianist, Sara Suttel, who played one of her own compositions and several Liszt numbers. Schumann-Heink graciously stayed over to give a second concert to accommodate those who couldn't get tickets. Schumann-Heink liked Bay View and returned in 1913 for a second appearance on August 4. Hall paid the superstar $4000 which he personally guaranteed. The 1910 ticket price had been one dollar but, by 1913, the price had doubled to two dollars. Again, there was a sell-out crowd of over 2100. With the proceeds and a passing of the hat among those gathered on the lawn outside the auditorium, all expenses were easily covered and the assembly netted a profit of $500.

That summer Schumann-Heink followed her Bay View appearance with a special concert at the Native American Greensky Hill Methodist Church near Charlevoix. The late church member Odawa Jay Oliver remembered how taken his parents were with her. The woman with the Wagnerian voice so impressive on the large Bay View stage was captivating in the little log cabin church when she sang "Stille Nacht," described by Sanford as "full of wistfulness and lightness of touch."

As unforgettable as Schumann-Heink's 1913 performance was, the thirty-three-year-old Helen Keller's appearance on August 9 made a great impact on the community. Her Saturday lecture brought in an enormous crowd and made a $1200 profit, the largest of the 1913 assembly season. "Whenever I think of Helen Keller, the picture that comes to mind is the way she walked with her face uplifted and lighted with a faint smile and eager expression that seemed to be reaching out to drink in the sunshine," Sanford wrote years later.

Not knowing what to expect at first, the audience was hushed by the sound of her voice. Soon there came a

***W.E.N. Hunter designed Recreation Hall and Clarence J. Place built the building in 1911.*** *(Author's Collection)*

*Grace Hemingway, Ernest's aunt, told children's stories everyday for a week at Epworth Hall in 1910. She toured Chautauqua assemblies each summer. During the winter months, she taught in schools with under privileged children.* (Courtesy of James Sanford)

flood of questions. People asked how she knew to stop talking during the applause. Keller told the audience in a fluid voice that she knew when they were clapping from the vibrations in the wooden floor. When Mrs. Macy (Anne Sullivan) interpreted those questions from the audience, Miss Keller would often begin answering before Mrs. Macy had finished the "manual" interpretation."[36]

Swift, the Bay View ticket-seller, was put off by this "finger" language which spelled words out in Keller's hands. When Keller asked to go for a walk in the Bay View Woods, deaf teacher Leance Otebrecht asked Swift to accompany her. He reluctantly agreed. "I was dumbfounded! She knew the trees! She would feel the bark, and she knew many of those trees by the feel of the bark and the leaves," said Swift. While on one of her walks, Keller was recognized by a childhood friend, a black woman whose father had been a slave on the Keller's Alabama plantation. The two women embraced and shared childhood memories.

Before she left for Harbor Springs, Keller was entertained at Wayside by Leon Marx, violinist from the Chicago-based Theodore Thomas Orchestra, and pianist William K. Breckenridge of the Oberlin Conservatory, both on the staff of the Bay View Conservatory of Music. Sanford recalled the day: "Miss Keller placed her teeth against the instrument [violin] and she could enjoy the music by feeling the vibrations. Mr. Breckenridge played the piano for her by placing her fingers on the piano. Again, she said she could hear the music by feeling the vibrations. In spite of all her handicaps, Helen Keller was an enthusiastic person who seemed to enjoy life. She even said she enjoyed the things she could not see. When the Bay View sunset was described to her, she said she enjoyed seeing it and thought it was beautiful."[37]

In the summer of 1917, Sanford began courting Hemingway's sister Marcelline. He was finishing his engineering degree at U-M, provided for by Hall's estate, and had rented a room at Evelyn for the summer. Marcelline was staying with then well-known Chicago editor Trumbull White while she played viola in the Bay View Orchestra. Sanford had a Packard Touring Sedan. Quite the envy of many, one day he gave Marcelline a ride back to White's farm overlooking Round Lake east of Bay View. Intrigued with each other, the couple began dating. In 1919, Sanford joined Detroit Edison as an engineer, and they were married in 1923. The couple never returned to Bay View, but in 1924 bought a cottage on Walloon Lake where their family continues to summer.

The last time Sterling and Marcelline saw her brother was at Dr. Clarence Hemingway's funeral in 1928. In his 1969 biography of Hemingway, Carlos Baker cites Sanford as the one who paid for "Papa" (Clarence) Hemingway's funeral (with his inheritance from Hall). Baker also pointed out that Ernest considered Sanford to be "rich," "whereas he [Ernest] lived by his pen and had for some years been more or less an outcast."[38]

During the winter of 1919-20, Ernest spent time in Bay View. He rented a room in Petoskey at 602 State Street in October of 1919 to write and recover from war injuries sustained during his time in Italy. A very persuasive individual, Ernest talked Bay View's superintendent of grounds, Charles Ditto, into letting him use the little room with the wood furnace on the southeast corner of Evelyn Hall to write.

"He seemed to enjoy the peace and quiet of the place," Marion Stark, Ditto's daughter later recalled to Bay View Archivist Jane P. Doerr. After writing for a while, Hemingway would take off to Petoskey on the "high road," as they called Arlington Avenue in those days. Often, he stopped at the Little Bakery or Jesperson's for butterscotch ice cream.

Baker documented that Hemingway threw a party one fall at Dr. Ramsdell's Bay View cottage at Block 2, Lot 18. A fire in March of 1918 had destroyed the original Ramsdell cottage along with several others, and Ramsdell had built a new cottage on the site directly across from the present post office. Ernest and his friends drank alcoholic cider and threw raisins out the back door. That evening, Irene Gordon of Petoskey was either his date or met him at this party. The two frequently played tennis together and kept in contact until Hemingway's death.

Hemingway's friends in Petoskey included the Ralph Connable family who owned Connable's Fish Market. In Toronto, Ralph, Jr., was the head of the Canadian branch of the F. W. Woolworth five-and-ten-cent stores. The Connables may have become acquainted with the Woolworth and Knox families in Bay View, thus establishing a friendship that enabled the younger Connable to gain the company's top Canadian position.[39] During the winter months of 1919 when Hemingway stayed with the Connable family in Toronto, Ralph, Jr. presented Ernest to the editors of the Toronto *Star* where Hemingway began his professional writing career.

Hemingway returned to Petoskey during the summer of 1920 and stayed at The Florence Cottage No. 2, a Bay View rooming house. There he received a scathing letter from his mother concerning his "lazy loafing and pleasure-seeking" attitudes. After he married Hadley Richardson in Horton Bay on September 3, 1921, Hemingway left Petoskey and his northern Michigan retreat. Years later, when Irene Gordon asked him why he had not returned to this area sooner, he said he was always disappointed when he returned to places he had loved, and didn't want that to happen here.[40]

The syndicated six-part German mini-series *Ernest Hemingway,* starring Stacy Keach in the title role and Stuart Whiteman as his father, was filmed in Bay View in August 1987. A co-production of Alcor Films and Daniel Wilson Productions, the documentary was based on Baker's authorized biography. Producer Linda

***The great opera diva Madame Ernestine Schumann-Heink appeared in Bay View in 1910, giving a second concert when the first one sold out. In 1913, when she was contracted for a return engagement, she made a special appearance at Greensky Hill Methodist Church in Charlevoix, something Odawa Jay Oliver said his parents found so moving. Her personal accompanist Katherine Hoffman, who was also Bay View's choral accompanist, accompanied Schumann in all of her Bay View appearances in 1910 and 1913.*** *(Liza Lee Collins' Collection)*

Marmelstein chose Bay View for the filming of Hemingway's early life because of its Victorian authenticity. The paved streets were covered with sand, and the Bay View Archives provided accurate information on authentic local dress of the times.

During the filming, Keach spent quiet time between scenes in the room at Evelyn Hall where Hemingway wrote during the fall and spring of 1919 and 1920.[41] While the actual wedding of Hemingway to Richardson (played by Josephine Chaplin) took place twenty miles away in Horton Bay, the movie's scenes were filmed on the porch and lawn of Epworth Hall with many Bay View residents as extras. Because of its resemblance to Hemingway's birthplace, the cottage at Block 25, Lot 1, was substituted in the film for the family's Oak Park home.

The influence of Hall and his assembly program on the Hemingway family and Hemingway himself was considerable because of the many times the Hemingway family visited the assembly grounds, a significant fact not previously investigated in the many books written about the Hemingways. It was Hall who hired Trumbull White to teach journalism in Bay View in 1895 and it was White who purchased *The Bay View Magazine* and encouraged Hemingway to pursue a writing career.

***Marcelline Hemingway with her famous brother Ernest.***
*(Courtesy of James Sanford)*

All who knew her cooking at first hand agree that her real talent was for contriving clever meals in no time flat out of whatever chanced to be handy around the place. (Marion believed that the Bay View vacations had been the great nurturer of this gift)."[42]

Although Unitarians, each summer Irma, her husband, and their two children left the St. Louis heat to enjoy the rustic atmosphere of northern Michigan. Accounts of their summer life show just how involved Irma and her family were in Bay View's recreation program and the Summer University. Edgar, a prominent St. Louis lawyer, took the entire summer off to spend with his family and play golf at the Petoskey-Bay View Country Club. Marion developed an avid interest in the environment. Irma took up fishing on Pickerel Lake and often entertained friends on rowboat trips. In 1916, she studied French with Madame P. Marlotte-Davies of Purdue, Indiana.

In 1910, Irma enrolled Marion in Anna Lagergren's "Sloyd for Children." Hall referred to this Swedish instructor of wood-making as the "fountain head of manual training." Lagergren had been trained at the Naas Normal School in Sweden, the Gothenburg Sloyd School and the Boston Sloyd School and taught in Bay View for nearly twenty years. She told Irma that her daughter was "the most patient and least gifted child she'd ever handled,"[43] Edgar, Jr. later signed up for Sloyd classes in 1917, but with another instructor.

Up to this time, the Rombauers had been renting. In February 1920, they purchased the cottage at Block 25, Lot 4, named *Sans-Souci*, meaning "carefree" in

***For the Hemingway documentary, Bay View residents Max and Jeannette Collins, dressed in period wedding garb, pose with Stuart Whitman (Playing Ernest Hemingway's father) in front of Epworth Hall.***
*(Courtesy of Maxwell and Jeannette Collins)*

Another person on whom Hall's program had a dramatic impact was Irma Rombauer. In 1910, Hall's new cooking instructor, Mrs. W. A. Johnson (Nannie Talbot), of Paris, Kentucky, took over as head of the Bay View School of Domestic Science. "After experimenting long, Bay View has found one of the most capable women in the land for this school," he wrote in *The Bay View Magazine* in May, 1911. "She was taken last year on very high recommendation and soon proved that she was both an accomplished woman in her specialty of cooking, and knew how to successfully convey her knowledge and methods to others."

Hall's style is often tedious, but, regarding Johnson, his comments could not be more accurate. At a cost of twenty-five cents, women signed up for her courses in droves, making her classes the largest in the Summer University. Rombauer signed up for a class at Evelyn Hall. While she was never a gourmet cook, she was Johnson's prize student who would later author *The Joy of Cooking.* She took several classes and particularly enjoyed cake decorating, developing a great skill at it according to her daughter Marion. Johnson published a pamphlet, *Cake, Candy, and Culinary Crinkles,* in 1912, a copy of which was later found among Irma's possessions. Rombauer biographer Anne Mendelson wrote: "Cooking in itself had scant charm for her except as another expression of the social gift that she so intensely bent on her acquaintance.

*Although her mother visited the Harbor Point resort in the 1890s, Irma Rombauer and her family didn't begin summering in Bay View until about 1910. She is pictured outside her cottage Sans-Souci at Block 25, Lot 4, with her daughter Marion and son Edgar, Jr.* (Courtesy of Ethan Rombauer Becker)

French.[44] Fond of gardening, Irma wrote to the Bay View board on October 16, 1920, complaining that her lot was cut off from the street and had no alley: "Immediately behind is Block 18, the property of the Association. A road leading to the stand-pipe cuts this lot in two. The ground is sloping and covered with small neglected trees and underbrush. I desire to lease that part of Block 18 that immediately adjoins the back line of my lot and stretches up to the stand-pipe road. My purpose is two-fold: First to leave an outlet to the street, independent of my neighbors. Second, for the purpose of cultivation and general improvements."[45] Even though Irma wanted to plant a flower garden in back of her cottage and did not plan to erect a shed or garage, the policy of the association was not to sell half lots. The issue must have been resolved, because in 1928 and 1929 Martin Beer, who was later a founder of Petoskey's St. Frances Credit Union, tended Irma's garden.

"She liked bachelor buttons and so I planted those for her. She paid me twenty-five cents an hour and made lunch for me. It was nothing unusual - tomato soup and a whole-wheat bread sandwich. She also bought me a subscription to *American Boy Magazine*. I worked six hours a day every day all summer for two summers," recalled Beer.[46] He also worked at the Petoskey-Bay View Country Club caddying for Edgar, Sr.

During the Rombauers' married life, Edgar frequently suffered from bouts of depression. In an undated letter to William DeVol, an officer of the association and owner of the Terrace Inn, Irma referred to her husband's illness and the need to sell one house. "Of course, we are keeping the cottage. We love it too much not to feel that it is there ready for our use. Our return will depend entirely on Edgar's improvement."[47]

Any improvement in his nervous condition was temporary and, in February 1930, Edgar R. Rombauer took a double-barreled shotgun and killed himself. At the time the event was considered so shameful that the members of the family were not told and even her grandson Ethan never learned of his grandfather's actions for decades. Irma was left with only about $6000, a mortgage payment due on her St. Louis home, some valueless stock from her husband's major client, and the Bay View cottage. She turned to her interest in cooking as an outlet for her sorrow,

*Rombauer Cottage looking as it did when the family owned it.* (Photograph by Author)

an interest developed some two decades earlier in those Bay View cooking classes. She decided to write a cookbook. "Worst idea we ever heard of," was the family consensus: 'Irma is a TERRIBLE cook,' was the reaction of friends."[48]

Despite discouraging remarks, Irma persisted and came to Michigan to write her book but did not stay at her cottage. Instead, she chose the out-of-the-way Dilworth Resort in Horton Bay where she was a stranger. She published her first cookbook in 1931. A commercial publication followed in 1936, and by 1943 *The Joy of Cooking* was a national success. When her daughter Marion Becker, so unskilled at Sloyd, joined the effort in 1951, *The Joy of Cooking* became the most important American culinary reference book and probably the most successful cookbook ever written. The 75th Anniversary Edition published by Irma's grandson Ethan Becker is considered by the New York Public Library as one of the 150 most important books of the twentieth century. For Rombauer to pursue an interest in cooking at a time when tragedy had left her desperate, it's clear that Hall had been right about his domestic arts instructor. Mrs. Johnson passed on to Irma a passion for cooking and, in turn, Irma, Marion, and now Ethan have passed on culinary joy to the world. Definitely, the family summers in Bay View had a marked effect.

Despite his obvious impact, Hall's personality is illusive. Glimpses come from only a few sources but provide a welcome balance from the unresolved conflicts between his supporters and adversaries. What he was really like is only conjecture. A reporter from the

**BROWNIES OR FUDGE SQUARES**

| | |
|---|---|
| ¾ cup butter | 1 cup flour |
| 4 squares of chocolate | 1 teaspoon vanilla |
| 4 eggs beaten | 1 cup nuts |
| 2 cups sugar | |

Melt the butter and the chocolate. Beat the eggs, add the sugar, flour, vanilla and the melted mixture. Beat the batter well and add the nuts. Spread it to the thickness of 1 inch in a shallow tin lined with waxed paper. Bake the cake in a slow oven 350 degrees for about 30 minutes. Cut it into oblongs.

***Irma Rombauer particularly enjoyed baking. According to her grandson Ethan Becker, her brownie recipe was a favorite in Bay View.*** *(From Joy of Cooking, Irma Rombauer, 1931, Used by permission)*

***Architect's rendering of the proposed auditorium in 1914*** *(Author's Collection)*

*W.E.N. Hunter (1868-1947) was employed to design the new auditorium. Hunter was a member of Detroit's Metropolitan Methodist Church where Hall worshipped.* (Courtesy of the American Institute of Architects)

*Michigan Christian Advocate* in the 1890s found him congenial. An 1893 writer at the *Daily Resorter* found Hall to be reticent. "It may be here remarked that although for eight years Mr. Hall has been at the head of the Bay View educational system he modestly shrinks from talking or writing about the work with which he has been so intimately connected, preferring to leave this to be done by others."[49] *Daily Resorter* reporter Paul B. Blanshard found him reluctant to be interviewed. On the other hand, Swift described him as peculiar: "He was in many respects quite after his own kind – as we say in Latin, 'sui generis.' He was smooth shaven, tall (six feet, four or five inches tall) very thin, and had a rather peculiar voice, which was rather shrill, but had great carrying properties. He also liked to hear himself talk, for he would continue his announcements beyond what would seem to be was necessary; in fact, people became fatigued with his announcements."[50] When foreign correspondent George Kennan was on the program in 1895, an annoyed audience began yelling "Kennan." Sanford was amused because Hall had no regard for what other people thought of him. "He was a man of enormous energy, a workaholic. He never stayed through an assembly program but would always hurry back to his desk on the first floor of Evelyn Hall to write letters or finish some business," remembered Sanford.[51]

Emma Lamb Barnes penned an amusing satire about this workaholic. It seems local cats were banding together to find a way of getting attention with an annual day of honor on the assembly program. The Howard House staff always took care of Hall's pet cat when he was out of town. The other cats couldn't find a way of getting the prestigious cat's attention since it was never alone.[52]

Other stories about Hall revealed him to be gregarious and mindful of others. He made sure his summer school faculty, the BVRC guests, the assembly entertainment such as Madame Schumann-Heink and Booker T. Washington, and the camp meeting speakers were properly entertained at Wayside. He maintained a constant schedule of receptions both at *Wayside* and at the Bay View House where he owned part interest. In 1910, the *Daily Resorter* reported that he was experimenting with a new sound system in the Old Auditorium to aid the hearing-impaired.

Particularly stirring is the story of how the John M. Hall Auditorium was built. When Reed and Shier first contracted Hall in 1887, a 2500-seat auditorium was hastily erected. "It was a sheep barn — generally known as a sheep barn. It was a wooden structure — flat roof, one story tall, very low ceiling — and an immense building with pillars (iron pillars) that went up and spread out…to support the roof. And towards the end the roof got very bad. The last year it leaked like blazes in the thunderstorm. We had them in those days. We don't have them now, it seems. But, it leaked badly, and you would see people put up umbrellas, listening to the lectures or listening to the music," remembered Swift.[53]

*As superintendent of Bay View grounds between 1914 and 1917, Clarence J. Place oversaw the construction of the John M. Hall Auditorium. He trained under builder David Seibert who constructed all of Bay View's wooden public buildings, but when Place constructed the Mineral Well in Petoskey and Bay View's Recreation Hall, he found that he preferred working with cement. He later joined the Michigan Department of Transportation building bridges.* (Courtesy of Mildred Place Panney)

*Son of Frank Vernor, F. Dudleigh Vernor, composer of* **The Sweetheart of Sigma Chi**, *on his Bay View cottage porch in 1973 shortly before his death. He was a musician on the Bay View staff from childhood until just before his death.* (Photograph by Author)

Worse yet, that old "sheep barn" had a few steps coming down to the speaker's platform in the front of the seating area being built on the natural amphitheater of the hillside, the site of the present auditorium. As Anne Sullivan and Helen Keller made their way to the platform in 1913, there was a thud and big gasp went up from the crowd. "Every-one thought it was Miss Keller and that she had taken a fall: but it wasn't her, it was her assistant [Mrs. Macy]," John S. Davis remembered in a 1969 interview.

Hall had been contemplating a new auditorium. With this near catastrophe, he realized the time had come to move ahead with his dormant plans. William Egerton N. Hunter (1868-1947), was contracted to design this new structure. It was to be a Greek revival with no steps into the auditorium, a barrier-free design like auditoriums at other Chautauquas. The Canadian-born member of Detroit's Metropolitan Methodist Church, was a self-employed architect who was known as the "church architect." When he came to Detroit from Hamilton, Ontario, in 1899, he worked with Joseph Kastler to design Saint Josaphat Roman Catholic Church. By 1909, he had opened his own firm and developed architectural plans for a Beaux Arts church, the celebrated First United Methodist Church of Hastings, Michigan, where Bay View's vice-president, Judge Clement Smith, attended. Smith, therefore, had first-hand knowledge of Hunter's work. So he became the Bay View board's choice.

Hunter was then working on the Jewish synagogue Shaarey Zedek at Brush and Willis in Detroit (demolished) as well as the Central Methodist Church of Traverse City. He began the Bay View project immediately afterwards. The John M. Hall Auditorium marks a radical departure from Hunter's former designs with its Ionic portico, more in keeping with national trends rather than with Bay View's Victorian character. Nevertheless, the building is neatly nestled into the sloping hill beside Hitchcock Hall and architect Oliver's Victorian masterpiece, Evelyn Hall.[54]

At the November 13, 1913, meeting of the Bay View board in Detroit, Secretary Frank Vernor made the stunning announcement of two gifts to the association, a new auditorium costing more than $15,000 and a new $4000 pipe organ given by Thomas Gordon. Gordon, had been Hall's business partner since the resurrection of the assembly in 1909. All the board had to do was to raze the Old Auditorium and prepare the site for the new building.

Fully believing that the new auditorium would be ready for the 1914 season, Hall forged on with his plans. That spring, though, when the builders tried to set the foundation for the buttresses, "...a discovery of great importance was made. Far below the surface a stratum of quick sand was accidentally found, and it was decided to tear out the original footings and construct new ones of concrete and steel. The new bases, three feet thick and twelve feet square, were then put in, so that the building is practically based on solid rock which would support a building ten times as heavy as this one," reported Blanshard.[55]

Mildred Place Panney was just two years old when her father, Clarence J. Place, took the job of building the new auditorium, but she remembered the times vividly. Her father had been apprenticed to Peter and David Seibert whose firm built the other campus buildings in the 1880s and 90s. In 1910, Place built Recreation Hall, finding that he liked working with cement and steel. After a controversy with the previous contractor, Place was hired as Bay View's new superintendent of grounds and contractor.

Immediately, he became concerned about the sandy soil and the many springs in the construction area. "Father refused to build the auditorium until those plans were changed," remembered Panney. Hunter came from Chicago to review the situation and agreed with Place. The plans were changed and Place resumed work with about twelve employees. However, construction was behind schedule. Swift gave a first-hand account of how far behind: "Then I came back in '14 – came back about the last week in June…And the auditorium was only about eight or six feet (the walls); the floor wasn't in, of course, and the men were putting up those great trusses….And one day, the first or second day I was here, John M. Hall came, and I said, 'Mr. Hall,' (he was very deaf) 'I suppose I will have to sell tickets in the grove by the table.' 'Oh, no, you won't! You will sell tickets right here in front.' 'Well', I said, 'all right. I don't see any evidence of it now.' Well, you know I did! He got things started. He hurried those men along….It was leaky in some places but we held meetings in that building that year…."[56]

The Williams' Jubilee Singers and two Bay View theater productions - *The Mikado* and an elaborate musical, *Joseph* - opened the new auditorium in 1914. The shows starred F. Dudleigh Vernor, composer of the *Sweetheart of Sigma Chi*, who was one of Frank Vernor's sons. Unlike the earlier years, by then Hall had won the respect of his constituency. At the 1914 association annual meeting, he was unanimously re-elected to the board by acclamation. Journalist Paul Blanshard recommended naming the building the John M. Hall Auditorium. Like the Hemingway and Rombauer families, Hall had had a profound effect on Paul and his brother Brand.

***The Williams' Jubilee Singers opened the newly-built John M. Hall Auditorium in 1914 entertaining their audience with popular versions of ballads, ragtime, classic selections, Negro melodies, river tunes, and jubilee songs.*** *(Author's Collection)*

— CHAPTER FIVE —

# The Blanshard Bros.

Legally, the assembly was absorbed in 1906 by Bay View Camp-ground Association of the Methodist Episcopal Church, but in actuality, in 1909 the resurrected assembly incorporated camp meeting functions - Bible institutes, ministerial unions and missionary conferences and a Bible department within the Summer University. To better coordinate the activities and topics, during John Hall's second tenure at Bay View between 1909 and 1914, he introduced thematic planning with four conferences each summer: the Bay View Bible Conference, the Missionary Conference, the Labor and Social Welfare Conference and the Health Conference. The conferences featured topics of national concern by eminent speakers. In depth coverage was needed and the *Daily Resorter* found two very capable Petoskey high school students - Paul and Percy Brand Blanshard. Recognizing the intelligence of these twins, the paper hired them for the following six years to cover the Bay View program. The twins worked together to write (in longhand) daily columns until Percy won one of the first Rhodes' scholarships to study in England. Paul continued writing until he finished his degree at U-M.

Using his middle name Brand, Percy became a philosopher, probably the most distinguished proponent of rationalism, and chairman of the department at Yale University. Controversy followed his ultra-liberal brother, Paul, throughout a variety of distinguished careers as a minister, civil servant, lawyer, writer and editor. Paul's relentless attacks on the Catholic Church in the 1940s and 1950s - as expounded in his radical exposé and bestseller *American Freedom and Catholic Power* - for what he called its "un-American involvement in the affairs of state education", served as the philosophical basis for federal bans on public school prayer and aid to parochial schools.[1] It was a philosophy Paul formulated in his youth reviewing famous lecturers at Bay View and in his educational experience in Petoskey.

These two luminous men definitely left their mark on American thought and philosophy and, as each twin pointed out in individual autobiographies and Paul's late son Rufus confirmed, the Bay View Assembly was a major influence. Through their coverage of Bay View events during the assembly's finest era, a very distinct philosophical picture of the Bay View emerges. Radical ideas advocated by many speakers left an indelible imprint on these two who, in turn, left their own immeasurable effect on the philosophical makeup of this country.

Paul and Percy Blanshard were orphans raised by their paternal grandmother, Orminda Adams Blanshard. They were born August 27, 1892, in Fredericksburg, Ohio, to Methodist minister Francis George Blanshard and his wife, Emily Coulter. When the twins were just eleven months old, their mother died in a freak accident when she stumbled down a staircase while carrying an oil lamp. Her luxuriant hair caught fire, and she passed away in her husband's arms the following day.

Shortly after the tragedy, the twins' grandfather, also a Methodist minister, passed away. The twin's father Francis accepted a pastorate in a church in Grand Rapids, Michigan, and Orminda took over raising her two grandsons. She suffered from hay fever so that when the family heard about the healing effects of the northern Michigan air, sometime in the mid-1890s, they rented rooms in the Methodist community and attended the Hay Fever Convention at Evelyn Hall.[2] From then on, the family retreated to its haven each summer and enjoyed what Percy referred to as an "admirable program of lectures, concerts, plays, and summer courses of study."[3]

***Paul, shown here, and Brand Blanshard attended school in Petoskey until they were accepted at the University of Michigan***

*Brand Blanshard. Both pictures were taken in Petoskey when the twins were in the eighth grade.* (Courtesy of Jane and Rufus Blanshard)

When the twins were twelve in 1904, tragedy struck again. Their father died in New Mexico of tuberculosis. Out of her meager Methodist pension of $450 a year, Orminda purchased a Bay View cottage at Block 32, Lot 8, in 1905. It had running water but no bathroom. She cooked on a wood-burning stove using logs the boys chopped. "For some years this little house, unlined within and built of rough pine boards, was our real home," Percy continued.[4] "Bay View meant even more to us on the intellectual side," wrote Percy about their jobs punching tickets at the Old Auditorium for fifteen dollars a week and ringing the bells for the Chautauqua season.[5] Both twins mention the many famous speakers and entertainers they heard during those years.

In 1908, the twins were given the newsstand concession which a local carpenter built to their "juvenile specifications."[6] In a business venture they called "Blanshard Bros.," the boys ordered newspapers from major US cities and sold them at a nickel a copy, making two or three cents on each sale.

"Then we launched our favorite enterprise, a daily Bay View news column in the Petoskey Resorter [sic], where, for a total of $5 a week, we were allowed to experiment boldly with the English language. We interviewed everybody of consequence who came to town, ranging from Ernestine Schumann-Heink -- she ended her concert with 'The Rosary' -- to William Jennings Bryan," wrote Paul.[7]

Bryan spoke on the Bay View platform twice while the twins were living in Petoskey and Bay View. Paul described Bryan's 1905 speech: "Bryan had a magic kind of talent based on two assets, a uniquely orchestrated voice and the capacity for repose on the platform. He stood foursquare in his black alpaca coat with scarcely a single gesture until, toward the climax, he would lift an arm slightly, bringing it down with the authority of Jove. On the printed page his words looked like Tom foolishness — he was an idiot in matters of currency and fundamentalism -- but nothing could negate the mysterious power of that voice."[8]

So intrigued was Percy with the Bay View speakers and their oratorical styles that he took notes and built a speaker's stand in the backyard of their cottage. There, he and Paul practiced giving the great speeches they had heard, imitating the oratorical style of Bryan and Eugene Victor Debs, the leader of the 1894 Chicago Pullman strike and the 1904 Socialist Party presidential candidate who spoke at Petoskey's Baptist Church. This backyard practice served as background for their later membership on the U-M debating team, where they both won the National Peace Oratorical Contest as undergraduates. The local paper described Percy as "That literary genius from the University of Michigan [who] will represent the Resorter at Bay View for his fourth consecutive season. He is the modest young man with glasses and an apparent touch of shyness (which is only imitation to aid him in getting all the news). He can get the 'stuff' and he knows how to write it right."[9]

This "literary genius" with the right "stuff" decided he wanted to study in England on an Oxford scholarship established in Cecil Rhodes's will. Percy learned Greek and Latin, both offered in Bay View classes, and, in 1913, became one of the first Rhodes Scholars. With a grant of $1500 a year, he went to Merton College at Oxford, England, where his friends included T.S. Eliot. The following year, when World War I broke out, Percy was studying in Germany. Detained by German officials and unable to return to England, he wrote letters in German to Paul in Bay View, which Paul summarized in the *Daily Resorter*. Finally, Percy was able to get out of Germany and went to India where he worked for the YMCA. He returned to America when the US entered the war. "He feels that if he is to serve he prefers to be under the Stars and Stripes," reported the local paper.[10]

Percy dropped his first name and, as Brand, became one of America's distinguished contemporary philosophers.[11] He received his PhD from Harvard University in 1921 and taught at the U-M, Columbia University (where he was a student of John Dewey) and Swarthmore

***As cars became prevalent, writer Paul Blanshard complained about the lack of enforcement by the Bay View board of trustees of the 10 mile-an-hour speed limit on Woodland Avenue (US-31).*** *(Author's Collection)*

College. At Yale University, he chaired the philosophy department.[12]

Brand was well known for his coherence theory that truth is apprehended not in parts but as a whole as expounded upon in his numerous books including: *The Nature of Thought, Reason and Goodness, Reason and Analysis, Reason and Belief, The Uses of a Liberal Education, and Philosophy in American Education*. He summarized it by saying, "The finest of all achievements, and the most difficult, I have come to think, is merely being reasonable. It is difficult because it runs counter to our love of the dramatic, the temperamental, the aggressive, and the spectacular, all of which we prize too highly. If men were reasonable, if they even tried to be reasonable, the world would be transformed overnight"[13] Dr. David Scarrow, Professor Emeritus from Kalamazoo College, described Brand as an old-fashioned traditional rationalist at a time of radical imperialism.[14] Brand is particularly remembered for his personal demeanor, which was "one of extraordinary graciousness."

John Sanford, Ernest Hemingway's nephew and son of Marcelline Hemingway and Sterling Sanford, studied ethics under Brand at Yale University. During a 1999 interview, John said that Brand never mentioned Bay View. It is regrettable that these two people whose lives were completely altered by their Bay View connection never conversed on the subject. Brand himself lamented this in a letter to John's father, Sterling dated November 1, 1975, on the occasion of the naming of Vernor Hall in honor of Brand's and Sterling's friend, Dr. F. Dudleigh Vernor: "Please give my regards to your son, who I didn't know was yours when he worked with me at Yale. . . . Since I haven't been back to Bay View in more than fifty years, I was glad to be brought up to date on it. Attendance on the lectures and concerts there meant a lot to Paul and me in those far-off days; I hope the Chautauqua program still continues in the summer. Paul visited Bay View briefly a few years ago, and said that things looked surprisingly the same. Our little cottage on the edge of the golf links was a clubhouse for a time, but is now occupied by one of the Abbey family who used to take trunks to and from the station in a horse-drawn wagon."[15]

After his brother left for England in 1913, Paul remained at U-M and continued writing during the summers for the *Daily Resorter* until he finished his undergraduate degree in 1914. His "experiments with the English language" in the *Daily Resorter* during his six years as a reporter gave him confidence in his ideas as he earned the respect of his area-wide readership. Not only were his columns read by some 5000 Bay View residents, but dignitaries who lived in the vicinity - vice presidents Charles W. Fairbanks and Thomas R. Marshall; politicians and senators such as William Jennings Bryan and his 1908 running mate Senator John Worth Kern; and, numerous governors, federal and state judges, college presidents and faculty members, teachers, ministers and businessmen. Armed with an evolving self-assurance that became more and more apparent after his brother's departure, Paul ardently supported litigious local issues such as the financially troubled Bay View Assembly program of Hall and Gordon. Paul never missed an opportunity to lavish praise on these two, even when the political leanings in Bay View were in the other direction. Zealously, he sided with Hall on issues such as women's rights in covering the BVRC.

As part of his newspaper job, Paul attended all assembly programs and covered news about everything on the grounds: the woods, the recreation program, the Women's Club, the new men's club, the hotels and famous visitors. One of those highly regarded speakers on the assembly program was Ida Tarbell, scheduled to appear in 1913 discussing her book on practices of the Standard Oil Company. Much to Paul's disappointment, Tarbell canceled for family reasons. Paul was obviously influenced by Tarbell's writings. Later in the 1930s, he wrote *What's Wrong with New York*, analyzing the corrupt Jimmy Walker administration. After Walker resigned, Paul was appointed by Mayor Fiorello H. LaGuardia as commissioner of New York City's Department of Investigations and Accounts. He earned a law degree at Brooklyn Law School and fiercely attacked racketeering and corruption. By 1935, twenty-two officials from Tammany Hall had been dismissed or forced to resign. Despite his successful attacks on the darker side of New York life, Paul retained his poise and dignity. Writer August Heckscher referred to him as a "graceful figure."[16]

As a college student, Paul was intrigued by the four annual conferences of the assembly: the Bible Conference, the Labor and Social Welfare Conference, the Conference on Missions and the Country Life Conference. His coverage shed light on the socialistic thought widely subscribed to by popular Chautauqua speakers during those years and the reception they received from the Bay View audience. Reverend Charles Stelzle, in charge of Bay View's Labor and Social Welfare Conference from 1910 to 1915, made an enormous impact on Paul. A social reformer and Presbyterian minister of New York's Labor Temple, Stelzle served from 1903 until 1913 as director of the Workingmen's Department of the Presbyterian Church USA and headed the Bureau of Social Services in New York City. He was the first minister to take up the cause of industrial reform, and his ministry was endorsed in 1906 by the American Federation of Labor. During his years in Bay View, Stelzle's fame spread worldwide, and he was the recipient of many awards from Europe. As his recognition grew, however, criticism intensified. The Presbyterian General Assembly forced him out of the Labor Temple in 1913, but Stelzle continued to appear in Bay View.

Lecturing in 1914 on the subject "Radical Movements Among Workingmen," Stelzle pleaded for more broad-mindedness in the church so that socialists, communists and anarchists might come through its doors, reported Paul in one of his daily columns in 1914: "Once each year Bay View needs a Charles Stelzle to break through its religious placidity. ...Mr. Stelzle points out with unflinching courage that the church has never been less attractive to strong young men than it is today. Mr. Stelzle challenges Bay View to heed the signs of the times and not remain satisfied under a ministry of contentment."[17]

Another speaker at the 1914 Labor and Social Welfare Conference was Charles Zueblin of Boston and the University of Chicago who spoke on the subject of "Economic Justice," espousing communist ideas of scientific production, equitable distribution of wealth, and discriminating consumption of goods. "He declared that the chief evils of present day production are unemployment, over-employment, and misemployment," quoted Paul. Zueblin also advocated an employment bureau so that "we may know of employment fluctuations as we know of stock market fluctuations."[18] Paul wholeheartedly agreed with these reformers and, in 1917-18, he was involved in a strike as educational director of the Amalgamated Clothing Workers of America and arrested in Rochester, New York.

Another radical on the Bay View platform was Dr. William K. Sadler, who at the time was head of the department of therapeutics in the postgraduate Medical School of Chicago. Sadler had worked with Dr. John Harvey Kellogg in Battle Creek and studied in Vienna with Sigmund Freud, Alfred Adler and Carl Jung. He formed what he called the "American School of Psychiatry." He was a professor and lecturer of pastoral psychiatry at McCormick Theological Seminary and chief psychiatrist at the Chicago Institute of Research and Diagnosis. In 1914, Sadler spoke in Bay View on eugenics, declaring himself against the propagation of the unfit. Paul reported that Sadler declared that properly enforced laws providing for sterilization of all feeble-minded children before the age of fourteen would eliminate 90% of the prostitutes of our cities. Sadler and his physician wife Lena, also from the Medical School of Chicago, conducted a Better Baby Contest at Loud Hall, giving many Bay View babies physical examinations and performance testing. The baby who scored the most points was selected as the "best" baby.

As appalling as the baby contest seems, Mrs. Mary Cummings Bliss's 1914 talk, "The Menace of the Immigrant", is just as unsettling and might have germinated Paul's later anti-Catholic stance. He summarized her remarks: "She reached the astonishing conclusion that the crux of the whole trouble with immigrants is Roman Catholicism. She gave four reasons why the present immi-

*Drs. William K. and Lena Sadler, both of the Chicago Institute for Research and Diagnosis, conducted a better baby contest at Loud Hall.* (Author's Collection)

gration is a menace: 1. Nine-tenths of the immigrants are Roman Catholic. 2. Every one of these immigrants swears allegiance to a foreign potentate and not to the Stars and Stripes. 3. The immigrants segregate in cities. 4. They do not believe in and patronize our public schools. She advocated the restriction of immigration immediately."[19] In his autobiography, Paul noted that in Petoskey he lived "a life separated from most of the Catholics simply because they went to a separate, parochial, school."[20] That experience of social separation, later reinforced during his days living on the East Coast, served to substantiate his staunch position against the Catholic Church and parochial education.

Another famous socialist, Helen Keller, had a profound effect on Paul. He met her when she spoke in Bay View on August 9, 1913. Their acquaintance grew when he attended Harvard Divinity School and became part of the freethinking Maverick Congregational Church in East Boston. In this World War I atmosphere of free love, pacifism and left-wing politics, one of Paul's U-M classmates, Peter Fagan, a reporter on the *Boston Herald*, fell in love with Helen. When Paul moved to Florida, Fagan asked him to help them elope. Paul found a clergyman to perform the ceremony. Fagan and the clergyman drove to Alabama to pick up Helen, but her family found out about the intended elopement and prevented her from meeting him. Paul later wrote: "Peter Fagan, with all his shortcomings, might have turned out to be the 'bright sun' she needed to illumine a darkened life."[21]

Illuminating what he called darkened lives was a lifelong crusade for Paul. As a teenager in Bay View, he frequently voiced his developing belief that the welfare of the whole is dependent on the well-being of the few. He continually made suggestions for improving the community. He abhorred the "shoot and kill" policy in regard to dogs. He applauded the cottage owners of Blocks 1, 20 and 21 for their improvement of the area's Fairview Park, and praised Terrace Inn's owner William DeVol for putting in the sidewalk leading to the post office. He hailed the board of trustees for the $2000 drainage system installed on the beach in front of Woodland Avenue's Kenilworth Hotel, but severely chided them for not enforcing the ten-mile-an-hour speed limit they had set for automobiles on Woodland Avenue (now US-31).

Paul suggested improving the low water pressure in east Bay View (where he lived) by limiting the hours west Bay View residents on the esteemed first terrace could water their lawns. He recommended hiring a landscape gardener to thin the trees in the gloomy beech grove in front of John M. Hall Auditorium so that grass could grow. He recommended that a concrete sidewalk be installed in place of the muddy path leading from Hall Auditorium to the Bay View House, the association's premier hotel. He advised changing the cemetery numbering system of blocks and lots to regular street addresses and put forth the idea of naming the new 1914 auditorium in honor of its donor, John M. Hall, a man Paul deeply admired. All of Paul's recommendations were eventually enacted.

While Paul refined a writing style that would serve him throughout his distinguished literary career, he did not garner a lasting regard for religion or an enduring faith that would survive the test of his intellectual pursuits. In his coverage of the Sixth Annual Bible Conference on July 23, 1914, Paul's liberalism was evident. Displaying profound respect for the conference leaders: religious philosopher Dr. Camden Cobern; the University of Chicago's Dr. Shailer Mathews; and Metropolitan Methodist Church's Dr. Merton Rice of Detroit, Paul wrote:

> *"...we could wish that Bay View audiences took a different attitude toward the Bible conference. At a place like this conference the great facts concerning the origin and nature of biblical manuscripts should be presented without apology. The revelations of higher criticism should be handled without gloves - for what should Christians seek more zealously than truth? But the typical Bay View audience becomes frigid when the Bible as an accurate historical document is doubted in any particular. Both Dr. Mathews and Dr. Cobern experienced this. We believe that it is time for some clear, strong voice to speak the truth which our great universities have known for a decade, that the Bible is a spiritual rather than a historical collection of documents. If this were done sanely and tactfully, the Bay View Bible conference audiences would think less about Jericho and more about making themselves into twentieth century Christs."*[22]

Upon graduating from the U-M, Paul married classmate Julia Sweet Anderson, the daughter of a former Illinois congressman. She became a prominent journalist. From Boston the couple went to Florida where Paul was ordained a Congregational minister but soon became an avowed atheist and left the ministry to join the Unitarian Church. "I have come to the conclusion that Christianity is so full of fraud that any honest man should repudiate the whole shebang and espouse atheism," he wrote.[23]

A conscientious objector during World War I, Paul served the US State Department during World War II in the Caribbean Commission. Afterwards, in 1949, he published his famous and controversial book *American Freedom and Catholic Power*. Published two years after the 1947 Supreme Court decision in Everson versus the Board of Education, upholding the reimbursement of parents of parochial school students in New Jersey for the transportation costs on public buses, Paul's book focused on the separation of church and state, radically redirecting

***Twins Paul and Brand Blanshard are pictured here before their deaths in the 1980s.***
*(Courtesy of Rufus and Jane Blanshard)*

American thinking and promoting future bans on aid to parochial schools and prayer in public schools. The book had a major effect on the country and more than a quarter a million copies were sold in over twenty-one printings. The Division of Public Libraries of the American Library Association selected it as one of the fifty outstanding books of 1949. However, despite this and the fact that it was on the *New York Times* bestseller list for seven months, that newspaper refused all advertisements for it.

Paul became associate editor of *The Nation* and, for a time, served as the magazine's Vatican correspondent. He became known even among Catholics as "something of a Catholic prophet" and, when America's first Catholic president, John F. Kennedy, was elected in 1960, Paul became a consultant to his administration.

The Blanshard family sold their Bay View cottage in 1937, but Rufus, Paul's youngest son, remembered how his father always spoke fondly of his Bay View years. In an interview on February 28, 2000, Rufus, a retired English professor from the University of Connecticut who held his doctorate from Harvard University, said that he felt Bay View was very influential in the lives of both his Uncle Brand and his father. In Paul's last column of 1913, he revealed his partiality as he bade a traditional farewell to all Bay Viewites: "This is the week of the exodus of the children of Israel and the rest of the children of Adam who are in Bay View. The trouble is that this time they are going from the land of Canaan to the land of bricks and straw instead of traveling by the famous reverse route. They must hang their harps upon the willows…."[24]

Paul must have taken his harp with him. Throughout his life, he continued to expound the socialistic ideas formed in his Bay View years, even when it cost him the loss of book contracts. While his brother Brand settled into the life of a great philosopher and dedicated teacher, Paul continually tried to move the mountains of injustice and unfair practices. Two very different individuals, equally brilliant, their Bay View experience prepared them for a life filled with momentous accomplishments. For Paul, his years in Bay View generated a lifetime concern for women's rights.

*Just how much good we receive*
*from the assembly as individuals and as a group*
*we shall probably never know. To measure it*
*is like trying to find how many dollars' worth of friendships*
*you have, or how many yards of milk you can buy.*
*An atmosphere of culture has no dimensions.*
*Its workings are silent. Its influence is unconscious.*
*It is like a wind that in the old phrase*
*'bloweth where it listeth' and only our idea of its value*
*is gained when we go out*
*with finer sensibilities and elevated minds.*

Paul and Percy Blanshard, *Daily Resorter,* July 15, 1912

— CHAPTER SIX —

# Women in Council

The Blanshard brothers were not the only ones influenced by the speakers and entertainment of the Bay View Assembly. It had an intangible impact on the women's movement in Michigan. Helen Stoddard, president of the Texas Woman's Christian Temperance Union and the Bay View union, compared Bay View with Boston, an extraordinary claim until we realize that national women leaders of the 1890s and 1910s stopped regularly in Bay View. As many as a thousand strong would come to hear these great women talk on subjects such as how to be a good homemaker, the importance of women's political rights, women's property rights, women's prisons, child welfare, the drug and white slave trade, and the enormous social ills of the country. Little recognition of the magnitude of the Bay View women's movement on these issues has been considered.

Carrie Burke Taylor was the kind of women who came to Bay View. The perfect icon of the "Chautauqua girl", Taylor sought a career beyond the societal expectations of marriage. Once a country schoolteacher in the small Michigan towns of Parma, Clinton and Mason, she moved to Jackson and then to Flint in 1893, where she became the first secretary of the BVRC venture, the Bay View Assembly, and the Summer University,

***Dr. Carrie Burke Taylor Stewart became the first secretary of the Bay View Reading Circle in 1893 and served until she entered medical school in 1901. Here she is enjoying her Bay View cottage garden.***
*(Courtesy of Burton Historical Collection, Detroit Public Library, and Wayne State University Walter P. Reuther Library of Labor and Urban Affairs)*

As assistant editor of *The Bay View Magazine,* she was in charge of organizing Graduation Day for BVRC members, had the added responsibility of the annual selection and contracting of assembly talent, and assisting with the Summer University professorship positions and the enrollment of students. One of her significant accomplishments came though her travels across Michigan during the winter months of the 1890s, encouraging women to participate in the Bay View correspondence course and advance their education. Building on the foundation of the network of WCTU "unions" already established and the literary clubs previously organized with the encouragement of Kalamazoo's Lucinda Hinsdale Stone, founder of the state's first women's club in 1852, Taylor further enhanced the readiness of Michigan women to enter the political scene and the working world. The growth of the BVRC circles in Michigan towns gives an indication of her success. Then, in 1901, she left her position to attend medical school to become an osteopath. After finishing her degree, she married and returned to Bay View in 1908 with her husband, Dr. Stewart. She opened an office in Evelyn Hall.

The Chautauqua movement with its nationwide labyrinth of assemblies became the means whereby women like Taylor found opportunities to expand their lives and become acquainted with the important issues that affected them. At thousands of assemblies connected by a railroad system that spider-webbed America after the Civil War, women leaders were able to reach throngs with their ideas. The extent to which the Chautauqua movement played in the spread of women's rights has had limited investigation. Harry S. McClarran's unpublished 1994 study of over three hundred fifty Chautauqua assemblies includes the names of women speakers and where they lectured.[1] It proves how within a few short weeks each summer these energetic crusaders traveled by train from their homes to numerous watering places. Religion at these camp meetings and cultural assemblies provided an umbrella of propriety, and the reading circles offered the goal of educational purpose. The Bay View Assembly, with its aggressive management in the 1890s, was considered one of the most successful Chautauqua assemblies and an important stop for these progressives.

During the latter half of the nineteenth century, the national stage was set for women's ascent to political and economic equality with men. In 1868, newspaper columnist Jennie June Croly and others founded Sorosis, the first professional women's club. In 1869, Mary A. Livermore and others founded the National Woman Suffrage Association, and a women's suffrage law was passed in

***Jennie June Croly, the first American woman journalist, came to Bay View as the founder of the General Federation of Women's Clubs. She wrote of her impressions in her 1898 book Woman's Club Movement in American.*** *(Author's Collection)*

the Wyoming territory. In 1870, the American Woman Suffrage Association sponsored the first issue of the *Woman's Journal*. In 1874, the WCTU was founded in eastern Ohio and met at the Chautauqua Assembly in New York. In 1870, the Michigan State Woman Suffrage Association was formed in Battle Creek, and a woman's suffrage amendment was passed by the Michigan legislature only to be vetoed by then Governor Henry S. Baldwin.

Women were making progress, however. That same year Dr. Mary E. Green of Charlotte, Michigan, was the first woman physician in the country to be admitted to a medical association with her election to the New York Medical Society. In 1875, the Michigan WCTU was formed at an historic women's meeting in Grand Rapids attended by Anna Smeed Benjamin and Mary Torrans Lathrap. In 1880, Dr. Anna Howard Shaw of Albion and Big Rapids became the first woman in the nation to be a fully ordained minister. In 1889, Hull House was begun in Chicago. Directed by Jane Addams, the organization made social work a paid profession for women. In 1890, the Michigan Women's Press Association was established in Traverse City with Belle McArthur Perry as president. That same year, writer Jennie June Croly founded the General Federation of Women's Clubs (GFWC) as a national parasol organization for the many women's clubs already in existence. In 1891, U-M conferred an honorary doctor of philosophy degree on Lucinda Stone who had become known by then as Michigan's "mother of women's clubs." In the summer of 1892, Stone was in Bay View making plans for a Michigan federation. The fact she chose Bay View shows the importance the assembly held among women of that day.

All of the women mentioned appeared on the Bay View platform. Between Lathrap's sermon at the initial 1876 and 1877 camp meetings and Frances Willard's historic visits in 1887 and 1889, up to 1920, when the women's suffrage amendment finally passed, over 200 national, state and locally-known suffragists, suffragettes, reformers, and temperance workers were featured on the program. Why so many of the great women leaders congregated in Bay View in the early days needs attention.

Many of these zealous workers have been overshadowed or forgotten leaders like Carrie Burke Taylor Stewart who quietly did much to spread the idea of education among Michigan women. Sadly, her picture at Burton Historical Library in Detroit has no provenance or biographical information. Frances Willard was the most famous woman in the world during her lifetime but her fame has been surpassed by Susan B. Anthony who was far less known in those days. Lathrap, who as president of the Michigan WCTU from 1882 until the early 1890s, organized Michigan women along congressional districts, paving the way for women to become politically active. Like many white women preachers in that era, she turned to administration and proved an effective leader. She

***Lucinda Hinsdale Stone.*** *(Courtesy of Larry Massie)*

expanded the number of "unions" throughout the state and focused attention not just on temperance but on other issues including the race question, labor problems, white slavery, child labor laws, drug problems, and women's prisons. In Jackson after the Civil War, she opened a school for "Negro" children at her own expense. Devoted also to the cause of "fallen women" (unwed mothers), she campaigned and received an appropriation of $30,000 from the Michigan Legislature to build an institution in Adrian, Michigan.

A powerful speaker, Lathrap argued vehemently against liquor traffic as the "great force in America that is pushing it to ruin." She traveled all over the world for the WCTU and, she was a member of the national Woman's Council in Washington, DC. She was a personal friend of Frances Willard, and English suffragette Lady Henry Somerset who wrote a character sketch about her. Today, little is known about her, and adding to the insult, her name is frequently misspelled.

One reason so many women met in Bay View may have been accessibility. The WCTU headquarters at Willard's Rest Cottage in Evanston, Illinois, was only a seven-hour train ride on the GR&I or a pleasant twenty-one hour trip on the steamship *Manitou*. Many of Willard's inner circle from the Chicago union were on the Bay View speaker's roster, indicating Bay View's importance. Both Caroline Buell and Zeralda Wallace came to Bay View when they were opposing Willard's leadership in the 1890s.

The Bay View Assembly never entertained the more radical suffragettes such as Carrie Nation, preferring these more "moderate", domestic and intellectual suffragists instead. Though moderate, these women did face a local atmosphere of resistant. The editor of a local paper believed that women were unfit to be entrusted with the safekeeping of public affairs. "They are too emotional, too prejudiced, and lack calm, deliberate reason, which is the only safe political guide."[2] Furthermore, in their historical accounts, Bay View President Dr. W. H. Shier and other historians, excluded accounts of the visits of these prestigious women. It took a hundred years for historian Keith Fennimore to recognize that women played a significant role, but his account is limited in scope and inaccurate.

Frances Willard's visits had a profound effect on the populace. She had assumed the national presidency of the WCTU five years after it was established, a position she held until her death in 1898. Willard annually toured the country's Chautauquas, leading CLSC round-table discussions and lecturing. Chautauqua Cottage in Bay View was completed in time for her 1887 visit and was the site of her CLSC meetings. She preached her famous theology of abstinence and social and welfare reform, women's suffrage and world peace. She also led study groups about diverse subjects such as Richard T. Ely's book *Political Economy*. During her second visit, she was on the verge of creating the world WCTU and was getting ready to move to England. That summer she and Livermore were preparing their exhaustive 1893 biographical compendium, *A Woman of the Century: Leading American Women*, and Willard's lectures centered on material for that publication, such as information about her idol, former First Lady Lucy Hayes.

When Willard could not attend the assembly in 1888, her close friend, Dr. Anna Howard Shaw, also a national leader and close associate of Susan B. Anthony, addressed the assembly. Her topic was "Woman's Enfranchisement Essential to a True Republic," which sounds a great deal like the seedling for her famous 1915 speech, "The Fundamental Principal of a Republic," a speech that ranks among the top 100 American speeches of the twentieth century. Shaw returned to Bay View in 1891 to speak about "Health, Its Relation to the Temperance Reform."

***Frances Willard was the most famous women in her day as president of the US Woman's Christian Temperance Union and the World Woman's Christian Temperance Union. She visited Bay View twice, in 1887 and 1889, appearances that inspired the building of Evelyn Hall for WCTU meetings.***
*(Courtesy of Larry Massie)*

Shaw had personally experienced gender discrimination. After growing up in the Michigan wilderness near Big Rapids, without any formal education she entered Albion College and then the theological department of Boston University in 1875. Years later, she applied to the New England Methodist Episcopal Conference for ordination but, although she was the highest scoring candidate, her application was denied. She appealed to the general conference in Cincinnati in 1880, but the refusal was confirmed. Shaw then applied to the Methodist Protestant Church for ordination and on October 12, 1880, she became the first fully-ordained woman minister in the nation. She earned a second degree from Boston University, a medical degree and took over the franchise department of the national WCTU in Washington, DC, the position she held when she came to Bay View. Later in 1904, Shaw became president of the National American Woman Suffrage Association and in 1919 was the first woman awarded the Distinguished Service Medal.[3]

As prestigious as Willard's and Shaw's appearances on the assembly program were, Mary A. Livermore's visits in 1890, when Willard was at Lakeside, and again in 1891, were no less noteworthy. Although she never achieved the personal fame of Willard, Livermore had been one of the founders of the National Woman's Suffrage Association movement, a founder of the Illinois Woman's Suffrage Association, editor of the *Woman's Journal*, president of the Massachusetts WCTU, and president of the American Woman's Suffrage Association. During the Civil War, she established the Soldiers' Aid Society and frequently went to the front to escort injured soldiers home to their families. Just before her Bay View appearances, her book *My Story of the War* was published, and she lectured about her experiences.

These women generated enough excitement to bring about the building of Evelyn Hall in 1890 to house WCTU meetings. Hall claimed that it was to be the WCTU's national summer headquarters. Considering the support coming from the country's leaders at that time and the

***Mary A. Livermore made numerous appearances at Bay View as a journalist, temperance worker, suffragist, and humanitarian.*** *(Author's Collection)*

close proximity of the national headquarters in Evanston, his claim was well founded. Bay View definitely became a regional headquarters for the WCTU, as historian Keith Fennimore pointed out.

Livermore, Shaw and Willard had considerable influence, but the Bay View WCTU would not have continued much beyond their visits had it not been for strong support from Michigan women. As early as 1877, only three years after the founding of the national WCTU, a Petoskey union, founded by Anna Smeed Benjamin of Portland, Michigan, was active and meeting at the Presbyterian Church. When Hall established the Bay View WCTU in 1886, Benjamin was there to head it up.

Benjamin attended the 1874 Grand Rapids women's convention where she was appointed chairman of a committee to draft a constitution and by-laws for a Michigan WCTU. She came to Bay View every summer between 1885 and 1908 where her managerial skills were put to good use. "[She] has built up white ribbon interests in the Bay View Assembly until that foremost summer camp has become a model for all others in that particular. Mrs. Benjamin is a notably excellent presiding officer and a skilled parliamentarian," wrote Willard and Livermore.[4] Benjamin was considered by several sources to be one of the best parliamentarians in America. Knowledge of this boring topic was crucial for 1890s women fighting for political recognition, educational opportunities, and the right to vote and work in their chosen fields. It allowed them to gain control of political and legislative meetings. During Bay View's annual WCTU Institutes, Benjamin held daily instructional sessions.

Beginning in 1890 WCTU institutes were held in Evelyn Hall. Since the WCTU evolved out of Methodist religious zeal for Christian duty, the meetings often began at nine a.m., with devotional activities including scriptural readings and prayer. The meetings lasted all day and were held for a week or more. In 1896, the WCTU Institute took place from July 16 through 24 and included an evangelistic conference, an investigation of the scientific side of temperance, personal finances, and a "school of methods," which was probably about political tactics.

Cultural entertainment such as a violin solo or a song such as "My Heart Ever Faithful" was always part of the program. Calisthenics, appropriate fashions, health seminars, evangelistic techniques, parliamentary usage and educational lectures were included. In addition to Mrs. Benjamin's talks on parliamentary procedure, Dr. John Harvey Kellogg and his wife Ella addressed the WCTU in 1890, 1891, 1892 and again in 1910 about dress reform, correct posture, good eating habits and the adverse effects of corsets. Kellogg often warned the WCTU women against corset wearing, using an apparatus showing the injurious results of lacing and constriction. In 1891 Kellogg told his audience: "The average civilized woman is a deformed woman. Uncomplimentary as this statement may appear, it is nevertheless demonstratively true. Corset wearing and neglect of physical exercise have produced such grave and almost universal physical deterioration among American women that scarcely one can be found who has reached the age of twenty years who is not more or less deformed."[5]

In 1895, Carrie L. Grout addressed the group on the monetary system, "the Silver Question versus the Gold Standard". In 1902, a Professor Hill spoke about property laws in the US. That same summer, Anna Boyle of Durango, Colorado, spoke about the benefits of the enfranchisement of women in Colorado that had been granted in 1893. As early as 1887, Angelia F. Newman of Nebraska spoke on the need for changes in the nation's penal system. Two years later, she again addressed the women just before becoming the subject of a national controversy as one of the five women delegates denied access to the Methodist Episcopal Church national conference. In 1898, 1900 and 1902, women's suffragist Jane M. Kenney of Port Huron, who was the WCTU national supervisor of prison work, addressed the institute about the need for women wardens in women's prisons. Mary Kuhl, the president of the Illinois WCTU, talked in 1909 about "White Slave Traffic."

When Helen M. Stoddard was president of the WCTU , each summer the women wrote a lengthy document reaffirming their stand against the "liquor traffic". Stoddard was a well educated and outspoken woman who for many years was president of both the Texas WCTU and the Bay View WCTU. She had had a difficult life, losing an infant son and her husband after only three years of marriage. She was left to raise her only living son at a time when there were few vocational opportunities for women, a fact which might explain her hardened attitudes. She taught at Ft. Worth University, but under the inspiration of Anna Palmer, a national evangelist who served as a president of the Michigan Federation of Women's Clubs and the first woman to serve on the Bay View board, Stoddard joined the WCTU. In Fanny Armstrong's biography of her, Stoddard's years at Bay View are mentioned with great fondness.[6]

In 1902 a young man named C. Donald Call, a resident of Bay View and Petoskey, was covering Bay View news for the *Daily Resorter*. Supposedly, a woman wrote a letter to the editor of the paper claiming to have visited Bay View and left greatly disappointed. She had come to meet a man but there just weren't any available. Her attempts to flirt with the only man she met ended in disappointment. Taking the story seriously, Stoddard answered the letter: "Of course the letter was true to life in its central theme, namely the absence of young men. It is true that young men are scarce here, and I am sorry that it is so. The details of the letter are what I object to especially. I didn't approve of the general tone in which the matter was treated. I have never felt like laughing at young people in love. Such matters seem to me too sacred for jesting. As for flirting, I have no words to express my contempt for

***John Harvey Kellogg spoke at Bay View numerous times warning the women of the detrimental effects of wearing corsets such as this example made in Jackson, MI.*** *(Author's Collection)*

young people who will thus deal with holy things....So far as fun is concerned I can see nothing humorous in the whole letter. It contained many objectionable details and incidents."[7] Stoddard's response illustrates the rigidity of some women leaders of that day, but, more importantly, it gives a graphic picture of the demographics of the association due to the very strength of the women's movement. There were few men on the grounds![8]

During Stoddard's presidency, interest in the WCTU waned. In the 1890s, attendance ranged in the hundreds and nearly a thousand at some meetings. By 1900, membership had dwindled to about sixty, while 150 ladies did attend the Bay View WCTU Institute that summer. Mrs. L. F. McWhirter, president of the Indiana WCTU, talked about methods for increasing attendance. In 1908, the WCTU Institute included several women from Petoskey and Harbor Springs as presenters. By 1909, Bay View's

*Margaret A. Sangster, editor of Harper's Bazaar helped organize the Woman's Council. (Author's Collection)*

interest in temperance and enfranchisement ceased as both causes were coming closer to being resolved by amendments to the constitution. Hall tried unsuccessfully to revive the WCTU in his 1909 assembly program.[9]

When Evelyn Hall was built in 1890, there was an open attitude toward new ideas and newcomers. The previous year, Mary Virginia Hawes Terhune had come to Bay View with her husband, author Dr. Albert Payson Terhune, to address the CLSC at Chautauqua Cottage (now the Woman's Council Building). A noted writer, she had published books about homemaking, etiquette, cooking and child care under her pen name, Marion Harland, and had organized women's clubs among urban factory women. The next summer, Terhune returned with her friend, Margaret A. Sangster, nationally known editor of *Harper's Bazaar*, to organize the Bay View Woman's Council. The WCTU did not claim exclusive rights to Evelyn Hall, and the first meeting of the Woman's Council was held July 30, 1890, just a week after the dedication of the building. Harland addressed the women with one of her then-famous speeches, "Ourselves and Our Daughters." The following day, Terhune's speech had to be scheduled at the Old Auditorium where 800 came to hear her. She explained her reasons for taking up the work of the Woman's Council: "I love women. I believe that the [future] of the world to a great extent depends upon its women."[10]

Overwhelmingly well received, Terhune returned in 1891, again with Sangster who addressed the women on the subject of the "Well-Equipped Woman," citing the importance of life-long learning and education achieved through membership in clubs like the Woman's Council. She closed the session with the topic, "The Open Secret of Success." Terhune concentrated her efforts on a speech about husband and wife relationships, advising women that "the carping discussion of his failings be prohibited by pride, affection and right taste." Sangster ran the 1892 session.[11] Mary A. Greene, counselor-at-law of Providence, Rhode Island, spoke about the rights of married women, and Kate Ford, a writer with the *Detroit Evening News*, served as president of the Woman's Council.

With the WCTU and the Woman's Council both holding meetings at Evelyn Hall, there were yet enough women in the area to support a third women's organization. On August 18, 1892, members of the newly formed national General Federation of Women's Clubs (GFWC) and Hall urged the formation of a statewide federation to "push the work of all the varied interests of women."[12] Lucinda Stone and Irma Theoda Jones of Lansing had just returned from the Chicago meeting of the federation where they heard Frances Willard and Ellen M. Henrotin, president of the GFWC, speak. Jones was president of the Lansing Woman's Club and the wife of Nelson Jones, a prominent Lansing businessman who was part of the group that developed Harbor Point Association in Harbor Springs, where the couple owned property.

*Irma T. Jones originally owned a cottage at Harbor Point as her husband was one of the Lansing businessmen that developed that resort. In the 1890s she became active in Bay View and took over as president of the Woman's Council to help organize the Michigan Federation of Women's Clubs. She was a founder of what is now the oldest women's club in Michigan, the Lansing Woman's Club. (Author's Collection)*

The following summer, in 1893, Irma Jones was elected president of the Bay View council with Elnora L. Porter of Lansing, secretary, and Mrs. D. F. Barnes of Bay View, treasurer. Jones called for the formation of a Michigan federation. All women of Bay View, Petoskey and neighboring resorts were invited to join. Mrs. Barnes of Kalamazoo, Mrs. Howard of Bay View and Petoskey, and Mrs. Anna Palmer of Saginaw were appointed to receive names for enrollment.

The following summer "on the advice of Mr. John M. Hall", Irma Jones invited Ellen M. Henrotin of Illinois to speak. Through the newly established *Bay View Magazine*, "an invitation was extended widely to club-women throughout Michigan," wrote Jones in her MFWC history. That letter invited all the women's clubs in the state to meet in Bay View on August 14 and 15, 1894, "to take steps toward organizing a Federation of Women's Clubs for the State of Michigan."[13] Representatives from twenty-five women's clubs came, including Martha Root, vice president of the Michigan Women's Suffrage Association and Bay View residents, Mrs. M. J. Brabb of Romeo and Mrs. Clement Smith of Hastings. The meeting, which was held at Evelyn Hall, resulted in a vote that set up a committee to prepare a constitution and formally organize the MFWC. Upon the recommendations of that committee, the MFWC was founded in March 1895 at the First Baptist Church in Lansing, Michigan. The following November, Jones was elected the group's second president. For several summers, the MFWC held its biannual meetings in Evelyn Hall.[14]

The summer of 1894 was significant for other reasons. Lucy A. Leggett of Washington, DC, the national organizer of the Women's Republican Organization and past vice president and corresponding secretary of the Women's National Press Association, addressed the Woman's Council. Helen Campbell of New York City, another featured speaker, talked about her investigative reporting for the *New York Tribune* on the working conditions of women and children in this country. Assembly women packed Evelyn Hall to hear her.

Woman's Council President Jones invited Jane Addams to speak on Tuesday and Wednesday, August 13 and 14, 1895. The *Daily Resorter* wrote that the speech would be "of interest to all who were interested in the betterment of the race."[15] The small dark-haired young woman addressed an audience of both men and women at an overflow crowd at Evelyn Hall about her controversial opinions on dancing and saloons. She told of her devotion to the inception and accomplishments of Hull House, located in Chicago's Nineteenth Ward, an area of Catholic and Jewish immigrant factory workers: "In the midst of this sin and suffering, a few practical reformers have voluntarily taken up their abode in the Hull House. The idea is to take cultivation, refinement, good manners and good morals where they are most needed, and by the coming in touch with society's outcasts be able to do something to help them."[16]

Her staunchly Methodist audience was shocked by her attitude toward saloons and dancing. "The Hull House dancing keeps the people until they get so that they can be kept out of the saloons by something better," she explained to listeners who disapproved of dancing. Addams told them that she "fully understood the dangerous and demoralizing influence of saloons and it is for this reason that she is helping to maintain coffee houses and places of social enjoyment to supplant the social instinct which brings men together if no more attractive place is provided".[17]

Due to the overflow crowd, Addams appearance the next day was moved to the large Old Auditorium where she talked of changing social customs of women's work in the home and the work place. She explained that, as a general rule, the most enterprising girls of a community go into factory work while the less enterprising go into household employment, which was then a changing social phenomenon in America. It was a subject of great interest to many Bay Viewites who relied on live-in help. Addams returned to Bay View in 1903 under the auspices of the Bay View Assembly Program and spoke at Hitchcock Hall.

By 1896, the GFWC included five hundred organi-

***Women were attracted to assemblies such as Bay View because of its emphases on morals, and its inherent respectability.***
*(Courtesy of Marion Caveny)*

zations in twenty states. That clubwomen were "better wives and mothers" was the philosophical viewpoint. "The great growth of the organization has occurred within the quarter of a century. In that time the club life has developed a new social order. It has uplifted and brightened the outlook of many thousands of women. It has lifted the tone of the morals of whole communities and its usefulness in all directions can never be measured," the newspaper reported.[18]

That summer Jones, who was still president of the Woman's Council, invited Louise S. Rounds, the president of the Illinois WCTU, to address the Bay View FWC and run the WCTU Institutes.[19] Rounds and Jones invited Jane Cunningham Croly to speak at the Woman's Council and participate in the biannual federation meetings. Croly, whose pen name was Jennie June, was making the circuit of Chautauqua assemblies that summer, as she also appeared at Lakeside. Croly was the honorary vice president and president of the New York State FWC and editor of the women's page for the *New York World*. "A valued feature of Michigan State Federation work is federation day in August in connection with the summer university courses at Bay View perhaps the most delightful spot in northern Michigan," Croly wrote of Bay View.[20]

Also, included on that summer program was Mary Mayo, leader of the Women's Work Committee for the Michigan Grange. Mayo was a pioneer in building the first women's dormitory, Abbott Hall, at Michigan State University, as well as establishing the first women's curriculum. In 1896 when she appeared at Evelyn Hall at the Woman's Council, she was at the height of her success with the Women's Sections at the statewide Farmers' Institutes, where over 5000 women learned the newest ideas on nutrition, homemaking and childcare.

Unfortunately, the records from 1897 to 1899 of the activities of the WCTU, the Woman's Council, and the Bay View FWC vanished, along with several years of *Daily Resorters*. The next mention of the Bay View Woman's Council is in 1900 when Reverend F. L. Thompson, leader of the Bay View camp meeting, spoke to a group of mostly preachers' wives at Hitchcock Hall, urging them to meet regularly if possible. Hall's departure in 1898 and the chaotic management in the Bay View Association had affected the Woman's Council, and the group ceased holding regular meetings.[21]

As the time for the passage of the women's suffrage amendment grew closer, there was a complacent attitude among the women toward their rights. In Bay View where the women's rights issue was forcefully expounded upon from the assembly platform and heavily supported by assembly superintendents and religious leaders Reverend H.M. Joy and Albion College President Lewis R. Fiske, and where the Bay View Reading Circle was serving to educate thousands of women nationally, association leadership was confined to men. Despite the influence of these women's rights advocates and the fact

***From very early in it's history, women made up a majority of the property owners on the grounds.*** *(Author's Collection)*

that women formed the majority of the membership, Bay View women voted for men for their governing board, while they could easily have elected a woman.

As early as 1852, the state constitution granted Michigan women the right to own property. During the initial days of the assembly, though, cottage owners were predominately men. With the tremendous growth of the Summer University, that quickly changed and, by 1890, nearly half of the leaseholders were women. In the 1890s, Summer University librarian and English Professor M. Louise Jones reported that three-fifths of the people in Bay View were women. By 1912, a Bay View survey indicated that sixty-percent of Bay View cottage owners were women.

For whatever reason, the Bay View board apparently paid little heed in the 1880s and 1890s to the relationship between property ownership and trustee membership. The Reverend D.F. Barnes was elected to the board of trustees and served as president of the association between 1882 and 1884, even though his cottage was in his wife's name. Watson Snyder bought and sold many cottages on the grounds and was listed as a leaseholder during his presidency from 1884 to 1886, even though his cottage was in his wife's name. When State Senator John Moon was elected president of the association 1886-7, his cottage was listed as belonging to Alice M. Moon, his wife. Like Snyder, Moon also purchased and sold forfeited cottages for the association and may or may not have been a leaseholder during his administration. Dr. Shier, Bay View's longest-serving president, transferred his cottage to his wife's name in 1883 while he was a trustee. When he became president of the association in 1887, he transferred the property back to his name. One must wonder about his wife's reaction.

Women did not have the legal right to serve on community boards in Michigan until 1902, when the Michigan legislature, spurred on by the MFWC, changed the law. It was not, however, until 1909, that the first woman, Anna E. Palmer, a president of the MFWC, was elected for a two-year term to the Bay View board, an event mentioned in only two sources. In contrast, the Bay View Cottagers' Improvement Association, which met from 1893 until the 1920s, had various women presidents, and the Bay View Library Board consisted entirely of women.

The energy of the Bay View women's movement of the 1890s and the turn of the century mirrors the history of women's clubs across America. Inspired by national leaders, the movement grew rapidly, highlighting the issues of women's rights, women's suffrage and economic opportunity as well as welfare reform. During the first decade of the twentieth century, however, Bay View women lost interest in the gains made by their dynamic foremothers, turning away from politics to less disruptive activities of self-improvement. Historian Fennimore suggested that the reason was that national leaders were focused on Washington as the time for passage of the nineteenth amendment drew near. Curiously, the number of women in influential positions nationally during this same period in America declined.[22]

***Mrs. Anna A. Palmer was fourth president of the Michigan Federation of Women's Clubs and the first woman to be a Bay View trustee.***
*(Author's Collection)*

Clearly, the situation in Bay View related to a lack of local leadership after assembly superintendents Hall left in 1898 and Horace Hitchcock died in 1903. By then, women's association, so active in the 1890s, had ceased meeting, and Jane Addams was one of only a few prominent women featured on the assembly program after the turn of the century. Not only did the management change in the late 1890s affect the Bay View women's movement, but so did the official cancellation of the Bay View Assembly and Summer University. By 1908 the WCTU, the Woman's Council and the Bay View FWC had become simply the Women's Club. That year, the club season was highlighted by two special events: a social affair at Evelyn Hall where a silver tea service was given to the club as well as Chautauqua Cottage as a clubhouse. Evelyn Hall was being used by that time, with donor Peters' consent, by other organizations as a result in the decline in interest in women's clubs. Chautauqua Cottage was, perhaps, compensation for the women.

With renewed spirit, the ladies immediately began putting on dime socials, candy pulls, and social teas to raise funds to get their "cottage" fitted up. The candy pull brought in $40. A baby show was attended by over 300 people and brought in more than $70 - something that indicates how many young families there must have been on the grounds. Then, on July 30, 1910, another tradition of today's Woman's Council was begun. The season was opened with a tea to which every lady in Bay View and the surrounding area was invited.

The new president, Mrs. W. B. Street, planned the 1912 meetings, providing an educationally and socially centered program. She engaged Caroline Abbot Stanley to speak about her book, *The Modern Madonna*, and a story that she sold for $1000 to the *Ladies' Home Journal*, "The Missionary Bell." One hundred fifty members signed up, and the club prospered financially. When the summer ended, membership had increased from fifty women to 252.

In 1913, the membership fee remained at 25 cents, a very low fee even at that time. A practice begun by Hall was reestablished. A manager, Edna M. Wright of Indianapolis, kept the clubhouse open daily. Plans continued for the bazaar, which became an annual event. The women contributed handmade items for sale to the public, raising $150. At the president's day program, President Mrs. W. B. Street told about her work with neglected children of the North Carolina mountaineers. The club ended the season $347 richer for needed improvements to Chautauqua Cottage including an improved kitchen, a new platform, new dormer windows, closets and a paint job. Bay View women did rally to celebrate "woman's suffrage day" in 1914, an event organized by the Petoskey Woman Suffrage Association. The gala included a children's march through the grounds and a ride on the gaily decorated ferryboat, *Columbia*.

As the decade came to an end, the First World War severely disrupted programming. The lake steamers and trains were needed to transport supplies, the young men in responsible positions enlisted for service, and the women were needed to furnish medical supplies for the Red Cross. By 1917, all social activities ceased at Chautauqua Cottage. That August the *Daily Resorter* reported: "The work of the Bay View annex of the Petoskey Red Cross chapter is progressing well under the general direction of Mary V. Osborn of St. Louis. There is someone knitting all the time at the Women's club building. Red Cross work has superseded all else with this organization, but it is possible that there may be a reception or two later, although nothing to that effect has as yet been definitely decided on."[23]

Added to this, the association's 1918 overhaul of the assembly program gave Bishop Theodore S. Henderson of the Michigan Methodist Church and his assistant, social engineer Dr. John G. Benson, free rein to manage the Bay View Assembly and Summer University. Benson demanded control of all buildings to house religious students and conduct seminars. To great dismay, the successful Evelyn Hall Tea Room was closed and Chautauqua Cottage was taken away from the women. In return, Benson promised a financially successful program for the

***Edith Buffett is the only woman president of the Bay View Association and served from 1992 to 1994.*** *(Author's Collection)*

1918 season. The Women's Club ceased to meet and the Women's Home Missionary Society and the Women's Foreign Society became active.[24]

That summer, there was a public outcry for leadership change within the Bay View management. The elderly but feisty Emma Lamb Baker Barnes spoke out at a public meeting recommending that the Bay View board get a woman to organize things. Even though women cottage owners outnumbered men by nearly five to three, the women voted for men to fill vacancies on the board even when displeased with their performance. Not until 1941 did a second woman, Ruth E. Heseltine, joined the administrative board. Over 100 years after Lathrap gave her opening camp meeting sermon and Willard led the CLSC meetings, would a woman, Edith Buffett, be elected president of the association.

The community's women represented the middle class. In 1877, the local paper described a camping scene in Bay View: "Ladies who do but little work at home have cooked, washed, hoed and dug."[25] These privileged women were a devoted group and, yet, as the fervency of reform issues such as women's suffrage was raised to national heights, to the new generation was complacent. In 1917, Superintendent Trumbull White attempted to infuse some fire into the women by scheduling Juliet V.

Strauss, the "Country Contributor" for the *Indianapolis News* and the *Ladies' Home Journal*. She spoke on the topic, "How Mother Gets Her Halo," hardly a topic that would have appealed to the 1890s women.

A 1917 incident over the election of the Bay View board illustrates the extent of disinterest. Of the some 420 cottages in Bay View in 1912, 254 were owned by women and only 166 by men. John S. Weidman, a lumberman and president of the Mt. Pleasant State Bank, was elected to the board of trustees. It was discovered that he was not a member of the association because the cottage was in his wife's name. Weidman submitted an application and the trustees appointed him to a one-year term. He ran again the following summer as a member and was re-elected by his decidedly feminine constituency.

Women's activities began again in 1922, when the GFWC held its annual meeting at Chautauqua, New York. Fifteen thousand women out of the national membership of two million, attended. Mrs. George Leavenworth of Bay View and Greenville, Mississippi, was there. Influenced by what she saw, when she returned to Bay View she assembled a group of women to make plans for a Bay View women's group. A Women's Club Day was held Friday, August 3, 1923, at Evelyn Hall. Dorian M. Russell, of Grand Rapids, Michigan, president of the MFWC, her vice president, Mrs. Charles E. Vowels, and former president, Mrs. Edith V. Alvord, addressed the sessions, introduced by Mrs. W. B. Lawton of Petoskey. In the 1890s, the Bay View Woman's Council and Hall were the motivators behind the formation of the MFWC. In 1923, the MFWC became the catalyst for the re-establishment of the Bay View Woman's Council. The *Petoskey Evening News* summed it up: "As an outcome of Women's Day at Bay View Friday of last week, the Bay View Women's [sic] Council was permanently organized. Club women of 12 states were represented at the rally and, in their short talks, indicated the tremendous power of womanhood in the mass and the opportunity Bay View presents as a crystallization center for the development of club leadership."[26]

***In 2005, the Federation of Women's Clubs – Michigan returned to Evelyn Hall, the site of its organizational roots, to dedicate a plaque. From all over Michigan, 104 women attended the ceremony and luncheon led by then President Linda Clark standing on the right. Geneva Wiskemann, former Michigan state archivist, shown in the middle, represented the historic Lansing Woman's Club. The event was organized by Mary Sue Hansen of Bay View and Big Rapids, on the left, now a trustee of the association.*** *(Photograph by G. Randall Goss)*

Irma Rombauer, who later authored *The Joy of Cooking*, became the council's temporary president and addressed the Petoskey FWC in an informal meeting at the Hotel Roselawn.[27] Mrs. Leavenworth explained that the purpose of the new Woman's Council was to provide programs that would attract clubwomen from all parts of the country. MFWC President Dorian M. Russell took charge of the meetings for 1924. Mrs. Percy V. Pennybacker, a former president of the General Federation, spoke on "What Can I Do to Serve My Country in a Civil Way?"[28]

The Woman's Council was firmly re-established and again had charge of Chautauqua Cottage. This time, however, the women insisted on a contract with the association, giving them the right to use the building in exchange for its internal upkeep. At a reception at the Terrace Inn, the Woman's Council paid special tribute to Mrs. Leavenworth, who "conceived the idea of a club house and finally succeeded in arousing sufficient interest among the Bay View women, and Anna B. MacElwee of Washington, DC, through whose untiring efforts the council building became a reality."

MacElwee, or Mother's Mac, was a moving spirit in the reformation of the Woman's Council. She had first come to Bay View in 1878 when her husband, Methodist minister Reverend Samuel J. MacElwee was preaching in Charlevoix. Shier and Reed suggested he build a Bay View cottage. The couple purchased two lots on Fairview Avenue, "far away from any other cottage." They had a son, Dr. Roy S. MacElwee, and a daughter, Mrs. W. L. MacFarland. Reverend MacElwee died in 1893, so, in 1899 Anna MacElwee went to Germany, where her talented daughter could study music. In Berlin, Mary Bannister Willard, Willard's sister-in-law, encouraged her to open a home for American girls. She ran it for eighteen years. Her son, Roy, a lecturer on economics for the Columbia School of Business, held a doctorate in economics from Berlin University and was in the US consular service when the World War I broke out. His wife had a German father and an English mother. In 1916, she had to leave Germany with her American husband after losing a brother in the German army at the same time her uncle, a colonel in the British army, was injured. In 1917, anti-German sentiment in Bay View was so strong that MacElwee was investigated by the Emmet County sheriff after an incident at the Southern Hotel where someone accused her of being a German sympathizer. Nothing came of the charges. MacElwee continued her volunteer work despite the unsettling affair.[29]

Evelyn Hall was the original home of the Woman's Council, but Chautauqua Cottage was the preferred home because it was not used by other organizations. MacElwee oversaw repairs to the leaky roof and the installation of bathrooms on the second floor at a cost of $2500. She made the building presentable for the opening reception of 1925 with delphiniums, poppies, and phlox around the newly painted ivory walls and orange floors, and new "dull blue" rugs and draperies.

In 1926, Mrs. G. G. Hunter, President of the MFWC, led the annual institute in Bay View called "Women's Week." Emma A. Fox of Detroit and Vice President Mrs. Edward Franklin White of the General Federation were featured speakers. White addressed the women on "Law Enforcement", and Fox talked on "Parliamentary Usage." Membership fees were raised to $1, and Tuesdays were set aside for regular meetings. To raise money, the Woman's Council planned a recital by Florence Mulford, formerly of the Metropolitan Opera Company.[30]

In the late 1920s, through Mrs. Walter W. Seymour's leadership as president, the council had regular "state" days when the women from each state were honored. For the 1931 Michigan Day, Dr. Carrie B. Stewart, the first secretary of the BVRC, hosted Mrs. Wilber M. Brucker, wife of Michigan's governor. Fundraisers and bridge parties were held at the Petoskey-Bay View Country Club. On August 3, 1928, the council had its annual bazaar with some odd entertainment for a Methodist community: a character analyst, Sari, and her assistant, a crystal gazer.

Repeating its success with the 1926 concert, in 1930 the Woman's Council sponsored Mr. and Mrs. Ossip Gabrilowitsch for a duo concert at Hall Auditorium. The celebrated couple owned a summer home on Mackinac Island, and arrangements were made through the close friendship between the couple and McElwee's daughter, Mrs. W. L. McFarland, who had studied music in Berlin with Gabrilowitsch. The August 8 performance was considered the biggest event in Bay View since Madame Schumann-Heink. Mrs. Gabrilowitsch was Clara Clemens, the middle daughter of Mark Twain. The contralto was accompanied by her husband, Russian conductor of the Detroit Symphony Orchestra. Her songs and his piano solos and compositions were interspersed with stories about her famous father. The couple donated their time and dedicated a piano to the Bay View Association. Sales from the concert netted $1117.50 in profits for the council, a significant accomplishment during the Depression.

In 1934, the Woman's Council opened its building to a new group, the New Leisure Group. For three seasons, about sixty men and women from Harbor Springs, Bay View, Boyne City, Harbor Point, Petoskey, Roaring Brook and Wequetonsing met to learn more about antiques, fine arts and collecting as well as other educational topics - an unusual hobby during the Depression Era. Speakers included specialists on oriental rugs, pastels and watercolors, fine china, antiques, knitting, quilt making, gardening,

***The Daughters of the American Revolution was one of the many women's groups that held annual meetings in Bay View. Here is the DAR pictured in front of the Terrace Inn in 1916.*** *(Courtesy of Little Traverse Historical Society)*

flower growing, astronomy, needlepoint and painting. Even Ella Petoskey, relative of Chief Petoskey, was asked to demonstrate how she made porcupine quill boxes. After three seasons, the group's president, Mrs. Roland Solomon, of Middletown, Ohio, died and the group disbanded.

The people of Bay View were joiners. They formed every kind of social group imaginable, and proudly displayed their membership with countless numbers of pins on dresses, coats and shirts. "It was a fashionable caper to wear your assembly season ticket tied to your button hole with a white ribbon if you are a WCTU or a 'Y' a white one with a crimson line through it if you are an Epworth Leaguer, a purple one if you are a King's Daughter or a King's Son," the *Daily Resorter* reported in 1894.[31] One of the groups begun in 1885, even before the Bay View Assembly and Summer School, was a northern Michigan organization of college fraternity and sorority members. The meeting of the Delta Tau Delta fraternity took place at the cottage of Ralph Connable.[32] Enthusiasm continued, and each summer a reception was held at Petoskey's Arlington Hotel. In 1896, Dr. John M. Coulter, president of the Bay View Summer University and professor at the University of Chicago, served as toastmaster. The event, which culminated with dancing in the hotel's casino, continued annually through the turn of the century. Methodists may have forbid dancing on the grounds but didn't hesitate to take part at Petoskey's luxury hotel. Panhellenic was reestablished in the 1920s as an area-wide club for local sorority women. In the 1979, the newest women's club was formed when younger women wanted morning meetings. The Bay View Woman's Council was then split into two entities, the Woman's Council and the Morning Council.

Of the many women's organizations which have met on the grounds - WCTU, the Woman's Council, the MFWC, Panhellenic, YWCA, the Michigan Woman's Press Association, the Women's Home Missionary Society, the Women's Foreign Society, PEO, the Daughters of the American Revolution (DAR), and the Morning Council there are three that are still thriving. They serve servicing an open membership, raising funds for local charities and association needs, and providing stimulating programs, all activities in the spirit of the "uplift movements." They represent the heritage of the past and the enormous role Bay View, the Chautauqua movement, and the reading circle craze had in spreading issues of women's rights across Michigan and America. In this little community, off the heavily populated Chautauqua routes of nearby Midwestern states, women were attracted not by the sublime climate but by the philosophical atmosphere. It is, therefore, ironic that then Vice President Marshall, who vacationed in this atmosphere for nearly three decades and presided over the Senate was opposed to women's suffrage. On June 4th, 1919 the US Senate finally passed the legislation by two votes. Had it been a tie, Marshall would have voted against it.

***This picture of Evelyn Hall shows the distinctive Victorian painting style accentuating architect F. X. Oliver's decorative design. David Seibert of Petoskey built the structure in 1890. It was the site of the formational meeting of the Federation of Women's Clubs - Michigan and several years ago was deemed Emmet County's most significant building by local architects.*** *(Author's Collection)*

— CHAPTER SEVEN —

# The American Way

Fortunately Marshall's opinion did not prevail. So, in 1914 when women's suffrage was close to becoming a reality, the Bay View idea was thriving with high enrollment in the Summer University, large crowds at the high profile assembly, and peak enrollment in the BVRC. Though delayed, the new John M. Hall Auditorium was scheduled for completion for the 1915 season. The dedication ceremony was planned after the new organ from Kentucky's Pilcher Organ Company was installed. Then, everything came to a halt.

On December 20, 1914, one snowy Sunday afternoon in the second floor master bedroom of his stately Boston Boulevard home, in Detroit John Manley Hall died at the age of 63 of pneumonia, the result of typhoid fever. It was on a day when he had planned to entertain needy Detroit children with a Christmas party. The January issue of *The Bay View Magazine* carried the news of his death to the nationwide readership: "Only a month ago we were gathered together around the Study Lamp, some thousands of us, the beloved leader, Mr. John M. Hall was talking with us about our call to a higher and more useful service that comes to us through the Bay View work. Who could foretell that before another month he would have answered the call of the Master and be today in his Father's house? His was indeed a life of service. So quietly did he walk among us, so unostentatious was he and so averse to publicity that to go into any detailed account of his many deeds of kindness would be against his wishes. Sufficient to say that he was a true friend, and that his life was one of continual service to humanity in the Master's name."[1]

The news saddened the Petoskey people too. The City of Petoskey carried this resolution: "In the death of John M. Hall, at the City of Detroit, on the 20th day of December 1914, Bay View loses her most imposing and foremost figure, and the whole Little Traverse region a most valuable friend. That a large share of the growth and prosperity of Bay View in the last thirty years has been due to the unceasing and energetic labor of Mr. Hall cannot be doubted. That the interests of Petoskey are in a large measure interlinked with those of Bay View is admitted by every observing person. Therefore, we, the official representatives of the City of Petoskey, recognizing the community of interest that exists between our neighbors and ourselves and that we have suffered a joint loss, do hereby give public and official expression to our sense of loss and our sorrow in the departure of our friend."[2]

Hall had been a zealous reformer whose lifetime endeavors were totally centered on ideas and philosophies for self-improvement. He was a champion of women's rights, however when he died, he died intestate - without a will to provide financially for his widow Mary. When three of his relatives contested the estate, Mary Hall had to go to court to secure a monthly income for living expenses.

During his tenure as president, Thomas Gordon, Jr. had become Hall's closest associate so he oversaw the completion of the new auditorium and negotiations between Bay View, the lawyers for the Hall estate and the probate court. Mary Hall was ordered by the court to sign over her Wayside Cottage to Bay View and Thomas Gordon, as well as her husband's interest in the Bay View House "for payment of debts." Approximately forty-five days later, her cottage was sold to the Bleazby family, proprietors of the Harbor Springs Kensington Hotel. Despite colossal changes in her financial condition, Mary Hall honored her husband's commitment to Bay View and paid $45,000 to complete the John M. Hall Auditorium. When the estate was legally settled in 1917, Mary Hall's portion of her husband's estate was about one-third of his wealth. A decade later, the Hall family mortgaged its East Boston Boulevard home in Detroit for $40,000 - nearly the same amount given to Bay View.[3]

The then eminent writer and editor, Trumbull White of Petoskey, eulogized Hall in the October 1915 issue of *The Bay View Magazine*: "Every such institution needs a man, a personality, who may typify the work, who will saturate himself with it, submerge himself in it, give his heart and mind and strength to it."[4] Such a man was John M. Hall. He had carried the responsibility of the university and assembly with such assurance that no one was prepared to take over. The leaders of the early days had passed away and new leadership was needed. The community would find it in the fortuitous election of Dr. Hugh Kennedy to the Bay View board in 1916.

For the interim summer of 1915, Nelson O. Wilhelm, an experienced manager from Orange, New Jersey, was hired to take over the assembly and university. In Detroit, Mary Hall hired Trumbull White to edit *The Bay View Magazine*. The following year, he purchased the magazine and assumed the superintendency of the Bay View Assembly and Summer University. During his long career as journalist, author and editor, White had been a war correspondent and editor for the Chicago *Sun-Times*, and magazines such as *Everybody's Magazine* and *Appleton's*. He authored books on the World's Columbian Exposition in Chicago in 1893, the Spanish American War of 1898, the Russo-Japanese War of 1904-5 and the San Francisco earthquake. In Bay View, he taught journalism and edited *The Bay View Assembly Record* in 1895. He summered regularly in Emmet County and had a retirement home on Round Lake, just east of the community. As a longtime and close friend of the Hemingway family, White encouraged Ernest to pursue a writing career. A

***The John M. Hall Auditorium has been in continual use for nearly 100 years with only minor updates and maintenance. Presently, plans are underway for much needed improvements to the stage facilities, sound system, and seating,*** *(Photograph by Charles Ditto)*

1930 *Petoskey Evening News* article published White's list of writers he deemed most significant. Hemingway topped his list.

White attempted to maintain the level of programming Hall had provided while staying within the budget. He brought in the incomparable Howard Barlow as the director of assembly music with an outstanding roster of musicians. He continued the concept of the conferences set up by Hall in 1910. The Sadlers led the annual Health Conference. Dr. Otterbein O. Smith of Chicago and child welfare specialist Dr. George B. Mangold of Washington University headed up the Town and Country Industrial Conference. That conference also featured ex-Milwaukee mayor Amil Seidel, the first elected socialist official in the US. For National Conference Day, E. J. Millington of Cadillac represented President Woodrow Wilson, speaking on the subject of the president's handling of the sinking of the *Lusitania*. The crowd-pleaser of the season was Sir Douglas Mawson's illustrated lecture.

Mawson's "Antarctic Adventure" included moving pictures taken on Lieutenant Ernest Shackleton's 1908 trip to the Antarctic, an expedition of which Mawson had been a member. The presentation was especially timely because in August of 1916, Shackleton was on South Georgia Island attempting to rescue twenty-two of his men imprisoned by Antarctic ice on the southern hemisphere's Elephant Island. "I remember the speaker well. I was just four but he brought penguins with him and I have never forgotten those penguins," said Mildred Place Panney, daughter of C. J. Place who built Hall Auditorium.

Those thrilling pictures brought much more to the assembly than penguins and the exciting account of Shackleton's failed attempt to be the first to reach the South Pole. The presentation ushered in the age of silent movies. "With a view to economy, a machine was rented from a Detroit concern at a cost of thirty dollars, and the trustees were notified that if they cared to own the outfit it could be bought for $165," reported the *Daily Resorter*.[5] They bought the machine.

The silent movies being shown at Petoskey theaters - the Palace, Hollywood and Casino - were mounting formidable competition for the still financially ailing assembly program. Audiences, now with a choice of venues, were opting for glittering bright lights over the more cerebral pursuits of university classes, biblical lectures, chalk talks, classical music and the "high-class" films of Lyman H. Howe. The editor of the *Daily Resorter* noted in the August 25, 1916: "While it is true that more persons come to the shores of Little Traverse Bay for physical recreation than for any other purpose, it is strongly felt that these

# *The Beauty and Allure of Bay View Today*

CAPTURED BY PROFESSIONAL PHOTOGRAPHER ROBERT CLEVELAND

B20 L31

1877

1886 AD
1794

1888

D. GAZSO & G. DENNIS

thousands can be drawn to the Auditorium. Although the 'back bone' of the program must be the serious, it is probable that much will be introduced next year to obtain financial returns from those who want to be amused rather than forced to think. While some Bay Viewites were wending their way to the Auditorium on Assembly nights this summer, many of their neighbors were on their way to the bright lights and picture shows in Petoskey...."[6]

***Dr. Charles H. Swift, L. O. Odebrecht and Joseph M. Lewis ran the movies series in 1917 and featured the* Last Days of Pompeii.** *(Author's Collection)*

While movies raised eyebrows of some Bay View highbrows, given the accumulated debt by the 1916 season, fiscal responsibility took center stage. Despite conservative opposition, assembly leaders purchased the projector. Three young men - Dr. Charles H. Swift, L. O. Odebrecht and Joseph M. Lewis - teamed up to furnish the films, run the projector and provide the advertising. The silent movies selected by these young men brought in crowds of 750 each evening for the special movie week.

Bay View assembly-goers always enjoyed illustrated lectures, whether they featured chalk talks or stereopticon slides. The first stereopticon show was presented at the Old Chapel on August 10, 1885. It included sixty views of missionary work in China and was given by Miss Frances Baker, a preacher. The first slide show in the Old Auditorium was H. H. Ragan's "The Rhine and Switzerland" on August 1, 1887. During the 1890s, Jacob Riis showed his famous photographic collection. In 1890, the Bay View Camera Club was formed and continued for many years. Photography classes were always part of the Bay View Summer University curriculum. Vitagraph and Biograph films were shown at the Old Auditorium at the turn of the century just as they were at other summer assemblies such as Martha's Vineyard. The *Daily Resorter* described the offerings in 1900:

> *Mr. Bert Kimball of Haverill, Mass. exhibited four groups of American Biograph pictures aggregating more than a score of films. This was a novel treat to Bay View people, and many words of commendations have been overheard. The pictures of the war scenes in South Africa and Manila seemed to receive the most noticeable approval and applause. The Christmas pantomime "Cinderella," as presented by the Drury Lane Theatre Co. of London is 450 feet long and has fifteen exposures to the foot. Every one of these nearly seven thousand miniatures was colored by hand.*[7]

These visual treats were not repeated until the assembly was re-established in 1909. Then, from 1909 until 1915, Bay View booked the popular, high-grade filmmaker, Lyman H. Howe. His features always filled the auditorium, as it happened with a 1912 film by adventurer Paul J. Raney who photographed wild animals in the African jungle.

After Swift and company's initial success with the 1916 movie week, in 1917 the assembly secured eight film classics from the Kleine establishment in Chicago: *Spartacus, Julius Caesar, Antony and Cleopatra, Quo Vadis, The Last Days of Pompeii, Othello, The Lion of Venice* and *Vanity Fair*. When Dr. John Benson took over assembly planning in 1918, he scheduled more than one or two evenings a week for movies. Dr. Sidney D. Eva, Associate Pastor of Simpson Tabernacle Church in Detroit, was instrumental in drafting a "law" (in the Methodist Episcopal Church) covering the use of motion pictures for religious, educational and scientific purposes. Eva conducted the movie presentations for the 1918 season, which were hyped in the 1918 *Bay View Mirror*: "No effort nor

[sic] expense has been spared to secure the highest class of films for the Bay View visitors this season. Each program contains one educational film."[8] In the early 1920s, the library board took over movie week and used the proceeds for the depleted library building fund. Moving pictures became an integral part of the programming of the association. Many years later, researcher Robert Carter remarked that the assembly had become an assembly of movies.

To make the silent films more enjoyable, Tin Pan Alley song lyricist J. Will Callahan and his wife Nannie entertained between reels. Helen Woodruff Marin was just ten in 1911 when she first met "Uncle Will." Every morning, she would stop off at her swing by the Speaker's Stand on her way to the Bay View House to pick up the mail. One morning there was a stranger sitting in her swing. She stared at him until he asked her if she would care to join him. "I got in and eventually told him it was really my swing, because that's where I always swung," she said.[9]

This was the beginning of a memorable friendship between Helen and this tall, lanky man with the green visor and dark glasses. All the children loved Uncle Will and always asked him if they could lead him, but Helen developed a special relationship with the childless couple, Will and his wife, Nannie. She often visited them at their Forest Avenue cottage, at their Indianapolis home, and then at their winter home in New Smyrna Beach, Florida. When Helen was a teenager, she frequently drove Uncle Will around in her 1914 Templar to his eye appointments with Dr. Burns in Petoskey, to the Petoskey Opera House where he directed the Petoskey Band, and to Harbor Springs where he sang at Juilleret's Cabaret.

People came from all over northern Michigan during the 1920s to Juilleret's to hear Ange Lorenzo's band, The Tunesters. Detroit was the home of the world's largest sheet music publisher, Jerome H. Remick & Co. Writers and composers such as Richard A. Whiting, who collaborated with Lorenzo on *Sleepy Time Gal,* gathered at the Harbor Springs restaurant. Callahan, a tenor, soloed with the band.

Callahan was born on a farm near Columbus, Indiana, on St. Patrick's Day in 1874 and graduated with highest honors from Columbus High School in 1893. He then studied law under James F. Cox, US senator from Indiana. He moved to Indianapolis in 1895 and, in 1900, married Nannie Brinton Wallace, also of Columbus. He practiced law and sold real estate and insurance until deteriorating eyesight compelled him to abandon his career. With a natural gift for rhythm and verse, he began contributing poetry to several magazines and newspapers: *Smart Set, Sunny South Magazine, Out-Door Life, The Indianapolis Journal* and *The Boston Transcript.*

Callahan also had asthma. In 1902, when he and Nannie heard about the delightful Petoskey weather, they joined the annual trekkers wishing to escape the Indianapolis summer humidity. Within just a few years, Nannie and Will purchased the Hoosier Cottage at Block

***Like so many hay fever sufferers, J. Will Callahan came to Petoskey seeking relief. He and his wife soon bought a cottage on Forest Avenue in Bay View. Although blind, he wrote the lyrics to some 300 songs over four decades at his summer retreat.***
*(Author's Collection)*

23, Lot 30 and he began writing poetry to tunes. Callahan published almost 300 songs during his lifetime, a great number of which were written in Bay View. For many of those songs, he teamed up with some of the biggest names in the sheet music business: Ernest R. Ball, Egbert Van Alstyne, Granville English, Frank C. Huston, H. W. Petrie, Neil Moret, Paul Pratt, Paul Biese, and Max Kortlander of Grand Rapids.

Public adoration of Callahan was evident inside Will's cottage where the walls were papered with postcards from all over the world. Friends and admirers sent him cards from their travels since he and Nannie were never wealthy enough to travel themselves. Will's only source of income was from his song royalties and his movie-house singing. He became a member of ASCAP (American Society of Composers, Authors and Producers) in 1924, and the union collected all his fees and looked after his financial interests.

Outside the couple's cottage located beside the Bay View woods, came more inspiration for his "bird songs." Nothing is known about these songs other than that they might have related to "birdman" Charles Crawford Gorst's appearance on the Bay View Assembly program in 1922 where he imitated the sounds of many birds.

Not only did the natural environment of Bay View influence him, but Callahan was also aware of its philosophical climate. He teamed up with women composers when they were being ignored by the general production companies. In 1909, Callahan wrote the lyrics to *Dusty Rag*, composed by May Aufderheide, one of the more famous women ragtime composers of the day. Between 1916 and 1932, he collaborated on several songs with Blanche M. Tice from Sioux City, Iowa. When she opened a publishing firm in Denver, Colorado, one of her first pieces was *While the World Sleeps On,* a collaboration with Callahan. In 1933, Callahan's song, *In a Porch Swing*, was written with Mildred White Wallace.

Callahan also ventured into black Americana even when the music was not published in the US. In 1914 he collaborated with black composer Billy Johnson on *Swing Me Honey, Swing Me*, published in Australia. Also published in Australia was a 1918 edition of *Mammy's Lullaby* featuring a black woman on the cover who was knitting and *Mama Can't Pray for Us Now* picturing a black railroad attendant with three white orphans.

The Callahan's woods side cottage was also the scene of frequent parties. They entertained not only relatives but musicians such as ragtime composer Paul Pratt, who stayed in Bay View during the summer of 1914 where he wrote his hit *Hot-House Rag*. The previous year, in 1913, the pair had scored a hit with the song *Gasoline*, reflecting the growing importance of the fuel.[10]

*Callahan's greatest hit was* **Smiles** *in 1917 which was written in Bay View and published at Jerome H. Remick & Co. sheet music plant in Detroit. It sold millions and was recorded by many famous singers including Judy Garland.* (Author's Collection)

During the 1916 summer season, Callahan penned the words to his most famous song, *Smiles*. Lee S. Roberts, an executive for QRS (the largest piano-roll manufacturer in the US), wrote the tune and published the piece. Panney, daughter of Bay View's then superintendent, remembered that summer well: "One day, Will came over and told my mother about this new song he had written. He played it for her on our piano. It was *Smiles*. He said he had sent it in and was waiting to hear from the publisher."

He would have to wait awhile. The sheet music lay unnoticed on a jobber's shelf in New York for a year until a young Jack Robbins (later head of Robbins Music Corporation) found it. He brought it to the attention of Mose Gumble, editorial director of the Detroit office of Jerome H. Remick & Company. Gumble purchased the song for Remick in 1918 and turned it into a huge success, selling over two million copies.[11]

Roberts and Callahan went on to publish more songs but none achieved the popularity of *Smiles*. In 1918, the

*"Dear Edith: Hope you're having big sales on 'Smiles'. It is certainly going tremendously everywhere. Kindest regards from Mr. C. and myself. Your friend, J. Will Callahan."*
*Note: Edith Loftin was the head of sheet music sales at Kresge's in downtown Indianapolis.*
(Author's Collection)

year *Smiles* was published, the pair teamed up on a piece that didn't have the same sentimental appeal called *Ching Chong*. It was about the Chinese opium world of San Francisco, a far cry from the ever popular *Smiles* or the religious atmosphere of Bay View.

As soon as World War I broke out, Callahan joined the effort and wrote a number of poems to war tunes. His song *Story of Old Glory, The Flag We Love* was set to music by famous composer Ernest R. Ball (*When Irish Eyes are Smiling).* It was featured by prominent singers all over the US. Vice President Marshall heard it vacationing in Petoskey and wrote a personal letter to Callahan praising the song. *Write a Letter Home to Mother,* first sung by Frank H. Clemens at Petoskey's Methodist Episcopal Church on Mother's Day in 1917, was taken up by the YMCA and sung in army camps across America throughout the war.

Sacred songs were also part of Callahan's output. *Alone with Thee* was written for Henry D. Tovey's tune at the request of the publishing house. Wilbur T. Starr, Bay View's theatrical baritone and director of assembly music from 1913 to 1915, sang it often in his concerts. In 1922, Tovey joined the Bay View music faculty, and he and Callahan met for the first time. In their honor, contralto Florence Hallberg sang *Alone with Thee* at a Sunday evening vesper service. In 1939, Callahan teamed up again with Roberts to write two religious pieces, *God's Highway* and *Father, Hear Us While We Pray*.

The *Petoskey Evening News* referred to Callahan's ballads in 1924 as being of a "better grade." "Blues and Jazz songs are waning in popularity. 'This does not mean,' Callahan says, 'that good snappy and tuneful dance numbers are dying out but that the unmelodious and trashy music that for a time held sway is being tabooed by lovers of real melody and sensible lyrics.' "[12]

When *The Hoosier Romance* opened the 1919 summer season, there couldn't have been a more perfect film for the couple to accompany. Callahan had been a protégé of his Indiana neighbor, James Whitcomb Riley, as well as his accountant, before becoming a nationally famous song lyricist, movie-house singer, song-slide demonstrator (forerunner of song videos) and song plugger. "The world will one day be proud to recognize Mr. Callahan's genius," Riley told the *Indianapolis News* in 1918.

Nationally known artists Edith Bideau Normelli, John Barnes Wells and Reinald Werrenrath - performed Callahan's songs in their concerts as well as on their recordings and during radio appearances. World-famous tenor John McCormack recorded *The Gateway of Dreams* on Red Seal Victor records. Before he died, Callahan enjoyed hearing Judy Garland's version of *Smiles* and *Tell Me* in her 1942 film, *For Me and My Gal*. Local hotel orchestras The Tunesters and the Roselawn Orchestra often played them. They were performed at Petoskey's Casino Theatre where Callahan sang.

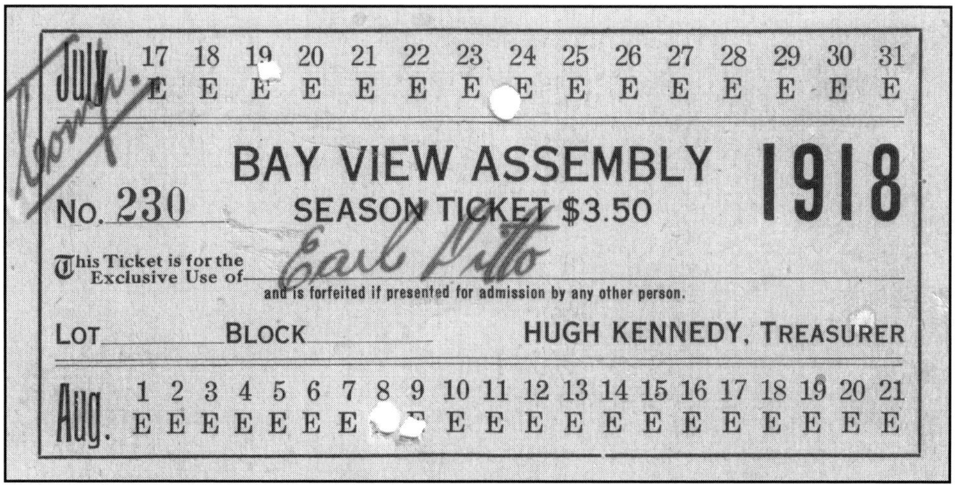


***During the early decades the assembly was so popular season passes were required. Charles Ditto was the superintendent of the grounds from 1914 until 1947.*** *(Courtesy of the Ditto Family)*

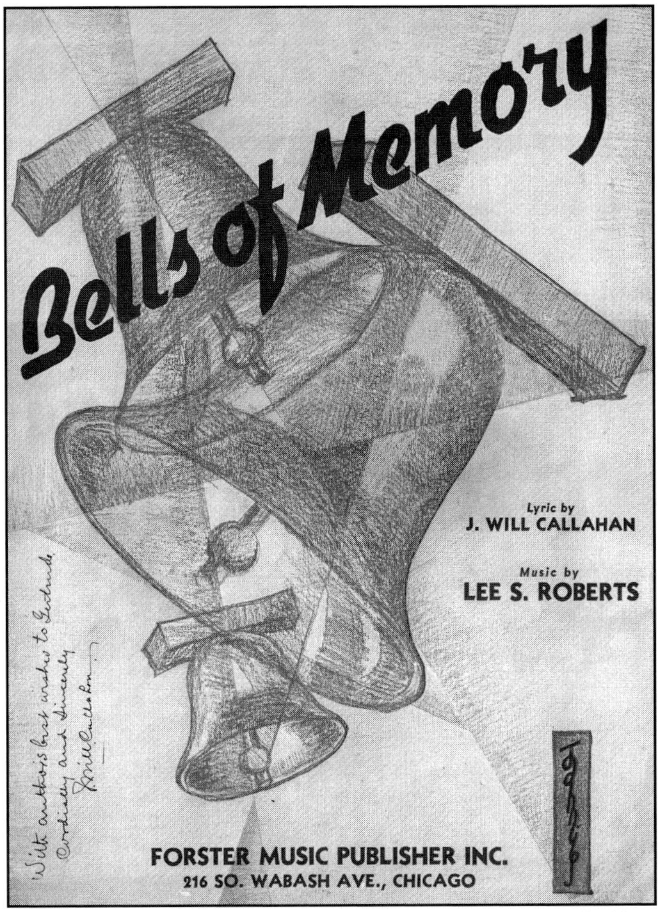


***Before he left Callhan wrote this in memory of Bay View and inscribed it to Gertrude Solms.*** *(Author's Collection)*

Although his music was featured regularly at Bay View concerts, the Callahans sold their Bay View assembly tickets each summer. This was the dark side to this tall slender man who was never seen without his felt visor and dark glasses. Will was unable to attend performances at the auditorium because the lights were too bright for his sensitive eyes. Callahan had glaucoma, a disease that caused hardening of his eyeballs, leaving him unable to tolerate even the smallest amount of light. Helen Marin found the lamps in his cottage covered with cloth and the blinds forever pulled down. It was so dark inside that she could hardly see to walk or enjoy his postcard collection.

Helen recalled what happened when the couple received a tune from a publisher. Will dictated words to a tune to his wife, and she would write them down. "I mean they would get some music sent to them from someone, and he couldn't see at all then. He would sit there, and she would play the piano and he would speak the words that came, or sing."[13]

Callahan's disease worsened even though he continued under Dr. Burns' care in Petoskey. They summered in Bay View for thirty-four years until poor health confined them to their retirement home in New Smyrna Beach, Florida, in 1937. That summer he and composer Roberts teamed up to write *Bells of Memory*, an obvious tribute to Bay View. Before he left, Callahan also penned a copy of *Smiles* signed "with all good greetings" for his good friend, cellist Herbert Weiss of the Cincinnati Orchestra, a Bay View music staff artist (1927-1945). On December 9, 1943, the Callahans finally sold their cottage. Callahan lived in Florida until his death in 1946.

Despite the popularity of the Callahans and the silent films, the assembly was still in the red in 1917. Superintendent White had secured a variety of entertainers, such as Arthur Guy Empey with his famous World War I lecture, "Over the Top and the Best of Luck"; a return engagement of sculptor Lorado Taft; and Juliet V. Strauss, the Country Contributor of the *Ladies' Home Journal*. The *Daily Resorter* reported that the assembly program and summer school cost $6665 due to the extra talent Barlow and Marx brought in to improve the performances of the Bay View Music Festival. The total disbursements of the season were between $9000 and $10,000, and the season deficit was $4193.50.[14]

The Hall-Gordon-Association agreement was to conclude in 1918. It had not been successful because the board never enforced the ten dollar assessment on cottagers. Consequently, the association failed each season to provide half of the agreed-upon amount. In 1917, the Cottagers' Improvement Association recommended that a Detroit accounting firm be hired to audit the financial records.

People were again questioning the value of continuing the costly assembly program. A writer for the *Daily Resorter* asked the questions on everyone's mind: "What should be the character of the Bay View Assembly program? What do Bay View cottagers and transients come north for? What is the fundamental principle that underlies what all Bay View has been doing for so many years? Is Bay View merely a place of recreation for physical man, or is its fundamental idea cultural development?"[15]

Petoskey druggist Charles Fallass, then secretary of the association, remembered the dire situation back in 1907 and 1908. He spoke out at an August 27, 1917, meeting in favor of the assembly, warning everyone that without it, property values would drop fifty percent. That certainly scared cottagers! Then an unexpected event took place. Newly elected trustee Dr. Hugh Kennedy took over as treasurer of the association in 1917, just as a new management team was hired to head up the entire program.

Bishop Theodore S. Henderson of the Detroit area Methodist Episcopal Church and his social engineer, Dr. John G. Benson, made a formidable impression on the Bay View community which was desperately searching for another "Hall." Both had confident take-charge personalities, and the board liked their plans to make Bay View a national religious center. But, the pair would accept the position only if specific demands were met: The Gordon-Hall-Association contract had to be abrogated, the successful Evelyn Hall Tea Room was to be closed, the association lodging rooms would be available as free housing for the Benson-Henderson staff and Bible students, a cafeteria was to be set up to serve inexpensive meals since Henderson and Benson considered the food at the hotels and boarding houses far too expensive, and the Bay View Association - not Henderson, Benson, or the Methodist Church - would assume all debts resulting from their management at the end of the 1918 season.

As the new assembly program began in 1918 under Benson and Henderson, with Dr. Hugh Kennedy now chairman of the education committee, the unpopular ten dollar fee was repealed. Harlan J. Cozine of Albion College directed the Bay View Assembly Chorus, and Professor H. J. Barnum of DePauw University brought that university's orchestra to perform for the season. Henderson and Benson provided a religious program headlined with the appearances of no less than five Methodist Episcopal Church bishops, and featured a Christian Workers' Institute, a Bible Conference and a Conference for Religious Educational Workers. To keep things financially viable, they programmed more of the popular silent films, continued Hall's conference ideas with a Country Life Conference, the fifth appearance of politician William Jennings Bryan and the long-awaited appearance of Vice President Thomas R. Marshall.

While Chautauqua, New York, has long been a place visited by US presidents, at this time, Bay View was the site of vacationing vice presidents. From Cleveland's Vice President Hendricks' first visit to northern Michigan on July 27, 1885, the resort area attracted the country's second-in-command. Charles Warren Fairbanks, Teddy Roosevelt's vice president from 1905 to 1909, owned property in Harbor Springs and was married to Cornelia Cole who vacationed in Bay View with her relatives, the John Cole family at Block 20, Lot 31.

Charles's nephew, George, married Bay View music staff member Ella May Smith's daughter Helen. During the 1916 Republican convention in August, the name of Mrs. Henry W. Ford appeared on the Bay View registration list as did that of Mrs. George Fairbanks. While not definitive, it gives further credence to the persistent rumor that Henry Ford stayed with the Smiths on Knapp Avenue at Block 22, Lot 19, or possibly the cottage next door. Ford had expressed an interest in running for office, perhaps vice president. Fairbanks ended up accepting the nomination with Republican presidential nominee Charles E. Hughes, a team that only narrowly lost its bid for the White House.

Running against Fairbanks was incumbent VP Marshall. Marshall had appeared on the Bay View Assembly program in 1896 when he was practicing law in Indiana and his family owned the cottage possibly at Block 24, Lot 5. He and his wife continued to summer in Petoskey after he was elected governor of Indiana in 1909. As Woodrow Wilson's vice president, he traveled with his wife in their private Pullman rail car to Petoskey each summer, staying at the Cushman House for as long as three weeks at a time.

Although the regional audience was probably not interested in a five cent cigar[16], on August 25, 1918, Marshall did appear before a crowd of 2500 at a Bay View bayside service. Even though he was opposed to the US involvement in World War I, Marshall backed Wilson and endured the president's disparaging attitude toward him. Spurred on by the need to garner support for the war effort,

*After many invitations, Vice President Thomas R. Marshall finally addressed the Bay View Assembly on the beach in 1917.* (Peggy Child Smith Collection)

Marshall talked that evening about the sacrifices young men and their families were making. The vice president compared it to a religious war: "The time has arrived when the strong man must help the weak, and thank God, we are doing it. Heaven did not bless me with a son, but if it had I'd rather see his name in the casualty list than to have him at home as a lounge lizard."[17]

Some anonymous Bay Viewites thought their new assembly superintendent, Dr. Benson, was a lounge lizard. At the beginning of the 1918 summer season, Benson received hate mail from aggravated cottagers who were offended by his uncensored remarks the previous summer about Bay View needing a president who was not on vacation. Hoteliers and rooming-house owners were insulted by his crude comments that their food was too expensive. Music lovers were unhappy with the departure of Howard Barlow and their beloved violinist Leon Marx. The Women's Club ladies were angry over losing their clubhouse, Chautauqua Cottage, and the popular Evelyn Hall Tea Room. However, by the end of the 1918 summer season, Benson had accomplished the impossible. He had raised $3500 from 179 donors to save the assembly. Despite Benson's insults, President Thomas Gordon was among the donors.

The religious team did not return for a second season. Henderson joined Lakeside in Ohio when he took over leadership of the Cincinnati Area of the Methodist Episcopal Church and returned to Bay View for many years as a preacher. Benson left to pursue a career in hospital administration, although he did return in 1952 to address the association. With their departure, Bay View needed another restructuring for the 1919 season. An alliance with Albion College was completed in 1918, and Dr. Clarence Wilson Greene of Albion College assumed management of both the assembly and the university. He had the help of Bay View trustee Dr. Hugh Kennedy, still chairman of the education committee. In 1919, Dean Robert G. McCutchan of DePauw College assumed the reins of leadership of the music department from Harlan J. Cozine.

Since becoming a trustee in 1905 and president of the association in 1908, Thomas Gordon had supervised the resurrection of the assembly program and university in 1909, negotiated the affairs of Hall's estate and the building of John M. Hall Auditorium, established the religious affiliation of the Bay View Assembly with the Methodist Church, and had managed the alliance between Albion College and the Bay View educational system. Then in 1919, the Howell businessman retired as president, although he remained on the board.

Silas Hays became president with Kennedy as treasurer and chairman of the education committee. Kennedy was a Methodist minister at the Asbury Methodist Church in Traverse City when he first came to Bay View in 1900 to lead the Epworth League meetings at Epworth Hall. By 1916, he was so well-known and liked that he was elected to the board. Having been in the community when Hall managed the assembly and a board member under President Gordon, he was well qualified. After nine years, Silas Hays stepped down, and Kennedy assumed the responsibilities of all three positions: president of the Bay View College of Liberal Arts; superintendent of the assembly; and president of the association. It was more official responsibility than any other president had assumed,

*Dr. Hugh Kennedy continued Bay View's emphases on equal participant political involvement in his assembly plans inviting senators, governors, and political activists every summer.* (Author's Collection)

***The grand balcony on the Cushman House where Vice President Thomas R. Marshall stayed.*** *(Courtesy of Little Traverse Historical Society)*

although Gordon had carried many of the responsibilities unofficially.[18]

Kennedy witnessed the end of the camp meetings and the establishment and decline of the Bible conferences. He replaced them with daily "Morning Watch Services" and "Bible Studies and Devotional Hours" held at Evelyn Hall beginning in 192l. In 1926, Dr. William W. Whitehouse, then a sociology professor at Albion College, joined the faculty of the Bay View College of Liberal Arts and began making regular appearances at daily worship services.[19] His colleague at Albion College, historian Dr. Royal Hall, came to Bay View in 1929. Immediately, the daily devotional services were focused on world affairs. Whitehouse spoke on subjects such as "America's Democratic Destiny," considering the success of the American democratic experiment and reflecting upon philosophically-divided American attitudes toward the American way of life. In a 1940 lecture, he considered how quickly Hitler was carrying out his aims outlined in *Mein Kampf*: "Today we see them realized almost ahead of schedule. Never in a single year has there occurred more general interlocking and intensive retrogression of human culture. We are forced to think of large issues and momentous problems. 'Must America mortgage her democracy?' is not merely a rhetorical one, but a very real dilemma in the world of totalitarian controls."[20]

Besides making religious studies contemporary and relevant, Kennedy featured world missionaries in the Bay View pulpit as well as some of the greatest preachers from the country's seminaries, colleges and pulpits. In 1933, a young Dr. George Arthur Buttrick began preaching at the East Jordan Presbyterian Church near his summer home in the Sequanota Club on Lake Charlevoix. The Englishman had just taken over Dr. Henry Sloane Coffin's pulpit in 1927 at New York's Madison Avenue Presbyterian Church and begun summering in northern Michigan. Buttrick had already published two books, *The Parables of Jesus* and *Jesus Came Preaching,* which had been well received nationally.

That summer, from August 4 to August 6, Dr. E. Stanley Jones appeared in Bay View, drawing many visitors. Among them were the noted Quaker Dr. Douglas V. Steere of Haverford College, Pennsylvania, as well as Buttrick. The next summer, 1934, Dr. Hugh Kennedy contracted Dr. Ralph W. Sockman of Christ Methodist Church in New York, author of such well-known books as *Live for Tomorrow* and *The Highway of God.* He was known also for his radio addresses, being among the first to effectively use that medium. In 1935, Kennedy succeeded in booking Buttrick as a regular preacher. While Steere preached many times in Bay View, and both Buttrick and Sockman appeared nearly every season for decades.

Dr. George A. Buttrick was dubbed the "preacher's preacher" for his profound sermons and writings. In 1947, he became editor of the twelve-volume *Interpreter's Bible* and the four-volume *Dictionary of the Bible.* In 1955, he left the Madison Avenue Presbyterian Church and was appointed pastor of the Harvard University Memorial Church. Buttrick did not have a master's degree. So Harvard University voted him one to enable him to accept the Plummer Chair of Christian Morals, which Buttrick humorously dubbed the "morals chair of Christian plumbing."[21]

In Emmet County, Buttrick might have been known as the "people's preacher." He preached forty-two times at the East Jordan Presbyterian Church and nearly every summer between 1935 and 1977 in Bay View, with the exception of 1974 and 1975 when he was ill.[22] In August of 1945, the end of World War II required a celebration and a speaker on short notice. Since he was already in northern Michigan, Dr. Buttrick delivered the message. "No one thought to find out his views on the war," recalled Dr. Jonathan Amy, a Bay View resident and chemistry professor at Indiana University. Buttrick was a pacifist and his

Bay View Association

BAY VIEW, MICHIGAN

Stones and Songs

I removed rocks
And fallen logs
From our little stream,
And the brook
Lost its laughter
And forgot its song.

Then I understood
Why, when I prayed,
"O Lord,
Take all my troubles away,"
The answer came,
"Are you sure
You want this,
My child?"

-Harold E. Kohn
in BEST WISHES

AUGUST 13, 1972

***Poem and Art by Harold E. Kohn used at the Kohn Memorial in the Bay View Woods.*** *(Used by permission of Carolyn Minch)*

opposition to World War II had caused such furor that President Franklin Roosevelt invited him to the White House to discuss his opinions. Buttrick never changed his stance.

In the early 1940s, *The Christian Century* included both Sockman and Buttrick on its list of the six "most effective" preachers in the US. In 1999, Buttrick was ranked by *Preaching Magazine*, a bimonthly journal based in Jackson, Tennessee, as the third most influential preacher of the twentieth century behind Scotsman James S. Stewart and Billy Graham. Civil rights leader Martin Luther King, Jr., was ranked fourth, and fifth place went to Harry Emerson Fosdick. Sockman was ranked eighteenth, not an uncomfortable ranking considering that E. Stanley Jones was ranked sixteenth.

When Dr. Ralph Sockman retired in 1963 from his nationally syndicated column "A Lift for Living," he named Reverend Harold E. Kohn of Charlevoix as his successor. Kohn had accepted the ministerial position at the First Congregational Church in Charlevoix in 1952 when he was diagnosed with a brain tumor. In the less frantic northern Michigan surroundings, the tumor subsided and his health improved. In the 1960s, he frequently preached at Bay View and provided copies of his black and white etchings for the programs. He published eight books and was a nationally respected artist.

On July 26, 1968, while he was preparing to preach in Bay View on the subject "Finding Certainty in an Uncertain World," he discovered that the tumor had returned. With it came numerous operations at the U-M Hospital. Through all of his pain and discomfort, he continued writing and publishing his books which were translated into numerous languages. He turned to watercolors when it was too difficult for him to continue his black and white artwork. He never lost his sense of humor and was the hope and inspiration for millions through his writings and his counseling sessions with the depressed, confused, sick, and downtrodden. With never ending, increasing pain, the growing tumor eventually blinded him in one eye. He completely lost his sight the last year of his life. He died May 9, 1975, and was mourned by his international public and the many who knew him in northern Michigan. In the Bay View woods there is a memorial to him with one of his poems, "Stones and Songs", burned into a wooden memorial, an inspiration to all who visit it.

Traditionalism and correlating views were not the criteria that Superintendent Kennedy used for selecting assembly guest talent. Unafraid of controversy, when Kennedy first took over assembly programming on short notice in the spring of 1922, he planned a pioneering Child Welfare Conference featuring Dr. Owen R. Lovejoy. Lovejoy was a graduate of Albion College, general secretary of the National Child Welfare Committee and president of the American Association of Social Workers. In 1928, he scheduled a debate between R. N. Holsaple, superintendent of the Michigan Anti-Saloon League, and Detroit Attorney Walter A. Rice on the subject "Can the Law Be Enforced?" The talent that appeared during the 1930s and 1940s was extraordinarily diverse and widely representative of American culture. As Charlotte Canning, professor at the University of Texas, commented "Refinement and respectability were important concerns of every performance of the time."[23] Harry Harrison, the Redpath-Chautauqua booking agent, remarked that the people at the Bay View Assembly "were more interested in poets and poetry, art, literature and polite travelogues."[24]

***Rev. Dr. Harold Kohn of Charlevoix was a prolific writer and artist and preached in Bay View many times.***
*(Courtesy of Carolyn Minch)*

Most baffling is the association's changing attitude toward its black assembly guests. In 1894, Booker T. Washington stayed at the Oriental Hotel in Petoskey when he appeared on the assembly program.[25] Hall entertained him at Wayside on his return visit in 1913. Some of the other black talent - the Fisk Jubilee Singers, the African Boy Choir, the Virginia Jubilee Singers, and the Williams' Jubilee Singers – are listed on the register at the Bay View House where Hall was a financial partner. However, by 1931 and 1932, when black poet Countee Cullen appeared on the assembly program, Hall was deceased, the Bay View House lay in ruins from a fire and area hotels were not accepting African-American guests. Both times he came, Cullen stayed at the home of Homer Larsen - outside of Bay View.

*Jonathan Amy's father, Dr. Ernest Amy (member of the Bay View Summer School faculty) did this drawing of Carl Sandburg when the poet was on the Bay View program in 1936.* (Photograph by G. Randall Goss)

Larsen knew from personal experience the prejudices that blacks suffered. Prior to World War I, his father was principal of the LeMoyne Normal Institute in Memphis, Tennessee, an African-American school run by the American Missionary Association of the Congregational Church. Local discrimination focused on whites who associated with blacks. Just because his father worked at the school, ten-year-old Larsen was thrown over a wall by a mob, breaking his arm in two places, injuring his leg, and causing convulsions. "Even today when I get tired, my leg will start to drag. Friends told my parents that they feared to think about what might happen to my sister. After that my sister and I stayed at home. Bay View provided the only opportunity for us to have a normal life with children our own age. We attended the Boys' and Girls' Club. This became our mainstay and our anchor," remembered Homer during an interview in 1987.[26]

When Larsen wanted to attend college, he needed chemistry, physics and math. By this time, his father was teaching in Alabama. So fifteen-year-old Larsen violated Alabama law by attending a black high school where his teachers held degrees from Ohio State University and the University of Michigan. "Ironically, I had better teachers there than I would have had at the white schools," Larsen went on. "But, there is no record of my having attended high school."[27] With the education provided by his mother and the knowledge received at this Alabama

*The Bay View House burned amid rumors of arson in September of 1929 just before the stock market crash. It was under insured and was never rebuilt. The site is now called Sunset Park.* (Courtesy of the Little Traverse Historical Society)

black high school, Homer passed the entrance exams at Oberlin College.

After serving in World War I, Larsen taught at Tougaloo College in Alabama from 1923 until 1943, earning about $1300 a year. Out of that meager pay, he had to spend $100 a year to send his daughter to school in Jackson to escape the dangers of local prejudice at the white schools where his two sons attended. At Tougaloo, he coached baseball with black athletes who he felt could have played in the major leagues, but this was before Jackie Robinson broke the color barrier, and the athletes had no hope of playing professionally. At Bay View, Larsen considered it a privilege to entertain Cullen. "We enjoyed having Cullen in our home and since he did not have a ride to Mt. Pleasant for his next speaking engagement, I drove him down there," said Larsen.[28] In addition to Cullen, other poets who appeared in Bay View during this time were Michiganders Edgar A. Guest, Douglas Malloch (*Michigan, My Michigan*), Barton Rees Pogue, Anne Campbell and Carl Sandburg.

Sandburg was living in Michigan when he came to Bay View in 1936. He was finishing his work *Abraham Lincoln: The War Years*, which netted him the Pulitzer Prize for history in 1940. At his afternoon appearance, Sandburg read his poetry and answered questions about his writings. Dr. Jonathan Amy believes his father arranged for Sandburg's appearance. At Ohio Wesleyan, the senior Amy ran a lecture series for students to meet and talk with contemporary authors. Amy knew Willa Cather and was good friends with Robert Frost. While Sandburg was on the grounds, Amy, also an artist, drew a sketch of the great poet.

Kennedy featured politicians as well as entertainers. Among the politicians were Michigan Governor Wilbur M. Brucker, Michigan Congressman John C. Ketcham, ex-Indiana Senator James E. Watson, North Dakota Senator Gerald P. Nye, Ohio Senator Simeon D. Fess, Michigan senators Woodbridge N. Ferris and Grant M. Hudson, and the Czechoslovakian political leader and congressional Senator Vojta Benes. Kennedy also booked humorists Strickland Gillilan and Arthur Welwyn Evans; foreign correspondents Mark Sullivan (*Collier's Weekly*) and Will Irwin; authors Gay MacLaren and Sydney R. Montague, a member of the Royal Canadian Mounted Police; and the respected Drew Pearson. Adventurers and world explorers such as Charles E. Lofgren of the Byrd's South Pole Expedition; environmentalists and conservationists such as Canadian bird specialist Jack Minor; and photographers such as Carveth Wells of the Royal Geographical Society were also popular. Roselle Brewer and her seeing-eye dog, Lady Luck, and numerous magicians and puppeteers added entertainment for children. The "multiple mentalist", Harry Kahne, demonstrated six mental operations simultaneously on the platform.

In 1940, Kennedy contracted atheist philosopher and later Pulitzer Prize winning historian Dr. Will Durant, author of the *Story of Philosophy* and the eleven-volume *Story of Civilization*. Durant spoke on "A Blueprint for a Better America," telling his audience that he thought the answer to the biological problem of the feeble-minded would be to give them a choice between self-segregation and sterilization: "After responsible medical investigation persons found biologically unfit, they should promise to give up parentage. I would encourage the birth rate of the ablest by doubling the income exception for every child born. Reproduction as well as production should be financed."[29] In 1941, Kennedy featured Rabbi Jerome Daniel Folkman of Temple Emanuel in Grand Rapids in a debate with Catholic priest Dr. John A. Meade, a former member of the Illinois Department of Labor, and Protestant clergyman Dr. Stanley B. Crosland, a member of the Illinois State Conference on Social Action. Their topic was "The American Way."

For nearly three decades, even after his health began failing, Dr. Hugh Kennedy lead Bay View through difficult times. True to the Chautauqua ideal, if not entirely to the Bay View idea, Kennedy developed his program within the local community, augmenting it with road shows and booked entertainment. He brought a multi-faceted program to northern Michigan with few resources and no outside support. While both Hall and Kennedy booked talent through Chicago's Redpath-Slayton Lyceum Bureau, as shown in the Redpath documents at the University of Iowa Archives, the two leaders differed. Hall went out and contracted the talent he wanted while Kennedy maximized his resources and personal connections. Hall was flamboyant, entrepreneurial, intellectual and financially resourceful while Kennedy had a consistent managerial style that inspired his staff and maintained the association through World War I, the Depression, World War II, and the advent of the radio and television age that eroded the nation's interest in assemblies.

Historian David Glick, former senior administrator at Henry Ford Museum and Greenfield Village, estimated that as many as 292 national independent assemblies were founded before 1912 and thousands more Tent Chautauquas. Most had folded by the 1930s. In this national environment, Kennedy's most stunning achievement was financial. When he took over as treasurer in 1917, the assembly was in financial stress. In the following decades of wars, tight money, and depression, when sister institutions were in bankruptcy, in 1933 Kennedy lowered the assembly ticket price to thirty-five cents and the crowds increased along with the revenues. On August 2, 1934, the *Petoskey Evening News* reported that receipts for the year had totaled $41,528.34. Dr. Kennedy commented. "When institutions such as Chautauqua, New York; Boulder, Colorado; Lakeside, Ohio; and Winona Lake, Indiana, are in financial difficulty, we have much to be grateful for. On March 31, we had no indebtedness and a balance of $18,394.72." In 1935, an even more incredible announcement was made at the annual meeting:

"President Kennedy declared that the Board of Trustees planned to make refunds to the cottagers on their annual rentals of $1,689.11. This still allows the association treasury to maintain a reserve fund of $20,000. All bills were reported paid."[30]

During these years when a college education might not have been at the forefront of the minds of many, enrollment in the Bay View College of Liberal Arts was on the upswing. In 1932, two innovative students, Ronald A. Brunger and his classmate Henry Brown, serious about finishing their degrees but pinched for money, pitched a tent in the Bay View woods. Brunger wanted to skip his senior year of college to save money. On Bay View's "back street," the pair cooked their meals over a gasoline stove and used the creek as a refrigerator for milk, butter, and other perishable items. "In the seven weeks I spent in Bay View, my share of the grocery cost was $7.96. We ate for $1.14 a week," Brunger later wrote.[31]

Enrollment in the college grew under Kennedy until 1946, when 377 students registered, aided by the GI Bill of Rights tuition for veterans. The trustees then capped the enrollment at 250 students because of limited classroom and dormitory facilities. In 1947, students from thirty-five colleges and fifteen states enrolled. Albion led the list with nearly a third of the students, while students from the University of Arizona and the University of Colorado also registered.

During Kennedy's years in office, from his election to the board of trustees in 1916 until his retirement as superintendent of the assembly in 1945, every department flourished. The Bay View Summer College of Liberal Arts and Music School was accredited and experienced consistently high enrollment. The Bay View Music Festival attracted the nation's top musicians. The library board was reorganized and the library building constructed. A men's club was organized and plans for a building made. The Woman's Council was re-established at the Chautauqua Cottage, now the Woman's Council Building. The Recreation Department was organized with regularly scheduled programs for children of all ages and the waterfront developed for swimming. The dock was reconstructed of concrete. A theater program for young people featured Shakespearean drama. Two young people's orchestras and a band were regular features.

Kennedy's most admirable attribute was the loyalty he elicited from his colleagues and department heads who remained in their positions during his administration. Dr. Roscoe Sleight, who headed the Bay View Summer School for over twenty years, retired in 1947. Music director William Reddick remained in Bay View for twelve seasons until his New York career became too demanding, and he reluctantly resigned. Fred Patton followed Reddick as music director but left when Kennedy retired. Charles Ditto, superintendent of the grounds, retired in 1947.

Upon Kennedy's resignation as president in 1944, his boss in the Methodist Church hierarchy of the Detroit area of the Methodist Church, Bishop Raymond J. Wade, said, "Dr. Kennedy "was one of the best administrators and secretaries that we had in the United States."[32] His departure from Bay View marked the decline of the Chautauqua era's diverse and broadly-based assembly program. His boss, Bishop Wade, took over.[33]

*As the pool inside Recreation Hall was dysfunctional, a second pool was built alongside the building in the 1930s for the small children.* (Photograph by Charles Ditto)

— CHAPTER EIGHT —

# The Flying Bishop

When Bishop Raymond J. Wade assumed the presidency of the Bay View Association after Dr. Hugh Kennedy retired, he was involved in a project overseeing the immigration of ministers from the Baltic states to Michigan pulpits of the Methodist church, where they would be free of Soviet persecution. Wade had been appointed head of the northern European Area of the Methodist Church in the late 1920s. When the war broke out, he was in the US and unable to return to his comrades. He was assigned to the denomination's Detroit office as resident bishop and joined the Bay View board in 1942. At this time, he was honored for his work in international Christian service and listed in the 1942-43 edition of *Who's Who in America*. By 1944, he assumed the presidency of Bay View and, in 1945, took over all three positions from Kennedy: president of the association, superintendent of the assembly program, and president of the summer colleges of music and liberal arts. In Bay View, he found an association also affected by war - where gas rationing had closed nearly half of the cottages and financial constrains allowed for few excesses.

The Hoosier preacher was born in La Grange, Indiana, on May 29, 1875, at the time Michigan Methodists were exploring possibilities for a campground. Wade's father, Reverend Cyrus U. Wade, also a Methodist minister, and his mother, Mary, first came to Bay View in 1894 as part of a large Indiana contingent which journeyed north each summer. That year, Raymond was ordained a minister and continued his studies at DePauw University, from which he graduated in 1898.[1]

After graduation, the young Wade served several churches in the Indiana Conference.[2] He married Ella L. Yarian in 1901, but she died prematurely in December 1909, leaving him to raise their three children: Elizabeth E., Mary Elouise, and Paul Raymond. Wade's parents owned a cottage at Block 23, Lot 1, in Bay View. While visiting them one summer, he met Myrtle Mudge of Elkhart, Indiana, at an ice cream social. She became his second wife in 1913. In 1921, the couple bought their own cottage, the Octagonal Cottage at Block 19, Lot 10.

Wade's career was becoming an international one. In 1922, he became the corresponding secretary of the Board of Benevolence for the Methodist Church. The following season he was invited back to Bay View to speak on "Living at Our Best" and "Christ the Outdoor Man." In 1925, Wade again returned, this time as executive secretary of the World Service Commission. Between 1924 and 1928, Wade served as secretary general of the Conference of the Methodist Church and editor general of the *Conference Journal*. During this time, he was elected to the Bay View board and became vice president, but, his appointment as Bishop of the Methodist Church for Northern Europe took priority, and he resigned, moving to Stockholm, Sweden.

Wade arrived in Europe in October, 1927, just in time to participate in the Jubilee Missionary Celebration in Riga, Latvia, an event that would be significant in Bay View history. It was held at the Methodist Episcopal Church at 15 Elizabeth Street in Riga, where Lithuanian-born Sergei Mosienko was ordained as a minister, and the American members of the Riga Methodist community honored American missionary Dr. George Albert Simons with a communion set commemorating his twenty years of missionary work in Russia. The set of four vessels, inscribed in English, was left behind when Simons returned to the US years later. Thus began a seventy-year period when this communion set touched the lives of people in three countries and across two continents and became part of Bay View's history. Shortly after the Riga celebration, Bishop Raymond J. Wade officially assumed

***Bishop Raymond J. Wade, president of Bay View 1944 to 1961.***
*(Courtesy of Gaylor W. Jones)*

***Bishop and Mrs. Wade dining family style at the Terrace Inn in the 1940s.*** *(Courtesy of Patty Rasmussen Rave)*

his new position and became acquainted with the brave ministers who lead the church in the Baltic states - a relationship that would take on greater importance in the decades to come.

Wade was a strong leader and, by 1930, he had charge not only of the Methodist conferences in Sweden, Norway, Denmark, Finland, Russia, and the Baltic and Slavic countries but was chancellor of the Scandinavian School of Theology. He soon assumed charge of the church in France, Spain, the Madeira Islands, Algeria and Tunisia - a position encompassing congregations speaking sixteen different languages in countries under thirteen national flags. Reverend Eduard Eidins, who was fluent in six languages, served as his interpreter.

In the years leading up to World War II, Wade's influence widened. His granddaughter, Linda Jones Matthews, wrote that, "He and Mrs. Wade were presented to the King and Queen of Norway, received a framed picture and gifts from the King of Denmark, and knew the King of Sweden."[3] In 1929, the *Paris Herald* ran an article about the Wades' contribution to European life. During these years, Wade traveled so often by plane to oversee his charges that he earned the title among the Methodist hierarchy of "The Flying Bishop."

Baltic Methodist churches flourished under Wade's leadership. Then came three invasions: the Russians, the Nazis and the Russians again. Church officials were harassed and persecuted, and the property of the Methodist Church was confiscated. Ministers were imprisoned, killed or driven out of their homes and homeland. When the Russians arrived in 1940, Mosienko, the minister who was ordained at the celebration in 1927, was found guilty of being hostile to the Russian government as a representative of an American Missionary Society. Fleeing Lithuania, he sought refuge in Germany but was picked up by the Gestapo and placed in a concentration camp. Fluent in seven languages, he was forced to work as an interpreter and sent to the Russian front with the German army.

As the war was ending and the Germans were retreating from Latvia as they were being pursued by the Russians, one of Wade's ministers, Fricis Timbers, who was superintendent of the Latvian District of the Methodist Church, secretly left Riga by rowboat across the Baltic Sea. He carried with him a frayed envelope, carefully tied with a string, and the communion set that had been presented to Simons at the 1927 ceremony. Timbers followed the retreating German army and made his way to Switzerland, ahead of the advancing Russians. In Basel, he met Methodist Bishop Paul Garber and gave him the well-worn envelope. Inside it were the deeds to the Methodist properties in Riga, which had come under

*The four-piece Communion Set was made in Riga, Latvia, in 1927 and inscribed in English. It was a gift from Americans of the Methodist Church in Riga to Dr. George Albert Simons for his missionary work in Russia between 1907 and 1927.* (Photograph by Author)

Russian domination. "When I hand them to you, my commission will have been fulfilled. I have kept the trust committed to me as the superintendent of the Methodist Mission at Latvia," he announced to Garber.[4] For unknown reasons, Timbers kept the Simons Communion Set. No mention of it is made in that meeting. Instead, Timbers took it back to Germany where he used it to serve communion in the German displaced persons' camps.

At this time, in 1948, Wade retired from the Methodist Church and went back to Frankfurt. Realizing that many ministers in the camps faced deportation back to their home countries now occupied by the communist USSR, Wade worked with Dr. Gaither P. Warfield to arrange for their emigration to the US and resettlement in Michigan congregations. Some have estimated that Wade arranged for as many as fifty ministers and their families to come to Michigan, but Wade's granddaughter Linda Jones Matthews placed the number at close to 100.

*Bishop Fricis Timbers, superintended of the Methodist Church in Riga, smuggled the set out of that country after World War II. He took it to Germany and eventually to Lakeview, Michigan when he and his wife were relocated by Bishop Raymond J. Wade.* (Courtesy of Keith Willison)

Janis Laupmanis, Eidins, Timbers, Mosienko and their families were a few of those who settled in Michigan. Laupmanis took a pulpit in Kalamazoo.[5] Eduard Eidins, Wade's faithful interpreter, accepted an appointment in Bad Axe. Mosienko served a congregation in Ubly and then spent seventeen years at the Bethlehem Methodist and Woodmere Methodist churches in downtown Detroit. He bought a Bay View cottage at Block 41, Lot 3, and summered there until ill health confined him to Florida in the 1990s. Timbers was assigned to the Methodist congregation in Lakeview, Michigan. After a few years, he moved to California. "He never used that communion set in our church," Keith Willison, a church member, reported years later.[6] However, Timbers must have had the communion set with him during his relocations.

With the settlement of these ministers and their families in Michigan communities, Wade focused his attention on the needs of Bay View. During World War I, the Great Lakes steamers were taken off their normal routes to serve the war effort, limiting transportation to resorts like Bay View, but cars quickly became the alternative. The Depression did not affect Bay View as severely as it did other national Chautauqua assemblies which either disappeared altogether or lost possession of their land. World War II had the most far-reaching effect on Bay View when all transportation was cut off by the lack of available trains and streamers and gas-rationing of cars.

However, it was not as severe as many have speculated. The *Petoskey Evening News* summarized the 1943 season: "Hit by the war and by the gasoline rationing Bay View authorities had not anticipated much more than a 60 per cent attendance this season but according to Charles Ditto, superintendent of grounds, more than 82 per cent of the cottages are open this season. The survey, Mr. Ditto said this morning, disclosed that of the total of 436 cottages on the grounds proper, 358 are now occupied or have been occupied during the present season. This is 97 per cent of the total number of cottages occupied last season. In addition, three hotels are open, and hotels and the smaller eating places report a good business. The membership in the Woman's Council is 140 thus far for this season while for 1942 the total membership was 130. The Campus Club membership is only slightly less than last season at this time, with a good interest being shown in all of the club's activities."[7]

By the end of the war, however, nearly half of the cottagers did not return, leaving many vacant homes. Older residents had passed away, and young families were unable to get away summers. Wade faced the challenge of revitalizing the association by taking two separate approaches. First, he emphasized a strong recreation program, and then he took a path familiar to many ministers wishing to revitalize their churches: he started a building campaign.

The first building constructed under Wade's administration was the Campus Club. Originally called the Men's Club, the Campus Club dated back to the early part of the twentieth century and was a direct attempt to increase the number of men on the grounds. The Blanshard reporters described its beginning in 1912:

> *"Hush ye Amazons! No longer shall the female phalanx rule our fair city. Bay View is to have a real Men's club! There will be no beer or billiards or even cigars about it; nevertheless it is guaranteed 101 per cent [sic] genuine. The club will be composed of any Bay View men who are interested in the welfare of the resort. A big banquet has been arranged for next Saturday night at the Howard House to begin at eight o'clock and to cost just fifty cents. An executive committee has been appointed to launch this promising organization which is the first of its kind ever started in Bay View. This*

***In the 1920s, the men in the association were interested in promoting sports such as roque and more organized activities for the young people.***
*(Courtesy of the Little Traverse Historical Society)*

*committee is composed of W. J. DeVol, G. W. Childs, S. A. Hays, E. A. Wallace, H. I. Ruth, and R. M. Brunson."*[8]

**Stanley and Dorothy Kresge donated $60,000 in memory of Paul W. Voorhies, the first president of the Kresge Foundation (1924-1952).** *(Courtesy of Bruce Kresge)*

Even Hall and Dr. William H. Shier attended the inaugural banquet on August 15, 1912. Judge Silas A. Hays of Greencastle, Indiana, was elected the group's president.[9] Not until 1916 was there another meeting. At that time, Mr. Hathaway attended a trustees' meeting concerning Bay View's population being three-quarters women. His remedy was to attract men by building a men's clubhouse, and he offered $3000 toward the project. President Thomas Gordon offered another $3000 but Bay View had serious management issues and no building was constructed. In 1919, Henry Vogt succeeded Hays as president of the Men's Club. Because the early records were unavailable, Vogt has long been thought to be the Men's Club's first president. A constitution was drawn up and adopted July 26, 1920, although the group had no official clubhouse.

The men were very much interested in sports. Horseshoe pitching, roque and croquet were located on the center campus grounds for members in 1921. In 1924, the checkers pavilion and the drinking fountain were installed, along with another shuffleboard court and a croquet court. By 1926, they had three roque courts, several horseshoe courts, two shuffleboard courts, a clay croquet court and two checkers pavilions – one for boys and one for men. In 1927, lawn bowling became popular, and the first court was constructed. "Men's only" bowling became the most popular sport. By 1939, Bay View youth were using the roque court for badminton. Then, on August 21, 1940, the name of the Men's Club was officially changed to the Campus Club. Women were allowed to play shuffleboard, and activities increased substantially.

With the Campus Club building completed in 1952, next on Wade's agenda was a lecture hall for the daily Religion and Life Hour Bible lectures. While on the faculty at Wayne State University, Dr. William W. Whitehouse was attending Detroit's Metropolitan Methodist Church. There, he met Stanley S. Kresge and his wife Dorothy McVittie Kresge, long-time members of the church. Stanley Kresge's father, S.S. Kresge, founded the K-Mart Corporation. The Kresges were ardent admirers of F. Dudleigh Vernor, organist at both Bay View and the Detroit church. Mrs. Kresge's relationship with Bay View went back to 1887 when her grandfather, Alexander McVittie, was a pallbearer at the funeral of Bay View's first treasurer, Detroit Banker David Preston.

In 1910, at a very sad time in her childhood when her own father passed away, she and her family began summering in Bay View, staying at the Ramsdell cottage at Block 19, Lot 8. Extremely vivacious and very athletic, Dorothy was the leading woman bowler at the beachfront bowling alleys in Recreation Hall. She and Stanley's sister, Ruth Kresge, are listed in 1916 as sopranos in the Bay View Chorus. In 1917, Dorothy studied violin with Bay View staff artist Leon Marx. During this period, Stanley Kresge played centerfield for one of Bay View's three baseball teams.

The family of Paul W. Voorhies also spent time in Bay View during these years.[10] Later, Voorhies became prosecutor for Wayne County and attorney general of the state of Michigan. Also a prominent member of Metropolitan Methodist Church in Detroit and a trustee of Albion College, he knew many Bay View people. He was the first president of the Kresge Foundation, serving from 1924 until his death on January 8, 1952, an event that was the impetus for a substantial gift to the Bay View Association. Through the Kresge Foundation, a $60,000 grant for a new auditorium was made in his honor, to be called the Paul W. Voorhies Hall. As he did in many places, Kresge honored his wife Dorothy with the gift of a $7000 Baldwin electronic organ for the new building. The Kresges attended the dedication of Voorhies Hall on June 28, 1953. In 1984, Bay View resident and *Detroit Free Press* writer Bill Laitner (Block 23, Lot 24) interviewed Kresge and wrote this account:

> *The ties are deep and well-known between the Bay View Association and Stanley S. Kresge, one of Michigan's most famous Methodists. I believe his generosity to the Association, at least in part, stemmed from some of his earliest, fondest summer memories — those of summer days spent at Bay View. I refer in particular to the days when young*

*Stan Kresge got to know a certain young lady from Detroit. This is how it happened, as Mr. Kresge told me in an interview in June of 1984.*

*The occasion was my visit, as a reporter for the* Detroit Free Press, *to Mr. Kresge's office at the Kresge Foundation, in Troy, Michigan. He was happy to see me but understandably uncomfortable about the subject of the interview — the disappearance and presumed murder of his granddaughter, Carol Kresge DeArment, whose body was never found. Her husband, though never charged by police, remained a suspect until he died years later from cancer.*

*Naturally, before discussing the difficult matter at hand, Mr. Kresge and I both welcomed the opportunity to make some small talk. After an interchange about mutual friends and family members, to get things rolling I mentioned that I was having a great summer, having just returned from a wonderful place where I had just bought a cottage. When I said it was Bay View, Mr. Kresge's entire face lit up. I knew Bay View meant something special to him. Although he was 84 and using a wheelchair, he remained a very lively, animated conversationalist.*

*'Bay View! Wonderful place. Wonderful place. I met my wife there!' he began.*

*With that, Kresge launched into a half-hour litany of Bay View's virtues, spiced with a recollection of his playing softball 'on that big open park, you know, down near the center of things.' It was during a softball game that the young Kresge, who was then by his description a short but rock-solid adolescent from Detroit's upscale Boston-Edison neighborhood, slugged a notable hit while aware that on the sidelines watching was a cute young lady, also from Detroit, named Dorothy McVittie.*

*Kresge's comments to me that day have sparked a debate that may remain forever unsettled. Family members, including Bruce Kresge in a statement to me in 1997, maintain that Stanley met Dorothy on a tennis court at a Methodist parsonage in Detroit. That account appears in Dorothy Kresge's obituary, published in the Detroit Free Press in 1988, which states that Stanley was 14 and Dorothy 13 on the date of that fortuitous tennis match.*

*It may well be, however, that the young Stanley and Dorothy first crossed paths at Bay View sometime before that first official date. They may have met informally at Bay View. At the time Mr. Kresge discussed Bay View with me, I failed to inquire about the details of his social life as a youngster. It seems clear, however, that young Stanley Kresge spent many a pleasant summer day at Bay View. And it's equally clear that he recalled for me, vividly and fondly, that he showed off on the ball diamond for his future sweetheart.*

*Stanley S. Kresge died on June 30, 1985, one year to the month after I interviewed him. That summer, with the encouragement of then Bay View President Ben Vanden Belt, Jr. and Archivist Director Jane P. Doerr, I*

**The Paul W. Voorhies Hall was a gift from the Kresge Foundation to the Bay View Association. It was completed and dedicated in June, 1953. E. W. Prieb was the architect for the building.** *(Author's Collection)*

*drove to Lake Angelus, Michigan, an hour north of Detroit, to visit Dorothy Kresge and talk about Bay View. My goal was to record her reminiscences for the archives and to suggest that she support Bay View's fundraising efforts. Unfortunately, Mrs. Kresge, although very friendly, was too frail to respond thoughtfully to my questions. She died a year later.*[11]

After Voorhies Hall was completed, Wade undertook the construction of a Boys' and Girls' Club in 1955. The recreation program was quickly outgrowing the two historic but inappropriate buildings in the center of the campus, and the club needed a place for rainy day activities. A redwood structure, with a fireplace in the center of a large community room, was to be called the Ernest D. Gray Boys' and Girls' Club.

Immediately after the Boys' and Girls' Club was completed, Wade embarked upon his next mission: new seating for the John M. Hall Auditorium. Association members donated funds for new upholstered seats and the old wooden "opera" seats were removed. The renovation reduced the auditorium's seating capacity from 2100 to 1708. Chairs from the 1887 Old Auditorium were used in the balcony.[12]

To help finance this energetic building campaign, Wade started the tradition of Appreciation Night in 1953. During William Reddick's time as director of music in the 1920s and early 1930s, an annual tradition of an "Old Fashioned" concert was begun, combining some old popular songs with a touch of humor. Fred Patton expanded the idea during his tenure as director of music, and the artists began an annual "Fun Night." When Harold Tallman of Wayne State University took over as music director, he replaced Fun Night with black-faced minstrel shows. Wade seized upon the popular idea to begin an annual fund-raiser to help defray the costs of his building campaign.

Wade's proudest hour came after he stepped down as president of Bay View in 1962. He planned a special reunion called Patriotic Week to include many of the Baltic refugee pastors of the Methodist Church whom Wade had relocated in the US. Five of the ministers, including Sergei Mosienko, spoke to the association. Timbers was by then living in California and could not be there, but he sent the Simons Communion Set to be used for a combined memorial service and Holy Communion in honor of this special occasion. In appreciation for his help in establishing their new lives in America, the Baltic ministers presented the set as a gift to Bay View and Bishop Wade. When Bishop Wade was too frail to return to Bay View, he left the Simons Communion Set in the large oak bookcase in his office on the second floor of John M. Hall Auditorium, much the way Simons had left it behind in Riga.

Wade died January 23, 1970, in Florida, The legislature of the state of Michigan passed Resolution 177 on February 19, 1970, honoring him for service to the Methodist Church in Europe and the United States and as president of the Bay View Association. Two years later, the Bishop Raymond J. Wade Memorial Bell Tower was designed and erected through donations by the Wade family. Bay View's three bells were tuned and hoisted into the tower. The clappers were wired so they could be electronically controlled from the president's office in John M. Hall Auditorium.

Over the past century, the three cast bells have come to symbolize the association's important events. Each evening in the early days of the camp meeting, the bells reminded campers of sunset. The great bell was always rung for "ordinary occasions," the full peal meant "a very important gathering" and the sustained peal meant a dreaded event such as a fire. The bells also have been rung to commemorate great national events – the end of World War I, D-Day, the surrender of Japan and the end of World War II, and each year's Independence Day.

Originally mounted on a cement slab in the center of the campus just south of the present Wade Bell Tower, the bells have long been a wonderful, never-ending source of pranks and mischief for the younger generation and the forever-younger generation. Since the bells first arrived, boys, girls and older pranksters have had to be constantly chided for ringing those bells at disturbing hours of the

***To prevent pranks by misguided young campers in the early days, the bells were shrouded in fencing and foliage.*** *(Author's Collection)*

day and night. "The boys at Bay View have formed an unpleasant habit of destroying slumber by ringing the church bells at unreasonable hours," complained the *Daily Resorter* in the1888.[13] The pranks were frightening since they disturbed the sleeping masses with the fear of fire and aroused Bay View's volunteer fire brigade needlessly.

By 1889, the mischief makers had a new trick. They took the clappers out so the bells couldn't be rung for the sunrise camp meeting services. Later, when the same trick was done, in 1910, Paul Blanshard wrote humorously: "Perhaps you will notice that the big ding-dong on the campus does not make quite the big melodious racket to rouse everybody in the vicinity. The reason for this is that some fellow who is terribly lacking in veneration for established institutions decided to violate Section X of the Decalogue and purloined the clapper from the throat of the big bell. The doctor tried to cure this throat trouble by putting a sledge hammer in place of the old tongue but the bell has been hoarse ever since."[14] During the years when college students were housed on the grounds, the bells were the source of constant amusement, and many times Wade had to investigate. It was fitting to have the tower built in his honor, though it has hardly served to keep the pranksters away.[15]

Wade was well-known for his sense of fairness and ability to get things done. An ardent conservative in a denomination full of free thinkers, Wade "often disagreed with the liberal views expressed in the [*Christian*] *Advocate*, but he did not attempt to interfere because he was convinced of the necessity for freedom of the press", wrote historian Douglas MacNaughton.[16] An innovative president, he had overseen the largest building campaign the association had undertaken since the 1880s and 90s. When he retired in 1961, the emphasis was no longer on a wide variety of talent and diversity of lecturers in the assembly or on the importance of serving the entire area-wide audience, something that distinguished the assembly of the earlier days. For financial reasons, the assembly in the 1950s pretty much consisted of ministerial lectures, local travelogues and movies. The music festival had remained intact with artists-in-residence, but the budget did not allow for special events. Ticket demand was minimal and there was no need for season passes. The Summer University, which had become the Bay View College of Liberal Arts, was booming but its days were numbered. The recreation program, however, was thriving.

***The Bay View Bells were the symbols of the Assembly since its first season in 1887. Mr. and Mrs. Charles J. Ditto sent this Christmas Greetings out during the 1930s.***
*(Photograph by Charles Ditto Family)*

— CHAPTER NINE —

# The Bay View Way

Both Bay View presidents Kennedy and Wade realized the association's future depended on its youth and heavily supported their legacy from John M. Hall, the recreation program. While athletics had been a community goal since the 1890s, in 1931, when President Hugh Kennedy hired Ernie Gray, a tenacious young man from Albion, Michigan, the program was formalized. From then on, it grew continuously. Today, it is the only such program among national Chautauqua assemblies.

Children grow up in Bay View attending the recreation program, making lifelong friends and enjoying summers while living with their extended families. It is an experience that most campers want their children to share and becomes a major reason for their return later in life. *GQ Magazine* writer John Sullivan recently reminisced in a *Graphic* interview about his childhood days in Bay View when he formed enduring friends from all parts of the country. Attending the Boys' and Girls' Club, he competed in the Ernie Gray Olympics and appeared in Bay View theatrical productions. Strongly affected by those memories and especially Petoskey's legacy of great writers - Hemingway and Bruce Catton - Sullivan embarked on a literary career. His first book, *Bloodhorses*, *Notes of a Sportswriter's Son,* received favorable reviews from the *New York Times* and *Sports Illustrated*. Sullivan also realizes how affected he has been by both the proximity to the Odawas and the heritage of the utopian concept of the Chautauqua idea, and contemplates writing about the place his family has summered for six generations.

Back in the 1880s, for founding families like Sullivans, once their summer city of Bay View was primarily built, the residents were ready for some fun. While recreation in those times was more re-creation and organized sports were chiefly left to the imagination of the campers, games and leisure activities were prevalent, though restricted to what the association could afford and what the Bay View founding fathers deemed proper - things like candy pulls, bonfires, hayrides, picnics, and rowing. Swimming was frowned upon and the subject of local jokes. The *Grand Traverse Herald* poked fun at the trustees in 1895: "Bay View has always borne the reputation of being one of those modest of all the summer resorts in the country but this summer she has certainly out done all efforts. The rules and regulations say 'Bathing is allowed but not encouraged.' But, really, now you know that's pretty tough. If a man were a Chinese or a Turk once or twice a year might do, but free-born American citizens will certainly object to doing without their customary ablutions all summer. It's hard on the Petoskey merchants who have laid [sic] in a larger stock of soap than ever before in

***The early wooden docks extended northwest out into Little Traverse Bay 300 to 600 feet in order to accommodate the draft required by the transportation ferries. Winter storms were disastrous and many of the docks didn't last more than two seasons. Although primarily for transportation, the docks were a center of recreation and leisure time.*** *(Author's Collection)*

***In the late 1800s, there were several crudely built structures housing rowboats on the Bay View beach.*** *(Author's Collection)*

anticipation of a big resort season. Superintendent Hall and the trustees of the resort should be seen and induced to reconsider."[1]

Since bathing was "frowned upon" and the beach was rocky, in the 1890s, many resorters swam along the Kegomic shoreline east of Bay View, the sandy banks of Petoskey State Park, and the Menonaqua Beach areas at the east end of the bay. At Kegomic there a bathhouse erected with two changing rooms, one 9x12, and the other 7x12. The cost was $1 for a private swimming lesson and twenty-five cents apiece for a class of three. That beach was so popular that the *Daily Resorter* observed in 1887: "It would have taxed the accommodations of half a dozen bath houses to care for all who were enjoying a dip in the crystal waters."[2] With the lack of adequate facilities, resorters took to the woods. At the Bay View beach, a boathouse was erected in 1887 and was open from 6 a.m. until 9 p.m. for boat rentals and rowing lessons. The crude structure also served as the living quarters for the recreation director.

Mary Farnsworth described her memories of the 1890s in a 1964 letter to her relatives:

> *On the beach there was a boat house large enough to accommodate the family "navy" and also my grandfather's hobby – stone polishing. The "navy" consisted of a rowboat large enough for the whole family, and heavy enough to require two pairs of oars; a duck boat in which we children learned to row, and which we were allowed to operate on very calm days and not more than about 200 feet from shore; and a very light and extremely tippy bark canoe which my father had bought from the Indians. It could carry one passenger guaranteed not even to "bat his eyes" during the trip. We used to say that father invited only people with their hair parted in the middle. The other half of the boat house was furnished with two grindstones revolving through water and several boards covered with felt impregnated with some chemical – for grinding and polishing the Petoskey stones which then could be picked up by hundreds along the beach....*
>
> *There was no sandy beach at Bay View for wading or swimming,so we rowed across to the "Sand Banks", usually with a picnic lunch. The tannery was over there and we sometimes brought back sacks of tan bark for surfacing garden paths.*
>
> *Mr. Seely who had a very superior Roque Court [near today's Stafford's Bay View Inn] where the old gentlemen of the neighborhood assembled every day. There was a tacit agreement between Mr. Seely and the children that if we were very careful not even to step on the pristine surface of the court, to say nothing of ever*

*running across it (!) we would be privileged to play croquet on it the day before it was sprinkled and rolled (a bi-weekly ritual).*[3]

The number of young people was sizable. As early as 1888, there were fifty-four children who attended the children's Sunday services. In 1900, nearly 350 children took part in the Children's Day. With that many children on the grounds and literally no organized sports, the do-it-yourself style of recreation was taken literally by the young boys who found their own form of wreck-creation. Trouble erupted when the boys amused themselves by cutting tent ropes, breaking lamps, ringing bells at odd hours, and engaging in other pranks. In 1890, a Mrs. Kennedy began Young People's meetings in an effort to curtail the mischief.

Children's activities in those days were what the adults thought they should enjoy. Horace Hitchcock took up the cause and organized the first Boys' and Girls' Club - through the university with professors teaching the sessions! Activities included the study of stone quarries, sand dunes, forests and lakes through picnics, excursions, and illustrated travel lectures - informative but certainly sedentary. The cancellation of the program in 1907 and 1908 meant there were no organized children's activities. But by 1909, children's classes included Sloyd (woodworking) and art. A Miss Andersen took over the Boys' and Girls' Club of forty-five children in about 1910 - emphasizing Norwegian folk dancing.

With a kindergarten for the little children, woodworking and Norwegian folk dancing for the elementary age children, the teenagers and college students needed action, and so they formed a social group, the Marshmallow Club: "Two enterprising young men [R. O. Austin and C. O. Davis] inspired by the greatness of the cause, collected this dormant force into one mighty organization 'which is to go down in the annals of history,'" is how Hall described it in 1896.[4] The goal of the club was to "drive dull care away." Membership reached a maximum of seventy-five for the moonlight excursion on one of the bay steamers. The club had officers and a membership pin which was a badge of birch bark inscribed with the letters MMC. There was a five-cent tax on all members for food for picnic outings. Meeting notices were tacked to a tree outside Loud Hall. The season ended with a 6 a.m. rowboat trip on the bay.

***Recreation and fun were left to the campers' imagination in the early days. Here at the Octagon Cottage, Ralph Apted made a toboggan slide for his family to enjoy.*** *(Author's Collection)*

*Tennis was one of the earliest sports enjoyed by the campers. The first court was built on the site of the present courts.* (Author's Collection)

Tennis was one of the earliest organized sports. In 1891, the Bay View chapter of the YWCA built a tennis court in Fairview Park for the association members, increasing the total number of association courts to five or six. That meant that at least one clay court was in good enough condition for "skillful" playing. Cottagers themselves arranged for tournaments between Wequetonsing and Harbor Point on a sporadic basis.

The newspaper often chided the Bay View team for its lack of commitment and organization. "If Bay View is to make any showing in the coming tennis tournament, her players should get down to work, and be in the best possible shape for the event. Bay View has plenty of good material and is abundantly able to cope with any of the surrounding resorts. The trouble will lie, if anywhere, in lack of practice....[5], the *Daily Resorter* assessed in 1891. Compared to the surrounding resorts there was a lack of enthusiasm. To improve the situation, Superintendent Hall began the Department of Physical Culture in 1891 under the Bay View Summer University. The *Daily Resorter* approved: "This increase in athletic interest is to be commended for it affords the young people of Bay View an opportunity for profitable spending of their many idle hours, which are now to a great extent wasted in hunting for something to do."[6]

The affable Reverend A. Bowen of the U-M was hired to head the new athletics department, and he instituted Bay View's first tennis tournament in 1893. It included gentlemen's singles and doubles. The following year, Bowen ran open tennis tournaments for men's and ladies' singles, and men's doubles. The Bay View tennis team competed against the teams from nearby resorts. That summer, Bowen added two new clay tennis courts at the waterfront, which the association took charge of maintaining and renting to the public. Turf courts rented for fifty cents an hour, while clay courts rented for seventy-five cents an hour. Of course, each rainstorm meant delays to recondition the clay courts.

After three seasons, Bowen took a pastorate at a Boston Methodist church, and the tennis courts fell into disrepair. Tournament play was discontinued. In 1900, Charles G. Maywood was hired as tennis manager and he laid down rules for the courts: "No person shall go on the courts except with tennis shoes. Periods of play shall be even hours governed by the clock on the grounds."[7] Tariffs were set at $1.25 for the season, eighty cents for two weeks' play, fifty cents for one week, and ten cents for an hour's play, which was a reduction of the charges in the Bowen days. Despite Maywood's efforts, association courts were dilapidated, and the number of courts dwindled to three. Fed up with the situation, Aaron T. Bliss, nephew of Michigan's governor, turned the lot adjoining his cottage at Block 16, Lot 4, into a tennis court in 1906. The family held tennis tournaments for men's singles, junior singles and doubles, with prizes for the winners.

Despite the inconsistent conditions, outstanding tennis players were attracted to the area. In 1908, Hal C. Malone, who represented Georgetown University in the eastern tennis tournaments, and Charles Benton, Cleveland's junior champion, played for Bay View.

Benton went on to win the Ohio doubles championship and the Michigan singles championship. In New York, he won the Great Lakes Championship and, at Cornell University, he was the singles champion. In Bay View, he oversaw the building of two new tennis courts in 1909 and formed the first Bay View Tennis Association in 1910. In 1912, Benton returned to Bay View to manage the Bay View tennis courts and tennis thrived.

In 1908, court rates were raised to five dollars a court for the season, and by 1913 costs were up to six dollars for a doubles court. With the added interest, rules had to be enforced. "Contrary to the custom in other years, privilege of playing on the doubles courts must be bought by all four participants in the game at once, instead of piecemeal purchasing with vacancies left for other purchasers," the newspaper reported.[8]

In 1914 when Benton was no longer on the grounds, tennis became known as a "mournful affair." Complaints were that the five association courts at the waterfront and in Fairview Park were in such deplorable condition that star players would not come. "The only court which has approached worthiness this year is the Bliss private court on Beech street [sic] and even this court is marred by neighboring trees, bushes, and banks," writer Blanshard reported.[9]

Finally, in 1918, the association reinstated the Bay View open tennis tournament. The Thomas Gordon, Jr. Challenge Cup was a handsome sterling silver trophy valued at over $100. Virginia, Cordelia and Beatrice DeVol of the Terrace Inn helped organize the event, along with Edgar Rombauer, Jr., son of Irma Rombauer. By 1923, tennis competitors were coming from twenty-five states, universities such as Yale, and local communities such as Mackinac Island to compete on the waterfront courts. There were six singles and six doubles events, and players included nationally ranked stars. The annual tennis tournament, which followed the United States Lawn Tennis Association rules, was held yearly from 1918 to 1941.[10]

Later in the 1970s, Dave Berles, coach at Grand Rapids High School, took charge of the tennis program. Berles had a long connection with the Petoskey area being the grand nephew of U.P. Hedrick, author of the 1948 national bestseller about his youth in Harbor Springs, *The Land of the Crooked Tree*. With only a few players and very little interest, Berles built up the tennis program over twenty-four years. During his tenure, Berles was Michigan Class A Coach of the Year in 1980 and was inducted into the Michigan High School Tennis Coach Hall of Fame in 1994. In 2001, he retired from his Bay View position after three decades of successful club management. Membership, including people from the entire surrounding Petoskey area, was over 250. It is so busy that during "high weeks," all seven courts were in constant use and more courts were added in 1980 and 2006.

Tennis wasn't the only sport enjoyed by early residents. By far the most popular was America's favorite pastime – baseball - which captivated the Bay View people as well as the entire northern Michigan region. In 1888, the resort boasted three teams: the Bay Viewites, the Bay View Juniors, and the Bay View Babies. By 1893, the Bay

***The Young Women's Christian Association (YWCA) built the tennis courts in Fairview Park where Voorhies Hall is now located.*** *(Author's Collection)*

Viewites were competing against teams from Elk Rapids, Pellston, Oden, Petoskey, Charlevoix and Traverse City as well as the Wequetonsing and Harbor Point resorts. Over the following decades, the squads played teams from the Detroit Athletic Club (DAC), Sault Ste. Marie, the Mackinac Island soldiers, the long-haired House of David team from Benton Harbor, and the engineers from the U-M Douglas Lake research camp.

Rivalry was fierce. For a game between Petoskey and Bay View in 1895, they secured an "unbiased" umpire up from Chicago, while Bay View tried to get a pitcher from Pittsburgh who failed to arrive in time for the game. Bay View then secured a pitcher from Washington University in St. Louis for the rest of the season. When the Bay View team beat the Hustlers of Traverse City, Harbor Point sent a telegram congratulating them. In 1908, Bay View finally won a game against Wequetonsing, to everyone's astonishment including the *Daily Resorter* reporter: "Sneak, knockers, sneak. Throw away your hammers, and get ye to the woods, for Bay View defeated Wequetonsing yesterday on their opponent's grounds. Rigged out in their handsome new suits, the Bay View team traveled to Wequetonsing on Tuesday afternoon, and in a game marked by brilliant plays and team work on Bay View's part, defeated the Wequetonsing team to the tune of 15 to 3."[11] Two days later Wequetonsing returned the favor.

In the 1890s, competition was moved from the eroding beachfront to Fairview Park. The teachers'-versus - preachers' game, though, drew a large crowd, and the cracking bats and cheering crowds annoyed the Fairview Park cottagers. After several seasons of complaints, Coach Reverend Alexander Cooper, president of the Hay Fever Association, pleaded for a proper field: "What we need most of all is a good diamond to play on. I believe that our baseball team will never be the perfect success it ought to be until the patrons of Bay View, who are abundantly able to do so, come to our aid and give us a good diamond. At a very small expense a diamond could be made in Fairview Park. This park was planned for recreation and then some trees were put in to stop recreation. If we could raise this small amount necessary to put a diamond in shape in the park we could give the people of Bay View free games as they do at Chatauqua [sic]."[12]

Regardless of appeals, the Fairview Park residents were resolute. So Cooper quit and the baseball team faltered. After several years, he reassumed management, renting Petoskey's Recreation Park for all area teams to compete. Through the efforts of Charles Fallass, owner of Petoskey's Fallass Drug Store, the field on Knapp Avenue, away from the unreceptive cottagers, was made available. The association needed to use part of the field as a "rick" yard to store and sell wood, so the baseball diamond was not entirely cleared. Despite the complications, games were played on a roughed-out Knapp Avenue field (now Swift Field), in 1908 and the team won the regional championship. In the 1912 and 1913 seasons, Bay View didn't lose a single game which made it difficult to schedule games since the other teams would no longer play them.

Then in 1923, Irma Rombauer's husband Edgar and Dr. Charles Swift, chairman of the recreation committee, raised $4000 to fully develop the field. After that, Bay View had its strongest teams. They were resort champions nearly every season for two decades. The most famous player was Stanley S. Kresge, who played centerfield. His son Bruce said Kresge was such a good player that he considered a professional career in baseball. Fay Thomas, who pitched for Bay View during these years and had a twenty-two game winning streak, pursued a professional career with a Los Angeles team in a Pacific coast league. The last time Bay View participated in the local baseball league was in 1956 when they had a baseball team sponsored by Capital Airlines. Now, from time to time there are competitions in tennis and sailing, but the friendly rivalry created between the local communities and resorters of the early days is gone.

Bowling was popular during the first decade of the twentieth century, but it was also the subject of controversy. Many opposed it, claiming that, under its charter, the association could not legally sponsor such a "sport." Others protested because in most cities bowling alleys were attached to saloons or associated with gambling. W. B. Chew commented for the local paper: "The danger is that it will lead to other things."[13] What it led to was a gift by Hall in 1910 of Recreation Hall, which included four bowling alleys and a heated swimming pool. Perhaps to the horror of the conservatives, the board of trustees eagerly accepted the gift, and Recreation Hall was built near the pier on the beach.

The alleys came under the management of the athletic director, who had his office in the front of the building. Boys were hired to replace pins in the alleys and tournaments were held regularly for years. Dorothy McVittie was the most eminent bowler, winning the girls' bowling championship each summer from 1910 until 1917. She won so often that the athletic directors refused to give her prizes. Later, she married Bay View's centerfielder, Stanley S. Kresge.

The waters of Little Traverse Bay were polluted from the residue of the many steamers and cruise ships that plied the waters, the raw sewage that Bay View and other communities dumped daily into the bay, as well as from the scum from the Tannery Factory in East Bay View and the Bear River lumber mills. The lake's frigid temperature as well as the pollution added to the need for a heated swimming pool. Recreation Hall's swimming pool had a capacity of 15,000 cubic feet and ranged from three to eight feet deep. Directors boasted that it had a diving platform and changing rooms. Swimming lessons were offered to all age groups every day from 9 a.m. to 9:30 p.m. In addition to lessons, for twenty-five cents a swimmer could get a suit, a towel and a bath.

While the pool was a wonderful addition to the

grounds, there were problems from the start. The very first season, a crack caused by the winter ice developed in the concrete. Then, there were the widely fluctuating Great Lakes water levels. The hall was built at a time when the lake levels were extremely low. Within a few years, the water rose so dramatically, it continually flooded the cellar where the pool's machinery was located, and the building foundation rotted after only six seasons. In 1916, the board of trustees considered a plan of running a dock along the building or placing stone-filled cribs along the beach to protect the building. Ruined by the constant flooding, that summer the pool's heating system had to be replaced. So, the pool was closed. Since it was a very hot summer, people began swimming again in the bay. By 1917, the lake level was three feet above the pool which was closed again for the season. Then, the young men who managed the recreation program started leaving to join the armed forces in World War I. The supervision provided by these athletes was evidently missed. In 1918, a young boy, Gerald Curley of Petoskey, drowned at the Bay View dock despite the life saving efforts of five local physicians who were on the beach.

Hall and the board of trustees were not entirely imprudent in building Recreation Hall at the beach. The building was designed by W.E.N. Hunter, the competent Detroit architect who later designed the John M. Hall Auditorium, but there were no engineering or feasibility studies or public records of lake levels that would have alerted them to the extreme variations in water levels and severe erosion. Since 1875, Bay View has lost 600 ft. of shoreline east of the Bay View dock and 300 ft. west of it.

The popularity of Recreation Hall with its pool and bowling alleys made it profitable for the association. On July 8, 1914, Bay View Treasurer Thomas Gordon reported that in the first three years of operation, the building had brought in $767.28 which was put in the constantly evaporating library building fund. Writer Paul B. Blanshard described the atmosphere: "It is the fusion of recreation and educational advantages which make Bay View the happiest place on earth to spend a vacation."[14]

During the early years, the athletic department was headed by Methodist ministers and later, by "letter" men from various colleges and universities. While directors for the men's sports were always young men, a woman directed women's sports. For a few years, an intriguing character, Madame Alberti of the Madame E. Alberti School of Expression in New York City, led women's athletics. She was followed by a succession of women physical education directors. By 1925, Bay View was turning to Petoskey for help with its recreation program. Walter J. MacMillan, physical education director of the Petoskey schools, was hired to direct the recreation program. The cost was ten dollars for Petoskey children and fifteen dollars for Bay View children. The parents had to provide transportation to and from activities, which didn't go over very well. At the urging of members of the Men's Club, Bay View hired its own professional recreation director with trained assistants from the University of

*It was always a big day when the circus came to town. Here the performers are pictured in front of the Bay View depot, taking the elephants to the fairgrounds east of Bay View.* (Courtesy of Marion Caveny)

*Ernie Gray was known as a "fresh air" person when he arrived in the early 1930s to take over the recreation program.* (Courtesy of Luella Gray)

Wisconsin. "If the parents of the community cooperate there is no reason why Bay View cannot have a recreational program that will fulfill a long-felt want," said Dr. Roscoe Sleight, chairman of the Recreation Committee.[15]

The year 1931 was a momentous one in Bay View's recreational history. Dr. Kennedy, president of the association, and Dr. Roscoe Sleight, dean of the Bay View College of Liberal Arts, hired Ernie Gray of Albion to take over the boys' program. The girls' program was still under the leadership of women counselors. Gray was described as six-foot two- inches tall and a fairly slender "fresh-air type of person" with an athletic background as a coach at Albion High School.

After only a few years, Gray took over the entire program, for both girls and boys, and began meeting in 1937 in the old bookstore and Speaker's Stand on the campus. The growing program created renewed interest in the beachfront. Since the initial days of the camp meetings, when the steamers delivered worshippers, the beachfront had been important to Bay Viewites. As early as 1879, one of the trustees, A. P. Moors, built a wooden dock to allow the steamers to unload camp-meeting goers. Since then, the association has spent millions on new and renovated docks and breakwaters. Transportation needs and sports such as fishing, swimming, row boating and sailing have always justified the expense.

The history of the Bay View dock reflects man's age old struggle with nature. Who was winning depended on the moment. Beginning with Moors' dock, new docks have been repeatedly built and subsequently destroyed in storm after storm. It seems as soon as a dock was built, Mother Nature would take it out. An 1888 *Daily Resorter* writer remarked how extraordinary it was that their present dock had weathered two winters. Even when the dock remained intact though, there were constant complaints from the draymen about the rotten boards, which made it difficult to safely unload baggage and passengers from the steamships. In 1897, a young girl drowned at the dock falling off the ferry as she was unloading.

One of the worst storms came in the fall of 1916, when the dock was hit by a large tidal wave and com-

*Since the early days, the waterfront has been a place for recreation.* (Author's Collection)

pletely destroyed. Much to the consternation of the locals who enjoyed fishing and strolling, it took several years to completely repair it. During this time, there were some swimming activities at the beach other than bowling.

During the 1920s, the newest dock was forever being fixed but was somewhat usable. In 1921, just after World War I, Raymond Edmunds took a job waiting tables at the Howard House (now Stafford's Bay View Inn). A Virginian, he was a former member of the US life-saving crew and a veteran of the war. Obviously, he was in great physical shape. In August, he decided to swim Little Traverse Bay. Horace B. Rose, co-proprietor of the Howard House, and several others took Edmunds to Harbor Springs, where they advised him against making the crossing because of the high winds and waves. Sure of his abilities, an unwavering Edmunds dove off the Harbor Springs pier about 2:30 p.m. in heavy winds and white caps. Accompanied by two row-boats, he arrived on the Howard House beach three hours and twenty minutes later where Rose, who had driven back from Harbor Springs, and a crowd of reporters and spectators greeted him with cameras.

Fame caused Edmunds some dismay. Local papers reported that the "black" man was the first person to swim Little Traverse Bay. Some people claimed that a "black" man could not have accomplished the feat. Then, the local and national press referred to him as a "Negro", when in fact he was one-quarter American Indian, one-quarter Hawaiian, and half white. A few weeks later at the Bay View dock, Edmunds had to give a "demonstration to a crowd of 300 of his abilities in life saving, fancy diving, speed and long distance swimming strokes".[16]

In 1928, another storm dismantled the latest dock. This time, the trustees decided to shore up the dock near the beach and abandon the outermost cribs since the steamers were no longer servicing tourists and the automobile was meeting transportation needs. The dock was now needed for recreation, not transportation.

Then the Depression hit. So it was not until 1934 that a new dock was put in when Katherine Foley, Civilian Works Administration (CWA) director for Emmet County, applied for state funds for major projects around Little Traverse Bay. Unemployment in Emmet County was between forty and forty-five percent, and work was desperately needed. So the Bay View pier was included in the Emmet County CWA projects. That new Bay View dock cost $2431.50 in labor and $41,786.81 in materials. This time it was concrete, not wood.

This new dock was not entirely what Bay View had hoped for. So in 1937, Charles Ditto, superintendent of Bay View, finished the work with twenty truckloads of boulders which were placed on the west side of the dock. By 1939, the cottage owners were discussing a more permanent dock at the annual meeting. So every few years, more concrete was added to the dock surface to keep it usable.

With a usable dock and lots of interest, the growing swimming program needed a warm shallow pool for lessons for young children. The broken down swimming pool in Recreation Hall was boarded over in 1924 with a wooden plank floor and was unusable. So, in 1938, a wading pool and sandy area were created on the waterfront side of Recreation Hall. Ten years later, a storm took it out. With continuous repairs a second one lasted until the 1980s, when a new pool was installed. It too fell victim to Lake Michigan's viciousness. Finally, in 1999, a new 40x16 foot rectangular pool, $1^1/_2$ x $3^1/_2$ ft. deep, was built. This pool was located in front of the Recreation Hall.

*During the Kennedy years a concrete dock was built to withstand the harsh Lake Michigan weather. (Photograph by Author)*

With the problems at the dock and the cold water, sometimes the swimming program was conducted at the shallow and warmer east end of the bay. In 1940, tragedy struck Bay View's swimming program again when eight-year-old George Beeson, Jr., of Bay View and Crawfordville, Indiana, drowned at Menonaqua Beach. He disappeared while wading with nine companions in waist-high water. The other boys immediately ran to tell their leader, Ordel McElhaney, but the camp leaders could not find little Georgie. An airplane from Emmet County Airport was brought in to join the search. Dr. George Maksim of Burns Clinic believed Beeson had suffered from "cold shock," since he was found in water where he could easily have stood up. Leaders have always felt that he had had some sort of seizure. Recreation director Ernie Gray's oldest daughter Jane said her father was affected the rest of his life by this experience even though nothing could have been done to save the young man. At the beachfront, his philosophy and slogan, "Fun and Recreation for All", took on a deeper meaning. As a result of this tragedy,

Gray developed the "buddy system", and campers were forbidden to swim alone. "We are responsible for the other fellow" became known as the "Bay View way."

Fortunately tragedies were never as prevalent as storms and bad weather. In the spring of 1952, Recreation Hall now called the Rec. Club, sustained severe damage from several tidal waves. As it had in the early days, water seeped in under the floor. This time the trustees decided to raise the floor of the building two feet. Much to Gray's relief, the old 1911 pool was finally cemented in, and the entire building was deemed safe for use.

Wishing to rekindle the interest in sailing of the early days, in 1955, the recreation department purchased the "Windjammer," a wide-bellied Rebel that was good for giving sailing lessons to the campers. This purchase sparked a phenomenal growth of sailing. Some sixty sunfish and sailfish were housed at the Rec. Club and, in the 1960s, Bay View boasted the largest fleet in Michigan. A Bay View Boat Club was organized in 1961 for the purpose of promoting waterfront activity, encouraging safety and teaching good boat-handling and sailing skills.

It was not the first such effort. In 1910, the Bay View Yacht Club was organized with Commodore Charles X. Robinson and a team of officers. However, without a permanent dock for safe mooring for the boats, that club was short lived. The 1961 club organized regular races for teenagers, and invitational meets were scheduled between Bay View, Harbor Springs, Wequetonsing, Roaring Brook, Walloon Lake and Boyne City. Again, recreation was the means that brought about interaction between the resorts. Gray wrote in 1965, "As I look at our small harbor I am amazed at the number of craft anchored and used. This has been the biggest year for our boating area."[17] With the rise in interest in sailing among the young people and the introduction of the sailfish and sunfish, the back of the Rec. Club, where the pool had been located became the Bay View Sailhouse. With this success, by 1967 activity on the waterfront had reached an all-time high and so had the car traffic on Woodland Avenue (US-31). A walking bridge was constructed to give children safe access to the beach.

The tremendous enthusiasm for sailing among the young people was abruptly halted at the end of the decade when the water level of Lake Michigan reached another all-time low, thwarting both swimming and sailing. Then a 1968 storm took out the back end of the Rec. Club, and a concrete boat dock of sheet plate metal pilings was put in, something that would have saved the heated swimming pool had it been possible fifty years earlier.[18] The erosion continued until 1995 when Bay View undertook a project costing over a million dollars to bring in armor stones to stabilize the dock and the shoreline. It was financed through a self-imposed special assessment of the association members.

One benefit of the millions spent on the Bay View waterfront was the continued success of the recreation program. In 1955, the association raised $11,000 to build the Boys' and Girls' Club in honor of Ernie Gray and his contributions. A redwood building was erected at the edge of the trees on the field adjacent to Knapp Avenue. Since Dr. Charles Swift had been chairman of the 1923 Recreation

***When the lake levels were high in the1960s and 70s, sunfish races between the different resorts were extremely popular among young people.***
*(Photograph by Author)*

***Recreation has been a priority of Bay View since the early days and the program has continued to be a major reason why families return generation after generation.*** *(Photograph by Dr. Beverly Brandt)*

Committee when the field was first cleared, it was named Swift Field in his honor.[19]

With the new clubhouse, recreation continued to expand. Each year, Gray reorganized the program, making necessary changes to accommodate the popularity. Originally, when the club was meeting on the campus in the 1930s and 40s, it was divided into two groups, boys and girls. At the time of the dedication of the clubhouse in 1955, there were about 330 young adults and children enrolled under the direction of fifty-three staff members. Club counselors dreamed up the names of Chipmunks, Skunks, and Squirrels for the girls and Antelopes, Cubs and Bears for the boys, and the campers were divided not only by gender but by age. In 2003, the program had grown even more, so that two new groups were added, the Bunnies and the Wolves. That caused some controversy, because the name "Bunnies" has come to have other connotations. The Fawns included the five and six-year-olds, while the Tot Lot comprised of three- and four-year-olds.

In the early 1950s, Marcia and Harry Bethea began teaching craft projects to the campers in the old bookstore, pounding copper, doing block printing and making lanyards. Mary Spayde, a supervising teacher from Michigan State University took over with just a basket of lacing for lanyards, some junk, and a lack of money. She wanted to offer creative opportunities for youngsters who weren't athletic or interested in playing baseball or other sports. In 1992, a generous donor gave the money for a new craft building. Since then, the program has increased so much that two additions, also given by generous donors, have been built for storage and to house the electric machines safely away from the children.

The craft house staff is challenged by the task of creating projects for more than sixty children a day and some 240 campers weekly with a limited budget. The storage area is filled with recycled items such as stamps, cheese boxes, birch logs, meat trays, yarn, fabric, string, golf balls, paint and cardboard tubes, out of which such things as yarn octopi, paintings, hand plaster moldings, stick puppets and masks are made. Wood projects include a gumball machine fashioned out of peanut butter jars, a basketball game, stringed puppets, birdhouses, bookends, picture frames, airplanes and all kinds of boats. A tumbler for Petoskey stones runs twenty-four hours a day, seven days a week, just as the Farnsworth tumbler did a century ago.

A very popular event has taken place each summer since the 1960s, when a young man named Thomas

***In 2005, Mary Spayde was honored for longtime service to the recreation program. Seated next to her is her husband Sam Spayde, a former director of recreation and behind her are John Higgins, Bryan Shaw, Stephen Turkal, and Roy Harvey, all former recreation directors.*** *(Photograph by Author)*

*A swimming demonstration at the Bay View dock in 1960 when water levels were high.* (Photograph by Maxwell H. Doerr)

Shearer suggested holding an Olympics Day for all campers. Gray immediately acted on the idea and since then regular competitions have been held each summer. Originally, it was called the Tom Shearer Olympics, but Tom eventually changed the name to the Ernie Gray Olympics to honor the long time recreation director.[20]

The recreation program is an eight week program which services some 500 young people from Bay View and the surrounding area. However, because the staff is large (around seventy employees) the salaries are low, and most young people have to work other jobs during the summer. Since the program accepts all children, the staff serves campers who may be academically challenged, developmentally disabled, or have various syndromes. A system of awards equalizes success for all children. Former Director Roy Harvey summed up the meaning of the Bay View recreation experience and the 'Bay View way' saying: "it means caring for others and putting the other guy first. It is what the counselors most hope each camper will remember about their Bay View days."

The Bay View Recreation Department teaches children the benefits of a healthy lifestyle. On July 5, 2004, world class gymnast and United States Olympic gold medalist Mary Lou Retton paid a surprise visit to the Boys' and Girls' Club. In her talk to the campers, she bade them to follow their dreams, be all that God had made them to be, and to go ahead with their passion, even when people said they would fail. Impressed with the Bay View Recreation Program, she called it an ideal place for children, just like writer Blanshard had decades earlier. Now that national statistics show that the country's adolescent obesity rate is approaching 30%, in a country where busing has eliminated the necessity of walking to school and many communities have no sidewalks, and where financially-strapped school districts often cut physical education and the arts from curriculums, the recreation program is vital to the community.

***In the 1960s, Arthur Anderson, Bo Morley, Jack Whaley, Peter Sparling, and Tom Gattle formed their own band King Arthur's Court. Today as adults, they return each summer from all parts of the US to perform and raise money for the recreation program.*** (Courtesy of Arthur Anderson)

— CHAPTER TEN —

# Grace Notes

Not only has recreation always been important to cottagers but so has music and drama. The Bay View Music Festival, the oldest continuously operating music festival in the US, was begun in 1886 as part of the Summer University. In the 1930s and 40s when most orchestras offered only nine-month contracts and the country had few summer festivals, the Bay View festival boosted some of the most famous musicians in the country. However, the decline of the Chautauqua movement, competition from larger and widely funded music festivals, year-around orchestra contracts, as well as the changes in Bay View budget priorities in the 1950s, adversely affected programming. With careful planning, though, the department has continued to offer scholarships to talented students from all over the world and present quality performances to a receptive northern Michigan audience. Today, a young Director of Performing Arts Chris Ludwa is breathing new life into the program with an eclectic mix of popular and classical music, a variety of programming with innovative ideas that are attracting crowds and donors.

***Stafford Smith, owner of Stafford's Bay View Inn, was a close friend of Dr. F. Dudleigh Vernor. He attended Albion Summer School and worked for Dr. Roy Heath at the Bay View Inn.*** *(Photograph by Author)*

John M. Hall was so keen on having music as part of his first assembly program in 1886 that he invited his Flint church choir to stay at his Wayside cottage. He climbed out the second floor window each morning to let the women dress. The effort was worth it. While other independent Chautauquas imported entertainment, none were offering music education in conjunction with concerts at this early date - not even Chautauqua, New York, had a music school until 1889.

In Flint, Hall found Professor E. E. Stephens to head up the department. Prof. Stephens invited singers from the surrounding area to join in daily rehearsals in the amphitheater on the Bay View campus. Stephens stayed for two summers and Professor Calvin B. Cady from the faculty of the Ann Arbor Conservatory and the first director of U-M's Choral Union, took over in 1888. During these years, lessons were offered in voice, violin, piano, organ, mandolin and other instruments to as many as fifty students each summer, making the department one of the most successful in the Summer University.

Then, in March 1889, Hall found a director for the assembly music and separated that job from that of the director of the department of music in the university. Chautauqua had formed its own department of music and C. C. Case, who had inaugurated the vocal music tradition at the New York campground in 1879 by directing massive choirs in classic oratorios and published then widely-used collection of music, *Harvest of Song*, was not included. Seizing the publicity opportunity, Hall advertised that Bay View had accomplished a real coup by hiring Case away from Chautauqua. In the *Bay View Assembly Herald* he claimed that Professor C. C. Case, one of the "greatest chorus conductors and best music teachers in this country, has been engaged for Bay View for a series of years. Our School of Music with an already fine reputation will go up several notches higher."[1]

Case was on the staff from 1889 until 1906 and again from 1910 to 1912 until poor health prevented his return. Despite his length of service and a number of historical glimpses, little is known about him - not even his first two names. What is known is that he was from Kinsman, Ohio, and lived in various cities in that state, ending up in Oberlin. He had directed a 1000-voice choir in Kansas City for Dwight L. Moody and spent twelve years with the great evangelist.[2] Other reports place him in Boston, where he directed enormous choirs at various Methodist churches. In August of 1912, a chorus of male voices sang his Progressive Party campaign song, *The Old Red Bandanna*, at the national convention in Chicago.

Case generated enthusiasm in Bay View with his magnetic personality. Newspaper accounts tell how fans greeted him at the train when he arrived escorting him and his wife to their quarters in the upper floors at either Loud Hall or Hitchock Hall and back to the train three-weeks later. Each morning at 9 a.m., throngs of two to three hundred would gather in the Old Auditorium to rehearse the great oratorios. Case even took over the "Sunbeams," the children's chorus of 200.

Socially, these rehearsals and oratorio concerts were the main event. "It seems that at this period people sang because they loved to," F. Dudleigh Vernor remembered. "Before the automobile disrupted the peace and quiet of daily life, the joy of being together to sing was a great recreation: hence, the great choruses of those bygone days."[3] The quality of these early oratorio performances is uncertain. A concert-goer compared the 1935 production of *Elijah* with Case's 1912 rendition. "I remember 25 years ago there was scarcely one-third of the audience remaining when the oratorio was finished. I doubt if 25 persons [sic] left the auditorium during this production last evening."[4]

Talent for the conservatory came from Chicago and Boston, as well as Michigan. The Detroit Symphony Orchestra was not fully established until 1919, but the Theodore Thomas Orchestra, forerunner of the Chicago Symphony Orchestra, was reputed to be the finest orchestra in America. Harbor Springs was a mere twenty-one hour trip on the *Manitou* from Chicago, or a half-day's journey on the GR&I. With little competition, Hall succeeded in another coup. He hired the concertmaster of that orchestra, Max Bendix, to be Bay View's violin soloist, advertising this with a full-page picture in *The Bay View Magazine.* Bendix, a Detroiter, had been Thomas' first choice for concertmaster. "It is no exaggeration to say that he is the greatest orchestra player in the country and it is possible excelled nowhere in the country," wrote the editor of *Brainard's Musical World* in 1897.[5]

This early music program was remarkable for the quality of its artists. In 1891, the soprano, Genevra Johnstone Bishop, from Chicago's Second Presbyterian Church, made her Bay View debut, the first of many appearances spanning twenty-five years. Between 1905 and 1910, Katherine Hoffman of St. Paul, Minnesota, was Bay View's choral accompanist. As Madame Schumann-Heink's personal accompanist, she traveled with the great diva for over twenty years and performed her two 1910 Bay View concerts and the singer's return appearances in 1913. Allen Spencer, dean of the faculty and professor at the American Conservatory of Music in Chicago from 1892 until the late 1920s, was another early staff member. The pianist, who summered at Wequetonsing near Bay View, joined the staff about 1900. He represented Chicago's Kimball Hall, so Kimball pianos were shipped to Bay View each summer.

Other assembly pianos were shipped from either Detroit or Chicago. In the 1890s, J. Whitney & Co. of Detroit furnished Hallet & David pianos, including two grand pianos. Later, Chase Bros. of Detroit furnished Steinway pianos. In 1892, an organ was shipped from the Ann Arbor Piano and Organ Company for assembly use. In 1901, a Kimball pipe organ, furnished by M. B. Harner, manager of the Petoskey Music Store, was installed in the Old Auditorium. The 6000-pound, 393-pipe organ had two manuals - a Great organ with three stops and a Swell organ with three stops.

***Baritone Irving Prescott was a soloist for many years on the Bay View music staff. When he retired from the stage he worked on the administrative staff.***
*(Photograph by Author)*

In 1899, when Horace Hitchcock took over from Hall, the music program thrived. In 1901, Henry Eichheim, concertmaster of the Boston Symphony Orchestra, joined the conservatory. In 1902, the very popular violinist Leon Marx joined the staff. As a ten-year-old, Marx had toured the US and studied in Berlin with the famed violinist Joseph Joachim. Upon his return, he joined the Thomas Orchestra for thirteen years, leaving to become concertmaster of the Chicago Opera Company orchestra.

Marx must have had a generous personality. He remained loyal to Bay View through the difficult years leading up to the cancellation of the assembly program in 1907. He was exceedingly popular with the audience, and had as many as eight or ten violin students each season. Dr. F. Dudleigh Vernor, Bay View's longtime organist and composer of *The Sweetheart of Sigma Chi,* made his pub-

*Mary Valenti-Parsons was Liza in Pierce's 1980 production of* **My Fair Lady.**
*(Photograph by Author)*

lic debut on the Bay View stage in 1906 as a pianist performing with Leon Marx.

No doubt Marx and his wife loved the north country. They spent their free time picnicking and entertaining friends at Menonaqua Beach, with homemade dinners seasoned with sand and smoke. After an absence of about six years, Marx returned to Bay View in 1913 and formed a successful alliance with the theatrical assembly director, Wilbur Starr, conducting the pit orchestra for Starr's elaborate stage productions.

Starr came to Bay View as the assembly's baritone soloist in 1909. He liked it so much he purchased a tiny cottage at Block 17, Lot 14, and named it *The Music Box.* A native of Greencastle, Indiana, he was a graduate of DePauw University. He and his wife, a cellist and singer, were leaders of the Starr Grand Opera Company which toured the US during the lyceum days prior to Tent Chautauqua. He was a captain in the Spanish American War, the son of a captain in the Civil War, and a grandson of an army colonel. Besides his appearances on the assembly program, he helped out with music at Petoskey's Methodist Episcopal and Presbyterian churches. When Case did not return in 1913, Wilbur Starr took over as director of assembly music and totally changed the emphasis from static choral works to fully staged theatrical extravaganzas featuring large choruses and huge casts.

The accomplishment was far more monumental than it would seem. In the 1890s, static tableaux were in style, and elocution was the most popular subject taught in the university.[6] In 1892, for instance, Professor B.W. King's classes had the highest enrollment with receipts totaling $400. However, religious opposition to live theatre prejudiced the Bay View audience for decades against theatre arts as a vital part of the total program. The Ben Greet Players broke through the resistance nationally when they began touring the Chautauqua assemblies in 1904. Three years later, when Hall returned to Bay View management, he contracted the Players for the 1907 season.[7]

***The Ben Greet Players began coming to Bay View in 1907 doing a different Shakespearean play each day for a week. Ben Greet wrote letters from the Bay View House where the group stayed.*** *(Author's Collection)*

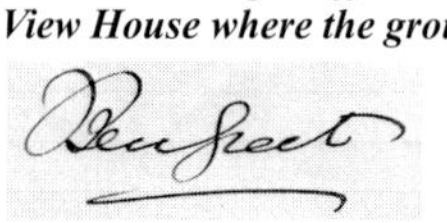

Acting on the interest in theatre created by the Shakespearean troupe, Starr produced two shows each summer - *Queen Esther* and *H.M.S. Pinafore* in 1913, *Joseph* and *The Mikado* in 1914, and *The Bohemian Girl* and *The Chimes of Norway* in 1915. The 1913 *H.M.S. Pinafore* production featured the Bay View Assembly Chorus; F. Dudleigh Vernor as Sir Joseph Porter; John Davis as Ralph Rackstraw; Starr as Captain Corcoran and Homer Larsen as the technical director. Blanshard reviewed the production in the *Daily Resorter*. "Mr. Starr's judgment in choosing Pinafore was vindicated by the large chorus of over a hundred voices which took part in the performance and the immense audience which filled the Auditorium to the doors....The hit of the evening was made by Dudleigh Vernor in the part of Joseph Porter, K.C.B. Mr. Vernor's inimitable mannerism kept the audience in continuous laughter. Maxwell Martin as Dick Deadeye and Miss Margaret Johns as Buttercup rendered several very pleasing solos. The other leading parts were successfully carried out by John Davis as Ralph Rackstraw, Harold Wright as boatswain and Mrs. Mary R. McBride as Cousin Hebe. The large chorus of sailor maids and sailor lads looked well and sang well and did credit to Mr. Starr who trained them and Bay View which claims them."[8]

Particularly impressive during the 1914 season was *Joseph*, an immense production for a cast of hundreds produced in the then unfinished Hall Auditorium. The musical about the biblical character was compiled from operatic scores of Haydn, Mozart, Gounod, Wagner, Bellini, Rossini, Mendelssohn and Verdi by the Chicago-based composer and playwright, William Dodd Chenery. The leads - Ridgely Hudson, Elmer Kneale, and Maxwell Martin of the Chicago Opera Company - sailed to Bay View on the *Manitou* along with six hand-painted sets and Oriental gauze costumes for a cast of 300. Local youngster George Ruth played the young Joseph. Children from Petoskey and Bay View formed the children's chorus featured in the first act at the Temple of Karnak. The Bay View Amateur Orchestra under Leon Marx accompanied the show.

The mammoth cast performed four shows - one night a week for four weeks. They followed it with a production of *The Mikado*, a formidable feat in itself. The dauntless Starrs rehearsed their huge cast at their tiny cottage and in the larger assembly rooms at Loud Hall and the Woman's Council. "If you don't know something is hard, then you don't know it is impossible," was how professional actress Terry Amy, a graduate of Chicago's Goodman School of Drama (now the Theatre School of DePaul University), characterized the enthusiasm.

Blanshard summed up the 1914 season's sensation, "Another great assembly has come to its close and Bay View can take a retrospective view. Few there are who rejoice that the five delightful weeks are past and many long for more of the knowledge and entertainment which this assembly has afforded. Although Bay View has been favored with equally fine programs in other years, not one of the twenty-five great assemblies here has drawn such large audiences or given such universal satisfaction. Ten times the great auditorium has been filled to capacity in accommodating the unusually large audiences....It is generally believed that the climax of the season was the opera "Mikado" [sic] which drew the largest crowd of the season and evoked enthusiastic applause."[9]

Tragically in January of 1916, Starr died in Wolf Creek, Ohio. "His adherence to the slogan 'make the date at any cost,' cost him his life. It was in the old Lyceum days and, crossing a swollen river, he was swept from his vehicle and was drowned," Martha Brockway wrote in a letter to her nephew Bruce Brockway on October 8, 1950. Starr's memorial service took place the following summer in the finally finished John M. Hall Auditorium with the Reverend Seth Reed, Judge Hays and the Reverend Lewis H. Manning presiding.[10]

After Starr's untimely death, Howard Dunham Barlow, a talented twenty-four-year-old scholarship student at Columbia University and director of the Modern Music Society of New York, replaced him. This ambitious youth was viewed as a refreshing change from his predecessors. He had an impressive habit of dressing in formal attire for concerts. "Director Barlow is a young man – in his twenties – and is proving popular with the young people who form the larger portion of the chorus. He is of the modern school of music and is putting aside old classics and oratorios and turning to compositions by today's composers," reported the local paper in 1916.[11] Barlow formed an artistically impressive team with Leon Marx who conducted the orchestra in 1916 and 1917.

Marx brought several professional musicians from Chicago orchestras to organize the first Bay View String Quartet and to augment the amateur orchestra. Among them was violist Herbert Butler of the Chicago Symphony Orchestra and the faculty of the American Conservatory of Music. Like Marx, he had studied with Joachim. Marcelline Hemingway Sanford, Ernest's sister, described what it was like playing in the orchestra:

> *My big thrill of the summer was being invited to visit the Trumbull Whites in Bay View, a mile from Petoskey. While staying with them - Mr. Trumbull White was the manager of the Bay View Chautauqua that year – I rehearsed and played with the Bay View Orchestra. I sat at the same stand with a violist from the Chicago Symphony Orchestra, one of the nucleuses of professional musicians who made up the Bay View summer orchestra. We amateurs added numbers but probably not too much else to the total musical effect. The learned*

*gentleman next to me - possibly tortured beyond endurance by my performance – offered to tutor me in the viola parts if I would stay after the regular rehearsals for an hour each day. I was grateful for his help. We put in several extra hours rehearsing together. On the night of the final concert that season, when we finished the last program, he patted me on the back. 'You kept right in time," he said kindly, "and I don't think you made more than half a dozen mistakes all the way through. It was wonderful!' That from a member of the Chicago Symphony was praise indeed."*[12]

Barlow directed the Bay View Assembly Chorus, rehearsing the choir members six mornings a week. Although he called for at least three hundred people his first summer, only sixty-four joined up. In 1916, he presented the choral and orchestra works, *The Peace Pipe* from Longfellow's *Hiawatha* and Rossini's *Stabat Mater.* In 1917, he led the orchestra and assembly chorus in Bruch's *The Cross of Fire* and, on Opera Night, the chorus joined the soloists in selections from *Faust* and *Lucia di Lammermoor*, an extraordinary accomplishment for an amateur choir. Ruth Kresge, whose family founded the Kresge Corporation, and Dorothy McVittie, future wife of Stanley Kresge, were both in his choir.

Mildred Place Panney, whose father was superintendent of the grounds, remembered Barlow. She lived at the superintendent's house where her mother had a box grand piano. Barlow liked that piano better than those on the stage. "I was just four at the time but I remember him coming over three days a week to do his composing at that piano" she recalled. Barlow composed *Marpessa* the summer of 1917, a tone poem for orchestra and tenor that premiered August 16. "It is an ambitious piece of work, thoroughly modern in methods and musical values. It is highly rhythmic and very effective in its representation of the clash between mortal and immortal love. It made a tremendous hit and at its conclusion the young composer was called forward again and again," reported newspaper.[13] *Musical America* reviewed the festival in its September 8, 1917, issue calling it an impressive event and Barlow's tone poem "an imaginative bit of writing, finely conceived and effectively written." Barlow later renamed it *Song of Idas*.

The soloist for the premiere was distinguished tenor George Rasely of the Bay View faculty and soloist at New York's Fifth Avenue Baptist Church. Vernor performed the piano parts in the orchestra.[14] To show their appreciation, the Bay View Assembly Chorus presented Barlow with a silver loving cup at the final music festival concert.

Unfortunately, a strong music program was not a priority of the Benson-Henderson management team that took over. At a public meeting on August 20, 1917, George W. Childs, owner of the Bay View House who was defeated in his bid for reelection to the Bay View board, asked newly-elected Trustee Silas Hays how Benson and Henderson's plans would impact Barlow and Marx and their plans to make Bay View "the greatest musical center in the United States." Hays replied that Dr. Benson had received a very high impression of Barlow and his associates, but "somebody had given Barlow a free hand and the music bills aggregated $2,100. Miss Onelli had received $500 for two appearances, Mme. Sundelius had received $500 for one, Miss Loveland got $50 and Miss Harman received $50."[15]

Barlow, who was only paid $250 for the entire season, joined the armed services in France. He subsequently became America's first great conductor and later gained fame as the conductor of the Columbia Broadcasting System (1927 to 1943) and conductor of the *Voice of Firestone* orchestra (1943 until 1958).[16] Ironically, his imaginative plans for a nationally significant Bay View Music Festival and his contemporary ideas on organization were implemented after his departure, and the size of his music staff was surpassed within just a few years.

Barlow wasn't the only martyr of administrative fiascos. Bay View's beloved violinist Marx left to continue his career with Chicago's Opera Orchestra and Lyceum Arts Conservatory. Dr. Charles H. Adams of Oberlin College, who had headed the music department since 1900, and his wife, Margaret J., also a singer and professor, left. They had given voice lessons, presented concerts for the assembly, ran the conservatory, secured the music staff, and were even on the grounds in 1907 and 1908 when there were no formal assembly or university classes. Vernor lamented their departure, as they left with bitter feelings.

Professor Frank H. Shaw, director of the Cornell College Conservatory of Music and organist on the Bay View faculty, took over from Adams. The following season, in 1918, Harlan J. Cozine, Director of the Conservatory of Music at Albion College, filled the position while the Bay View trustees overhauled the entire Bay View Assembly Program and Summer University. Attempting to fill the tremendous void left by the departure of Barlow, Marx and the Adamses, Cozine took over the Bay View Assembly Chorus, and Professor Howard J. Barnum of DePauw University brought his university orchestra to perform for the 1918 season. No assembly vocal soloists are mentioned, and there were few music classes offered.

When negotiations with Albion College were completed to form the Bay View Summer College of Liberal Arts and School of Music in 1919, Robert Guy McCutchan of DePauw University in Greencastle, Indiana, became the first dean, a position which combined the duties of both the university music classes and the assembly program responsibilities. He brought an impressive roster of some

*Director of Music William Reddick with one of his students Virginia Sangston. (Courtesy of Deborah Sangston Hindle)*

fifteen musicians to teach piano, voice, organ and instrumental music.

A most significant event occurred on July 28, the first Sunday night of the 1919 season. An open-air vesper service was planned for the beach, but rain spoiled the festivities and the concert was moved to the auditorium where the university artists "were heavily encored and a great many of those present expressed the hope that similar concerts might be given on coming Sunday evenings."[17] McCutchan combined this concert format with religious vesper services, a longtime tradition of the camp meetings. These vesper concerts were organized in the style of the John Philip Sousa concerts, where performers and soloists sat on the stage and proceeded to the front for their virtuoso solos. It was the beginning of the Sunday evening vesper concerts, still a popular tradition in northern Michigan.[18]

After seven seasons, McCutchan resigned on November 7, 1925. In a letter to the Bay View board dated November 5, McCutchan complained of lack of adequate funding for new artists: "The demand for them has increased very greatly and I do not find it possible to do as I have done in former years and secure them for a very small amount of money. I am of the opinion that the time has come for a very radical change to be made in the musical scheme and feel that it probably should be done now. I think it would be well to have some other man take over this problem and let him work out a plan along entirely different lines than have been followed for several years."[19]

His talented pianist William Reddick became the "other man" who replaced McCutchan. Like Barlow, Reddick was an exceptional musician. Before joining the staff, he had toured under the Redpath-Lyceum Bureau with Chautauqua singer Alice Nielsen, performing sometimes as many as 118 consecutive concerts in a summer. It was a prestigious position even though Nielsen was temperamental. In 1915 and 1916, Nielsen was the highest paid act on the circuit and had her own private railroad car in which she traveled sometimes as many as 20,000 miles a summer.

As music director, Reddick's congenial personality and an understanding of finances complimented his high professional standards. His staff included four vocalists, three pianists, an organist, a violinist, a voice teacher, a harpist and a music theory instructor. He conducted the Bay View Assembly Chorus, the University Choir and a small orchestra. Continuing the long tradition of presenting choral works, like Barlow, he turned to contemporary works such as *The Golden Threshold* by Liza Lehmann. Reddick preferred a small select choir of about twenty experienced singers. This smaller choir frequently performed on Sunday evenings, and a larger choir performed the oratorio work for the finale. Judging from Reddick's future reputation as a conductor, these ensembles had to have been exceptionally fine.

Reddick, his wife Irma, a staff contralto, and their son Bill enjoyed family summers together with Irma's parents, the Reverend and Mrs. A. M. Hootman. Hootman was minister of the Petoskey Methodist Church and an Emmet County school commissioner. Reddick and his young son were particularly fond of bait and fly fishing on Crooked River and Burt Lake. Many warm sunny days were spent with close friend Richard Vernor, brother of Dudleigh, on his boats, first the twenty-five-foot day cruiser *Nokomis* and, later in the 1940s, the thirty-eight-foot Chris-Craft, *Simokon*. The ships' logs give poignant accounts of adventurous trips to Good Hart and Five-Mile Creek on Lake Michigan. In 1926, the Reddicks remained on the grounds into September and, in heavy seas, they sailed to Charlevoix, East Jordan and Holy Island where they enjoyed a corn roast. Calling himself coxswain on some cruises and the purser on others, Reddick jokingly complained on the July 6, 1929, trip that "there was not a bathing suit on the boat." Irma referred to the boat as part of "Bay View's Fatal Attraction."

Born in Paducah, Kentucky, Reddick grew up on the Mississippi River listening to African-Americans singing their spirituals and spinning yarns, leaving him with a deep appreciation for the genre which he arranged into a book called *Roustabout Songs.* Once in a rehearsal with the New York Philharmonic, Conductor Walter Damrosch carped at him, "Young man, let me show you how the composer intended those songs to be played," as he took Reddick's place at the piano. The chorus and orchestra members snickered. Someone informed the red-faced Damrosch that Reddick was the composer.[20]

Artists on the assembly program often performed Reddick's works. Soprano Lucia Chagnon sang *The Velvet Darkness* at her August 20, 1919, recital. Tenor Arthur Boardman sang *April Ecstasy*, *Spanish Serenade* and *To a Little Child* in a recital on July 22, 1924. Baritone John Lester sang *Trav'lin' to da Grave* at a concert July 28, 1933. John Barnes Wells, Frederick Jagel and Nevada Van Der Veer also performed his songs in both New York and Bay View. As recently as 2005, staff artist Kelly Hale performed his piano solo *Espanharlem*.

During this time, grand pageants with casts of hundreds carried on the theatre tradition kindled by Starr. In 1918, Esther Bloomfield Merriman of the Northwestern University School of Oratory mounted a production entitled *America, Yesterday and Today.* The show had several episodes, the first featuring the Harbor Springs Camp Fire Girls in Indian dances. The second represented the wilderness and involved children as daisies, poppies and butterflies followed by the story of the state of Michigan and World War I. The final scenes included 150 people carrying Allied flags, dressed in national costumes and marching to the tune of various national anthems. Merriman, dressed as Old Glory in a white robe, narrated the show to an audience of 2000 people. Merriman's 1920 pageant, "Ye Olde Story Book", ended humorously when the lights went up, the curtain came down and the audience instinctively left, missing the final scene, "The Judgment of the Books" - much to the disappointment of Director Merriman, author of the show. Merriman continued to mount expansive pageants in Bay View with increasingly better stage settings and lighting effects. Ruth Mougey Worrell, a nationally known director who mounted one of the largest indoor pageants ever produced for the Red Cross, came to produce the 1925 show. She returned in 1950 to produce the seventy-fifth anniversary pageant.

In 1933, Reddick left Bay View because of career demands in Detroit and New York. In 1935, he was invited to direct the "Telephone Hour" and, in Detroit in 1936, he became the producer-director of the highly successful Ford Sunday Evening Hour, a program that featured the world's greatest musicians performing with the Detroit Symphony Orchestra. The weekly national broadcast reached an estimated audience of thirty million over 110 radio stations. Reddick gained a country-wide reputation as the director of the critically acclaimed Ford Sunday Evening Hour Chorus. Toscanini and Stokowski of the NBC Symphony Orchestra noticed his success and hired him to produce their radio show in 1942. In 1943, he took over for a student as conductor of the hit Broadway musical *Oklahoma!* After the war, he returned to Detroit to again direct the Ford Sunday Evening Hour.

These career demands proved excessive, and he and Irma divorced in 1941. Irma remarried in California and Reddick in New York. The breakup of the marriage left a deep impression on young Bill, as did the absence from their summer home. "I always regretted it when my father resigned from Bay View," William Reddick, Jr., once revealed.[21]

Through all of his career changes and personal conflicts, Reddick never ceased making annual excursions to Bay View to visit friends like Dutch Pailthorp (Hemingway's friend) and Dick Vernor. Many summer trips were spent entertaining celebrated opera stars like Gladys Swarthout and John Charles Thomas when they performed in Bay View. In 1948, Reddick left New York and finally, in the 1950s, bought a place on Walloon Lake.[22]

In the late 1920s, there was a national movement to establish instrumental music camps to foster music instruction among high school students. The National High School Orchestra Camp was founded at Interlochen in 1928, and, in 1931, Frederick Lewis of Ann Arbor, Michigan, founded the American High School Band. Arrangements were made for it to be held at the Recreation Building and perform in Bay View, Harbor Springs and Petoskey. More than forty students and eleven staff members assembled at Recreation Hall, using the space between the building and the tennis courts for marching practice. Three times a day they marched to the Hilton Hotel for meals. The following summer, the camp was expanded to include an orchestra, and concerts were given at the Bay View Auditorium, Petoskey's Pennsylvania Park, the Perry Hotel and Ramona Park.

In 1933, the name was changed to the American Band and Orchestra Camp. Lewis was assisted by Alexander Shuster of Michigan State College; D. C. Ryan, director of the Ypsilanti Normal College; and Alvin Davidson, director of instrumental music at the Petoskey Public Schools. Lewis planned to expand both the orchestra and band to one hundred members. Recreation Hall proved inadequate, and the camp was moved to Cheboygan in 1934 to a new facility, the Damrosch Bowl, although concerts were still given in Bay View. Later, in 1939, cottager Gilbert H. Wilkinson organized the Young People's Orchestra to entertain audiences at the association's annual meeting and at the Bay View Players' performance of *Mrs. Wiggs of the Cabbage Patch*. During the 1940-41 seasons, the group of between twenty and thirty high school students performed each Saturday evening before movies.[23]

Student bands and orchestras were not the only arts activities for young people. The Depression era was Bay View's golden age of theatre. The legendary DeWolf Hopper made a return visit to Bay View in 1934 with his own theatre company productions of *H.M.S. Pinafore* and *The Mikado*. Hopper's performance as Dick Deadeye is one of the earliest memories Dr. Jonathan Amy has of Bay View. His father, a professor in the Bay View College of

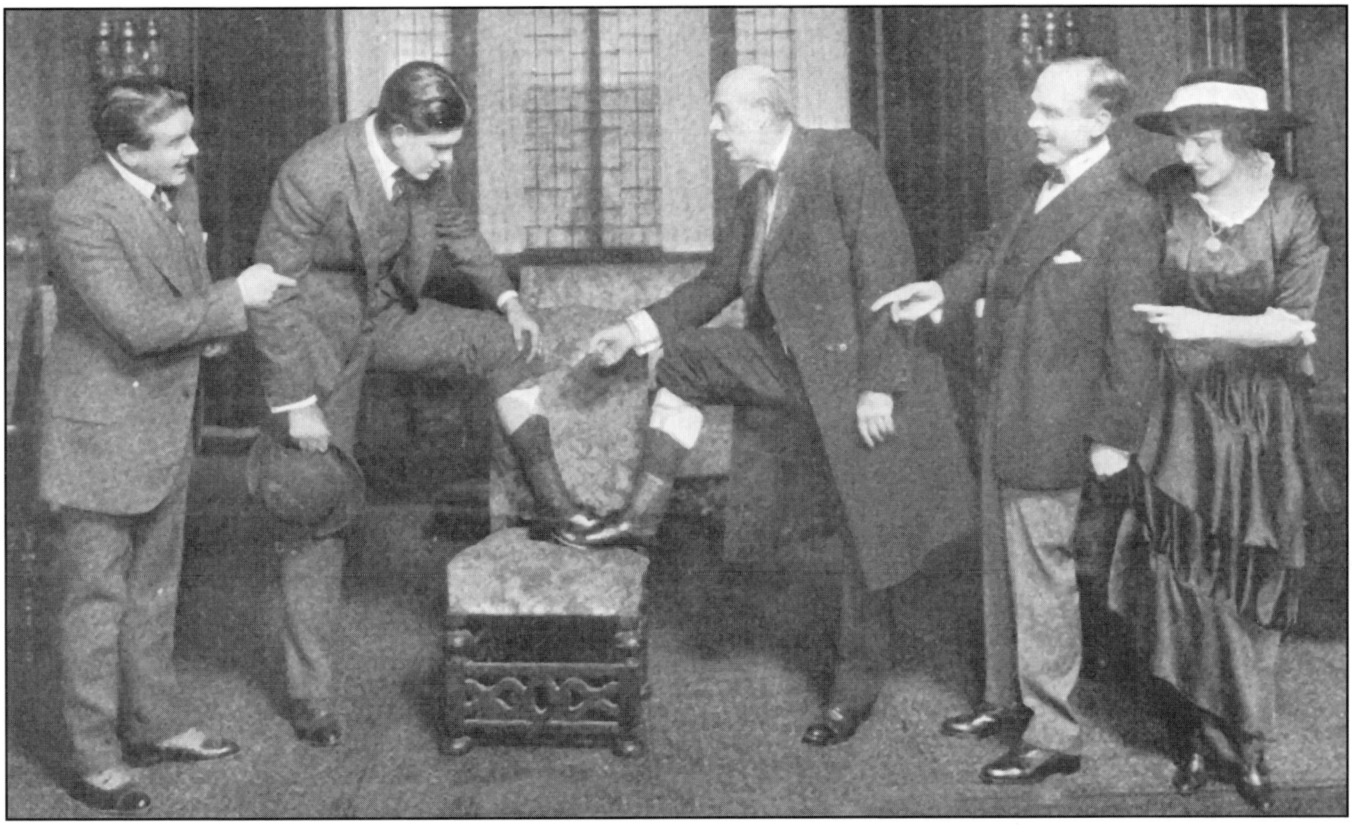

*The play "It Pays to Advertise" was one of the road shows on the program in 1931.* (Author's Collection)

Liberal Arts and Ohio Wesleyan, got him out of bed and took him to the balcony of the auditorium where they joined an audience of 1900 people to see the seventy-six-year-old veteran. When the show was over, Hopper recited *Casey at the Bat*, his famous encore.

The eminent Russian director David Itkin brought the DePaul Players to Bay View in 1936 and 1937. In 1936, the company performed *Holiday* and *Three Cornered Moon*. In 1937, the company presented *Fresh Fields* and *Holiday* again. For five years during the 1930s, the DePaul Players were that school's traveling troupe. Terry Amy said Itkin was an old-world teacher. "The basic principles of theatre at that time were the same in acting as they are today but the acting style was more of a presentational one rather than realistic."

In 1937, Professor Rollin C. Hunter joined the Summer College of Liberal Arts to teach *Fundamentals of Speech, Acting and Makeup* and *Principles of Play Selection* and *Production*. At the time, the Bay View board stated: "The proposed activities of the summer are an experiment to determine the interest of Bay View Residents [sic] in a permanent summer theatre. Long range plans are being formulated and will be carried out should the community response justify the present feeling of the Trustees that this enterprise will add materially to the attractiveness of Bay View as a summer home and make a substantial cultural and recreational contribution to the summer program of activity."[24]

Hunter formed the nucleus of the summer community theatre with Ohio Wesleyan students who starred in that school's spring productions and were therefore precast for the summer roles. Those actors received credit and free tuition for their Bay View courses. Bay View residents took part by "acting, building and painting scenery, making costumes, properties, lighting and general production."[25] Of the productions staged in the 1930s and '40s, Dr. Amy remembered elaborate costuming but noted that the sets were simple and easily accommodated in Hall Auditorium. "We had to move into the auditorium on Friday, rehearse that evening and present the show Saturday evening and then take the sets down for Sunday church."[26]

The effort was worth it. In 1938 *Rip Van Winkle* was presented on July 29, *Hamlet* on August 12 and a one-act play on August 13. In 1939, *As You Like It* was the featured production and a group of one-act plays was presented, in addition to Kate Douglas Wiggins' *Mrs. Wiggs of the Cabbage Patch.* That was particularly appropriate since Wiggins had been a lecturer in Bay View in the 1890s. Amy said, "President Kennedy [of Bay View] was a strong supporter of theatre and it flourished . . . It was Depression time, but we did have quality in our programs."[27]

Don Eyssen, also from Ohio Wesleyan, directed *Twelfth Night* and *Our Town* in 1940. In 1941, George Wilner of the University of Wichita took Hunter's position and presented both *The Tempest* and *Ten Nights in a Bar*

*Fred Patton had the connections with the great opera starts of the 1930s and 40s and each featured one of them concert such as James Melton and Jennie Tourel. (Author's Collection)*

*Room*, a favorite of the temperance movement of the nineteenth century. In 1942, Hunter returned to present *Brittle Heaven* and *A Midsummer Night's Dream.* Doris Hunter Mauch, who came to Bay View with her father, explained why the troupe stopped coming after 1942: "The students were not available for the plays. I think that the war kept everyone from traveling."[28]

Fred Patton, head of vocal music at Michigan State College, took over for Reddick in 1934. An opera singer, Patton had sung with James Melton on national radio in the *Revelers,* the singing group of the Cities Service Program, and for two seasons at the Metropolitan Opera. The Pattons enchanted everyone on the grounds. Their daughter, a model, fascinated young people like Virginia Crouse, later a heavy contributor to the festival. Mrs. Patton, a champion bridge player, won tournaments at the Petoskey Bay View Country Club. Under Patton's direction, the choir increased from forty to over 120 singers and their cottage at Block 40, Lot 4, was the scene of many parties and rehearsals. "He was about 46 years old at the time, about 5 ft. 8 in. tall, and 165 pounds. He was an engaging man but not beautiful," remembered Max Smith. Smith was a clarinetist on the music staff from 1940 to 1948, music director with the Charlevoix Public Schools and, later, director of instrumental music for the Petoskey School District. "He made things joyful for everyone on the staff."[29]

Like Reddick, he was a fine choral conductor but entirely different in style. "I think of all the people who have influenced me the most, it would be Fred Patton," said Donald Allured, nationally known organist, composer and handbell expert. "Patton had a very passionate way of conducting that brought out the beauty of the music. I find myself even today being influenced by my memory of him." At ten, Allured studied organ with Dr. Vernor and joined the Bay View Assembly Chorus, which rehearsed during the 1920s, 1930s and 1940s at Petoskey's Methodist Church.[30]

Musicians had few summer prospects, so Patton was able to enlarge the staff with many fine musicians. He formed an assembly quartet of vocal soloists, the Bay View String Quartet and the Bay View Male Quartet. Other instrumentalists included a harpist, three clarinetists, a flutist, a xylophonist, an organist, several pianists, and sometimes a cornet player and a trumpeter. He improved public relations by providing entertaining programs for local service clubs such as Kiwanis and Rotary, and wrote publicity columns called "Grace Notes."

After a six-year absence, organist Dr. F. Dudleigh Vernor returned in 1934. Together with Archie Black, he continued the popular duo piano tradition started by William Reddick and Allen Spencer in 1923. Most popular were their two-piano arrangements of Gershwin's *Rhapsody in Blue* and Handel's *The Arrival of the Queen of Sheba*. On Sunday evenings, Black and Vernor modulated musical interludes between concert numbers because both could improvise spontaneously.[31]

Patton is best remembered for bringing Metropolitan Opera stars to Bay View. When Hall contracted Madame

*James Melton*

*Etta Moten, the first African American to entertain at the White House, the real voice behind many films in 1930s, and Gershwin's first choice to sing Bess in his opera* **Porgy and Bess,** *gave a recital in Bay View in 1941 at Patton's invitation.* (Author's Collection)

Schumann-Heink in 1910, he began a tradition that Patton had the eminence to continue. He knew the singers personally and contracted Amri Galli-Campi, Frederic Baer, Anna Kaskas, Gladys Swarthout, Helen Jepson, Richard Crooks, John Charles Thomas and James Melton, who all filled the auditorium to capacity with each concert. During World War II, these singers needed work, but it was Patton's charisma that enticed them to venture to Michigan's North Country.

A highly significant recital Patton arranged for was that of the mezzo-soprano Etta Moten, who should have been a Metropolitan Opera star. A graduate of the University of Kansas in vocal performance, she was a personal friend of both Marian Anderson and Paul Robeson, and, at Eleanor Roosevelt's invitation, she was the first black singer to entertain at the White House. She also broke the color barrier in Hollywood, dubbing songs for movie stars Barbara Stanwyck and others. Moten was George Gershwin's first choice for Bess in his opera *Porgy and Bess* in 1934, but she didn't think the role was right for her voice and it went to Ann Brown. On July 28, 1941, Moten performed in Bay View a combination of African-American spirituals and classical vocal literature to a crowd of over 700.[32]

Patton also scheduled opera performances. In 1940, he joined forces with Hunter and Eyssen to mount a fully staged production of *Faust*, featuring himself as Mephistopheles with staff soloists Floyd Townsley as Faust and Thelma Von Eisenhauer as Marguerite. Two of the three were soloists at the Metropolitan Opera, so that production must have been noteworthy.

Patton also succeeded in bringing famous violinists to Bay View as well. Perhaps the greatest artist to join the Bay View music staff was the Russian-born violinist Michael Press, who came in 1935. A virtuoso noted in Boris Schwarz's book *Great Masters of the Violin*, Press had been on the Moscow Conservatory faculty from 1915 to 1918 and was decorated by six European rulers for his extraordinary talent. With his violin, he escaped after the Russian Revolution and immigrated to the US in 1922. He joined the staff of Curtis Institute and then the faculty of Michigan State College where he was the teacher of Dorothy DeLay, who later joined the Juilliard School faculty and taught Itzthak Perlman. Press commanded an astounding fee of $72 an hour for lessons and enthralled audiences of over 2000 every Sunday evening. "Press had a Stradivarius and the sweet sound of that violin is something I will never forget," remembered Allured.

"He was an incredible virtuoso," said Max Smith, who had studied violin at Michigan State College with Press and performed with him in both Lansing and Bay View. "Tradition was that at the Sunday concerts there was no applause," said Smith. "Michael was used to being a star. He expected the applause and he always got it."[33]

Press frequently commented that his Bay View summers were some of the happiest in his life. One of his stu-

*Violinist Hugo Gottesmann, longtime soloist with the Bay View Music Festival, was known throughout Europe for his interpretation of chamber music. As a Jew, however, he was forced to immigrate to the US from Austria before World War II.* (Photograph by Earl Child, Courtesy of Anne Sheaffer)

dents from Michigan State College, Marjorie Hoyt, the daughter of Reverend Myron E. Hoyt, pastor of the Community Methodist Church in Okemos performed with him playing a duet, Sarasate's "Navara" and other numbers. Then, on April 16, 1938, Press received a contested divorce from his first wife with whom he had three daughters, (one of whom, Dorothy became secretary to Detroit radio celebrity Karl Haas). In late April, the 65-year-old Russian eloped with his 23-year-old pupil.[34]

The couple's marital bliss was short-lived. Press suffered a heart attack that summer just before music week but insisted on appearing at the final vesper concert to play Saint-Saens' *Swan Song.* He told Patton that it would be his Bay View swan song. He passed away December 22, 1938, in Florida. Press was deeply loved, and finding a replacement was difficult. Frank Kneisel, son of the celebrated Boston violinist Franz Kneisel, succeeded him for the next three seasons. In 1941, 21-year-old Robert Mann, winner of New York's Naumburg Prize and, later, founder and first violinist of the Juilliard String Quartet, was the featured violinist. Then, in 1942, Patton found Hugo Gottesmann.

Like Press, Gottesmann was also an expatriate Jew. He was forced to leave his Austrian homeland in 1936 just before World War II. He and his wife Lia immigrated to New York where he conducted the Ballet Russe de Monte Carlo. He founded a quartet which played over the NBC Blue Network at the Academy of Music in Brooklyn. He became the fourth member of the famous Busch Quartet, with Adolph and Herman Busch and Bruno Strauman, concertizing worldwide and recording for Columbia Records. Pianist Rudolph Serkin performed with the group.

Unquestionably Gottesmann was Vienna's premier violinist prior to World War II. He was concertmaster of the Vienna Symphony Orchestra under conductors Richard Strauss, Bruno Walter and Wilhelm Furtwängler. He performed Beethoven's *Violin Concerto* for the centennial celebration of the composer's death with the Vienna Philharmonic at the Theatre an der Wien where the concerto premiered. Gottesmann excelled as leader of the Gottesmann String Quartet and was noted throughout Europe for his interpretation of chamber music literature. In Vienna, his ensemble performed the Schubert string quartets for the city's centennial celebration of that composer's death. In Bay View, Gottesmann took over the leadership of the string quartet, working with Felix Resnick in 1948 and Daniel Majeske in 1949 and 1950:[35] "I was a young man at the time and it was a rewarding experience working with someone like Hugo," said Resnick, leading violinist with the Detroit Symphony Orchestra for over 50 years. "He had a rich wonderful background which he brought to music. Working with him, I found the summer to be an intensely interesting one."[36]

Sixteen-year-old Detoiter Daniel Majeske joined the Bay View String Quartet in 1949. The child prodigy was studying with Ivan Galamian at Clevelands's Curtis Institute and debuted with the DSO in 1948. "Everyone was so excited to have someone of his talent playing here," remembered Thomas Shearer. "I distinctly remember his wavy hair. He was impressive." Bay View resident Ruth Dyer remembered how he played with his eyes closed. Gottesmann must have transferred his knowledge of the chamber music literature to the young musician. After leaving Bay View, Majeske joined the Cleveland Orchestra in 1955. In 1968, he became concertmaster, a position he held until 1993, performing under conductors George Szell, Lorin Maazel and Christoph von Dohnanyi. He was first violinist of the Cleveland String Quartet.[37]

Fred Patton left Bay View in 1944 for "health reasons." He had brought some of the country's greatest musicians and brightest young talent to the Bay View stage. Besides those mentioned were violist David Dawson of Indiana University; Clark Brody who later became principal clarinetist of the Chicago Symphony Orchestra; soprano Thelma von Eisenhauer of the Chicago Civic Opera Company and winner of the 1940 Chicago Opera Auditions; mezzo-soprano Winifred Heidt, winner of the 1939 Metropolitan "Auditions of the Air", and Metropolitan opera soloist Ellen Repp. Building on Reddick's foundation, Fred Patton had accomplished what both Barlow and McCutchan had wanted to do. He had built a nationally recognized music staff of outstanding musicians. Patton himself had had a major career as a singer at the Metropolitan Opera and on radio, been chairman of vocal music at Michigan State College and director of a very successful Bay View Music Festival. In the 1950s, his hometown high school finally awarded him a diploma.

Hardin Van Deursen of the U-M and the First Methodist Church of Ann Arbor replaced Patton in 1945. In three summers, he established the Bay View Opera Workshop and hired vocal coach Walter Taussig in 1946 and 1947 to work with students. Taussig worked at the Metropolitan Opera for more than fifty years and even coached Cynthia Munzer, wife of later Bay View Director of Music Gary Glaze. In Bay View, he found a quality group of soloists and students. He directed Opera Nights with scenes from *Carmen, Madame Butterfly, The Magic Flute, Lohengrin* and *Aida*, with himself as accompanist. Later, he worked with contralto Ellen Repp at the Metropolitan Opera. Taussig was such a valuable artist on the music staff that he was allowed to break one of the hard-and-fast rules of the association. "When they sent me the contract, it said 'no cats at Epworth Hall,'" remembered the ninety-year-old musician. "I wrote back and told them 'No cat, no Taussig'. They let me bring my cat."[38]

Bay View had survived both World War I and the Depression through Dr. Hugh Kennedy's skillful leadership. By the 1950s, Wade's building campaign garnered renewed interest and support from cottagers, but the diminished budget no longer allowed for the appearance of major stars. By the time Dean Harold Tallman, head of the

*Willard Pierce established the theatre arts program in Bay View utilizing talent from New York, the music staff, music students and thespians from all over Emmet County. In 2005, he was given the "eddi" Award by Petoskey's Crooked Tree Arts Council.* (Photograph by Amer Mufti)

Wayne State University music department, re-placed Van Deursen in 1948, the festival featured fine artists but not famous ones. Tallman brought in popular music and focused on youth with six appearances of the Detroit-area "WJR Make Way for Youth" with Don Large. Seated in the top row of the balcony at a 1952 show, Milton Anderson was inspired to establish The Young Americans, a highly popular and successful singing and acting troupe that appears each summer at Boyne Highlands Ski and Snowboard Resort near Harbor Springs and in Bay View and now has troupes performing all over the world.[39]

In the cash-strapped years of the 1950s, without funding for professional leadership, theatre was a void. After Hunter left in 1942, Bay View did not sponsor live productions for fourteen years until two local teenagers, Pauline Shambes and Linda Jones, wrote a musical comedy with choreography which assembly tenor Willard Pierce voluntarily arranged. "The young people were complaining that they didn't have enough to do, so they wrote their own show," remembered Pierce. "This gave them lots to do."[40]

By the 1950s Bay View had become pretty much of a closed community, like modern resorts today. Existing for the purposes of its membership, it had lost the vision of the early days. There was no longer the variety of famous lecturers, and the assembly consisted mainly of movies and preachers. Beginning with this group of teenagers, Pierce developed a broad concept of theatre which included casts and crew made up of people from all over Emmet County. He realized that Bay View needed the resources of the entire area-wide community if theatre arts was going to succeed. He began holding open auditions and selling tickets for productions in the Petoskey business district, eventually increasing sales to fill the Hall Auditorium for three nights each summer. He discovered new talent, trained local actors and actresses, and provided them confidence and experience through working with professionals that he brought in from New York. He developed a corps of loyal volunteers who worked with limited facilities and inadequate supplies to accomplish the impossible. His foresightedness was a cultural renaissance leading Bay View back to its original commitment of cultural opportunities for all.

"Willie," as he was affectionately called, was a Depression kid who was born in Richmond, Virginia. Raised by his mother, he was a boy soprano who began his stage life at the age of eight. On Saturdays, he performed on a radio program for which he was paid in gallons of ice cream. When World War II broke out, Pierce enlisted in the Army because a friend promised him a job in Special Services, assuring him he would be able to remain in Richmond. Instead, Willie was shipped to Louisiana and then to England. Twenty-four hours after D-Day began, the seventeen-year-old found himself under fire on the Normandy beaches. He then endured some of the war's worst fighting at the Battle of the Bulge.

*The musical* Where's Charlie? *in 1978 was one of Willard Pierce's successes.* (Photograph by Author)

*The House in the Woods was built in 1915. Later the name was changed to the Hilton Hotel and it was run by Mrs. Hilton and her daughter and son-in-law, Fred Sanquist until 1969 when they made it available to the Bay View Association for music student housing. The name was then changed to Crist Hall in honor of Robert and Ruth Crist of Wequetonsing and Chicago, benefactors of the Bay View Association who provided financing.* (Courtesy of Fred Sanquist)

Willard Pierce could never stay off the stage. In Germany after the war, he mounted shows for the troops. When he returned to the US, with funds from the GI Bill, he studied voice and theatre at Juilliard School, Richmond Professional Institute and the American Theatre Wing. "I regret now that I did not finish my college degree. The opportunities to work were so plentiful at the time that I chose to work and began touring the country," said Pierce.[41]

Pierce became the tenor soloist at Radio City Music Hall, toured the country with Columbia Artists and the Broadway production of *Annie Get Your Gun.* He began his longtime solo position at New York's Central Presbyterian Church and was music director at Christ Episcopal Church in Ridgewood, New Jersey, where the controversial Episcopalian Bishop John Shelby Spong was head minister.

Pierce auditioned for Harold Tallman in 1955 and was hired. He came to Bay View for three seasons. Then, in 1958 and '59, he appeared in *The Most Happy Fella* at the Paper Mill Playhouse in New York. When he returned in 1960, he decided that mounting shows in the large John M. Hall Auditorium with its time constraints was "for the birds." So that season he produced *Charlie's Aunt* at Voorhies Hall, a smaller venue where shows could run without the necessary late Saturday night clean up. "President Kilpatrick told us that Voorhies Hall was not being used enough and 'would we please, please use it for the play as well as rehearsals,' " said Pierce, remembering those days. "We had to do plays that people knew, nothing with a message. When we started in the 1950s, President Bishop Wade told me, 'You will do productions suitable to the community of Bay View.' So, in the early days we had to cut lines and change words in the scripts. For instance, Coke was used instead of wine. I still have my copies of some of those scripts."[42]

Then in 1963, tragedy struck again. Tallman, who had served as dean of music since 1948, was hit in the head with a saw blade and died of his injuries. The trustees then turned again to DePauw University and hired their Dean of Music, Milton S. Trusler. Trusler is credited with beginning projects that would set the stage for redevelopment of the Bay View Music Festival. In 1965, he produced the first fully-staged opera in twenty-five years, *Hansel and Gretel.* Third-generation Bay Viewite Liza Lee Collins remembered appearing in the children's chorus. "I'd only acted in small church and grade school plays up to that time," she said. More fascinated with the back stage preparations – the lighting, the scenery, and the trans-

*Josephine Hilton who built the Hilton Hotel in 1915 and her daughter and son-in-law Mr. and Mrs. Fred Sanquist Sr.* (Courtesy of Fred Sanquist)

*Mr. and Mrs. Ruth E. and Robert C. Crist.*
*(Courtesy of Ruth Crist Dyer)*

formation of the characters by soloists such as baritone Irving Prescott who played the father. She later majored in theatre.[43]

Three years later, Trusler resurrected the Bay View Orchestra under violinist Hugo Gottesmann for the purpose of establishing a Bay View musical. By this time, Pierce was directing the Bay View Players but took on the added responsibilities of directing and producing *Carousel*. "In his sweet, kindly manner, Trusler asked me to direct this production," said Pierce. "He wasn't asking me a question, though. I knew that I was GOING to direct *Carousel* that summer." By 1973, Pierce was producing two shows a season, a play and a musical. The Bay View Department of Theatre Arts Department was formally established, with Pierce as director, sixty years after Wilbur Starr mounted his elaborate productions.

As Bay View began mounting its own musical productions, Albion College severed its ties with the Bay View Summer School and School of Music in 1969, and Bay View was again forced to reorganize its educational program. The Bay View Conservatory of Music was formally re-established. Ruth E. and Robert C. Crist, who had generously provided the landscaping surrounding Voorhies Hall in the 1950s, donated the money to buy and renovate the old Hilton Hotel to house conservatory students. It was renamed Crist Hall. When longtime organist, Dr. F. Dudleigh Vernor, retired in 1969, Music Hall was officially named Vernor Hall in his honor.[44] After these achievements, Trusler resigned, and Dr. Ernest Sullivan of Alma College became the next director of music.

By this time, the music festival had fallen to an all time low. The college had been closed, and so the music staff was small and there were less than a half a dozen students. The music department had always maintained a number of students, but they were never professionally-oriented. "I never really had an ambitious student here," recalled clarinetist Max Smith. Soprano Elizabeth Humphrey from Juilliard School, a former Bay View staff member who is organist at the Congregational Church in Charlevoix, put it in perspective. "We had students but they were not of the caliber they have at the conservatory today."[45]

Dr. Ernest Sullivan turned the dire situation around – with lots of hard work. The Bay View Opera Workshop was re-established, and the music faculty was increased to include instrumentalists and an orchestra. The Bay View Woodwind Quintet was formed, and, with a gift from music student Adrian Boyer and others, the Bay View Concerto Competition was established. The student

***Before his death Robert Crist purchased two matching Steinway grand pianos for the Bay View stage. The organ was also a gift from the Mr. and Mrs. Crist.*** *(Courtesy of Ruth Crist Dyer, Photograph by Ralph Bransby)*

scholarship endowment fund increased from a paltry $10,000, to over $100,000 still a minimal sum. Weekly radio broadcasts on WCMU-FM were supported financially by the Petoskey business community. "It was so disheartening at first. I would call up potential musicians for the music staff and offer them a job and they would say 'I don't think so,'" remembered Sullivan.[46]

In 1974, when Dr. Sullivan featured noted pianists Ruth Slenczynska and John Wustman, his efforts were hampered by poor quality pianos. Just before his death in July of 1975, ninety-year-old Robert C. Crist gave $50,000 for two matching nine-foot Steinway concert grand pianos.

***Donald Allured began coming to Bay View in the 1930s. In 1977, he created the Bay View Handbell Workshop. He is pictured here with his wife Melissa and a recent workshop in front of John M. Hall Auditorium.*** *(Courtesy of Donald Allured)*

In 1978, Robert's widow Ruth E. Crist gave Bay View a greatly needed new four-manual, 51- rank, 2844-pipe, $150,000 Schantz organ in memory of her husband. This new organ replaced the $5000 Pilcher Organ Company instrument of 1915. That old organ served the association for sixty-three years with only one renovation in 1952 of a new console and an increase in the number of pipes. The new one was the largest in northern Michigan.

In 1977, Sullivan initiated one of the festival's distinctive features. Internationally-renowned handbell expert Donald E. Allured began a handbell workshop at the end of the season. The workshop began with twenty-five new directors and inexperienced ringers. As the national level of sophistication increased, the workshops began attracting experienced directors and performance-oriented participants, and each week culminated in a full performance. Enrollment now includes over 100 highly skilled handbell ringers who perform on hand chimes and multiple units of six-octave handbell sets, totaling over 800 bells. Composer Carl Wiltse, of Scotland, who was the registrar for the workshops for over twenty-five years, has taken over for the retired Allured.[47]

By 1984, enrollment in the Conservatory of Music was up to 119 students. One of Sullivan's vivid memories was of a student riding a motorcycle from New York to Bay View to attend a class with the great singer, Ré Koster of the Paris Opera Comiquè. That student went on to sing with the Metropolitan Opera. Another student, Rebecca Cook, joined the San Francisco Opera.

Dr. Will Nichols, also of Alma College, followed his

***The student chamber orchestra is a vital part of the music program.*** *(Photograph by Author)*

*Continuing its tradition of featuring the great operatic stars, each summer Bay View has invited stars such as Sherrill Milnes for master classes with music students and to present recitals.* (Photograph by G. Randall Goss)

colleague to Bay View in 1985 as the new director of music. He introduced children's concerts to the Sunday evening vesper concerts, featured concerto winners with the orchestra, brought in established woodwind and string quartets as faculty members and re-established the tradition of the oratorios. Nichols' close relationship with Bay View's long time friend and generous supporter, Virginia Crouse, led to her endowment of the Bay View Music Festival with a special concert series. Virginia Crouse had studied voice with Fred Patton and remembered the great singers he had brought to the Bay View stage. She wanted to recreate that excitement. In 1988, she and her son Jay, trustee of the John E. Galvin Charitable Trust, set up a special $200,000 endowment for the Virginia Crouse Visiting Artist Concert Series. Each year, a nationally prominent artist is featured. Badly needed renovations to faculty housing at Epworth Hall and Harrison House were made possible through a grant of $300,000, also from the Galvin Charitable Trust. "I am doing this in memory of my mother and my grandmother who dearly loved Bay View," Virginia Crouse said.[48]

Nichols stepped down in 1993 but remained in the community as a cottage owner and continued to raise money through his singing trio, "Three for the Road." Dr. Kelly Hale from the College-Conservatory of Music of the University of Cincinnati took over in the interim. Hale, an extremely popular vocal coach-accompanist, organist, composer and conductor, had been with the festival since 1977. Versatile and talented, he is well known and loved for his dedication to the festival and especially his Sunday evening vesper concert sing-along.

The association conducted its first national search for a new director in 1994, and twenty-seven highly qualified candidates applied. Professor Gary Glaze, Chairman of the Vocal Arts Department of the University of Southern California, was hired. His high profile throughout the US and Europe as an operatic tenor at the New York City Opera, along with his extensive background as an administrator, made him a favored candidate. In just five seasons, interest in the conservatory reached another all-time high, with over 450 students applying for just thirty-five scholarships. Glaze programmed the Sunday vesper concerts with various popular musical styles and eclectic and contemporary numbers for the Wednesday evening chamber concerts. He re-established radio coverage by WCMU-FM and contracted legendary talent such as baritone Sherrill Milnes, flautist Eugenia Zuckerman, and promising young instrumental groups such as the Eroica Trio, the Ahn Trio and the Trio Voronezh. Other stars including Giorgio Tozzi, Ara Berberian, Martina Arroyo and George Shirley, conducted student vocal workshops.

During this time, Willard Pierce retired in 1996 after forty years. His foresightedness had enlarged the department to include youth theatre and dance. His shows were always profitable. In the 1950s, production costs were a meager $200. Despite gremlins in the opening

*Suzanne Smith was very active in helping the young people get the theatre arts department established with many years of service as a costumer, financial manager, and producer of shows.* (Courtesy of the Solms Family)

***The combination of music students, professional staff artists, and community participants make up the very popular Bay View Music Festival, now the oldest continuously operating music festival in the US.*** *(Photograph by Author)*

night house, his 1995 *Oliver!* was his most expensive show at $40,000 and ranked as his finest show, with opera director David Morelock as Fagan. [49] Pierce's last show, *Guys and Dolls,* was an economical $15,000. The show that always gave him the most trouble was *Blithe Spirit.* "It seems like that show was jinxed. I had nothing but trouble both times I directed it," he recalled.

During the four decades he mounted productions in Bay View; Pierce influenced a generation of young people and refocused Bay View on its Chautauqua traditions. In 2005, The Crooked Tree Arts Council in Petoskey honored Pierce with the "eddi" Lifetime Achievement Award for his contributions to the arts community in Emmet and Charlevoix counties. During his Bay View tenure, he directed 40 plays and 29 musicals, with a total cast and crew of 2175, for audiences numbering nearly 100,000. Most recently he was gratified that his former boss, Bishop John Shelby Spong, was a featured speaker on the Bay View platform.[50] Now Pierce enjoys retirement in Sarasota, Florida.

After his departure, the Bay View Theatre Arts Department was merged with the Music Department, forming the Bay View Department of Performing Arts. Tremendous challenges of funding, staffing and poor facilities led to the formation of The Friends of the Bay View Performing Arts, the first fund raising organization in Bay View's history. Donations are used to increase scholarships from sixty percent of student tuition to one hundred percent, keeping Bay View competitive with other national festivals in securing top talent.

Looking back on the Bay View tradition, former music director Dr. Will Nichols noted that the festival has become the oldest continuously-operating music festival in the US without public grants, significant debt or cost overruns, elaborate fund-raising, public or government support and without a publicist. Quietly and unobtrusively, Bay View has had a dramatic impact on youth and future thespians and musicians offering musical and theatrical opportunities for everyone - either free or at nominal prices. Clarinetist Max Smith summed up its importance: "The Bay View people love their culture and want their children and grandchildren to have the same experiences they had."[51] On September 21, 2001, the Crooked Tree Arts Center recognized Bay View with the "eddi" Arts & Cultural Organization Award for its contribution to the arts and culture in Charlevoix and Emmet counties. Following theatre director Willard Pierce's lead, Bay View was again reaching out to serve the interests of the community. The Chautauqua ideal was again the model.

— CHAPTER ELEVEN —

# Changing Times

Following Willard Pierce's lead in renewing the vision of "the Bay View idea" and working its way back to "the Chautauqua ideal" within a society that has taken over its historic contributions has not been easy. Of the three parts of the "Bay View idea," the reading circle had ended in 1922, and, by the end of World War II, the assembly was reduced to lectures and movies. The recreation, a spin-off of the university, was doing well on its own, and the music program was continuing as part of a separate school within Albion College of Liberal Arts. Overall college enrollment was at an all time high. Eventually, the extremity of the 1960s counterculture didn't play well with the board. Also, competition from year-around state-funded college classes being offered in Petoskey by the newly established North Central Michigan College (Emmet College) and other state schools, forced the cancelation of the college. The community has held to its self-imposed commitment to education with adult education classes and lectures by Pulitzer Prize winning authors and other notables, despite financial restrictions.

The Summer University, established officially in 1888 with the erection of Loud Hall, was an unqualified success in the 1890s, attracting as many as 900 students and featuring professors from distinguished East Coast schools and even England. Beginning in 1899, though, the summer after Superintendent Hall resigned, the number of students and the level of courses declined. Historian Keith Fennimore attributed this to competition from emerging summer schools at the state's major universities and colleges. Roscoe Sleight later wrote: "Many of the members of the faculty of the School of Liberal Arts were teachers in high schools rather than in colleges and universities. As a result some of the departments were offering high school subjects only."[1] Considering that at the time only one in ten Americans had a high school education, perhaps those high school courses were exactly what the population needed, even though they were not representative of a university. During the difficult first decade, the cancelation of the assembly forced the cancellation of all classes.

When Hall re-established the assembly in 1909, he did not bring in famous professors from England and the East Coast as he had earlier, but hired professors from state universities. His program was successful, and, by 1914, enrollment was back up to 879 students from twenty-seven states. A diverse selection of classes included primary teaching methods, history, physical culture, psychology,

***Some of the most popular classes in the Bay View Summer University from its inception were art and drawing classes.*** *(Author's Collection)*

***Julia Alvord Cole did this sketch of a Bay View cottage in an art class.** (Courtesy of Betsy Fleming Kittle and Elizabeth S. Ewing)*

philosophy, sociology, arts and crafts courses, languages (French, German, Latin, Greek and English), nature study, library work and, of course, cooking, the subject that had been so popular.

Hall's death in 1914 brought chaos to the entire program. A professional manager was hired in 1915, and the then famous editor Trumbull White of Petoskey took over both the assembly program and university in 1916, placing major emphasis on the assembly program, which had an accumulated debt by this time. Adding to those financial woes, in 1916, the Michigan State Department of Education informed Bay View that the upper rooms at Evelyn, Hitchcock, Loud and Epworth halls could not be used for sleeping accommodations until fire escapes were installed. The restrictions left only one room at Hitchcock, one in Loud, seven in Epworth and ten in Evelyn that could be rented to students and faculty.

Despite the fine program Trumbull White and Howard Barlow had provided, their contracts were not renewed. Before White left, he reiterated a valuable suggestion in the local paper: "He would drop the university idea and take steps to attach the school to Albion, Hillsdale or Oberlin, so students could get credits for their summer work. This would draw students to Bay View he thought."[2] The idea was not new. On July 30, 1900, the *Daily Resorter* reported a movement to affiliate the university with an institution which would supervise the classes and give credits to the students. This time the board listened. They took White's recommendation and, in 1917, the education committee consisting of Chairman Dr. Hugh Kennedy, Dr. John G. Benson, Thomas Gordon, Jr., Dr. Charles Swift, and Judge Clement Smith began negotiations with Albion College, the most likely institution to ally itself with Bay View. Dr. Clarence Wilson Greene of Albion College became the president of the Summer University with mathematics professor Dr. Roscoe Sleight as secretary.[3]

The Albion alliance was informal, but expectations were high that accredited classes would allow students to work toward degrees. Since the Bay View program offered the only college level classes in northern Michigan, the issue was exceedingly important. Newly-constructed fire escapes allowed the association to resume lodging students in Loud Hall and Evelyn Hall for seventy-five cents to two dollars a week. The faculty was housed in Epworth Hall and Hitchock Hall.

"Bay View has the greatest opportunity for a summer school of any resort in the United States," Dr. John G. Benson, the new superintendent of the Bay View Assembly, told the local paper. With the war going on in Europe, there was some talk around the country of banning all assemblies. "It was my privilege to go before Secretary of War Baker and persuade him to make them centers of patriotic propaganda instead." Benson stated.[4] Despite the war, 179 students enrolled in classes that summer. Within two years, enrollment was up to 250 students, who signed up for forty-one different classes.

In the summer of 1918, an ardent attempt to endow the Summer University was made through a tax of one and a quarter percent levied on the Bay View constituency. Dr. Benson was to be in charge of this endowment fund, but the community voted down the proposal. Desperate for funding, at the end of the 1920 season, the Bay View trustees and Dr. Green, dean of the Bay View Summer University, requested a special meeting with the Petoskey board of education. They wanted a portion of the township school taxes to be applied to the Bay View Summer University and Associated Schools. Judge Clement Smith, vice president of the association, who had successfully secured the return of a segment of Bay View's portion of Petoskey road taxes the previous year, reminded Petoskey officials that Bay View had paid $34,000 in taxes over the previous five years. He told them, "The Bay View trustees freely admit that all real estate must pay a school tax, the only difference of opinion is being where and how that fund shall be used. They believe that a plan of co-operation can be devised where by Petoskey and Bay View get together on the matter to their mutual advantage, and they are not averse to Petoskey's assumption of part of the control and administration of Bay View's educational institution."[5] The trustees felt the request was justified since not one student from Bay View attended the Petoskey schools, but many Emmet County residents took classes in Bay View.

Reaction to the request was swift and adverse. Homer Sly, president of the Petoskey Board of Education, stood firm in his belief that it was illegal to divert public funds to a private institution. Mayor A. B. Klise said, "the people of Bay View should take a little broader view of life and consider themselves as citizens of the United States of which Bay View is an infinitesimal part." He went on: "Bay View is a private corporation and as much comes in the same category with every other private corporation. If Bay View desires public funds for its schools, the first move is to give up its charter and come under the general regulation. The public school laws require a school to be maintained a certain number of months in the year that it may have standing. The Bay View school cannot qualify under these regulations.[6] During the winter of 1922-23, a bill was introduced in the state legislature concerning separate school districts for resorts. An article in the *Petoskey Independent* on March 16, 1923, suggested that Bay View members prompted it, since the bill would have given resorts like Bay View the power to become separate school districts.

Nothing came of the issue except ill will. Had it been possible to work out the legalities, the outcome would have had enormous ramifications. Bay View would have been obliged to relinquish its independent nature, winterize its operation and submit to state codes on public education. Petoskey would have had to redirect some of its tax funding but the city might have had a local college decades earlier that it ultimately did. As it was, not until Emmet College was established in 1959, did the county have year-round college classes.

The ambitious Dr. Greene accepted the presidency of Hedding College in Illinois and resigned in 1922. Dr. Phil H. Hembdt of Albion College took over and increased the number of departments to seven. About this time, Thomas E. Johnson, Superintendent of Public Instruction for Michigan, wrote: "I have gone over your request for approval of summer school conducted at Bay View. We will be glad to accept credits toward the renewal of certificates."[7] Unfortunately, this statement applied only to teachers who needed to earn college credits to renew their teaching certificates, not to general accreditation. With the shortage of funding, full accreditation pending, and lack of leadership due to Dean Hembdt's absence for several seasons during the Roaring Twenties, the summer school dwindled in size to an all-time low in 1928 of seven faculty members and thirty-eight students. Then, Dr. E. Roscoe Sleight took over officially.

Under Sleight, the kindergarten and the school of methods, fine arts and art methods, public speaking, physical education for girls, commercial branches, tutoring and other high school subjects were spun off and separated from the college. The name was officially changed from the Bay View Summer University and Associated Schools to Bay View Summer College of Liberal Arts and School of Music. Despite frequent attempts to attract the attention of the state's department of education with invitations to its superintendents beginning as far back as 1888, the Bay View program was still not fully accredited. No state charter was awarded to Bay View like it was to the Chautauqua Institution. The association with Albion College had not brought about the general acceptance of credits for which Bay View had hoped. Some institutions accepted the Bay View credits, but the large majority did not, because the Bay View Summer University was not listed with a major accrediting association. People were recommending that Albion College completely take over the management of the Summer University to "secure credits in more colleges and universities than at present."

In his efforts to expand the scope of the newly named College of Liberal Arts and increase the likelihood of its accreditation, in 1929, Dean Sleight began hiring more qualified professors, and by 1930 the Michigan State Department of Education reiterated its acceptance of all credits earned in Bay View applying toward the renewal of teaching certificates. Dr. Ernest Amy, an English professor at Ohio Wesleyan, joined the faculty to teach English literature for a flat fee of $600. Amy was listed in *Who's Who in America* and had been on the lecture circuit of the Chautauqua assemblies during the 1920s. But, with the success of radio, his speaking opportunities had all but disappeared. At the time he was working on the *Oxford English Dictionary* and was soon be the American editor of Thomas Hardy's novel *The Mayor of Casterbridge*. Besides being an expert on Hardy, he was also known as a Chaucer scholar. Another distinguished professor who came to Bay View in 1928 was Dr. Royal G. Hall. Hall, a graduate of Park College, had received his master's degree from the University of Kansas, his B. D. from Auburn Theological Seminary and his Ph.D. from the University of Chicago. In 1939, he was the American lecturer at the Honfleur International Conference in France. He traveled extensively in Europe, Siam, Hawaii and China before World War II and fascinated his Bay View audiences with his predictions about world events as they led up to World War II. In Bay View, he taught history and philosophy. Dr. William W. Whitehouse took charge of the department of economics and sociology in 1930. Like Hall, he was from Albion College, but spent several years at Wayne State University. "Dean Sleight's purpose was to elevate the Bay View Summer school to a level where it would be recognized by major universities and produce credits which could be transferred. This meant that he needed a faculty with credentials beyond those of Albion College teachers, so he recruited a mixture from the Midwest. And, it worked - after U of M accepted credits, everybody else did," said Dr. Jonathan Amy.[8]

Finally, in 1934 at a conference at U-M, Sleight and Whitehouse convinced the dean of U-M's College of Literature, Sciences, and Arts to accept Bay View credits. Arrangements with similar Michigan institutions followed. The State Department of Public Instruction did a survey in 1935, and the Association of Michigan Colleges conducted a second one in 1938. As a result, Albion College expressed its willingness to assume a closer relation to Bay View Summer College of Liberal Arts College and accept all credits earned.

With these hindrances surmounted, the summer college was increased to nine departments, taught by a faculty of fifteen. The number of weeks in the summer session was extended to nine by 1944, and the number of required hours for accreditation was achieved by offering double sessions and Saturday classes. In 1947, students from thirty-five colleges and fifteen states enrolled. Albion headed the list with nearly a third of the students, while students from the University of Arizona and the University of Colorado also registered. Dean Sleight and the Bay View administration continued their contacts with the State Board of Education, entertaining the assistant superintendent of Public Instruction of Michigan and school officials from Petoskey on July 24, 1942 at a luncheon at Terrace Inn.

During the 1950s, college enrollment was steady. Dr. Howard E. Pettersen taught for the school. "Ferris State didn't offer physics in the summer at that time and so many of their students came to Bay View to get their credits," said Pettersen.[9] He described the program as a low-key, laid-back atmosphere which was very enjoyable. He joked that he had two kinds of students in those days – "A" students and beach students.

***Dr. Roy E. Heath, owner of the Bay View Inn in the 1950s was one of the intellectual giants that were attracted to Bay View. Heath was a brilliant chemist who had worked on the Manhattan Project in Chicago and joined Northern Michigan University after World War II. His sister Stella Teegarden owned the Terrace Inn. When responsibilities at Northern Michigan University increased, he sold the hotel to Stafford Smith with an exchange of the keys and a handshake.***
*(Courtesy of Cheryl Bryant)*

Dr. Keith J. Fennimore took over as dean of the Bay View Summer College of Liberal Arts in 1964, when Dean Dr. Joseph J. Irwin stepped down after seventeen years. An associate professor of English at Albion College, Fennimore was also a Bay View cottager. He received his B. A. from Albion College, his M. A. from the University of Michigan and his Ph.D. from Michigan State University. In his 1975 history of Bay View, Fennimore wrote that he "took special pride in the quality of his staff, often presenting a faculty more than half composed of departmental chairmen on their home campuses.... Under his leadership, problem courses (such as chemistry with its laboratory requirements) were weeded out of the curriculum and field courses (such as geology, in an area rich in fossils) were reintroduced to a student body still divided about evenly between Albion College transfers and other enrollees from widely scattered colleges across the nation."[10] Enrollment during the 1960s was a consistent 140 liberal arts students. Sixteen faculty members, twelve of whom had doctorates and six who headed their home college departments, taught thirty courses.

Despite satisfactory enrollment and qualified faculty, problems emerged that brought about the demise of the college. Competition was coming from North Central Michigan College, and local summer courses offered by Central Michigan University and Michigan State University. Then, in 1969, Albion College withdrew its formal affiliation wishing to establish its own summer school. In a 1969 article, the *News-Review* quoted Reverend Russell King, president of the Bay View Association, as saying "the college was being closed with regret because of a number of factors - the last one being a decision by Albion College to terminate its academic affiliation on Sept. 1."[11] Dr. King explained that Bay View could not meet state requirements for buildings and housing because of capital expenditures for a college that operated only eight weeks a year. The Michigan State Department of Education announced that it was resurveying the Bay View operation. In its contact with the department, the association was informed that the its charter did not give it the right to operate a college. Dr. Pettersen believed that the reason was "the arrangements with the state board were not tight, Albion College wanted to improve the facilities, and the social environment of the 1960s adversely affected the Bay View board of trustees."[12]

Dr. King said, "It is a sad commentary when we consider that we are trying to produce more college classrooms to meet needs today and Bay View, which has operated all these years with no expense to the taxpayers is being closed.... We are no longer rendering a service to cottagers that we were 50 years ago. There is a junior college now in Petoskey and extension courses are available. There isn't the crying need as there was years ago when many teachers got their certificated [sic] validated here. I guess it's one of the changes of the changing times."[13]

Believing that education should be affordable and available to everyone, Bay View had always kept its tuition low. By 1969, the downside of that philosophy caught up with them. The association never took enough overhead costs from college receipts to repair buildings, upgrade facilities or buy supplies. For instance, in 1917, the faculty received seventy-five percent of the tuition with twenty-five percent for registration. Even in 1969, at the time the college was closed, fees were twenty-five dollars for registration and twenty dollars per credit hour. With no reserve funding or outside sources to cover the now enormous cost of upgrading the facilities to meet state standards, and without Albion's support to meet the accreditation requirements, it was impossible to continue the Bay View College of Liberal Arts. The board voted to close the college. The College of Music was allowed to continue as the Bay View Conservatory of Music under different state regulations.

Without a state charter, without full accreditation until 1935, without governmental funding or grants, and despite the burden of separate Bear Creek Township school taxes, the Bay View Summer University and College of Liberal Arts thrived for eighty-three years, helping to educate thousands of students. During that time,

*Lumberman Henry M. Loud provided financing for an education building in 1888 named Loud Hall in his honor. (Author's Collection)*

it provided local teachers with the opportunity to validate teaching certificates without moving downstate, enabled local students to take entry-level college classes, and permitted students from across the country to continue their studies during summer months. Petoskey resident Dr. John Fochtman summed up the college's importance very simply in a letter published in the *News-Review*. In 1955, the St. Francis High School graduate was attending Notre Dame, "and the Bay View summer school and my course in quantitative analysis got me into medical school…Again, Bay View, thank you for making my life more meaningful to me."[14]

Though inevitable, the closure of the summer school was a significant blow at a time when Bay View was approaching its centennial celebration in 1975. Instead of being able to boast of its achievements, it was a time when all three parts of the Bay View idea (the assembly, the university, and the reading circle) were defunk. The music program was at an all time low while only the recreation and religion departments were thriving. The disappointing closure of the college did not mean, however, that Bay View would abandon its educational goal of lifelong learning.

That summer, Education Committee Chairman Dr. Wesley Hager arranged for questionnaires to be sent out to cottagers to assess possible interest in adult education classes. Classes were then arranged in art, furniture refinishing, literature, nature and history and met from one to four times a week for six weeks. In subsequent years, the adult education program carried on the tradition of the Bay View Summer University.[15]

Hager first came to Bay View to preach in the 1960s. He was elected to the board of trustees in 1969 but, like Bishop Wade, he was appointed to a foreign position as minister of the American Protestant Church in Antwerp, Belgium, and resigned. When he and his wife Charlotte returned to Michigan in 1975, he accepted the presidency of the Bay View Association, and the couple made Petoskey their permanent home. Born in 1905 in Minneapolis, Hager earned undergraduate and doctoral degrees from Hamline College. He received his Bachelor of Divinity degree from Union Theological Seminary and earned a master's degree in Christian Education from Columbia University in New York City. He also did graduate studies at the University of Edinburgh. An eloquent writer, he authored four books - *Mastering Life with the Master, Conquering, They were There,* and *God Hath Joined Together*, which was reprinted more than seventeen times. Assuming his new position, he immediately noticed in his second floor office at Hall Auditorium the now well-tarnished communion set in an antique bookcase. The inscription on the pewter-like chalice was in English, so he was unaware of its Latvian background and how it came to Bay View. He decided to use the holy vessels to inaugurate regular communion services in the west side of Evelyn Hall beginning June 19, 1977.

Dr. Hager set high standards for himself; standards that all agree that he more than lived up to, both personally and in his leadership of Bay View and in Petoskey. When he was president, he told his eventual successor, Dr. Robert Stephens, that he wanted to see Bay View totally immersed with the northern Michigan community, definitely a goal that would take Bay View back to the Chautauqua idea and away from the concept of a modern day resort that it had become. He hoped to make every effort to keep the Bay View program closely allied with world events while at the same time upholding the foundation and high ideals upon which the community was founded. When he died in 1994, Petoskey resident Ernie Mainland, Ernest Hemingway's nephew, described Hager: "I remember him as being one of the most dynamic speakers I'd ever heard in my life. Not only would his message move you, but his delivery of his message moved you."[16]

Hager was the last Bay View president to leave a prominent historic legacy since term limits were inaugurated in the late 1970s. After Hager retired, the position of president and director of the assembly (then religious activities) was again divided, as it was before 1928. Presidents carried the administrative duties and served behind the scenes, while the director of the assembly and religious activities officiated on the platform. The increase in activities after Hager's retirement required a larger staff

***Reverend Dr. Wesley Hager, president of Bay View from 1975 until 1984.***
*(Courtesy of Judith Hager Bryan)*

and more feasible administrative facilities. So, twenty-seven years after his death, another memorial to Bishop Raymond Wade was built in the form of a much-needed administration building. The Wade family and friends led the campaign and, in August 1997, a new $800,000 Raymond J. Wade Administration Building was dedicated. Mr. John R. Edman, former vice president of GM and president of GMAC, headed the fund-raising campaign and the new building was dedicated on August 3, 1997.

Bishop Wade and Dr. Hager remain two of Bay View's most revered presidents for very different reasons. They were hardly acquainted, but their Bay View legacies are interminably intertwined through the Simons Communion Set, so gratefully given to Wade and so valued by Hager. In 1991, the General Board of Global Ministries of the United Methodist Church in New York reiterated its request to the Bay View Association that the Simons Communion Set, then being used weekly in the new Crouse Memorial Chapel, be given to the newly re-established Methodist Church in Riga, Latvia. With the fall of communism and the destruction of the Iron Curtain, the property deeds carefully smuggled out of Latvia by Timbers over the cold Baltic Sea and presented to Bishop Garber in Switzerland were again significant. The papers had been stored for some fifty years in a safe at the United Methodist Church headquarters in New York City and were being used to reclaim ownership of the Latvian Methodist properties where the church was located in 1927.

For both Hager and Mosienko, the Latvian minister who was ordained in 1927, the set held special meaning, and they both felt it belonged in Bay View.[17] Mosienko said the set was a gift from Americans to an American, Missionary Simons, and was not Latvian. Hager believed it was a gift to Bay View. Hager passed away at the age of eighty-nine on October 13, 1994, and Mosienko died shortly thereafter. In late August 1996, the Bay View board sent the Simons Communion Set to the newly re-established congregation at Riga's Akas Street United Methodist Church, with the consent and blessing of the Wade family.[18]

By the time Hager left office in 1984, the "Bay View idea" was evolving into the "four pillars"– religion, recreation, culture, and education. Kennedy had emphasized all areas, Wade strengthened recreation and facilities, and Hager rekindled the religious spirit with the creation of endowed lectureships and education with the establishment of adult educational seminars. However, the preservation of the community and its traditions would soon be challenged as it had never been before. Dark days lay ahead.

*Petoskey resident Dr. John Fochtman*
*summed up the college's importance in a letter*
*published July 30, 1999, in the* News-Review.
*In 1955, the St. Francis High School graduate was attending*
*Notre Dame and wanted to go to medical school.*
*"And the Bay View summer school and*
*my course in quantitative analysis got me into medical school...*
*Again, Bay View, thank you*
*for making my life more meaningful to me."*

# Bay Views

Pulitzer Prize winning author Bruce Catton visited Petoskey his hometown on July 30, 1965, and appeared at the John M. Hall Auditorium. The event may have been a milestone in the community's return to its historic heritage. He told his audience: "We have only to live up to our own past - - and do our honest best to create the magnificent future which that past lights up."[1] Knowledge of past history is always the prerequisite for the creation of a future.

By the time Catton came, the Bay View community had taken an inward turn like most of the Chautauqua communities, and it took a combination of events to refocus priorities. The theatre arts program began taking a county-wide approach with the musicals. At the same time, the Bay View Archives was officially organized for the preservation of historic documents, making them available to the public. Finally, state and national historic preservation officers recognized Bay View's significance through various designations, most notably the National Historic Landmark. Next, the judgment by the US Sixth Circuit Court of Appeals developed the "Bay View criterion" regarding national historic properties which has had a major impact nationally.

Bay View people in the past were aware of their history. A 1916 newspaper article mentioned the Bay View archives when founder Reverend Seth Reed requested to view documents relating to the history of the Methodist Church in Michigan. These documents were stored at the newly constructed John M. Hall Auditorium, but no catalogue of the contents of the collection is known to exist. That collection was moved to the Bay View Library when it opened in 1932, along with John M. Hall's papers donated by his daughter Dorothy McClintock. In the 1960s, Bay View librarian Mary Bobbitt mentioned to Jane Park Doerr, then Bay View Library Board president, that there was a valuable collection of documents that needed proper care. So in 1968, the Bay View Archives Commission was officially established with Mary Bobbitt as chairman. Having just published her book, *With Dearest Love to All – The Life and Letters of Lady Jebb*, in England, Bobbitt had the interest, time, and professional qualifications to assume the new position. Inspired by her leadership and with help from Dr. Charles Swift, Doerr embarked upon an oral history campaign to interview the many "old timers" still living on the grounds about their early memories. Dr. John Perkins, then president of the University of Delaware, conducted the interviews, while Doerr made the arrangements and did the audio taping. The tapes were then transcribed and added to the library's collection. Doerr also began a taping service of all lectures and concerts on the grounds. With her interest and knowledge of oral history, Doerr helped found the Michigan Oral History Association.

***Jane Park Doerr was Director of the Bay View Archives' Commission from 1977 until 1989.*** *(Author's Collection)*

Dr. Keith Fennimore, acting chair of the English department at Albion College, took over as chairman of the archives commission in 1973 and set about writing a history of the association for the 1975 centennial celebration. *The Heritage of Bay View*, was a substantial addition to the other histories published by the association - those written by Clark Wheeler and Dr. William Shier. After the celebration and publication of his book, Fennimore stepped down as director and Doerr took over. By this time, there had been a large influx of materials into the collection from donors now aware of the importance of the papers and the available place for safekeeping and public research. The collection needed to be catalogued, properly preserved and stored in fireproof files.

Even though she was in her 60s, Doerr approached her new career professionally. To learn proper techniques, she attended archival management classes taught by the well-known professional, Dr. Philip P. Mason, at Wayne State University. She then offered seminars each summer for volunteers. Once trained, individuals were assigned to various tasks in the archives. For the preservation of the materials, Xerox Corporation was contracted to microfilm the collection, and copies were placed at the Bentley Historical Library at the University of Michigan. For her work in establishing the Bay View Archives, on September 19, 1984, the American Association for State and Local History presented Doerr with a Certificate of Commendation. She was also honored by Mackinac Associates for "furthering historic preservation of the Straits of Mackinac region."

One of Doerr's projects was to arrange for cleaning and restoration of the oil portraits of Bay View's founding fathers. Under a grant from the State of Michigan and funds donated by friends and relatives of the founders, paintings were restored at the Detroit Institute of Arts. These paintings are on display for the public in Hall Auditorium, Evelyn Hall, and in the Bay View Archives.

Then in 1983, Dr. Kathryn Bishop Eckert of the History Division of the Michigan Department of State approached Doerr concerning the possibility of Bay View becoming a National Historic Landmark. Bay View was first listed on the State of Michigan Register of Historic Sites on June 5, 1957, and became a National Historic Site on March 16, 1972, and was eligible for the highest honor. The archives took charge of the process. Members and cottage owners filled out descriptions of their properties on forms prepared and collected by volunteers. Pictures were taken and added to each form. Dr. Ellen Weiss, professor of architectural history at Loyola University, wrote the introductory essay to accompany the Bay View application. The community effort marked the largest landmark effort ever mounted in Michigan, and Doerr was recognized for her leadership with the Diamond Award of Excellence from the Michigan Historical Commission.

The official designation came during Ronald Reagan's presidency on December 23, 1987. It was Michigan's first in sixteen years and began a resurgence of interest in historic properties throughout the state. On July 9, 1988, the Director of the National Park Service, William Penn Mott, Jr., came to Bay View to make the presentation. Mott did not usually present awards personally, but in Bay View's case he made an exception. His wife Ruth had grown up in Bay View and wanted to see her childhood summer home again.

For the landmark dedication ceremony, a special anthem was commissioned by Marion Stark, daughter of Bay View's longtime caretaker, Charles Ditto. *Psalms of Summer* was written by Bay View's organist, Tom Robin Harris, and performed by Bay View music faculty members. In conjunction with Jack Kausch Photography of Birmingham, Michigan, Helen Guittard produced a video documentary on the history of Bay View, "In Celebration of Bay View", written by Mary Jane Doerr and Guittard to music recorded in Bay View by WCMU public radio. Francis A. Blouin, Director of the Bentley Historical

***In a special ceremony at John M. Hall Auditorium on July 9, 1988, Jane Park Doerr and Ben VandenBelt, Jr., then President of the Bay View Association, accepted the National Historic Landmark Plaque from William Penn Mott, Jr., Director of the National Park Service.***
*(Photograph by G. Randall Goss)*

Library of U-M recommended the video for the Hamer-Kegan Award from the American Society of Archivists. It was judged to exemplify the "best use of archival materials for public consumption" produced in the US in 1987, and the award was presented to Bay View archivist Jane Park Doerr.

The landmark validated Bay View's significance in our country's history. The mood of the celebration in 1988 was festive, but the road to the award was fraught with turmoil and complications. During the four-year application process, community members expressed concerns about the possibility of federal control. Resistance resulted from the designation's inclusion of Bay View's entire property of 337.33 acres, including the Bay View woods, a tract of land of approximately 167 acres. At that time, there were suggestions that the woods could be developed for condominiums to increase Bay View's tax base. That possibility would be precluded by the designation.

Those in favor of the preservation of the woods found support in some of Bay View's history. While as early as 1876, Reverend Bird of the Petoskey Methodist Episcopal Church indicated that the Bay View's founders intended that the area now known as the Bay View woods would be subdivided eventually, because the founders felt that if the association were to survive, it needed a large membership like the Ocean Grove, Lakeside, and Chautauqua. On June 23, 1876, the *Emmet County Democrat* reported: "Rev. Mr. Bird told us that this is designed not only for a Camp meeting ground, but will be made a summer resort for those who will come and spend a portion of the hot weather, not only in the worship of God, but in rest, and relaxation; and he ventures the assertion that at no distant day there will be erected one thousand or fifteen hundred summer residences and occupied a portion of the season by that number of families."[2] But, within a few years, the trustees reversed themselves. On October 25, 1880, they voted to reserve the Bay View woods as a natural park.[3]

The perplexing issue of possible federal control was addressed during a visit of Benjamin Levy of the National Park Service (later director of the national landmark program). Levy explained the relationship between a landmark property and the National Park Service. Of the nation's then 2,341 landmarks, Bay View would be one of 1,124 privately owned and one of 436 district landmarks.[4] Some landmarks are private, such as Windemere Cottage, Hemingway's summer home on Walloon Lake, and are not open to the public, while others, such as George Washington's home at Mt. Vernon, are privately owned and managed but open to the public. According to Levy, landmarks are free to manage their own properties. As a landmark though, Bay View would be eligible for federal funding for rehabilitation and other federal tax incentives. Since the association had never sought or received any federal aid, the point was moot. More importantly, Levy described the meaning of the designation: "The National Historic Landmark designation is the federal government's way of recognizing a site or building as possessing the highest significance in the nation's history. It signifies that an historical property has a high degree of physical integrity remaining from its period of historical significance. It certifies that the events and people associated with these places and structures are of the highest importance in the history of the United States."[5]

More opposition came from a roadway issue. During the early decades of the twentieth century, the levying of property taxes, dissention-causing lawsuits, and disagreements over the roadway, Woodland Avenue (US-31), through Bay View had caused a schism between the once-close communities of Bay View and Petoskey. Early in the century, when Bear Creek Township began taxing Bay View residents, trouble began brewing, until 1983, when the landmark effort coincided with proposed widening of Woodland Avenue (US-31) in Bay View by the Michigan Department of Transportation (MDOT). Bay View was scheduled to receive the landmark designation in April, 1987, six months earlier than it did because Bay View's President Ben VandenBelt Jr. requested that the landmark designation be delayed to allow the association to vote on the issue. The delay nullified the mandatory federal review process for the proposed widening of Woodland Avenue as it would relate to Bay View as a National Historic Landmark. The landmark vote was placed on the annual meeting ballot on August 8, 1987, along with a vote on MDOT's three-lane highway proposal. Although the landmark was strongly supported (504-220), the highway proposal passed by a slim margin of twelve votes (367 to 355).

The highway vote culminated three years of intense disagreement within a deeply divided community. After the 1987 annual meeting vote, Bay View members Nancy Rajala and Stephen W. Guittard filed suit against James H. Burnley, Robert Farris and James P. Pitz of MDOT on behalf of the Historic Preservation Guild of Bay View. This was a group of Bay View members opposed to the widening of Woodland Avenue and represented almost half of the community membership. The case was argued by lawyers Gary R. Rentrop and Susan E. Morrison of Suidara, Rentrop, Martin, and Morrison, a Bloomfield Hills law firm. Elizabeth Merritt, then assistant general counsel for the National Trust for Historic Preservation in Washington DC, also argued the case in both the district and circuit courts.

In district court, Judge Richard A. Enslen abruptly dismissed the suit, granting "summary judgment" to MDOT in October of 1987, clearing the way for the development of plans to widen Woodland Avenue. The case was appealed to the Sixth Circuit Court of Appeals in Cincinnati. A request for an injunction against MDOT was denied in October 1987, and MDOT immediately began work on the project. Disturbed by the case, the circuit court reversed itself twenty months later and issued an injunction on May 1, 1989, against MDOT. By that time construction on the roadway was in progress, and work stoppage caused great inconvenience for local residents. Intense anger erupted against Bay View and the Historic Preservation Guild of Bay View, and the injunction was lifted and work resumed. A premium was then paid to H&D, the highway construction company for each day the work was completed ahead of schedule.

On December 15, 1989, after the project was complete, the circuit court ruled in favor of MDOT but clearly specified conditions relating to the issues of highway segmentation that were to be followed in all future cases concerning roadways and historic properties. The court expressed serious reservations concerning the lower court's "summary judgment:" "We do this with the understanding that no further widening of the questioned Bay View segment will take place without meeting federal environmental standards as they relate to a National Historic Landmark. Our decision is made without prejudice to the rights of plaintiffs (or others) to seek redress or modifications of the highway project at issue if serious adverse impact may be demonstrated on the Bay View Landmark by reason of construction and/or maintenance of this project."[6]

While MDOT prevailed, the judgment was not what Michigan's Assistant Attorney General R. Philip Brown, who handled the case for the state, had wanted. Brown said, "the decision still leaves open the question of who is the prevailing party." Gary Rentrop, lawyer for the guild, was encouraged by the court's decision regarding the future of the roadway. For its work on the construction of the three-lane roadway, the Petoskey firm of H&D was given awards by MDOT and the Michigan Asphalt Pavers Association - the First Place Construction Award in the urban streets category chosen from among fifty-eight entries in the state, and a first-ever Award of Distinction for "Outstanding achievement in 1989 on a bituminous paving project involving exceptionally challenging conditions."[7]

When the Bay View board agreed to a third lane in the widening project in 1987, Emmet County was considering a beltway to relieve traffic congestion through the downtown area. MDOT spent $5.5 million dollars in engineering and other studies on possible locations. However, residents of Emmet County could not reach a consensus on any proposal, and MDOT abandoned the project in favor of a "no build" option.

One of the biggest concerns was the danger to centennial family farms south of the city. MDOT announced its decision at a meeting in September 2002. Greg Rocine, its director at the time, was asked by local residents if Petoskey could solve its traffic problems by simply widening the existing roads instead of building a separate beltway or by-pass. Rocine responded by saying he was "under a federal court order not to touch Bay View," referring to the federal court judgment in the Historic Preservation Guild lawsuit which clearly stated that all future work in Bay View had to meet the standards set in the National Environmental Protection Act, the National Department of Transportation Act and the National Historic Preservation Act. The time for appealing the lawsuit had run out.

The US-31 Petoskey Area Improvement Study stated that: "Roadway capacity constraints remain along portions of US-31. The most significant constraints exist along US-31 within and north of Petoskey due to the inability to obtain additional right-of-way through Bay View, a National Historic Landmark."[8] The report also referred to comments received by MDOT opposing the study and expressing "a strong resentment of the protection afforded the Bay View National Historic Landmark that effectively required MDOT to only consider alternatives that avoid construction through Bay View." Apparently, the landmark designation was considered by those letter-writers to be an impediment to the area's progress. "The suit greatly affects the transportation options in the Bay View/Petoskey area," said Elizabeth S. Merritt, now Deputy General Counsel of the National Trust for Historic Preservation during a 2004 interview. "If I were to advise MDOT concerning the roadway through Bay View," she continued, "I would have to advise them, given the legal situation, not to touch Bay View."[9]

What was originally a local dispute had taken on national proportions. In the 1989 highway litigation statement, the circuit court opinion established the national rules upon which a highway project could be considered a segmentation issue – i.e., the practice of building sections of three and four-lane roadways up to a landmark, forcing heavy amounts of traffic onto the historic segment. In the subsequent years since that 1989 Sixth Federal Circuit Court decision, nearly 200 national court decisions have referenced the Bay View lawsuit, and the specifications have now become known as the "*Bay View* criteria." In a 2002 court case, the Ohio State Supreme Court characterized the 1989 US District opinion in blatant terms: "Furthermore, even in affirming the district court, the *Bay Guild* opinion boils with the displeasure of the Sixth Circuit at the grant of summary judgment: it seems the district court was affirmed only because the Sixth Circuit could not see how any remediation or mitigation of adverse [**36] effects could reasonably be affected [sic]."[10]

The Petoskey community-at-large continues to deal with the traffic issue and the now defunct beltway project. Bay View residents pay taxes to Bear Creek Township on 317.36 acres (including the roadway since MDOT does not hold the deed to the property). Of the 337.33 acres of land owned by the Bay View Association, 19.97 acres are tax-exempt for educational, religious, and cultural purposes. However, since Bay View members are not full time residents of Emmet County, they do not represent a voting constituency in Bear Creek Township and have no political voice in community affairs except through the judicial process: "The fact is that Bay View is a part of Petoskey and it is impossible to separate the interest of one from the other", wrote a journalist well over a century ago.[11] That statement is even truer today. The city of Petoskey continues to limit traffic access through the city, increasing congestion in the historic district with no alternative route or beltway. Local officials recently recommended further widening through the historic district despite the legal status. The issue is challenging, with national implications and legal ramifications, although few relish a repeat of the hostilities of the 1980s.

After spearheading the landmark process during the contentious highway dispute, Doerr retired from the Bay View Archives after the 1988 landmark ceremony. She received a Resolution of Appreciation from the Bay View Association for her service. Her longtime assistant, Mary

*Bay View has always been and continues to be a place where extended families get together.* (Author's Collection)

Andress, took over. Then in her eighties, Andress served as archives director for one season and continued to volunteer for another twelve years. For her service as a volunteer, the Historical Society of Michigan honored her with the Award of Merit for Distinguished Volunteer Service to the Bay View Archives Commission in 1998. Dr. John Weeks, professor of history at Adrian College, took over in 1990.

In 1997, when the Raymond J. Wade Administration Building was erected, it included the new Bay View Archives. Doerr and the new director Weeks were involved in detailed planning with Ann Arbor architect Richard Mitchell. Unfortunately, Doerr passed away on April 30, 1996, just months before construction began. She never saw the new archives for which she had labored so intensely. The main room was named the Jane P. Doerr Reading Room in her honor.

Not only is Bay View threatened physically with traffic issues, but differences of opinion on accepted Christian teachings confront Bay View's traditional philosophical stance. When the camp-meeting movement died in 1908, its activities were combined with those of the assembly. Religious speakers and ministers appeared on the same platform as the assembly's secular talent, thus combining two divergent perspectives. The auditorium was booked nightly with speakers representing various causes not necessarily reflective of the tenor of the Christian-based association. Speakers such as atheist philosopher, Dr. Will Durant, were as welcome as preachers such as Harvard University's World War II pacifist Dr. George Buttrick.

However, in 2003 when the announcement was made that Bishop John Shelby Spong, the champion of gay and lesbian rights had been contracted, an explosion of dissention erupted. Spong's stance on gay rights was not the issue. It was his teachings against the tenants of the Christian faith that caused the controversy. A group of Bay View members calling themselves the Committee for a Christian Pulpit objected to Spong's appearance at the Sunday morning worship service. "[Spong] has a number of what I would term disbeliefs about Christianity," said Dick Crossland, spokesman for the group.[12] Religious activities director Reverend Robert Kimes countered by saying that, "He gives expression to the Christian faith and his love for the church while not creating a new religion, but allowing the Scriptures to speak through him in ways that would reform the church that he loves."[13] In Petoskey, opposition took the form of the Little Traverse Christian Ministerial Association which scheduled nightly forums to contradict Spong's teachings. The conflict received extensive newspaper coverage. As a result, approximately 1200 people showed up daily for Spong's lectures which went on for two hours instead of the usual hour. Donations that week topped $1800, nearly six or seven times the usual amount.

The dispute over Spong's appearance presented a dilemma. Association leaders and the majority of members supported open-mindedness to the controversial opinions of this leader who raises serious issues about the divinity of Jesus Christ. While Bay View's position was in keeping with the Chautauqua tradition, if not the camp-meeting tradition or the contemporary Methodist Church, the intertwining of the two traditions (the camp meeting and the assembly) in the pulpit is an issue that will continue in what might be considered a reflection of the complex national issue between liberals and the right wing conservatives.

A tangent concern facing the association is membership. Although the activities of the association are totally open to the public, and assembly guests come from all faiths and backgrounds, the association requires prospective members be of the "Christian persuasion," a philosophical concept that evolves out of American historical thought and not easily defined. From the Spong episode, it is apparent that the association chooses to adhere to its Chautauqua roots of offering stimulating, enlightening and thought-provoking opportunities for all. A far more difficult matter is retaining a criterion for membership that brings people into the community who seek to continue that ideology of openness.

Heeding the advice of the great historian, Bruce Catton, despite the formidable physical and philosophical challenges to its existence, the future is one of hope. Based on its heritage, Bay View is a resort in the historical meaning of the word - as a watering place. While remaining a vacation spot where extended families of our transient society meet, membership and cottage ownership have obligations far beyond that of family or a vacation. Bay View remains a private organization as many National Historic Landmarks are, but the increase in activies requires leadership that surpasses what the salaried staff can provide. So, cottagers and friends are unreservedly encouraged to volunteer to help with events, show consideration for community traditions and respectfully preserve the architectural heritage. "In Bay View you don't just buy a cottage, you buy an opportunity to volunteer," remarked cottager Dr. Robert Docking. Jeb McGruder, of Watergate fame, was astonished that cottagers worked so hard and called it a vacation.

"We have nothing that quite equals it in the state," former director of Detroit Historical Department Solan Weeks told the local press a decade after Bruce Catton's visit. He was vacationing in northern Michigan with his wife, a descendant of Bay View founder Seth Reed. Weeks stated: "The closest we can come to it is our neighborhood associations. Here in Bay View, the community taxes itself to offer a [religious] cultural, education, and recreation program to the public-at-large at little or no cost to that public, and seeks no outside funding, no government grants."[14]

Like most Chautauqua assemblies, Bay View struggles to find a new voice in a society that has incorporated its traditions. However, in the Shakespearean idea, the past is always prologue to the future. So it is in looking back that a sense of purpose is gained. Continuing the Bay View idea, as in former times, with its financial commitment is formidable. Knowing that the Bay View people have successfully realized these self-imposed obligations throughout its history, despite controversy and financial risk, is reassuring of a strong future.

Bay View's first president Reverend Dr. Elijah Pilcher wrote in 1885:

> *This was designed as a place of summer resort where our people might gather and for a month or two in leisure and recreation for health and enjoyment with religious surroundings and associations. Most admirably does it answer its design and it has far exceeded the most sanguine expectations of its projections.*[xv]

Those words are even accurate today.

*Worthiness is not wasted.*

*Ours is a universe in which nobleness and magnanimity do not fail.*

Dr. George Arthur Buttrick, August 18, 1940, John M. Hall Auditorium

# Appendix I

## *Presidents, Bay View Association*

| | |
|---|---|
| 1875-77 | Reverend Dr. E. H. Pilcher |
| 1877-78 | Reverend W. H. Brockway |
| 1878-82 | S. O. Knapp |
| 1882-84 | Reverend D. F. Barnes |
| 1884-86 | Watson Snyder |
| 1886-87 | Honorable John W. Moon |
| 1887-07 | Reverend Dr. William H. Shier |
| 1907-19 | Thomas Gordon, Jr. |
| 1919-28 | Judge Silas Hays |
| 1928-44 | Reverend Dr. Hugh Kennedy |
| 1944-61 | Bishop Raymond J. Wade |
| 1961-65 | Reverend Dr. Lester A. Kilpatrick |
| 1965-73 | Reverend Russell R. King |
| 1973-75 | Paul Cook |
| 1975-84 | Reverend Dr. Wesley Hager |
| 1984-89 | Ben H. VandenBelt, Jr. |
| 1989-92 | Don C. Vogelsberg |
| 1992-94 | Edith Buffett |
| 1994-98 | Robert J. Blok |
| 1998-02 | Roy M. Talley |
| 2002-08 | Thomas C. Shearer |
| 2008- | Lawrence R. Ternan |

# Appendix II

| WOMEN SPEAKERS/BAY VIEW | LOCATION | ORGANIZATION/POSITION | YEARS/BV |
|---|---|---|---|
| Jane Addams | Chicago, IL | Hull House | 1895, 1903 |
| Anna P. Akins | Not Available | CLSC Speaker | 1892 |
| Edith V. Alvord | Highland Park, MI | Pres., MI FWC | 1923 |
| Margaret Angus | TX | Not Available | 1902 |
| Addie A. Austin | Chicago, IL | WCTU Publishers Assn. | 1897 |
| Leonae Ayrs | Not Available | Not Available | N/A |
| Mrs. Albion Fellows Bacon | IN | Writer, Ladies' Home Journal | 1914 |
| Miss Franc J. Baker | Morenci, MI | WFMS | 1885-6, 1891-92 |
| Florence Balgarnie | England | Int. WCTU | 1891 |
| Dr. L. Anna Ballard | Lansing, MI | MI State Social Purity, WCTU | 1887 |
| Carrie Barge | Delaware, OH | Nat. Officer, WHMS | 1912, 1917-20 |
| Mrs. H. M. Barker | Chicago, IL | WCTU | 1896 |
| Mrs. G.S. Barnes | Petoskey, MI | WCTU | 1876, 1892-93<br>1896-97, 1900-03 |
| Mrs. A. T. Barrett | Niles, MI | Pres. 4th Dist. WCTU | 1891-92 |
| Mrs. L. M. Beck | IN | Evangelism WCTU | 1896 |
| Mary E. Beedy | Chicago, IL | Speaker CLSC | 1891, 1895 |
| Anna Smeed Benjamin | Portland, MI | Pres. 5th Congressional Dist.<br>WCTU, Pres. MI. WCTU<br>Parliamentarian - Nat.WCTU | 1885, 1888-90<br>1900-02, 1908 |
| Margaret J. Bliz | Not Available | Med. Temperance Dept..<br>Nat. - WCTU | 1908 |
| Mrs. L. M. Boise | Grand Rapids, MI | Evangelism WCTU | 1890 |
| Sarah Knowles Bolton | Cleveland, OH | Author/ Lecturer-BVRC | 1886-87 |
| Maud Ballington Booth | | Reformer | 1898, 1914 |
| Anna Boyle | Durango, CO | Suffragist, Speaker | 1902 |
| Mattie A. Boughton | Athens, OH | Bay View Press Club | 1891 |
| Hattie Brand | IN | Corres. Sec. IN WCTU | 1901-02 |
| Marie C. Brehm | IL | Pres. IL WCTU<br>Nat. Superintendent WCTU | 1895, 1902 |
| Mrs. F. E. Britten | Albion, MI | Not Available | 1896 |
| Caroline Brown Buell | Chicago, IL | Corres. Sec.Nat. WCTU | 1891-93 |
| Mrs. Elmor L. Calkins | Kalamazoo,MI | MIState Supt. Non-Narcotics | 1897 |
| | Petoskey,MI | Pres., MI WCTU | 1900, 1910 |
| Vie H. Campbell | WI | Pres., WI WCTU | 1897-98 |
| Helen S. Campbell | New York, NY | Reporter, NY Tribune | 1894 |
| Mrs. R. A. Campbell | Northport, MI | WCTU | 1898 |
| Ida M. Cahoon | Not Available | Not Available | Not Available |
| Kate Upson Clark | Not Available | Suffragist, Speaker | 1913 |
| Mabel Conklin | Brooklyn, NY | Pres., Nat.White Cross Society<br>WCTU | 1900 |
| Sarah B. Cooper | San Francisco, CA | Kindergarten Movement | Not Available |
| Jane Cunningham Croly | New York, NY | Writer, NY *Sunday Times*<br>Pres., NY FWC<br>Founder of Sorosis, Hon. Pres. | 1896 |
| Mrs. Edmund Curry | Kansas City, MO | Woman's Suffrage Day | 1914 |
| Jessie Dalrymple | Philadelphia, PA | Not Available | 1891 |
| Mrs. Dandee | Chicago, IL | First Pres., IL FWC | 1912 |
| Mrs. E. Smith Davis | WI | WCTU | 1900 |

| | | | |
|---|---|---|---|
| Abby Morton Diaz | Boston, MA | Author, Speaker | 1896 |
| Mary Lowe Dickson | Not Available | Not Available | Not Available |
| Anna Downey | WI/IL | Evangelistic Dept., IL WCTU | 1896 |
| Nettie Dunn | Kansas City, MO | Int. Sec., YWCA | 1891 |
| Mrs. E. Dryer | Chicago, IL | WFMS | 1891 |
| Fannie K. Earle | WI | Corres. Sec., WI WCTU | 1895-96 |
| Mrs. Charlton Edholm | Oakland, CA | Representative, World WCTU | Not Available |
| Mrs. John W. Ela | Not Available | Not Available | Not Available |
| Anna O. Eldridge | IN | WCTU | 1898 |
| Carrie C. Faxon | Bay City, MI | Pres.Dist.WCTU VP MI WCTU | 1893, 1897-98 |
| Mrs. J. M. Flower | Not Available | Not Available | Not Available |
| Kate Brearly Ford | Detroit, MI | Writer, *Detroit Evening News* | 1892-93, 1896 |
| Emma Augusta Fox | Detroit, MI | Parliamentary Law, Pres. Det. | 1895-96,1904 |
| | | Women's Club, MI FWC | 1925-26 |
| Ada Iddings Gale | Albion, MI | Author, Educator | 1894 |
| Mrs. D.M. Garner | Davisburg, MI | Speaker, WCTU | 1891 |
| Mrs. S. H. Gibson | Kalamazoo, MI | WFMS | 1891 |
| Mrs. Gift | MS | MI WCTU | 1900 |
| Mary Read Goodale | LA | Pres. LA WCTU | 1901 |
| Anna A. Gordon | IL | Asst.Supt. Juv.Wk.Nat.,WCTU | 1887 |
| | | Companion to Willard WCTU | 1889 |
| Frances Graham | Not Available | Musical Director, Nat. WCTU | 1903 |
| Emma R. Greene | Detroit, MI | Supt. LTCS WCTU | 1893 |
| Mary A. Greene | Providence, RI<br>Boston, MA | WCTU | 1892 |
| Jessie Grosenbaugh | Petoskey, MI | WCTU BVRC | 1899, 1909 |
| Mrs. S. A. Grosvenor | Monroe, MI | WCTU Speaker | 1891 |
| Carrie L. Grout | | | 1895, 1898, 1899 |
| Alice Guernsey | Chicago, IL | Ed.,THE YOUNG CRUSADER<br>WCTU | 1890 |
| Mary Hadley | IN | WCTU | 1898 |
| Beatrice Forbes-Robertson Hale | New York, NY | Lecturer, Conf. Speaker | 1917 |
| Miss M. G. Hay | Indianapolis, IN | Treasurer, IN WCTU | 1892 |
| Ellen M. Henrotin (Mrs. Charles) | Chicago, IL | Pres. Nat. FWC | 1894, 1896 |
| Alice Henry | Australia, England,<br>US | Leader 20 Years Woman's<br>Labor Movement | 1917 |
| Mrs. S. M. I. Henry (Sarepta) | IL | Nat.Sup.Evang.Wk., WCTU | 1889 |
| Mary E. Heston | Not Available | Hygiene, Phy.Culture, WCTU | 1909 |
| Lillian Hollister | Detroit, MI | Juvenile Work, WCTU | 1888-89, 1893 |
| | | Sup. Dept. Y MI WCTU | 1895 |
| | | Supreme Commander-Ladies of<br>the Maccabees of the World | |
| Mary Hopper | IL | Corres. Sec., IL WCTU | 1901 |
| Helen L. Hood | Chicago, IL | England, WCTU | 1897 |
| Mrs. Houghton | Not Available | WCTU | 1900 |
| Mrs. P. J. Howard | Petoskey, MI | MI State Supt., WCTU | 1892-93, 1896-97 |
| | | District President, WCTU | 1900-02, 1909 |
| Ida Huitin | Not Available | Not Available | Not Available |
| Esther R. Hunter | St. Johns, MI | Pres., MI FWC | 1926 |
| Mrs. C. H. Johnson | Flint, MI | WCTU | 1891 |
| Irma Theoda Jones | Lansing, MI | Pres., MI FWC | 1893-98 |
| Martha A. Keating | Muskegon, MI | FWC | 1896 |
| Bessie Starr Keefer | Not Available | WCTU | 1888 |

| | | | |
|---|---|---|---|
| Mrs. John Harvey Kellogg | Battle Creek, MI | Lecturer Health, Nat. Supt.<br>Social Parity Dept., WCTU | 1890-1892<br>1910 |
| Mrs. R. M. Kellogg | Ionia, MI | WCTU | 1892 |
| Jane M. Kinney | Pt. Huron, MI | Nat.Supt. Prison Work/WCTU | 1898, 1900, 1902 |
| Mary S. Knaggs | Bay City, MI | Suffragist | 1895 |
| Mary H. Krout | IL | Chicago *Inter-Ocean* | 1898 |
| Mary E. Kuhl | IL | Pres., IL WCTU | 1898, 1900, 1909 |
| Leonora M. Lake | St. Louis, MO | WCTU, Irish Orator | 1898, 1905, 1913 |
| Mary Torrans Lathrap<br>(often spelled Torrance and Lathrop) | Jackson, MI<br>Temp. Worker,Pres. MI WCTU | Preacher<br><br>Sec. Nat. WCTU | 1876-77, 1892 |
| Sarah J. LaTour | Detroit, MI. | Supt. Press Dept., MI WCTU | 1892-3 |
| E. Corinne Law | Baraga, MI. | Organizer, WCTU | 1891, 1893 |
| Hattie Lawton | Petoskey, MI | Department Studies WCTU. | 1909 |
| Lucy A. Leggett | Wash. DC | Org. Women's Republican Club<br>VP Woman's Nat. Press Assn.<br>Prin., Sprague School of Journ. | 1894-95 |
| Mary A. Livermore | Chicago, IL<br>Boston, MA | Author, Editor, Suffragist<br>Pres., IL Woman's Suff. Assoc.<br>Org. Soldier's Aid Soc/Civil War<br>Pres. MASS WCTU<br>Pres. Am Woman's Suff. Assoc. | 1890-91 |
| Anna Lowney | Not Available. | Not Available | Not Available |
| Evelyn MacDougal | Not Available. | Delsarte Inst. Drills, WCTU | 1891 |
| M. Lena Marrow | IL | Supt. Scientific Temperance<br>Instruction, WCTU | 1896 |
| Fanny J. Mason | Detroit, MI. | Not Available | Not Available |
| Mary Mayo | Battle Creek, MI | Woman's Council<br>Supt. Woman's Sect., Michigan<br>Farmers' Institute | 1896-97 |
| Jennie McCherkin | Fair Grove, MI | WCTU Speaker | 1891 |
| Mary McDowell | Not Available. | WCTU | N/A |
| Kate McGowan | Chicago, IL | Temperance Worker.<br>Ladies' National Union, | 1877 |
| Miss McGuirk | Petoskey, MI | WCTU | 1908 |
| Luella F. McWhirter | Indianapolis,IN | Pres., IN WCTU | 1895, 1897-1900 |
| Rena H. Michaels | Leroy, MI. | Northwestern U. BV Press Club | 1891 |
| Cornelia C. Moots | Bay City, MI | Evangelism, WCTU | 1890, 1892 |
| Lucy F. Morehouse | MI | MI State Superintendent,<br>WCTU School of Methods | 1896 |
| Miss Morris | New York, NY. | YWCA. | 1891 |
| Lydia J. Newcomb | Not Available. | Desarte Inst. Drills, WCTU. | 1889-90 |
| Laura Newlin | Not Available. | Not Available | N/A |
| Angelia F. Newman | NE | NE Prison System, WCTU | 1887 |
| Josephine R. Nichols | IN. | Pres., IN WCTU | 1893 |
| Edna Chaffee Noble | Detroit, MI | Lecturer, Educator<br>Est.Train.Sch.Elocution and<br>English Literature | 1886, 1890 |
| Mrs. D. C. Osborne | Petoskey, MI | Leader of Music, WCTU. | 1909 |
| Alice Freeman Palmer | Wellesley ,U Chicago | Board Bay View Reading Circle | 1890s |
| Anna A. Palmer | Saginaw, MI | Author, VP Pres., MI FWC<br>1stWoman/BVBoard ofTrustees | 1896<br>1909 |
| Mrs. F. E. Palmer | Albion, MI. | WCTU | Not Available |
| Mrs. Franc H. Palmiter | Charlevoix, MI | MI Supt. Purity in Lit.Art WCTU | 1900 |

| | | | |
|---|---|---|---|
| Mrs. Samuel Shaw Parks | Chicago, IL | Nat. Pres., PEO | 1913-14 |
| Julia R. Parrish | Bay City, MI | Editor, Michigan Union<br>Corres. Sec. MI WCTU | 1896-97 |
| Belle McArthur Perry | Charlotte, MI | Assoc. Ed. Charlotte Tribune<br>First Pres., MI Woman's Press Assn. founded in 1890 in Traverse City, MI | 1892, 1896 |
| Miss L. L. Phoenix | New York, NY | Not Available | Not Available |
| Elnora L. Porter | Lansing, MI | Women's Club -Lansing | 1891 |
| | | Pres., Lansing Women's Club | 1893 |
| Mrs. E. C. Porter-Hillsboro | TX | State Supt. Mothers Meeting, TX WCTU | 1900 |
| Mrs. F. E. Preston | Detroit, MI | WCTU | 1908 |
| Esther Pugh | Chicago, IL | Treasurer Nat. WCTU | 1892-93 |
| Mrs. F. H. Rastall | Chicago, IL | Supt. Literature, Nat. WCTU | 1893 |
| Mary Palmer Reese | Saginaw, MI | Journalist, FWC | 1896 |
| Mrs. G. H. Read | IL | WCTU | 1898 |
| Mrs. Seth Reed | Saginaw, MI | WCTU | 1889 |
| Mrs. Clarence Rickenbaugh | Not Available | Woman's Council | 1900 |
| Mrs. Henry Wade Rodgers | Not Available | Woman's Council | 1899, 1900 |
| Mrs. J. B. Roe | Petoskey, MI | Supt. Scientific Inst., WCTU | 1887 |
| Martha E. Synder Root | Bay City, MI | VP MI Woman's Suffage Assoc. | 1894 |
| Matilda H. Ross | Not Available | Bay View Summer University | 1887 |
| Mary Jenny Rossiter | Not Available | Woman's Council | 1900 |
| Louise S. Rounds | Chicago, IL | Pres., IL WCTU | 1895-96, 1898, 1899 |
| Mrs. Dorian M. Russell | Lansing, MI | Pres., MI FWC | 1922-24 |
| Mrs. A. E. Sanford | Not Available | Not Available | Not Available |
| Margaret Sangster | New York, NY | Editor, *Harper's Bazaar* | 1890-92 |
| Mrs. May Wright Sewall | IN | Pres., Nat. Council of Women<br>Author, Suffragist, Founder: numerous women's orgs. | 1898 |
| Rev. Dr. Anna Howard Shaw | Washington, DC | Suffragist, Author,Minister,<br>Doctor, Public Speaker<br>Supt.Franchise Dept.Nat.WCTU | 1887-88 |
| Dr. Annnetta J. Shaw | Eau Claire, WI | Supt. Dept. Health Nat., WCTU | 1891 |
| Mrs. S. C. Smith | Not Available | Not Available | Not Available |
| Helen Ekin Starrett | Chicago, IL | Prin., Starrett School for Girls | 1913 |
| Katherine Lente Stevenson | MA | Rec. Sec. Nat. WCTU | 1894-95 |
| Dr. Sarah Hackett Stevenson | Not Available | Woman's Council | 1895 |
| Juliet V. Strauss | NY | Country Contributor<br>*Ladies' Home Journal* | 1917 |
| Mrs. W. B. Street | Greensboro, NC | Pres., Bay View Women's Club | 1913 |
| Julia Dexter Steward | Not Available | Not Available | 1890 |
| Helen M. Stoddard | TX | Pres., TX WCTU | 1893, 1899-1903 |
| Ellen M. Stone | Turkey | Missionary | 1902 |
| Lucinda Hinsdale Stone | MI | MI Mother of Women's Clubs<br>Founder, First Women's Club | 1892 |
| Corabel Tarr | Not Available | YWCA | 1891 |
| Mary Virginia Hawes Terhune | New York, NY | Editor, Author<br>(Mrs. Albert P.)<br>(Pen Name: Marion Harland) | 1889-91 |
| Eleanor L. Terry | WI | Evangelism WCTU | 1896 |

| | | | |
|---|---|---|---|
| Rev. Frances E. Townsley | Vassar, MI | Evangelistic Supt., Nat. WCTU | 1897, 1899 |
| | | Evangelist, Minister | 1901-02 |
| Lucretia Willard Treat | Grand Rapids, MI | Grand Rapids Kindergarten Association | 1897-98 |
| Mrs. L. M. Turner | TX | Editor, *White Ribboner* | 1901 |
| Mrs. Charles E. Vowels | Mt. Pleasant,MI | VP MI FWC | 1923 |
| Zeralda G. Wallace | IN | WCTU | 1891 |
| Dorothy Weaver | Ft. Worth, TX | Supt.Temp.Inst., TX WCTU | 1900 |
| Maria Weed | Chicago, IL | Nat. WCTU | 1903 |
| Kate Douglas Wiggins | CA | Author, Philanthropist | 1893 |
| Frances E. Willard | Chicago, IL | Pres. Nat. WCTU/VP Int.WCTU | 1887 |
| | | Pres. World WCTU | 1889 |
| Miss Wilson | WI | YWCA | 1891 |
| L. Helen Wood | Chicago, IL | WCTU | 1897 |
| Dr. Mary Wood-Allen | Ann Arbor, MI | Supt. Purity, World WCTU | 1895, 1902 |
| | | Medical degree - U-M 1875 | |

**LEGEND**

Bay View Reading Circle . . . BVRC
Chautauqua Literary and Scientific Circle . . . CLSC
Federation of Women's Clubs . . . FWC
University of Michigan . . . U-M
Woman's Christian Temperance Union . . . WCTU
Woman's Foreign Missionary Society . . . WFMS
Young Women's Christian Association . . . YMCA

# Appendix III

### *Some of the Notable People on the Bay View Assembly Program*

| YEAR | INDIVIDUAL/POSITION |
|---|---|
| 1877 | Dr. Jesse Lyman Hurlbut, Preacher, Author<br>Bay View Sunday School Congress |
| 1886 | Rev. Dr. John DeWitt Miller, Philadelphia |
| 1887 | Rev. Dr. John DeWitt Miller, Philadelphia<br>Frances Willard, President, National WCTU<br>Rev. Dr. Anna Howard Shaw, Preacher, Medical Doctor, Suffragist<br>Prof. Joseph Estabrook, Michigan State Supt. Public Instruction |
| 1888 | Bishop John H. Vincent, Founder, Chautauqua Institutions<br>Andrew J. Blackbird, Leader of the Ottawa Tribe of Little Traverse Bay<br>Rev. Dr. Anna Howard Shaw<br>Rev. Dr. John DeWitt Miller, Philadelphia |
| 1889 | Rev. Russell H. Conwell, Preacher<br>(first of many appearances)<br>Mary A. Livermore, Author, Suffragist<br>Rev. Frank W. Gunsaulus<br>(first of many appearances)<br>Frances Willard, President, National WCTU<br>Will Cumback of Indiana, ex-Congressman and ex-Lt. Governor |
| 1890 | Dr. and Mrs. John Harvey Kellogg of Battle Creek Sanitarium<br>Fisk Jubilee Singers, first African-Am.Entertainment group to tour US<br>Mary A. Livermore, Author, Suffragist<br>Margaret Sangster, Editor, Harper's Bazaar Magazine<br>George Washington Cable, Author, (Canceled)<br>Rev. Russell H. Conwell, Preacher (Acres of Diamonds)<br>Hon. Thomas W. Palmer, Senator, Michigan<br>Rev. Frank W. Gunsaulus<br>Hon. Major Wm. McKinley of Ohio |
| 1891 | P. B. Wachtel, Speaker of the Michigan House of Representatives<br>Dr. Jesse Lyman Hurlbut, Preacher, Author<br>Rev. Russell H. Conwell, Preacher (Garibaldi) (Jolly Earthquake)<br>Dr. Camden M. Cobern, Philosopher, Writer, Lecturer<br>(first of many appearances)<br>Fisk Jubilee Singers<br>Dr. and Mrs. John Harvey Kellogg of Battle Creek Sanitarium<br>Margaret Sangster<br>Rev. Dr. Anna Howard Shaw |
| 1892 | James Buckley, Editor and Orator<br>Dr. Richard T. Ely, Economist and Social Reformer<br>Bay View Summer University<br>Rev. Dr. A. J. F. Behrends<br>Lucinda Hinsdale Stone, Mother of Women's Clubs, Michigan<br>Dr. and Mrs. John Harvey Kellogg<br>Dr. Jesse Lyman Hurlbut<br>Leon H. Vincent, Speaker, nephew of Bishop Vincent<br>(first of many appearances)<br>Jacob A. Riis, Photographer, Social Reformer<br>Royal Hand Bell Ringers<br>Rev. Russell H. Conwell<br>Hon. Thomas W. Palmer, President, Columbian Exposition (Chicago 1893)<br>Ex-Gov. Cyrus G. Luce of Michigan |
| 1893 | Thomas Dixon, Jr., Preacher and Writer<br>Rev. A. J. F. Behrends |

Hon. John Temple Graves, Orator
Kate Douglas Wiggins, Author

1894........................................ Rev. Dr. A. J. F. Behrends
Booker T. Washington, Educator
John Brown Gordon, Brigadier Gen., Army of Northern Virginia
Martha Root, VP, Michigan Woman's Suffrage Assoc.
Fred Emerson Brooks, Poet
John Fiske, Historian
Major William McKinley, Ohio and General Gordon,Georgia

1895........................................ George Kennan, Senior Foreign Correspondent
Senator Julius Caesar Burrows of Michigan
Rev. Russell H. Conwell
Jane Addams, Hull House, Reformer

1896........................................ Will Carleton, Author
Jacob A. Riis, Social Reformer
Hon. John Temple Graves, Author, Editor
Hon. George R. Wendling, Orator
Bishop John H. Vincent, Founder, Chautauqua Institutions
Moses Coit Tyler, Champion Academic Freedom, Cornell University
Leon H. Vincent
Martha Root, V.P. Michigan Suffrage Assoc.
Jennie Cunningham Croly, President, New York State Federation of Women's Clubs, Hon. Pres. of Sorosis

1897........................................ Fisk Jubilee Singers
Rev. Dr. A. J. F. Behrends
Senor Gonzalez de Quesada
Representative of the Cuban Republic at Washington
Margaret Sangster

1898........................................ Maud Ballington Booth, Prison Reformer
William Jennings Bryan, Politician (unconfirmed)
Dr. Samuel Parkes Cadman, Preacher, Metropolitan Temple NYC (first of many appearances)
Dr. A. E. Winship, Editor, *New England Journal of Education*
Jacob A. Riis
Rev. Dr. R. S. MacArthur, Calvary Baptist Church, NY

1899........................................ Hon. John Temple Graves, Author, Editor
Dr. Samuel Parkes Cadman
William Jennings Bryan, Politician
Dr. Shailer Mathews, Preacher, Summer University (first of many appearances)
Rev. Dr. John DeWitt Miller
Rev. Frank W.Gunsaulus

1900........................................ African Boy Choir
Leon H. Vincent
Hon. George R. Wendling
Governor Leslie M. Shaw, Iowa
Montaville Flowers, Lecturer (Ben Hur)
Rev. Dr. Samuel Parkes Cadman, Pastor, Central Congregational Church
Mary French Field, daughter of author Eugene Field

1901........................................ Dr. George L. Robinson, McCormick Theological Seminary, Chicago
Rev.Thomas DeWitt Talmage
Dr. Russell H. Conwell (A Silver Crown)

1902........................................ Montaville Flowers, Speaker
Lorado Taft, Sculptor
Major General Fitzhugh Lee, nephew, Gen. Robert E. Lee (Introduced by Gov. Aaron T. Bliss of Michigan)
Rabbi Leo M. Franklin, Detroit

1903........................................ Lorado Taft
Rev. Dr. John DeWitt Miller

| | |
|---|---|
| | Jane Addams |
| | Hon. George W. Wendling |
| 1904 | Fred Emerson Brooks, Poet |
| 1905 | William Jennings Bryan |
| 1906 | Strickland W. Gillilan, Humorist |
| | (first of many appearances) |
| | James A. McCall, Blind, African-American Lecturer |
| 1908 | Chicago Glee Club |
| | Margaret Parry, Operatic Soprano |
| | Carry Lou Betz, Piano Artiste |
| 1909 | Gov. Robert B. Glenn, North Carolina |
| | Virginia Jubilee Singers |
| | Grace Hemingway, aunt of Ernest Hemingway |
| 1910 | Gov. Henry Buchtell of Colorado |
| | Senator John Worth Kern, Indiana |
| | (1908 VP Running mate of William Jennings Bryan) |
| | Senator Julius Caesar Burrows, Michigan |
| | Madame Schumann-Heink, Contralto |
| | Labor and Social Welfare Conference (first of several) |
| | Rev. Charles Stelzle, Presbyterian Minister of New York Labor Temple |
| | John B. Lennon, Treasurer, American Federation of Labor |
| | Hon. Perry F. Powers, Cong. Representative from Michigan |
| 1911 | Flying Machine Tournament (Baseball Park) |
| | Rev. Frank W. Gunsaulus |
| | Leon H. Vincent |
| | David Bispham, Baritone |
| | William Jennings Bryan (Prince of Peace) |
| | (Introduced by Gov. Thomas R. Marshall of Indiana) |
| | Dr. and Mrs. John Harvey Kellogg |
| 1912 | Cincinnati Orchestra (Canceled) |
| | Senator Frank J. Cannon, Utah |
| | Gov. Edward W. Hoch, Kansas |
| | David Bispham, Baritone |
| | Gov. Robert B. Glenn, North Carolina |
| | Booker T. Washington (Canceled) |
| | rescheduled for an unknown date in 1913 |
| | Maud Ballington Booth |
| | Kate Douglas Wiggins |
| 1913 | William J. Burn, American Detective (Canceled) |
| | Kate Upson Clark, Author |
| | Russian Balalaika Orchestra |
| | Leon H. Vincent |
| | Gay Zenola MacLaren, Reader, Author *(Morally We Roll Along)* |
| | Madame Schumann-Heink |
| | Henry A. Buchtel, ex-Gov. Colorado |
| | Helen Keller, Author, Public Speaker |
| | Gov. A. O. Eberhart of Minnesota |
| 1914 | Williams Jubilee Singers |
| | Mrs. Percy V. Pennybacker, Pres., Gen. Fed. of Women's Clubs |
| | Dr. Merton S. Rice (first of many appearances) |
| | Ida Tarbell, Author, (Canceled, replaced by Kate Upson Clark, |
| | Editor, *Leslie's Magazine*) |
| | Dr. Shailer Mathews, Dean, Divinity School, University of Chicago |
| | Thomas R. Marshall, VP of the United States (Canceled) |
| | Maud Ballington Booth |
| | John A. Lomax, President American Folklore Society |
| 1915 | Henry Pattengill, Director, Michigan Department of Education |
| | Dr. Merton Rice, Preacher, |

Dedication, John M. Hall Auditorium
Dr. Jesse Lyman Hurlbut
Boston Symphony Sextet
Evan Williams, Tenor
Fisk Jubilee Singers
Reinald Werrenrath, Baritone

1916........................................ Hruby Bohemian Orchestra
Lorado Taft
Marie Sundelius, Soprano

1917........................................ Dixie Jubilee Singers
Hruby Bohemian Orchestra

1918........................................ Howard Quintet
Metropolitan Male Quartet
William Jennings Bryan
Thomas R. Marshall, VP of the United States
Alice Schrode, Child Whistler
Dixie Jubilee Singers

1919........................................ Dr. Shailer Mathews, Dean, Chicago Dvinity School
Bertha Farner, Soprano
Mark Sullivan, Editor, *Collier's Weekly*

1920........................................ Orville Harrold, Tenor
Arthur Middleton, Bass-baritone
Republican Rally-Gov. Harding of Iowa, Cong. Montaville Flowers of California, William H. Smith, representing Gov. Sleeper of Michigan
Exhibit from Greek government of 400 photographs by Swiss photographer Frederic Boissonnas
Adolph Muhlmann, Basso, Lecturer

1921........................................ Issay Mitnitzky, Violinist
Arthur Middleton

1922........................................ Merle Alcock, Contralto and Lambert Murphy, Tenor
Will Irwin, War Correspondent
Dr. Owen R. Lovejoy, Nat. Authority Child Labor
Bay View Summer University Faculty
Dr. George L. Robinson, McCormick Theological Seminary
Senator Simeon D. Fess, Ohio
Dr. William C. Poole, Preacher, Christ Church, London, England
Vilhjalmur Stefansson, Arctic Explorer

1923........................................ Ex-Governor Henry J. Allen, Kansas
Dorian M. Russell, Pres. Michigan Federation of Women's Clubs
Mrs. Walter W. Seymour, 2nd VP of GFWC
Dr. Frank A. Poole, Michigan Department of Health
Edgar A. Guest, Poet
Theodora Sturkow-Ryder, Pianist, Robert Ambrosius, Cellist
Bishop John N. McCormick

1924........................................ Mrs. Percy V. Pennybacker, Past-Pres., Gen. Fed. of Women's Clubs
Mrs. William R. Alvord, Past-Pres. Michigan Federation of Women's Clubs
Jack Miner, Jack Miner's Bird Sanctuary, Ontario
Senator Simeon D. Fess, Ohio
Senator Woodbridge N. Ferris, Michigan
Ex-Gov. of Michigan, President of Ferris Institute
President E. C. Warriner, Central Normal College (CMU)
Edith Bideau Normelli, Soprano

1925........................................ Hon. Thomas E. Johnson, Sup't of Public Instruction of State of Michigan
Rev. Dr. Merton S. Rice

1926........................................ Rev. Edgar DeWitt Jones, Pastor, Central Christian Church, Detroit
Dr. Frederick W. Norwood, Minister, City Temple, London
John Barnes Wells, Tenor

| | |
|---|---|
| | Senator Grant M. Hudson, Michigan<br>Florence Mulford, Contralto<br>(sponsored by the Woman's Council) |
| 1927 | Hon. James Schermerhorn, Political Editor, *Detroit News*<br>Founder and proprietor of the *Detroit Times*<br>Dr. Edward DeWitt Jones, Editorial Staff, *Detroit News*<br>Max Pollikoff, Violinist<br>Hon. Pat M. Neff, Ex-Governor of Texas |
| 1928 | Constance Eberhart, Mezzo-soprano |
| 1929 | Lucia Chagnon, Soprano |
| 1930 | Ossip Gabrilovitsch, First Conductor of the<br>Detroit Symphony Orchestra, and Mrs.<br>Gabrilovitsch (Clara Clemens, Daughter of Mark Twain)<br>(sponsored by the Woman's Council)<br>Dr. John Timothy Stone, S.T.D., Pres. McCormick Theological Seminary<br>Max Pollikoff, Violinist |
| 1931 | Countee Cullen, African-American Poet<br>Governor and Mrs. Wilbur M. Brucker of Michigan<br>Mrs. Brucker (Woman's Council)<br>Frederick Jagel, Tenor (Canceled)<br>replaced by Barre-Hill, Baritone |
| 1932 | Countee Cullen<br>Benno Rabinof, Violinist |
| 1933 | Garrit A. Beneker, Artist (WWI Victory Liberty Loan Poster)<br>E. Stanley Jones, Preacher<br>Nevada Van Der Veer, Mezzo-contralto<br>Amri Galli-Campi, Coloratura Soprano<br>Dr. Ralph Sockman, Preacher<br>(first of many appearances) |
| 1935 | Dr. George Buttrick, Preacher, Editor, *Interpreter's Bible*<br>(first of 43 appearances)<br>Frederic Baer, Baritone |
| 1936 | Carl Sandburg, Author<br>Senator Gerald P. Nye of North Dakota<br>Julius Heuhn, Baritone |
| 1937 | Anna Kaskas, Contralto |
| 1938 | James E. Watson, ex-Senator of Indiana<br>Gladys Swarthout, Mezzo-soprano |
| 1939 | Drew Pearson, Author<br>Judge J. M. Braude, Authority on Juvenile and Adolescent Delinquency<br>Helen Jepson, Soprano |
| 1940 | Will Irwin, Author, Editor, Reporter<br>Dr. Will Durant, Author, Educator, Philosopher<br>Richard Crooks, Tenor |
| 1941 | Maury Maverick, U. S. Congressman (Canceled)<br>Etta Moten, Mezzo-Soprano<br>(first African-American to entertain at the White House)<br>John Charles Thomas, Baritone |
| 1942 | Reinald Werrenrath, Baritone<br>Dean of American Singers<br>John Temple Graves, II, Editor, Lecturer<br>Soo Yong, Actress, Lecturer<br>James Melton, Tenor |
| 1944 | Senator Vojta Benes |
| 1946 | Thomas L. Thomas, Baritone<br>Dr. Clarence T. Craig, one of the scholars who published<br>Revised Standard Version of the New Testament |

| | |
|---|---|
| | Dr. Frederick H. Olert, Preacher<br>(first of many appearances)<br>Douglas V. Steere, Preacher<br>Benno Rabinof, Violinist |
| 1947 | John Jacob Niles, Ballad Singer<br>Jennie Tourel, Mezzo Soprano |
| 1948 | Dr. Oilin Sewall Pettingill, Zoologist, U-M Biological Station, Pellston<br>Martha Lipton, Mezzo-soprano |
| 1949 | Fritz Krueger, Tenor, Philadelphia Opera Company<br>Joseph E. Ragen, Warden, Illinois State Penitentiary<br>Mrs. D. Leigh Colvin, Pres. WCTU<br>(Woman's Council) |
| 1952 | Mrs. O. R. Hurd, State Pres. WCTU<br>(Woman's Council)<br>WJR Make Way for Youth Chorus with Don Large<br>(Also appeared 1954, 1956, 1957, 1958, and 1961) |
| 1953 | 118th Annual Conference of the Methodist Church of Michigan<br>Stanley E. Kresge, Businessman<br>Dedication of Voorhies Hall<br>Mrs. George Buttrick, Woman's Council |
| 1954 | Mrs. Glenn G. Hays, Pres. Nat. WCTU, Woman's Council<br>Sen. Charles E. Potter of Michigan, member of<br>the McCarthy Committee on Un-American Activities<br>Nancy Williams, wife of Gov. Williams of Michigan<br>(Woman's Council) |
| 1955 | Mrs. Glenn G. Hays, Pres. Nat. WCTU, Woman's Council<br>Noble Cain, Choral Conductor, Composer |
| 1956 | Noble Cain |
| 1957 | Noble Cain |
| 1959 | Noble Cain |
| 1962 | "A Patriotic Week" Conference of Balkan Ministers<br>James M. Babcock, Chief of the Burton Historical Collection<br>Detroit Public Library, Sponsored by the Bay View Library |
| 1963 | Dr. Ione Catton, sister of Dr. Bruce Catton<br>(Woman's Council) |
| 1964 | The Swedish Youth Chorale |
| 1965 | Dr. Bruce Catton, Civil War Historian, Author, Editor<br>*American Heritage Magazine* |
| 1973 | RéKoster, Vocal Master Class |
| 1974 | Ruth Slenczynska, Pianist<br>University of Saarbrucker Choir<br>John Wustman, Accompanist, Vocal Coach<br>Wesleyan Bell Choir, Donald Allured, Conductor |
| 1976 | Mildred Dilling, Harpist<br>Eugene Bossart and Charles Fisher, Duo-Pianists<br>Detroit Symphony Orchestra |
| 1977 | Mildred Dilling, Harpist<br>Eugene Bossart and Charles Fisher, Duo Pianists |
| 1979 | Gwen Frostic, Writer, Artist<br>(Woman's Council)<br>Solan W. Weeks, Director, Detroit Historical Museums |
| 1980 | International Organ Competition<br>Diane Bish, Organist |
| 1981 | Marilyn Mason, Organist<br>Pierre D'Archambeau, Violinist<br>Meadow Brook Estate |

1982. . . . . . . . . . . . . . . . . . . . . . . . . . . . . . . . . . . . . . . . Glenn Miller Band
1984. . . . . . . . . . . . . . . . . . . . . . . . . . . . . . . . . . . . . . . . Moorhead C. Kennedy, Jr., Director
Council for International Understanding
1987. . . . . . . . . . . . . . . . . . . . . . . . . . . . . . . . . . . . . . . . Anne-Imedla Radice, Director
National Museum of Women in Arts
1988. . . . . . . . . . . . . . . . . . . . . . . . . . . . . . . . . . . . . . . . Diane Bish, Organist
Presentation of National Landmark Designation,
William Penn Mott, Jr., Director, National Park Service
1992. . . . . . . . . . . . . . . . . . . . . . . . . . . . . . . . . . . . . . . . Jeb McGruder, Preacher, returned-1997
Director, 1974 Nixon Re-election Campaign
1993. . . . . . . . . . . . . . . . . . . . . . . . . . . . . . . . . . . . . . . . James Wall, Editor, *Christian Century*
Huw Lewis, Organist
Balthazar Korab, Photographer
1996. . . . . . . . . . . . . . . . . . . . . . . . . . . . . . . . . . . . . . . . Esther Budiardjo Pickett, Pianist
Winner, William Kapell Piano Competition
1999. . . . . . . . . . . . . . . . . . . . . . . . . . . . . . . . . . . . . . . . Frederick Swann, Organist
2002. . . . . . . . . . . . . . . . . . . . . . . . . . . . . . . . . . . . . . . . Balthazar Korab, Photographer
Captain Al Haynes, Pilot, United Flight #232
Sung Sook Lee, Soprano
Diane Bish, Organist
2003. . . . . . . . . . . . . . . . . . . . . . . . . . . . . . . . . . . . . . . . Jack Rokave, Author
2004. . . . . . . . . . . . . . . . . . . . . . . . . . . . . . . . . . . . . . . . Bishop John Shelby Spong, Retired-Episcopalian Priest
2005. . . . . . . . . . . . . . . . . . . . . . . . . . . . . . . . . . . . . . . . Dr. Anthony Campolo, Author and Lecturer
Dr. Gordon S. Wood, Pulitzer Prize Winning Author
2006. . . . . . . . . . . . . . . . . . . . . . . . . . . . . . . . . . . . . . . . Dr. James A. Forbes, Jr., Pastor, Riverside Church
Judge John T. Noonan, Nineth Circuit Court
Berklee College of Music Jazz Ensemble
Ciaran Sheehan, Gay Willis, Eily O'Grady
Stars of *The Phantom of the Opera*
2007. . . . . . . . . . . . . . . . . . . . . . . . . . . . . . . . . . . . . . . . The Four Freshmen
Dr. Akhil Reed Amar, Author
Berklee College of Music Jazz Ensemble
2008. . . . . . . . . . . . . . . . . . . . . . . . . . . . . . . . . . . . . . . . Rev. Dr. Michael Ward, C.S. Lewis Scholar
Ethan Becker, Grandson of Irma Rombauer (Woman's Council)
Rev. Dr. John H. Thomas, Pres. United Church of Christ
Bishop John Shelby Spong, Retired-Episcopalian Priest
Dr. Rebecca J. Scott, Law Professor, U-M
2009. . . . . . . . . . . . . . . . . . . . . . . . . . . . . . . . . . . . . . . . Dr. Daniel Walker Howe
Bishop Peter Story
Rev. Walter Brueggemann

## VIRGINA GALVIN CROUSE VISITING ARTISTS

| | |
|---|---|
| 1989 | James Buswell, Violinist |
| 1990 | Jerome Hines, Bass |
| 1991 | Bach Aria Group |
| 1992 | Bolcum & Morris |
| 1993 | Lorin Hollander, Pianist |
| 1994 | Benjamin Mathews, Eddye Pierce Young<br>Leon Bates<br>Verdehr Trio |
| 1995 | Ara Berberian, Bass<br>Cleveland Duo |
| 1996 | Crofut and Brubeck<br>with Peter Madcap Ruth<br>Sherrill Milnes, Baritone |
| 1997 | Clear Fork<br>Eugenia Zukerman, Flautist |
| 1998 | Patricia Wise, Soprano<br>Cynthia Munzer, Mezzo-soprano<br>Cliff Jackson, Pianist<br>Martina Arroyo, Soprano<br>Opera Aria Master Class<br>Eroica Trio, Piano Trio |
| 1999 | Scholars of London<br>Giorgio Tozzi, Bass-Baritone<br>Opera Aria Master Class<br>Trio Voronezh |
| 2000 | Ahn Trio<br>Ara Berberian, Bass<br>Opera Aria Master Class<br>Trio Voronezh |
| 2001 | Bach Aria Group<br>Concert and Master Class<br>George Shirley, Tenor<br>Master Class<br>Boston Brass<br>Concert and Master Class |
| 2002 | Robert Stallman, Flutist<br>Concert and Master Class<br>The Martinu Quartet<br>Master Class and Concert<br>Virginia Zeani, Soprano<br>Master Class |
| 2003 | Allen Vizzutti, Trumpet<br>Master Class and Concert<br>George Shirley, Tenor<br>Master Class<br>Oleg Pokhanovski, Violinist<br>Master Class and Concert |
| 2004 | William Preucil, Violin, and Arthur Rowe, Piano<br>Master Class and Concert<br>Diana Soviero, Soprano<br>Master Class |
| 2005 | Verdehr Trio<br>Martin Katz, piano |

2006. . . . . . . . . . . . . . . . . . . . . . . . . . . . . . . . . . . . . . . . Antares Quartet
Virginia Zeani, Soprano
Master Class

2007. . . . . . . . . . . . . . . . . . . . . . . . . . . . . . . . . . . . . . . . American String Quartet
Concert and Master Class
Timothy Noble, Baritone
Master Class

2008. . . . . . . . . . . . . . . . . . . . . . . . . . . . . . . . . . . . . . . . Timothy Noble, Baritone
Master Class
Boston Brass
Concert and Master Class
Project
Concert and Master Class

2009. . . . . . . . . . . . . . . . . . . . . . . . . . . . . . . . . . . . . . . . Time For Three

# Endnotes

## Introduction

[1] See Mary Jane Doerr and Helen Guittard, "In Celebration of Bay View".
[2] See *Daily Resorter*, July 14, 1911.
[3] Speech, David McCullough, *Chautauqua and Its Place in American Culture*, 1993.

## Chapter 1

[1] As his grandson John Higgins tells the story – E-mail to Mary Jane Doerr, February 24, 2005. Used with permission.
[2] See *Petoskey City Record*, July 20, 1887.
[3] See Nancy Jarvis, ed. *Historical Glimpses*, Petoskey, MI: Little Traverse Historical Society, 1986. p. 97. In Petoskey there were some 22 hotels and thousands of rooming houses. By 1902, Petoskey hotels included The Arlington, (which rivaled Mackinaw's Grand Hotel in size) the Banghart, Bayside Inn, Clifton Hotel, Cushman House, Exchange Hotel, Imperial Hotel, National Hotel, Occidental Hotel, Hotel Perry, New Petoskey, and Ozark Hotel. Only the Perry Hotel remains today. Of the five major hotels in Bay View, there are two left – Stafford's Bay View Inn and the Terrace Inn – and one B&B, The Gingerbread House.
[4] See *The Bay View Assembly Record*, August 6, 1895.
[5] See *Petoskey Evening News*, July 31, 1911.
[6] See *Daily Resorter*, July 9, 1895.
[7] See Kenneth Brown, *Holy Ground, Too. The Camp Meeting Family Tree*, Pazleton, PA: 1997 p. 68.
[8] See *The Peterson Magazine*, January, 1895, p. 13.
[9] In the May, 1910 article in the *Bay View Magazine*, John M. Hall gives the year as 1874 which coincides more closely with the information that Knapp "took the first passenger train to Petoskey." That passenger service began in late 1873. However, Reverend McCarty did not approach the Methodist conferences until September of 1875, which would mean that Knapp waited a year before going to McCarty with his idea of a camp meeting near Petoskey. It is questionable that he waited a year before relaying his enthusiasm.
[10] The spelling used in this manuscript is that used by The Little Traverse Bands of Odawa Indians.
[11] See, John Halsey, "Jackson's Quiet Promoter" *Michigan History*, Nov./Dec., 1998 p. 19. S. O. Knapp was one of twelve children of a substantial New England family. He attended common schools until he was ten, when he was apprenticed to the woolen manufacturing trade in mills owned by Charles Payne (later, governor of Vermont). He worked in the mills for sixteen to eighteen years until he developed "brown lung" caused by inhaling unconfined wool fibers. His health failed.
[12] See *History of Rockland*, July, 1976, p. 9.
[13] While stockholders took millions in profits out of the mine, the company paid its workers an average salary of $30.46 per month.
[14] See Halsey, *Michigan History*. p. 20.
[15] See Dr. Margaret Burnham. *The Methodist Church in Michigan: The Nineteenth Century*, The Michigan Area Methodist Historical Society and William B. Eerdmans Publishing Company, 1967. p.307.
[16] Historians Seth Reed, Dr. Clark S. Wheeler, and the Reverend Dr. William Shier list the committee from the Michigan Annual Conference as McCarty, Brockway, Judge Aaron P. Moors and Samuel O. Knapp.
[17] Also included in this article but not mentioned in other sources are Reverend and Mrs. G. B. Joelyn of Albion; Reverend and Mrs. Hildreth; and Reverend and Mrs. L. R. Atwater of Grand Rapids; Reverend H. Worthington of Traverse City; and John L. Shaw and H. D. Wallen, both of the GR&I.
[18] Pilcher, Reed, Preston, McCarty, Brockway, Moors and Knapp represented the conferences. Visitors present were: James Gould, Silas Heyler and J. H. Pilcher of Jackson; Dr. J. W. Kermott, Reverend John M. Arno and D. Burnham Tracy of Detroit; and Perry Hannah of Traverse City. The committee elected McCarty, Pilcher, Brockway, Reed, Moors, Bird, Knapp, Preston and Tracy to the board of trustees.
[19] See DeLand's *History of Jackson County Michigan*, Jackson MI: 1903. and *Daily Resorter*, September 15, 1906.
[20] See Hon. Charles J. Pailthorp. "Speech to Petoskey Kiwanis Club." History Museum Archives, Petoskey: 1932.
[21] Wheeler lists Alice Cushway, John G. Harsha, Daniel and Mary Nakinashi (Nakenashe?), and Lewis (Louis?) and Sarah Shegwageshing as owners. Researcher Lowell Kosloskey added the names Catherine Ingalls, John B. Kizhigehenese and his wife, Ogawbaygezhegoquay (Margaret Wagley), and Francis Pirey (Priez?) also as owners.
[22] See Floy Irene Graham, *Petoskey and Bay View in Ye Olden Days*, Petoskey, MI: 1938.
[23] He chose Lot 15, Block 20.
[24] See Pilcher, *Elijah Pilcher Memoirs*, Burton Historical Collection, Detroit Public Library, 1885. p. 557. Benjamin F. Darling or L.D. Grosvenor (or both) planned the structure while William Samuel Batt of Petoskey built it.
[25] See *Emmet County Democrat*, October 1, 1875.
[26] See Ellen Weiss, *City in the Woods. The Life and Design of an American Camp Meeting on Martha's Vineyard.* New York: Oxford University Press, 1987. p. 38.
[27] See *Daily Resorter*, September 13, 1906.
[28] Olmsted's relative Mrs. H. B. Olmsted registered at the Bay View House, July 24, 1890 and today, distant Olmsted relatives are members of the association.
[29] See Garfield, 1908.
[30] See John Halsey. E-mail to Mary Jane Doerr, November 26, 2001. Used by permission.
[31] See Clark Wheeler, *Bay View*. Bay View, MI: Bay View Association of the Methodist Church, 1950. p. 23.
[32] See Kathryn Bishop Eckert, *Buildings of Michigan*. Oxford: Oxford University Press, 1993. p. 407.
[33] See *Daily Resorter*, September 15, 1906.

## Chapter 2

[1] Epworth Heights, another Michigan camp meeting site, was established at that location.
[2] See Floy Irene Graham, *Petoskey and Bay View in Ye Olde Days*, Petoskey, MI: 1938, p. 22.
[3] Letter dated October 8, 1950 to Bruce Brockway.
[4] See Charlotte Lockwood, *Church on Main Street, A History of the First United Methodist Church, Jackson, Michigan*. 1931-1943. Of 787 itinerant Methodist preachers who died in America before 1847, nearly half perished by the time they were thirty years old and most died within the first five years of service.
[5] See Brockway letter, 1950. Brockway's brother, Daniel and his wife settled in the Keweenaw Peninsula. His wife's diaries (1865 to 1897) are part of the Michigan Technological University Archives in Houghton, Michigan. Brockway Mountain Drive at the tip of the Keweenaw Peninsula is named for Daniel Brockway.
[6] See *Emmet County Democrat*, August 4, 1876.
[7] See Dr. William H. Shier, "Bay View History." *Golden Jubilee*, Bay View: Published by the Bay View Camp-ground Association, 1925. Pages unnumbered.
[8] This information about Pilcher and his involvement with the University of Michigan is taken from his handwritten 1885 autobiography at the Burton Historical Collection at the Detroit Public Library, the *Michigan Christian Advocate*, and Petoskey newspa-

pers. It is not confirmed by other sources such as Elizabeth M. Farrand's *History of the University of Michigan*, published in 1885. In William Ray Prescott's 1941 book, , the claim is made that the information from Pilcher is unreliable. More research about Pilcher is needed to confirm his claims.

9 See Pilcher, *Elijah Pilcher Memoirs*, Burton Historical Collection, Detroit Public Library, 1885. p.557. The present name, "Bay View Association of the Methodist Church," was adopted at the association's annual meeting August 5, 1936.

10 See *Emmet County Democrat*, August 4, 1876.

11 See Charles Edwin Jones, *Perfectionist Persuasion: The Holiness Movement and American Methodism*, 1867-1936, Metuchen, NJ: Scarecrow Press, Inc., 1974. p.16.

12 See *Bay View Herald*, 1884.

13 See *Daily Resorter*, August 29, 1906.

14 See *Daily Resorter*, July 8, 1902.

15 Ibid.

16 He built David Carpenter's cottage on Block 2, Lot 21, first. Later it was nicknamed the Bay View Cottage. It became the annex to the Bay View House and burned in 1929. Knapp's cottage was the second one built on Block 2, Lot 2. The Shier cottage at Block 2, Lot 8, was the third one completed. See Map.

17 See *Daily Resorter*, July 3, 1902.

18 See *Emmet County Democrat*, July 13, 1877.

19 The famous clergyman later wrote Hurlbut's Story of the Bible and numerous other books. Dr. Jesse Lyman Hurlbut returned to Bay View in 1891, 1892 and 1915 to lead Bible conferences.

20 Mary Torrans Lathrap helped found the Michigan union in Grand Rapids in 1875. Lathrap's name is spelled a variety of ways. In the annual reports of the WCTU at the Grand Rapids Public Library, the organization she was president of for fourteen years, her name is spelled "Lathrop." In her book "The Poems and Written Addresses of Mary T. Lathrap" at the Clark Library at Central Michigan University, her name is spelled with an "a." Torrans is also spelled differently is various sources.

21 See *Emmet County Democrat*, February 15, 1878.

22 The *Daily Resorter* of August 25, 1892, estimated that the local ferries transported about 75,000 passengers a month. Railroad travel was reported to be lower but the *Daily Resorter* of August 30, 1895 gave a figure of 1200 passengers arriving on the night train.

23 See *Daily Resorter*, July 25, 1887.

24 This railroad right-of-way was purchased a century later by the Bay View Association.

25 See *Daily Resorter*, August 6, 1883.

26 See *Emmet Country Democrat*, July 20, 1877.

27 See Frances E. Willard, *Women and Temperance*. Hartford, CT: Park Publishing Co., 1883, p 222 where she relates this story of Chief Petoskey referring to him as having seen "one hundred four summers." Other sources report that the chief died when he was in his 90s.

28 See *Daily Resorter*, July 18, 1892.

29 See *Daily Resorter*, July 29, 1889.

30 See *Daily Resorter*, July 24, 1891.

31 See *Daily Resorter*, August 26, 1896.

32 See *Daily Resorter*, August 24, 1891.

33 See *Daily Resorter*, July 18, 1895.

34 In recent years, the oil portraits of these early leaders were restored at the DIA through grants from the State of Michigan and funds raised by the Bay View Archives. Bowman's portrait now hangs with others done by Conely (John M. Hall, William H. Shier, Seth Reed and A. J. Richards) around the grounds. Samuel Knapp's portrait, donated by Mrs. Knapp, was painted by Jackson artist C. R. Wallace.

35 See *News-Review*, July 5, 1979.

36 See *News-Review*, June 17, 1982.

37 See *Daily Resorter*, July 15, 1902.

38 See *Daily Resorter*, July 9, 1895.

39 See *Daily Resorter*, July 11, 1892.

## Chapter 3

1 See Emma Lamb Baker, *Stories of Bay View*, Detroit: Published by author, 1925, p. 18.

2 Also known also as shin-tangle or yew.

3 M-59 or Hall Road, the retail and commercial center of Macomb County is named after the Hall family.

4 Hall's mother is thought to have had relatives in Flint including Florence, the wife of David S. Fox.

5 David Glick, former Senior Administrator of Henry Ford Village and Museum, was given this information by Henry Ford's sister.

6 See Mary Jane Doerr, "Bay View, A Michigan Chautauqua." *Michigan Connection*, Lansing, MI: Michigan Council for the Humanities, Winter-Spring, 1984, p. 8.

7 See *Petoskey City Record*, August 15, 1883.

8 Ibid. July 15, 1885.

9 See *Bay View Assembly Herald*, Fall, 1885.

10 See Cleveland *Leader*, August 8, 1887.

11 See *Frank Leslie's Illustrated Newspaper*, June 7, 1890.

12 See *Bay View Assembly Herald*, October, 1887.

13 See *Bay View Assembly Herald*, June, 1887.

14 WCTU members wore white ribbons.

15 See *The Union Signal*, November 15, 1888.

16 According to English Professor M. Louise Jones's 1916 account.

17 See Harry Harrison, *Culture under Canvas: The Story of Tent Chautauqua*, New York: Hastings House, 1958, p. 51.

18 Ironically in 2000 when Bay View was planning its 125th commemorative celebration, the cost of a return engagement of the Fisk Jubilee Singers was prohibitive for Bay View's budget.

19 See *Daily Resorter*, August 3, 1899.

20 His opponent was lawyer Clarence Darrow, nationally known for his defense in 1924 of child murderer Michael Loeb whose family summered in Charlevoix.

21 See Major James Pond, *Diary*, July 2, 1895. Used by Courtesy of David Eicher.

22 See Charles S. Wheeler, *Bay View*. Bay View, MI: Bay View Association of the Methodist Church, 1950, p. 77.

23 See *Bay View Assembly Record*, July 13, 1895.

24 See *Daily Resorter*, July 26, 1889.

25 See *Daily Resorter*, July 29, 1891.

26 Fabian "Joe" Fournier, upon whom the Paul Bunyan myth was fashioned, was a foreman at the H. M. Loud Lumber Company.

27 See *Daily Resorter*, July 13, 1891.

28 Ibid.

29 See *Daily Resorter*, August 8, 1889.

30 See Eugene Cittadina, "A Marvelous Cosmopolitan Preserve: The Dunes, Chicago, and Dynamic Ecology of Henry Cowles." *Perspectives on Science*. Vol. 1, No.3, University of Chicago: 1993. p. 527.

31 See *Bay View Magazine*, May, 1895.

32 See *Daily Resorter*, July 14, 1891.

33 On September 12, 1982, Bay View Trustee Win Hinman met with Dr. William Gilbert of Albion College regarding the "value and appropriate method of disposition of various plants, birds and rocks in Loud Hall." The Bay View board of trustees passed a resolution that " . . . the collection of birds, mammals, birds' eggs, rocks, shells, together with other paraphernalia, also the collection of C. W. Wheeler, Michigan plants to be disposed of at the discretion of the college." The collections were transferred to the Whitehouse Nature Center of Albion College. A carefully preserved passenger pigeon was among the items.

34 See *Bay View Assembly Herald*, May, 1890.

35 See *Daily Resorter*, July 28, 1891.

36 See *Daily Resorter*, August 26, 1892.

37 In 1906, Cobern returned to Allegheny College to teach religious philosophy. He remained there until his death in 1920 in Battle Creek, Michigan, except during World War I when he served in

Europe with the Red Cross.

[38] See Margaret Cool Root, Email and telephone communication with Mary Jane Doerr, July 19, 2001.

[39] See *Daily Resorter*, August 24, 1892. In 1918, the new board took over the popular "movie" week, which became known as the Ladies' Library Movies, and funds were again set aside for the future building. It took another fourteen years but finally by 1931, the Bay View Ladies' Library Board had raised $5,000 in cash and was busy securing the additional $3,000 needed for a new building. The Petoskey firm of Preston Feather erected the building during the winter of 1931-32.

[40] See *Daily Resorter*, August 3, 1889.

[41] See *Daily Resorter*, August 1, 1889.

[42] See *Daily Resorter*, August 2, 1894.

[43] See *Daily Resorter*, August 18, 1896.

## Chapter 4

[1] See Mary Jane Doerr, "Bay View, A Michigan Chautauqua," *The Michigan Connection*, Lansing, MI: Michigan Council for the Humanities, Winter-Spring, 1984, p. 9.

[2] See *The Graphic*, August 13, 1989.

[3] See *Daily Resorter*, August 26, 1900.

[4] See Mary Jane Doerr, *Bay View's Goodly Heritage*, Bay View, MI: Bay View Association of the United Methodist Church, 1976, p. 9.

[5] See Mary Jane Doerr, "Bay View, A Michigan Chautauqua," *The Michigan Connection*, Lansing, MI: Michigan Council for the Humanities, Winter-Spring, 1984, p. 9.

[6] See Mary Jane Doerr, *Bay View's Goodly Heritage*, Bay View, MI: Bay View Association of the United Methodist Church, 1976. p. 17.

[7] See *Daily Resorter*, July 22, 1896.

[8] The charge has since been refuted by every researcher including Bay View Archivist Jane Park Doerr (*The Bay View Man*), Robert M. Carter (*Forum on the Bay*) and Keith Fennimore (*Heritage of Bay View*). Analysis of the financial assets of Hall's estate, and the cost and circulation of the magazine do not substantiate the allegations.

[9] See *Daily Resorter*, August 26, 1914.

[10] See *Petoskey City Record*, August 15, 1894.

[11] When Bay View fulfilled its contract with the GR&I and was incorporated in 1890, the name was changed to the Bay View Camp-ground Association of the Methodist Episcopal Church. The final name change was made in 1936.

[12] See Mary Jane Doerr, "The Hall Years," *Beneath the Beeches*, Bay View, MI: Published by the Bay View Association, 2000, p. 46.

[13] This fact debunks the rumor that Ernest was the first man to stay at the all-women Evelyn Hall.

[14] Florence is thought to be Hall's aunt.

[15] When Hall died in 1914, his wife Mary Hall hired Trumbull White of Petoskey, a nationally known journalist, to edit *The Bay View Magazine*. Sources say White purchased the magazine from Mary Hall in 1915. Under his editorship, *The Bay View Magazine* was no longer keyed to the local interests of Bay View and the members of the reading circles. It became national in appeal and scope. In 1920, the magazine was sold again and ceased publication in 1922. "Like so many of the publications of this period, when the creator died, the magazine folded" journalist Donna Ullrich concluded in her review. Ironically, Flood's *The Chautauquan* stopped publication several years earlier.

[16] See *Daily Resorter* for July 9, 1901.

[17] See Mary Jane Doerr, *Bay View's Goodly Heritage*. Bay View, MI: Bay View Association of the United Methodist Church, 1976, p.16.

[18] See *Daily Resorter*, July 31, 1902.

[19] See *Daily Resorter*, August 25, 1902.

[20] See *John M. Hall Papers*, University of Iowa Archives. Iowa City, IA: University Libraries Special Collections: Redpath Chautauqua Collections, 1910-20.

[21] See *Daily Resorter*, August 24, 1906.

[22] See *Daily Resorter*, September 13, 1906.

[23] See Hugh Orchard, *Fifty Years of Chautauqua*, Cedar Rapids, IA: 1923. p. 225.

[24] See *Daily Resorter*, July 20, 1908.

[25] Ibid, August 5, 1908.

[26] See Mary Jane Doerr, *Bay View's Goodly Heritage*, Bay View, MI: Bay View Association of the United Methodist Church, 1976, p.15.

[27] See *Daily Resorter*, July 22, 1907.

[28] Petoskey druggist Charles Fallass was elected to the Bay View board of trustees on July 27, 1904, and served until August 2, 1939. He was secretary from 1914 to 1922, and from 1928 to 1939 he was the vice president. When he retired the association voted him the title of trustee emeritus as the longest serving trustee in Bay View's history.

[29] See Mary Jane Doerr, "The Hall Years," *Beneath the Beeches*, Bay View, MI: Published by the Bay View Association, 2000, p. 28.

[30] Ibid. p. 28.

[31] Ibid. p. 51.

[32] See John M. Hall Papers, University of Iowa Archives. Iowa City, IA: University Libraries Special Collections: Redpath Chautauqua Collections, 1910-20.

[33] See *Daily Resorter*, August 16, 1913.

[34] See *The Bay View Magazine*, Vol. 17 No. 8, May, 1910. Page 558.

[35] See *The Graphic*, July 11, 1985.

[36] See *Bay View Assembly Record*, October 4, 1913.

[37] See *The Graphic*, July 11, 1985.

[38] See Carlos Baker, *Ernest Hemingway: A Life Story*. New York: Charles Scribner's Sons, 1969, p.200.

[39] Records are inconclusive, but Mrs. F. Woolworth, a Canadian, could have owned property at Block 21, Lots 9 and 10 between 1881 and 1885. The Woolworths were Methodists as was their Michigan relative Seymour H. Knox, founder of the Canadian Woolworth stores. Louisa Knox, who owned property at Block 24, Lot 3-4, is thought to be Mrs. Seymour Knox.

[40] See *The Graphic*, July 15, 1999.

[41] The actual room was razed in the 1997 renovation of Evelyn Hall.

[42] See Anne Mendelson, *Stand Facing the Stove*, New York: Henry Holt and Co., 1996, p.128.

[43] Ibid. p. 57.

[44] In 2008, Ethan Becker, Irma Rombauer's grandson, visited the cottage for the first time. It had changed little since his grandparents had owned it.

[45] See *The Graphic*, June 17, 2002.

[46] Martin Beer, Telephone Interview with Mary Jane Doerr, September 2, 1998.

[47] See *The Graphic*, June 17, 2002.

[48] See Anne Mendelson, *Stand Facing the Stove*, New York: Henry Holt and Co., 1996, p. 84.

[49] See *Daily Resorter*, September 2, 1893.

[50] See Mary Jane Doerr and Helen Guittard, "In Celebration of Bay View." Bay View, MI: Video Published by the Bay View Association for the National Landmark Presentation. July, 1988.

[51] See *The Graphic*, July 11, 1985.

[52] See *Daily Resorter*, August 5, 1893.

[53] See Mary Jane Doerr and Helen Guittard, "In Celebration of Bay View." Bay View, MI: Video Published by the Bay View Association for the National Landmark Presentation. July, 1988.

[54] Researcher Robert Hamilton of Hamilton, Ontario, reports that Hunter came to Detroit to work in the offices of Albert Kahn. After designing St. Josaphat's Catholic Church in Detroit with Joseph Kastler and the original domed-North Woodward Methodist Episcopal Church (demolished) in 1901, at some point he joined the firms of Mortimer L. Smith and Son, John Scott and Company, and later Mason and Rice. He formed his own firm in about 1909. Through these years, he continued to design domed-Akron style churches such as the Hastings Methodist Church and many churches throughout Michigan, Indiana, Illinois, and several provinces in Canada. The Hunter domed-shaped churches bear dis

tinct similarities with Albert Kahn's Temple Beth El (Bonstelle Theatre) although Hunter's domed-shaped North Woodward Methodist Church predates the Kahn building by two years. If Hunter was in the Kahn offices during this period, he may have worked on the Temple Beth-El building. In 1913, Hunter was contracted to design Shaarey Zedek at Willis and Brush (demolished) in Detroit, a synagogue in the domed-Akron style. Hunter designed several homes on Chicago Boulevard (E.C. Kinsel, E. A. Laitner and F. M. Sibley) and perhaps John M. Hall's own home on Boston Boulevard. After the dedication of the John M. Hall Auditorium in Bay View on July 18, 1915, Hunter designed several arts and crafts churches - First United Methodist Church in Highland Park in 1917 and Royal Oak Methodist Episcopal Church in 1918. He turned to the Neo-Gothic mode with straight lines and arches (a feature of the Bay View auditorium) and even designed a wrap-around addition in 1921 to Jackson's First United Methodist Church, the site of the founding of the Bay View. In 1923, Reverend N. A. McCune of Petoskey and East Lansing hired Hunter to design East Lansing's Peoples' Church located next to the Michigan State University. Many of Hunter's churches (including the Bay View Auditorium) had a distinguishing feature, a sky light. Several churches have retained their beautiful stained glass window domes. Hunter designed Detroit's gigantic Metropolitan United Methodist Church, funded largely by Stanley Kresge, and the simplistic Historic Grace Episcopal Church in Mt. Clemens which were both completed in 1924. Grosse Pointe Memorial Presbyterian Church was finished in 1927 and Flint's Court Street Methodist Church House in 1929. Despite the Depression, in 1931 Detroit's Historic Trinity Evangelical Lutheran Church was completed when Hunter was seventy-three years old. Grosse Pointe Memorial and the Late Gothic Revival Historic Trinity Lutheran are elaborate and highly symbolic with sanctuary cross layouts. In 1936, Hunter supervised Detroit's Central Methodist Church when it was decreased in size as Woodward Avenue was widened. Robert Hamilton of Hamilton, Ontario, and Michael McCleer of Detroit are both researching this architect to assess his contribution to Midwest church architecture. So far 37 structures have been found that can be attributed to Hunter.

55 See *Daily Resorter*, July 8, 1914.
56 See Mary Jane Doerr, "The Hall Years," *Beneath the Beeches*, Bay View, MI: Published by the Bay View Association, 2000, p. 62.

## Chapter 5

1 See Paul B. Blanshard, "Obituaries," *Time Magazine*, February 11, 1980.
2 Reverend Francis Blanshard may have appeared on the Bay View roster in the 1890s.
3 See Paul Arthur Schlipp, *The Philosophy of Brand Blanshard*, La Salle, IL: Open Court, 1980, p. 9.
4 Ibid. p. 9.
5 Ibid. p. 9.
6 It was located on the campus near the site of the present Bay View Post Office across Encampment Avenue from the Bay View House. See map.
7 See Paul B. Blanshard, *Personal and Controversial, An Autobiography*, Boston: Beacon Press, 1973, p. 13.
8 Ibid, p.13.
9 See *Daily Resorter*, July 4, 1912.
10 See *Daily Resorter*, September 10. 1917.
11 See Blanshard, *New York Times Biographical Service*, January 30, 1980.
12 He married Frances Bradshaw in 1918. She died in 1966, and in 1969 he married RobertaYerkes. He had no children.
13 See *Who's Who In America*, 38th edition, Vol. 1, Chicago, IL: Marquis Who's Whos, Inc., 1974-75 p. 283.
14 Interview with Mary Jane Doerr, Aug. 7, 2000.
15 Used by permission of both families.
16 See August Heckscher, *When LaGuardia was Mayor*. New York, W.W. Norton & Company, 1978. p.106.
17 See *Daily Resorter*, August 3, 1914.
18 See *Daily Resorter*, August 5, 1914.
19 See *Daily Resorter*. July 30, 1914.
20 See Paul Blanshard, *Personal and Controversial, An Autobiography*, Boston: Beacon Press, 1973, p. 15.
21 Ibid., p. 36.
22 See *Daily Resorter*, July 23, 1914.
23 See Blanshard, *New York Times Biographical Service*, January 30, 1980.
24 See *Daily Resorter*, September 6, 1913.

## Chapter 6

1 See Harry S. McClarran, *A Flying Fish, A History of the Independent Chautauqua Assembly Movement*. Unpublished. Archives of the Chautauqua Institutions, NY: August 1, 1994.
2 See *Northern Independent*, August 5, 1884.
3 In her honor, a Bay View resident, Mary Sue Hansen, recently led a Michigan Federation of Women's Clubs (MFWC) to erect a statue of her in Big Rapids, one of only a few statues of women in the state.
4 See Frances E. Willard and Mary Livermore, *A Woman of the Century. Leading American Women*. Buffalo, NY: Charles Wells Moulton, 1893. p.88.
5 See *Daily Resorter*, July 28, 1891.
6 From Petoskey, Mrs. G. S. Barnes, Fannie B. Calkins and Mrs. P. J. Howard were extremely active. Howard was a personal friend of Louise Rounds from Chicago.
7 See *Daily Resorter*, August 29, 1902.
8 Call, the young newspaper reporter, went on to become an editor of the Lansing *State Journal*.
9 After 1910, no more meetings of the WCTU were held in Bay View until 1949 when Mrs. D. Leigh Colvin, then president of the WCTU spoke at a meeting of the Woman's Council. WCTU Institutes were held at the Woman's Council until 1957.
10 See *Daily Resorter*, July 31, 1890.
11 Terhune was visiting other assemblies such as Lakeside, Ohio.
12 See *Daily Resorter*, July 31, 1890.
13 See Blanche Blynn Maw, comp. *A History of the Michigan State Federation of Women's Clubs 1895-1953*. Ann Arbor: Ann Arbor Press for the Michigan State Federation of Women's Clubs, 1953, p. 4.
14 Jones was a founder of the Lansing Woman's Club, now the oldest woman's club in Michigan. A writer, she contributed to various publications besides being president of the Young Woman's Christian Association and the Lansing Industrial Aid Society. She was also active in the WTCU. Today, Lansing's Pilgrim Congregational United Church of Christ Woman's Fellowship continues to honor her each year with the Irma Jones Award.
15 See *Daily Resorter*, August 13, 1895.
16 See *Daily Resorter*, August 14, 1895.
17 Ibid.
18 See *Daily Resorter*, August 8, 1896.
19 Louise S. Rounds was the one who recommended Frances Willard for the presidency of the national WCTU.
20 See Jennie June Croly, *Woman's Club Movement in America*. New York: Henry G. Allen & CO, 1898. p. 717.
21 In 1903, under the leadership of Susan A. Hitchcock of Royal Oak, Michigan, wife of Horace Hitchcock then superintendent of the Bay View Assembly, a women's bazaar was held to help liquidate the indebtedness of the assembly. With the exception of the years between 1896-1903 and 1917-1924, these bazaars have been held annually.
22 Valerie Jane Millar, former Director of Public Education for PACE Communications in Emmet County, pointed this out in her 1999 doctoral thesis: *The Organizational Entry and Socialization of Women in Educational Leadership Positions: A Case Study*.
23 See *Daily Resorter*, August 22, 1917.

[24] In 1912, Carrie Barge, one of the national officers of the Women's Home Missionary Society of the Methodist Episcopal Church, led the Bay View Missionary Conference and the Women's Home Missionary Society. She returned each summer between 1918 and 1920 to lead the Missionary Congress.
[25] See *Emmet County Democrat*, July 13, 1877.
[26] See The *Petoskey Evening News*, August 8, 1923.
[27] Now Stafford's Bay View Inn.
[28] See *Petoskey Evening News*, July 30, 1924.
[29] See *Daily Resorter*, August 21, 1917.
[30] The federation then ceased its alliance with Bay View until 2005 when the Federation of Women's Clubs-Michigan returned to Evelyn Hall, the site of its organizational roots, to dedicate a plaque. From all over Michigan, 104 women attended the ceremony and luncheon, led by then President Linda Clark. Geneva Wiskemann, former Michigan state archivist, represented the historic Lansing Woman's Club, the club that helped found the MFWC and is now the oldest women's club in Michigan. The event was a reminder of the part women of the 1890s played in forming the federation that over the last century has worked to improve the political and economic welfare of Michigan women with its support of the juvenile court system, the organization of school boards, women's suffrage, the formation of local libraries, and the seat belt law, to name only a few issues.
[31] See *Daily Resorter*, August 2, 1894.
[32] See *Emmet County Democrat* on August 14, 1885.

## Chapter 7

[1] See *Bay View Magazine*, Vol. 22, No. 4, January, 1915, p. 223
[2] See Mary Jane Doerr, "The Hall Years," *Beneath the Beeches*. Bay View, MI: Published by the Bay View Association, 2000, p. 64.
[3] Hall's daughter Dorothy McClintock and her husband Wesley purchased founder Seth Reed's cottage at Block 2, Lot 9, in about 1928. In 1935, they presented the Bay View Association with Hall's papers and manuscripts concerning the early history. A letter from William DeVol stated that the gift was included with archival materials at the Bay View Library. However, the collection was not recorded or accessioned, so it is unclear what documents were in the compilation. In the 1960s, when the Bay View Archives was established there were no documents with the 1935 DeVol letter. When Dr. John Perkins, former chancellor of UCLA, and Bay View Archivist Jane Park Doerr began an oral history project in the 1960s, Hall's daughter Dorothy McClintock refused to participate, replying that everything she knew was included in the 1935 collection. Hall's great-grandson and McClintocks' grandson, David Bieber, summered in Bay View with his grandparents. He attended the Bay View Boys' and Girls' Club, became a camp counselor, starred in many of the early theater productions, and was a leader in the formation of the Bay View Department of Theatre Arts in 1973. He pursued a national career in television until his retirement in Florida. At various times, he managed some of the country's largest television stations for all three major networks and worked with the country's well-known entertainers just like his great grandfather.
[4] See *Bay View Magazine*, Vol. 23, No. 1, October, 1915. p. 46.
[5] See *Daily Resorter* August 18, 1916.
[6] See *Daily Resorter*, August 25, 1916.
[7] See *Daily Resorter*, July 18, 1900.
[8] See Clark S.Wheeler, *Bay View*, Bay View, MI: Bay View Association of the Methodist Church, 1950, p. 64.
[9] Helen Marin Interview with Mary Jane Doerr. *Graphic Resorter*, August 28, 1980.
[10] A part of the Smithsonian Collection of sheet music, the song is an example of how popular music mirrored the freedom brought on by the automobile.
[11] According to Nan Bostick, great niece of Charles N. Daniels, director at the Detroit Remick plant. Callahan had collaborated with Daniels himself on one of his earlier songs, *In the Shadow of the Alamo*, in 1914. Daniels composed under the name of Neil Moret.
[12] See *Petoskey Evening News*, June 4, 1924.
[13] Helen Marin Interview with Mary Jane Doerr, *Graphic Resorter*, August 28, 1980.
[14] See *Daily Resorter*, August 27, 1917.
[15] See *Daily Resorter*, August 25, 1916.
[16] Marshall had famously remarked that what the country needed was a good five cent cigar.
[17] See *Petoskey Evening News*, August 26, 1918.
[18] During his career, Kennedy typically juggled several jobs. He earned his B.A. degree from Northwestern University and his MA and an honorary DD degree from Albion College. In 1895, he was received into the Michigan conference and was stationed at Sherman, Michigan. He was ordained a deacon in 1897 and an elder in 1899. He accepted a position at the Asbury Methodist Church in Traverse City and, in 1909, became the first pastor of the Big Rapids Methodist Church. He stayed there until 1916, when he became pastor of the Methodist Church in Mt. Pleasant. Kennedy served as district superintendent of the Michigan conference for eight years: five in the Albion district and three in the Grand Rapids district. From 1919 until 1931, he was World Service executive secretary. About that time, he became a member of the Detroit area staff where he was recognized for devising "the Kennedy plan" for the support of educational institutions such as Albion and Adrian colleges and the Wesley foundations. In 1932, Dr. Kennedy became district superintendent of the Grand Rapids District and remained in that position until his retirement in 1935.
[19] Dr. Whitehouse was a member of the faculty of Albion College but left in 1939 to become dean of the College of Liberal Arts at Wayne State University in Detroit. He returned to Albion College as president from 1945 to 1960.
[20] See *Petoskey Evening News*, August 6, 1940.
[21] Dr. David Buttrick, Interview with Mary Jane Doerr. During his life, David's father Dr. George Buttrick was awarded twenty honorary doctoral degrees from major colleges and universities, although he never finished seminary and graduated from Victoria University in England with only a bachelor's degree in philosophy. He taught at numerous seminaries until he was eighty-six.
[22] In 1977, Bay View resident David J. Dykhouse, a prominent Michigan lawyer endowed a lectureship series in Buttrick's name. The pastor was scheduled to present the first two series of lectures in 1978 and 1979 but was ill. His sons Reverend Robert Buttrick and Dr. David Buttrick, who continue to summer in northern Michigan, presented them instead.
[23] See Charlotte M. Canning, *The Most American Thing in America: Circuit Chautauqua as Performance*. Iowa City, IO: University of Iowa Press, 2005. p 163.
[24] See Harry P. Harrison, *Culture under Canvas; The Story of Tent Chautauqua*. New York: Hastings House, 1958, p 51.
[25] See *Daily Resorter*, August 1, 1894
[26] See *News-Review*, July 8, 1987.
[27] Ibid.
[28] Ibid.
[29] See *Petoskey Evening News*, August 9, 1940.
[30] See *Petoskey Evening News*, August 8, 1935.
[31] Letter Courtesy of Suzanne Ternan.
[32] See *Petoskey Evening News*, August, 1944.
[33] Kennedy passed away in Grand Rapids on July 12, 1948.

## Chapter 8

[1] Later in 1910, Wade received a doctor of divinity degree in 1910. In 1932, he received a L.L.D. degree from Indiana's Taylor University.

[2] Ft. Wayne, Indianapolis, Arcadia, Nappanee, Kendalville, Richmond and Elkhart.

3 Letter to Mary Jane Doerr from Linda Jones Matthews. November, 1998.
4 See Roy Smith, "Fricis Timbers – Faithful," *The Christian Advocate*, July 18, 1946. p. 19.
5 Biruta Abuls, a Latvian native from Kalamazoo, is currently researching Laupmanis for the Latvian government.
6 Keith Willison, a member of the Lakeview congregation, Interview with Mary Jane Doerr.
7 See *Petoskey Evening News*, August 23, 1943.
8 See *Daily Resorter*, August 12, 1912.
9 Now Stafford's Bay View Inn.
10 They were registered at the Florence Cottage on September 1, 1923. During other summers, newspaper accounts listed them as renters at the Ramsdell cottage.
11 Used with permission of Bill Laitner, writer for the *Detroit Free Press*.
12 When the stage was enlarged in 1979 to accommodate the entire Detroit Symphony Orchestra for a concert, seats closest to the stage were moved to the back of the balcony where the old movie projector room was once located.
13 See *Daily Resorter*, August 20, 1888.
14 See *Daily Resorter* on July 18, 1910.
15 Although Bay View's bell tower came a century after Bay View's founding, bell towers were a common symbol of the nineteenth-century Chautauqua movement. For Bay View's first assembly in 1886, the Buckeye Bell Foundry of Cincinnati, Ohio lent the camp-meeting assembly a "peal of bells." On Recognition Day in 1887, the CLSC members decided to buy the bells and present them to the Bay View Camp-Ground Association. Donors included David Preston who gave $81, Senator J. W. Moon, $41.50 and the Hon. H. M. Loud, $25.
16 See Dr. A. Douglas MacNaughton, *The Methodist Church in Michigan: The Twentieth Century*. Grand Rapids: The Michigan Area United Methodist Church Historical Society and William B. Eerdmans Publishing Co., 1976, p. 213.

## Chapter 9

1 See *Emmet County Democrat*, July 17, 1895.
2 See *Daily Resorter*, August 18, 1887.
3 Mary Farnsworth letter, used by permission of Dr. and Mrs. James Beard.
4 See *Daily Resorter*, July 15, 1896.
5 See *Daily Resorter*, August 3, 1891.
6 See *Daily Resorter*, July 24, 1891.
7 See *Daily Resorter*, July 21, 1900.
8 See *Daily Resorter*, July 8, 1913.
9 See *Daily Resorter*, September 5, 1914.
10 Tennis was popular until the Depression but interest declined until 1942 when recreation director Ernie Gray instituted the Bay View closed tennis tournament for only the Bay View young people, a tournament won by Elizabeth Decker of Electra, Texas. Tennis remained a priority for Gray but it was limited to locals until 1958 when Mike Rosenow became tennis manager. He resumed competition between other resorts and teams such as Mackinac Island's Grand Hotel. After he left, interest dwindled. Today, tennis is fun for everyone at the Bay View Tennis Club. From four-year olds to septuagenarians, there are opportunities to find partners of the same level, play in tournaments at every age and ability level, and socialize with new friends. The program is so popular that another coach, Merv Kiesewetter, is teaching the juniors and the number of lessons given to four to eighteen-year-olds tripled from 359 in 1987 to 1122 in 2001.
11 See *Daily Resorter*, August 12, 1908.
12 See *Daily Resorter*, September 3, 1900.
13 See *Daily Resorter*, August 7, 1902.
14 See *Daily Resorter*, July 17, 1913.
15 *Petoskey Evening News* on July 11, 1929.
16 Researcher Lowell Kosloskey found the US Census Department census in 1920 listed him as a divorced mulatto, but the 1930 census does not list him at all. "He seems to have disappeared," according to Kosloskey. In 1971, Stanley Dickinson, Dave Trautman and Jerry Joneson of Petoskey accomplished the same feat as Edmunds, but it took them three hours and fifty minutes in calm seas. They were impressed with Edmunds' feat.
17 See *News-Review*, August 18, 1965.
18 Edward Neithercut, a Flint attorney, and Harold Child, a Grand Rapids businessman, co-chaired a committee called PROJECT WATERFRONT to raise $100,000 to improve the waterfront area for recreational use. A breakwater was planned to extend eastward to protect the swimming area. A boat launch was planned at the east end of the Rec. Club. The front breakwater was never built.
19 Swift made many contributions to Bay View. With his friends Joe Lewis and Homer Larsen he initiated the silent movies in 1916. That summer, he was thirty-five and became the youngest person ever elected to the Bay View board. From 1916 until 1928, he headed up the Recreation Committee. Later, in the 1960s, he supported and helped with the Oral History project, interviewing "old citizens" of the community. Those oral histories formed the basis of the award-winning video "In Celebration of Bay View." Swift was an extraordinary athlete of the mind. He did hold the walking record from Bay View to Harbor Springs of one hour and twenty-eight minutes. A strict Southern gentleman he was never seen even on the hot days without his three-piece brown suit, straw hat, and two gold watches. A licensed medical doctor and an intellectual giant in subjects such as botany and ornithology, he held three bachelor's degrees (history, Latin, and Greek) and two doctorates (anatomy and botany). He was an associate professor at the University of Chicago's Rush Medical School where his photographic memory was so keen that he could instantly recall former students' names and classes after nearly fifty years of teaching. Swift was born in Bluegrass Country on August 17, 1881, to William Swift, an artillery officer in the Confederate army who held degrees in law and medicine and taught in a Christian College in Kentucky. William taught his son to identify trees, flowers and birds. When he was growing up, Swift attended annual Civil War reunions with his father. Listening to the tales of the old soldiers and being an avid reader, he became an expert on the Battle of Gettysburg. The family took up the Chautauqua habit when they met William Rainey Harper, president of the University of Chicago and superintendent of the Chautauqua Summer School. They then moved to Chicago where they became acquainted with the famous botanist, John Merle Coulter, president of the Bay View Summer University. While Swift was attending medical school, the family began coming to Bay View. Swift met his longtime friend, Charles W. Fallass, an Albion graduate and Petoskey druggist, in a field west of Harbor Springs in 1903 when they were both overjoyed at finding a rare *Orchis rotundifolia*. Over the following forty years they made a vast collection of plants in Harbor Springs, Bay View, Oden, Carp Lake and Mackinaw City. Fallass kept a meticulous record of their findings. Together they drew up an annotated list of about 800 species found in Emmet County. In 1913, Swift found a purple-fringed orchid, *Habernaria psycodes*, at Round Lake, now in the herbarium of the Missouri Botanical Garden. Upon Fallass' death on November 5, 1942, the Fallass Herbarium was given to Albion College where Fallass attended school. According the Dr. Edward G. Voss of the Gray Memorial Botanical Association at the Botanical Gardens Association of the University of Michigan, 35 species of plants in Emmet and Cheboygan country were identified from the specimens in the Fallass herbarium, making the efforts of these two of considerable importance.
20 It was not the first time field events were sponsored by Bay View. In 1894, during his second summer, Bowen organized Bay View's first Field Day at Petoskey's Recreation Park. Over 100 contestants entered sixteen events: 20-yard hurdle; 16-pound shot put; hammer throw; standing broad jump; running broad jump; 120-yard hurdle; 440-yard run; hop, step, and jump; pole vault; 100-yard dash; 220-

yard dash; baseball throw; half mile walk; high jump; two-mile bicycle; and 100-yard dash open.

## Chapter 10

[1] See *The Bay View Assembly Herald*, March, 1889, p. 1.
[2] See *Daily Resorter*, July 20, 1900.
[3] See Clark S. Wheeler, *Bay View*. Bay View, MI: Bay View Association of the Methodist Church, 1950. p. 99.
[4] See *Petoskey Evening News* August 24, 1935.
[5] See *The Bay View Magazine*, May, 1897. p. 362.
[6] The history of Bay View theatre is inseparable from that of recreation. In 1896, the young people raised money for the waterfront and furnished the new Conservatory of Music building by mounting two tableaux, "Deestrick Skule" and "The Mistletoe Rough", featuring "Bay View Talent in Grotesque Costume and Comic Parts." Reverend Brockway's son Bruce starred in the show, along with Carrie Taylor, John M. Hall and other Bay View notables. These "entertainments," sponsored by the young people's social club called the Marshmallow Club, were popular for several years and brought in enough funds to erect both a boathouse and a bathhouse on the beach and purchase boats to rent.
[7] Over a period of a week, the Ben Greet Players typically performed five or six different plays on an open-air stage in the middle of the campus, mostly respectable Shakespearean dramas. That group was alternated with other troupes such as the John Nicholson Sylvan Players and the Coburn Woodland Players. In his book *Culture Under Canvas*, Redpath-Lyceum Bureau impresario Harry Harrison credits the Chautauqua movement with the change in American's religious attitudes and the Ben Greet Players for paving the way.
[8] See *Daily Resorter*, August 13, 1913.
[9] See *Daily Resorter*, August 20, 1914.
[10] Bay View's fledgling theatre movement seems to have died along with Starr, and the association began booking road shows to meet audience demand. By the 1920s, public tastes had changed from classical theatre to lighter Broadway fare, comedies and semiserious dramas. Groups from the Redpath Chautauqua Bureau in Chicago appeared each summer - Redpath Players, Coffee-Miller Players, Devereaux Dramatic Company, Bergman Players and Bob Hanscom Company.
[11] See *Daily Resorter*, July 14, 1916.
[12] See Marcelline Sandford, *At the Hemingways*'. Moscow, ID: University of Idaho Press,1998. p 151.
[13] See *Daily Resorter*, August 16, 1917.
[14] George Rasely later created one of the roles in Walter Damrosch's *Man Without a Country*.
[15] See *Daily Resorter*, August 20, 1917.
[16] See Edson L. Barlow, ed., *Barlow of Barlow,* Rochester, MI: May, 1994. p.129.
[17] See *Daily Resorter*, July 29, 1919.
[18] Gradually, various features now typical of the concerts were added. On July 20, 1924, staff pianist William Reddick began playing musical interludes or modulations between numbers to eliminate the applause which was taboo at Sunday concerts. The following year, on July 19, 1925, under Acting Dean Arthur Boardman, the Assembly Chorus began performing occasionally at the concerts. Reddick began the tradition of singing *God Be With You till We Meet Again*, at the closing concert on August 22, 1926, the year he took over as director of music. When Patton took over in 1934 the Assembly Chorus became a regular feature. The unusual and stylized Bay View vesper concerts are now the very heart of the Bay View Music Festival and its most popular attraction. Artists no longer remain on stage for the entire concert as they did in the early days and, since the 1970s, musical modulations have been eliminated. It is now acceptable for audiences to applaud each artist's performance. Attendance has ranged over the more than eighty-year history of the event from up to 2500 in the early days when the seating capacity of the auditorium was larger, to 1300 to 1700 today.
[19] See Mary Jane Doerr "Music," *Beneath the Beeches*. Bay View, MI: Published by the Bay View Association, 2000. p. 89. McCutchan became the editor of the 1935 Methodist Hymnal, publishing his own hymns under the pseudonym John Porter. One of his arrangements was of the famous hymn *Let All The World in Every Corner Sing*.
[20] See Bonnie Cave Bradley, *William J. Reddick, Composer-Musician*. Ph.D. Thesis, University of Kentucky, 1986.
[21] Ibid.
[22] In Bonnie Bradley's 1986 doctoral research, Eugene Ormandy of the Philadelphia Orchestra credited Reddick's finesse for the show's achievement of an ideal acoustical balance and tonal grading between the orchestra, chorus and the soloists. Dr. Leonard B. Smith, the Detroit Symphony Orchestra's principal trumpet who achieved worldwide fame for his performance of the "Lone Ranger" theme on radio, said, "Reddick was an excellent arranger, composer, conductor, pianist and overall musician." Longtime Bay View tenor soloist Willard Pierce remembered several occasions visiting with Reddick when he joined the Bay View music faculty. Both he and Reddick had worked at the Central Presbyterian Church in New York City.
[23] Mr. Wilkinson, principal of the John W. Cook School in Chicago, had led bands and orchestras for many years in various Illinois schools. Doris Hunter, daughter of theater director Rollin Hunter; cottagers Joe Britton and Lennis Britton Swift; and Donald Allured, Eleanor MacLaughlin, and Eleanor McFarland were a few of the young people in the orchestra. Rehearsal space was a problem. The Bay View College of Liberal Arts had very high enrollment and the campus buildings were in full use. At first, Charles Meinsinger's cottage was used, but in 1941 the orchestra rehearsed at Recreation Hall.
[24] Dr. Jonathon Amy, Email to Mary Jane Doerr, November 21, 1998.
[25] Bay View young people such as Jonathan Amy, Barbara Weber, John Springer, Bruce Blanchard and Harold Child had roles in *Taming of the Shrew* and other shows.
[26] Amy, November 21, 1998.
[27] Ibid.
[28] Doris Hunter Mauch lived at Epworth Hall with Donna Eyssen during those summers. She remembered the large and appreciative audiences and how much there was for young people to do in Bay View. "I have always felt warmly toward Bay View and fortunate to have been there."
[29] Max Smith Interview with Mary Jane Doerr.
[30] The John M. Hall Auditorium was too heavily booked to be used for rehearsals.
[31] Archie Black left Bay View to become the accompanist for the Metropolitan Opera Quartet and Kristin Flagstaff.
[32] Just after her Bay View appearance, Moten played the role of Bess on Broadway and then toured the country with the show. When she retired, she became involved with the Chicago Lyric Opera and Chicago's Field Museum, and represented the US in various African nations.
[33] Max Smith Interview with Mary Jane Doerr.
[34] See *Petoskey Evening News*, May 3, 1938.
[35] Gottesmann was looking for permanent employment when the Busch Quartet disbanded in 1952.While keeping his Bay View position he accepted a post as concertmaster of the Fort Wayne Symphony in Indiana and had a profound effect on that orchestra. "He taught the musicians how to interpret the classical literature," said violinist Edward Zala in a 1996 interview. During the 1970s, the Bay View Association produced a recording, "Hugo Gottesmann Memorial", in honor of Gottesmann's twenty-eight years with the festival. Violinist Ernest Zala, cellist Seymour Benstock and other staff members made the editing and recording arrangements. In 1953, Gottesmann was diagnosed with cancer at Petoskey's Burns Clinic and needed immediate medical attention at

Mayo Clinic in Minnesota. Robert C. Crist and friends in Bay View paid for Bertram Rowe, Bay View's baritone and licensed pilot, to fly him to Rochester where the cancer was treated. Out of gratitude, Gottesmann returned to Bay View every summer until his death in 1970 when the city of Vienna, Austria, put out an international press release commemorating Gottesmann's lifelong achievements.

36 Felix Resnick Interview with Mary Jane Doerr.

37 In 1993, Dr. Will Nichols, then director of the Bay View Music Festival, negotiated with the Cleveland String Quartet to appear in Bay View the following summer. Although Majeske wanted to return to Bay View, the quartet could not accept any engagements and Majeske died of cancer that November.

38 Walter Taussig Interview with Mary Jane Doerr.

39 The group trains in California during the winter months and now has seven groups touring the US, Europe and Japan.

40 Willard Pierce, Interview with Mary Jane Doerr. The seventeen-act show featured a pantomime by David Dykhouse, a magic routine by David Bieber, a solo by Sarajane Tallman, a boys' quartet, a ventriloquist, a banjo duet, singing and dancing ensembles, and the melodramatic skit, *The Lamp Went Out*. One performance was given on a Saturday evening at Hall Auditorium. Just as the Hunter group had done, the cast stayed up all night, striking the sets in time for Sunday church. David Dykhouse became a nationally known lawyer and the Michigan State Insurance Commissioner; David Bieber went on to a national career in television, working at different times for all three major networks, and Sarajane Tallman joined the choruses of several national television shows including The Perry Como Show and was a backup singer for major 1950s rock stars including Elvis Presley.

41 Ibid.

42 Ibid.

43 Liza Lee Collins Interview with Mary Jane Doerr.

44 Except for the years between 1928 and 1934, Vernor was a member of the Bay View music staff from 1915 until his retirement. At a vesper service August 4, 1967, the Bay View board of trustees honored him in a special salute for his long time of service. Vernor composed a set of variations to *The Sweetheart of Sigma Chi* for the occasion.

45 Elizabeth Humphrey Interview with Mary Jane Doerr.

46 Ernest Sullivan Interview with Mary Jane Doerr.

47 The Donald E. Allured Original Composition Award offers the opportunity to premier new compositions. Carl Wiltse's *Creator of the Light* was premiered August 15, 2002 at the John M. Hall Auditorium with Donald Allured conducting. Other winners are Cathy Moklebust, Hart Morris and Margaret Tucker.

48 See *The Graphic*, July 6, 1989.

49 During a final scene, the curtain literally fell on the stage, and the cast spontaneously finished the show with improvised adjustments.

50 Many students of Willard Pierce have gone on to professional careers. Rod Allen worked as a professional actor in Chicago; Charlie Hammond worked in the London theatre; Maureen McDevitt appeared on the professional stage in Detroit; Jane Millar became the director of programming for Pace Communications; Paul Nelson teaches music and theatre in an East Coast private school and is now Bay View Director of Theatre Arts; Peter Sims became director of music at the First Presbyterian Church of Harbor Springs; Mary Valenti joined the Young Americans; David Kitto became the director of marketing at Carnegie Hall and now is vice president of marketing at The Kennedy Center in Washington DC. In 2002, Shuler Hinsley (who appeared in *Most Happy Fella*) received every major award on Broadway and in London for his portrayal of Judd Fry in *Oklahoma! The New York Times* reported that he was the best actor to ever do the role, and he won the Tony Award for Best Supporting Actor. Eric Martsoff played "Elvis" with Donnie Osmund in the national tour of "*Joseph and the Technicolor Dreamcoat*." "He taught me everything," said Mary Catherine Dykhouse, chairman of the voice department at City Music Center at Duquesne University in Pittsburgh. Dykhouse made her debut as Gretl in the 1970 production of *The Sound of Music*. She went on to star in thirteen Bay View productions and majored in vocal performance. She has appeared with opera companies on the east coast and in the mid west. She returned to Bay View for a 2003 production of *The Sound of Music* to sing the role of the Mother Superior because "I wanted to give something back."

51 Max Smith Interview with Mary Jane Doerr.

## Chapter 11

1 See Clark S. Wheeler. *Bay View*. Bay View, MI: Bay View Association of the Methodist Church, 1950. p. 93.

2 See *Daily Resorter*, August 27, 1917.

3 After serving in World War I, Barlow went on to achieve fame as America's first great conductor. White sold his interest in the *Bay View Magazine* and retired to his farm overlooking Round Lake, Bay View and Petoskey.

4 See *Daily Resorter*, August 20, 1918.

5 See *Petoskey Evening News*, August 20, 1920.

6 See *Petoskey Evening News* on August 21, 1920.

7 See *Petoskey Independent*, March 16, 1923.

8 See Amy, Dr. Jonathon, email to author, February 13, 2001.

9 Dr. Howard E. Petterson Interview with Mary Jane Doerr, August 26, 2002.

10 See Fennimore, *The Heritage of Bay View*, 1975, p 113.

11 See *News-Review*, August 12, 1969

12 Dr. Howard E. Petterson Interview with Mary Jane Doerr, August 26, 2002.

13 See *News-Review*, August 12, 1969.

14 See *News-Review,* Petoskey, July 30, 1999.

15 In 2002, Robert and Mill Docking assumed the co-directorship of the department. Dr. Docking has had a long career in education as the former superintendent of Michigan's prestigious Bloomfield Hills School District and as a professor at the University of Detroit/Mercy. His wife Mill is a registered nurse who held a supervisory position at Henry Ford Hospital in Detroit. Classes have been greatly expanded and now some 800 students come from all over Emmet County. They have also expanded the concept with noted authors contracted each summer.

16 See *News-Review* of October 13, 1994. Hager was a reassuring preacher who endeared himself to everyone. His positive manner and uplifting approach brought happiness to brides and grooms and strength to the bereaved at the enormous number of weddings and funerals he conducted. So great was his appeal that when baritone Irving Prescott was interviewed about his forty years of service as a member of the Bay View music staff, he said that his proudest moment was when he sang at Dr. Hager's funeral.

17 They clearly stated their positions in separate articles in the *News-Review* September 5 and September 13, 1991.

18 The Simons Communion Set is in Riga, Latvia, at the Akas Street United Methodist Church. It is not used and has been stored since it arrived. The chalice is not with the other three pieces (the two plates and the pitcher) and its whereabouts is unknown.

## Chapter 12

1 See *News-Review*, July 31, 1965.

2 See *Emmet County Democrat*, June 23, 1876.

3 It wasn't until 1985, however, that the woods committee was established to sponsor educational lectures, build paths and provide maps to help everyone enjoy the natural environment. In a by-law change in July 2000, the Bay View membership voted to set aside the Bay View woods for preservation and nature study. It is now the oldest tract of woods left in Emmet County.

4 According to Kathy Duquette. *Town Crier*, July 26, 2002.

5 Benjamin Levy, Email to Mary Jane Doerr.

6 See *Historic Preservation Guild, Historic Preservation Guild of*

*Bay View vs. James H. Burnley; Robert Farris; James P. Pitz*, United States Court of Appeals, Sixth Circuit. No. 88-2080. (Cite as: 896 F.2d 985). December 15, 1989. p. 10.

[7] See *News-Review*, August 4, 1989.

[8] See US-31 Department of Transportation, Federal Highway Administration, and Michigan Department of Transportation. US-31 Petoskey Area Improvement Study, SUPPLEMENTAL DRAFT ENVIRONMENTAL IMPACT STATEMENT, Section 4(f)/6(f) Evaluation. August, 2001. p. 2-3.

[8] Elizabeth S. Merritt Interview with Mary Jane Doerr, National Trust for Historic Preservation Washington, D. C., January 10, 2005.

[9] See *Brewery District Society vs. Federal Highway Administration*. United States District Court for the Southern District of Ohio Eastern Division. Case No. 98CV00075 (211 F.Supp.2d 902;2002 U.S. Dist. LEXIS 19619), March 28, 2002. p. 11.

[10] See *The Petoskey City Record*, August 15, 1883.

[11] See *News-Review*, July 15, 2004.

[12] Ibid.

[13] See *Daily Resorter*, August, 23, 1979.

[14] See Pilcher, *Elijah Pilcher Memoirs*, Burton Historical Collection, Detroit Public Library, 1885, p. 557.

# Bibliography


Addams, Jane. *The Spirit of Youth and the City Streets*. New York: The MacMillan Company, 1909.

Allured, Donald. Interview with Mary Jane Doerr, August, 2001.

Ames, Dr. Donald. E-mails to Mary Jane Doerr regarding Dr. Roy Elmer Heath. June 10-14, 2004.

Amy, Dr. Jonathan. Interview with Mary Jane Doerr. Bay View, MI: August 10, 2000.

Amy, Dr. Jonathan. E-mail to Mary Jane Doerr. February 13, 2001.

Amy, Dr. Jonathan. *Theatre in Bay View, 1937-1942*. E-mail to Mary Jane Doerr, November 21, 1998. Used by Permission.

Amy Dr. Jonathan. E-mails to Mary Jane Doer concerning Dr. Roy Heath. June 2004.

Amy, Terry. Interview with Mary Jane Doerr. Bay View, MI: September 2, 2001.

Anonymous. *Darwinisn, Democracy, and the Public Schools*. Internet: http://www.freebooks.com/docs/html/gncf/Chapter07.htm,10/25/01

Anonymous. *Native of Latvia Comes Here as Methodist Minister.* Circulation-Member of Audit Bureau of Circulation. January 6, 1949.

Armstrong, Fanny L. *To The Noon Rest: The Life, Work and Addresses of Mrs. Helen M. Stoddard*. Butler, IN: L. H. Higley, Publisher, 1909.

Arnold, J.M. *A sketch of the History of Methodism in Detroit.* Michigan Pioneer Collections. Vol. 3 (1881) p. 225-243.

Asbury, Barbara. *Willard among the Stars.* Bay View, MI: August, 1992.

Avery, Helen M. and Nye, Frank W. *The Clubwoman's Book.* New York: Henry Holt and Company, 1954.

Baker, Carlos. *Ernest Hemingway: A Life Story.* New York: Charles Scribner's Sons, 1969.

Baker, Emma Lamb. *Stories of Bay View*. Detroit: Published by Author, 1925.

Barlow, Edison L., ed. *Barlow of Barlow.* Rochester, MI: May, 1994.

*Bay View Assembly Herald*. Flint, MI: Published by the Bay View Assembly, June, 1886 to June, 1894.

*Bay View Assembly Program*. Bay View, MI: Published by the Bay View Association, 1886-1901, 1909-11.

*Bay View Assembly Record.* Bay View, MI: Published by the Bay View Association, 1895.

*Bay View Bulletin*. Bay View, MI: Published by the Bay View Association, 1912-17, 1920 – present.

*Bay View Herald.* Published by the Michigan State Campground Association of the Methodist Episcopal Church. Grand Rapids, MI: Printing House of I. S. Dygert, 1884.

*Bay View Landmark Documents.* East Lansing, MI: Michigan State Historic Preservation Office.

*Bay View Magazine*. Detroit: Bay View Reading Circle, 1893-21.

*Bay View Mirror.* Bay View, MI: Bay View Association, 1901-06.

*Bay View Reflector*. Bay View, MI: Bay View Association, 1918-1919.

*Bay View, The Summer City of Michigan.* Bay View, MI: J. F. Arnold, 1894, reprinted, Bay View Historical Museum, 2002.

Becker, Marion Rombauer. Letter to Juanita and Don Vogelsberg. August 30, 1973. Used by permission.

Beer, Martin. Telephone Interview with Mary Jane Doerr. September 2, 1998.

"Bendix, Max." Chicago, IL: Chicago Symphony Orchestra: Rosenthal Archives. March 2, 1999.

BeVier, Thomas. "Our Man Paul." *Traverse Northern Michigan's Magazine*. January 2006.

Bieber, David. Phone Interview with Mary Jane Doerr. Ponte Vedra Beach, Fl: October, 1998.

"Blanshard, Brand." *New York Times*. Biographical Service, January 30, 1980.

Blanshard, Brand. Letter to Sterling Sanford. Nov. 1, 1975. Used by permission of the families.

Blanshard, Jane. E-mails to Mary Jane Doerr. 2000-Present.

Blanshard, Paul B. *American Freedom and Catholic Power*. Boston: The Beacon Press, 1949.

Blanshard, Paul B. Microfilm Collection. Ann Arbor: Bentley Library, University of Michigan, 1914-20.

Blanshard, Paul B.. "Obituary." *Time Magazine.* February 11, 1980.

Blanshard, Paul B. *Personal and Controversial, An Autobiography.* Boston: Beacon Press, 1973.

Blanshard, Dr. Rufus. Interview with Mary Jane Doerr. Storrs, CN: February 20, 2000.

Blinderman, Abraham. *American Writers on Education After 1865*. Boston: Twayne Publishers, 1976.

Bordin, Ruth. *Frances Willard.* Chapel Hill, NC: The University of North Carolina Press, 1986.

Bostick, Nan. Interview with Mary Jane Doerr. January 4, 1999.

Bostick, Nan. E-mails with Mary Jane Doerr. 1999, 2001.

Bradley, Bonnie Cave. *William J. Reddick, Composer-Musician*. Ph.D. Thesis, University of Kentucky, 1986.

*Brewery District Society vs. Federal Highway Administration.* United States District Court for the Southern District of Ohio Eastern Division. Case No. 98CV00075 (211 F.Supp.2d 902;2002 U.S. Dist. LEXIS 19619), March 28, 2002.

Brockway, Martha. Letter to Bruce Brockway. October 8, 1950.

Brockway, Porter Bruce, M.D. "The Brockway Family's Contribution to Albion (1897)."*Michigan Christian Advocate,* March, 1950.

Brockway, Porter Bruce, M.D. Letter to Jane Park Doerr. June 9, 1982.

Brown, Kenneth O. *Holy Ground, Too*: *The Camp Meeting Family Tree*. Hazleton, PA: 1997.

Brown, Kevin. "Wild Idea Born in 1960s May Bear Fruit in 1980s." *Mining Journal*. January 3, 1985.

Brown, Rose L. *Cavewomen to Clubwomen*. Philadelphia: Dorrace and Company Publishers, 1938.

Brunger, Ronald A. "William H. Brockway - A Varied Ministry." *Michigan Christian Advocate*. May 28, 1964.

Brunger, Ronald A. "Elijah Holmes Pilcher, M.D., D.D. *Methodist History,* July, 1964.

Brunger, Ronald A. "One of the Eminent Bay View Founders, William H. Brockway." *Michigan Christian Advocate*. March, 1950.

Brunger, Ronald A. "Seth Reed, Centenarian of Michigan Methodism." *Michigan Christian Advocate*. June 16, 1966.

Bryant, Cheryl Heath. E-mails to Mary Jane Doerr concerning Dr. Roy Elmer Heath. April 4, 2003 through June 27, 2004. Used by permission of Bryant.

Buttrick, Reverand David. Interview with Mary Jane Doerr. Six Mile Lake, MI: June 18, 2002.

Canning, Charlotte M. *The Most American Thing in America: Circuit Chautauqua as Performance.* Iowa City, IO: University of Iowa Press, 2005.

Carolan, Ann. "Hemingway's Michigan Home Welcomes a Film Crew." *Chicago Tribune Sunday*: September 13, 1987.

Carter, Robert M. *Forum on the Bay: Oral Communication Aspects of the Bay View Association: 1875-1965.* Ph.D. Thesis, Michigan State University, 1966.

Cattrell, Jacques, *American Men and Women of Science, Physical and Biological Science*. New York: Cattrell Press, R. R. Bowker Co. 1986.

Central Methodist Church, Pontiac, MI: *Dedication Program*, 1907.

Central United Methodist Church, Traverse City, MI: http://tccentralumc.org/

Cerf, Bennett, Cartmell, Van H.; comp. *SRO: The Most Successful Plays of the American Stage*. Garden City, NY: Doubleday, 1934.

Chambers, Jr., S. Allen and Hillary Rodham-Clinton. *National Landmarks, America's Treasures*. Washington, D.C.: John Wiley & Sons, 2000.

Chandler, Marilyn. *Bay View Week of Handbells, 1978-2002.* Bay View, MI: August 15, 2002.

*Chautauqua*. Vol. 13, #2. Dearborn, MI: Henry Ford Museum & Greenfield Village *Herald*, 1984.

*Chautuauqua News*. Vol. 4, Issue 1. Waxahachie, TX: Chautauqua Preservation Society. January/February 2003.

Christensen, Robert. E-mail to Mary Jane Doerr concerning WEN Hunter. March 28, 2005.

Cittadino, Eugene. "A Marvelous Cosmopolitan Preserve: The Dunes, Chicago, and the Dynamic Ecology of Henry Cowles." *Perspectives on Science.* Vol. 1, No. 3. University of Chicago: 1993.

*City of Detroit Michigan, The*. Vol. III. Detroit-Chicago: The S. J. Clarke Publishing Company, 1922.

Clarke, Don H. *Copper Mines of Keweenaw, No. 11 Minesota Mining Company*. Rockland, MI: Published by Author, 1978.

Cobern, Camden, M. D.D., Litt.D. *The New Archeological Discoveries.* New York: Funk & Wagnalls Co., 1929 edition.

Cobern, Camden. "*The Work at Tell El Hesy,* as seen by an American Visitor." Palestine Exploration Fund, Quarterly Statement for 1890. London.

Coletta, Paolo E. *William Jennings Bryan, Political Evangelist 1860-1908.* Lincoln: Universityof Nebraska Press, 1964.

Collins, Liza Lee. Interview with Mary Jane Doerr. Bay View, MI: September 16, 2004.

*Complete Chautauquan, The: A Guide to What 'Chautauqua' Means in America.* Jeffrey Scott Maxwell. http://members.aol.com/AlphaChautauquan/what.html

Connable, Ralph. Letter, Chautauqua Archives, Chautauqua Institutions, New York, NY: 1899.

Court Street Methodist Church, Church House.1929, University of Michigan Bentley Library, Records of Methodist Churches in Michigan. *Court Street Courier*, April 14, 1929.

Crathern, Alice Tarbell. *Courage Was the Fashion*. Detroit, MI: Wayne University Press for The Women's Achievement Committee, 1953.

Croly, Jennie June. *Woman's Club Movement in America*. New York: Henry G. Allen & Co., 1898.

Crouse, David. Telephone Interview with Mary Jane Doerr. November, 1988.

Crouse, Jay. Telephone Interview with Mary Jane Doerr. November, 1998.

Culpepper, Marilyn. *Mary Mayo: Leader of Rural Women.* Lansing, MI: Michigan Women's Studies Association, 1987.

Dagnall, Sally W. *Martha's Vineyard*. Oak Bluffs: Martha's Vineyard Campground Association, 1984.

Day, Eric H. "Sketches of the Northwest." *Michigan Pioneer and Historical Collections*. Lansing, MI: Robert Smith & Co., State Printers and Binders for the Michigan Pioneer and Society Collections, 16:205-56, 1890.

Davis, Charles H. S., M.D., Ph.D., and Cobern, Rev. Camden, A.B., S.T.B., Ph.D. *Ancient Egypt.* Meriden, CT: Biblia Publishing Co., 1892.

*Daily Resorter.* Petoskey, MI: Published by the *Independent Democrat* and the *Petoskey Evening News,* 1883-1917.

"Death of Michigan's Prohibition Leader: David Preston." Detroit, MI: *Detroit News*, April 15, 1887.

*DeLand's History of Jackson County Michigan*. Jackson, MI: 1903.

Dibble, Lewis C. "Rev. Seth Reed, Grand Old Man of Methodism, Nears 100th Birthday." *Flint Journal.* May 27, 1923.

Dickie, Mrs. Mary Brockway. *Reminiscences of William Brockway*. Undated.

Docking, Dr. Robert and Mill. Interview with Mary Jane Doerr. Bay View, MI: July 3, 2002.

Doidge, David and Mary. Interview with Mary Jane Doerr, Bay View, MI: Aug. 6, 2000.

Doerr, Jane, and Doerr, Mary Jane. *Bay View's Goodly Heritage.* Bay View, MI: Bay View Association of the United Methodist Church, 1976.

Doerr, Mary Jane. "Bay View, A Michigan Chautauqua." *The Michigan Connection*, Lansing, MI: Michigan Council for the Humanities, Winter-Spring, 1984

Doerr, Mary Jane. "Bay View's Current History continues Impressive Record." *Chautauqua Network News*, Vol. XIII, No. 2. Chautauqua, NY: April 1996.

Doerr, Mary Jane and Guittard, Helen. "In Celebration of Bay View." Bay View, MI: Video, Published by the Bay View Association for the National Landmark Presentation. July, 1988.

Doerr, Mary Jane. "Hall Years," *Beneath the Beeches.* Bay View, MI: Published by the Bay View Association, 2000.

Doerr, Mary Jane. "Music," *Beneath the Beeches*. Bay View, MI: Published by the Bay View Association, 2000.

Duquette, Kathy. "Did You Know That Bay View Was One Of Only 2,341 Landmarks Nationwide?" *The Town Crier.* Vol. X, Issue 9. Bay View: July 26, 2002.

Eccles, Richard L. and Inge. Interview with Mary Jane Doerr. Bay View, MI: July 1, 2002.

Eckert, Kathryn Bishop. *Buildings of Michigan*. Oxford: Oxford University Press, 1993.

Echert, Kathryn Bishop. E-mails from 2000 to 2005 to Mary Jane Doerr concerning buildings in Michigan and information concerning Bay View Landmark effort.

Edman, John R. Email to Mary Jane Doerr concerning the Raymond J. Wade Administration Building, January 14, 2005.

Edwards, Amelia B. *Egypt and Its Monuments.* New York: Harper & Bros. for the Bay View Reading Circle, 1891.

Ely, Richard T. *Ground Under Our Feet.* New York: MacMillan, 1938.

*Emmet County Democrat*. Petoskey, MI: Published by Rozelle Rose, 1875-86.

Engle, Dr. W. A. *Poems*. Chicago: Dibble Publishing Co.1883.

Farmer, Silas. *History of Detroit And Wayne Country and Early Michigan: A Chronological Cyclopedia of the Past and Present*. Detroit: Silas Farmer and Company for Munsoll &Company, New York, 1890.

Farnsworth, Mary. Letter. Phoenix, AZ: August, 1964. Used by Permission of Dr. James and Bernice Beard.

Farrand, Elizabeth M. *History of the University of Michigan*. Ann Arbor, MI. Register Publishing House, 1885.

Farrar, Hughes, Gladden, Gustafson, Ely, Cable, Riis, Mitchell, and Behrends. *My Brother and I.* New York: Hunt & Eaton, 1895.

Fennimore, Keith J. *The Heritage of Bay View, 1875-1975:* A *Centennial History.* Grand Rapids: William B. Eerdmans Publishing Co., 1975.

First United Methodist Church, Hastings, MI: http://my.voyager.net/07/7F/fumc/fumc/

First United Methodist Church, (Soul Harvest Ministries) Highland Park, MI: http://www.woodwardheritage.com/historicalsites/first.united.methodist.html

First United Methodist Church, Big Rapids, MI: http://michsite.state.mius/detlsite.cfm?ObjectID=11838

First United Methodist Church, Warsaw, IN: http://www.warsawfumc.org/church.htm. http://yesteryear.clunette.com/mechurch.html

"Four Methodists are named among the top preachers of the 20th century by Preaching Magazine." *United Methodist News Service*: December 17, 1999.

"Frank X. Oliver Victim of Stroke." *Daily Journal*. Flint, MI: August 12, 1911.

Gale, Martha Brockway. *Letters to Bruce Brockway*. October 8, 1950 and April 12, 1952.

Garfield, Charles W. *Semi-Centennial Celebration of Michigan State Agricultural College*. Lansing: 1908.

Gaustad, Edwin S., ed. *A Documentary History of Religion in America since 1865.* Grand Rapids: William B. Eerdmans Publishing Co., 1993.

*General Motors - Corporate Info – History-1900.* http://www.gm.com/company/corp_info/history/gmhis1900.html

Gildart, Robert. *Albion College, 1835-1960.* Albion, MI: Albion College, 1961.

Giel, Dorothy and Lawrence. *Anna Howard Shaw: Orator.* Lansing, MI: Michigan Women's Studies Association, 1987.

Glad, Paul W. *The Trumpet Soundeth: William Jennings Bryan and His Democracy, 1896-1912* Lincoln: University of Nebraska Press, 1960.

Glick, David. "The Independent Chautauquas, Then and Now." Dearborn: *Henry Ford Museum & Greenfield Village Herald.* Vol. 13, #2. 1984.

Glick, David. Email to Mary Jane Doerr. June 1998. Used by Permission.

Gordon, Anna A. *Frances E. Willard, A Memorial Volume*. Chicago, IL: Woman's Temperance Publishing Association, 1898.

Gorham, Reverand B. W. *Camp Meeting Manual*. Boston, MA: H. V. Degen, 1854.

Gould, Joseph E. *The Chautauqua Movement.* Albany: State University of New York Press, 1961.

Graham, Floy Irene. *Petoskey and Bay View in Ye Olden Days.* Petoskey, MI: 1938.

Guittard, Helen and Lewis, Anne. *Bay View Beginnings, the First 25 Years, 1875-1900.* Bay View: Bay View Museum, 2000.

Hager, Dr. Wesley. "The Hagers – Leaders in two communities". *The Graphic.* July 16, 1981.

Halsey, John R. "Jackson's Quiet Promoter." Lansing, MI: *Michigan History*. Nov./Dec., 1998.

Halsey, John R. "S. O. Knapp." E-mail to Mary Jane Doerr. November 26, 2001. Used by Permission.

Hamilton, Robert. E-mails to Mary Jane Doerr concerning

W.E.N. Hunter Churches in Ontario. April 12, 2005.

Hamm, Margherita Arlina. "Some Women Editors." *The Peterson Magazine*. Vol. VI., No. 6. New York: June, 1896.

Harrison, Harry P. as told to Karl Detzer. *Culture under Canvas; The Story of Tent Chautauqua*. New York: Hastings House, 1958.

Harvey, Roy. Interview with Mary Jane Doerr. Bay View, MI: June 13, 1999.

Heckscher, August. *When LaGuardia was Mayor*. New York: W. W. Norton & Company, 1978.

Hendrick, Illwood. *Lewis Miller, A Biographical Essay*. New York: G. P. Putnam's Sons, The Knickerbocher Press, 1925.

Hicks, Dr. Elizabeth M. Holtz. Interview with Mary Jane Doerr. Bay View, MI: June, 2003.

Higgins, John. E-mail to Mary Jane Doerr concerning Victor Blandford. February 24, 2005. Used with permission.

Hill, Eric J. FAIA, John Gallagher. *AIA Detroit. The American Institute of Architects Guide toDetroit Architecture.* Detroit, MI: Wayne State University Press, 2003.

Historic Grace Episcopal Church, Mt. Clemens, MI: http://www.gracemtclemens.org/docs/church.htm. http://www.gracemtclemens.org/docs/history4.htm

*Historic Preservation Guild of Bay View vs. James H. Burnley; Robert Farris; James P. Pitz, United States Court of Appeals, Sixth Circuit.* No. 88-2080." (Cite as: 896 F.2d 985). December 15, 1989.

History Museum Archives. Petoskey, MI: Little Traverse Historical Society.

*History of Jackson County, Michigan*. Chicago: Inter-State Publishing Co., 1881.

*History of Rockland Township.* Rockland, MI: Published under direction of the Bicentennial Committee, 1976.

*History of the Upper Peninsula of Michigan*. Chicago: The Western Historical Company, 1883.

Hollinshead, Ann. *Eminent and Interesting Albionians*. Vol. 1. Albion, MI: Albion College Alumni Association, 1955.

Howard, Joseph L. *Madame Ernestine Schumann-Heink, Her Life and Times*. Sebastopol, CA: Grizzly Bear Publishing, 1990.

Howard Barlow Collection. Danbury, CN: Western Connecticut State University, University Archives.

*Hugo Gottesmann gestorben*. Wiener Kultur-Notizen. Sonderdienst Der Rathaus- Korrespondenz. Nummer 26, 1970.

Humphrey, Elizabeth. Interview with Mary Jane Doerr. Ellsworth, MI: March 24, 1999.

Hunter, Kirk and Maureen Moore. *The Chautauqua Network Links Chautauquas Across U.S.* Vol. 4, Issue 1. Waxahachie, TX.: Chautauqua Preservation Society, January/February, 2003.

Hunter, WEN "Obituary." *Detroit Free Press*. Feb. 5, 1947.

Hunter, WEN "Obituary" *Michigan Society of Architects*. 1947.

*Independent Democrat.* Petoskey, MI: Published by Hampton, 1887.

Irwin, Alfreda L. *Three Taps of the Gavel: Pledge to the Future.* Chautauqua, NY: Chautauqua Institution, 1987.

Irwin, Alfreda L. Interview with Mary Jane Doerr. Chautauqua, NY: March, 1984.

*Jackson City Directory*. Detroit: R. L. Polk & Co., Publishers, 1875.

*Jackson City Directory and Business Advertiser*. Jackson, MI: James M. Thomas, 1876.

*Jackson County Michigan, Plat and Atlas for 1858*. Paul R. Peck, ed. Jackson, MI: LaRue Printing Co. for The Liberty Township Historical Society, 1974.

Jameson, Sheilagh S. *Chautauqua in Canada.* Calgary, Alberta: Glenbow-/Alberta Institute, 1987.

Jamison, James K. *The Mining Ventures of This Ontonagon Country*. Ontonagon, MI: Published by Author, 1950.

Jamison, James K. *This Ontonagon Country*. Ontonagon, MI: The Ontonagon Herald Co., 1948.

Jamison, Knox. *The History of Ontonagon County Towns.* Ontonagon, MI: Published by Author, 1967.

Jarvis, Nancy H., ed. *Historical Glimpses, Petoskey*. Petoskey, MI: Little Traverse Historical Society, 1986.

John M. Hall Papers. University Libraries Special Collections: Redpath Chautauqua Collections, 1910-20. University of Iowa, Iowa City, IA.

Jones, Charles Edwin, *Perfectionist Persuasion: The Holiness Movement and American Methodism, 1867-1936.* Metuchen, NJ: Scarecrow Press, Inc., 1974.

Jones, Edgar DeWitt. *A Man Stood Up to Preach.* St. Louis: The Bethany Press, 1943.

Kidd, Reverend David. Interview with Mary Jane Doerr concerning Memorial Garden. Bay View, MI: Aug. 4, 2002.

Krause, David J. *The Making of a Mining District: Keweenaw Native Copper, 1500-1870.* Detroit: Wayne State University Press, 1992.

Kresge, Bruce and family. Interview with Mary Jane Doerr. Bay View, MI: September 28, 2002.

Kynett, Alpha G. "The Bishops of the Methodist Episcopal Church." *The Peterson Magazine.* Vol. V. No. 1. New York: January, 1895.

Laitner, Bill. *Interview with Stanley Kresge*. Unpublished. Used by Permission of Writer and Family.1984.

Latiner, Bill. E-mail to Mary Jane Doerr regarding Stanley Kresge. February 11, 2005. Used by Permission.

Lane, Barbara Ingram. Letter to Mary Jane Doerr concerning J. Will Callahan and Ernest R. Ball, May 20, 2001.

Larsen, Homer, "A rendezvous with life." *The Graphic*. July 2, 1987.

Larsen, John C. " 'All This From Books We Could Not Own:' The Story of Michigan's Traveling Libraries." *Michigan History.* Vol. 61, No.1, Spring, 1977.

Leach, Dr. Morgan Lewis. *Grand Traverse Region*. Traverse City, MI: *Grand Traverse Herald*, 1883. Limited Ed.: Grand Traverse Pioneer & Historical Socicty of Traverse City, 1988.

Levy, Benjamin. E-mails to Mary Jane Doerr concerning Landmark. December, 2004 and October 31, 2004.

Lewis, Anne and Guittard, Helen. *Bay View Beginnings, The First 25 Years, 1875-1900.*Bay View, MI: Summer, 2000.

Lewis, Charles.A. "Latvians in Michigan." *Michigan History*. Vol. 40, No. 4. Ann Arbor: Michigan Historical Commission, Dec. 1956.

Linkugel, Will A., and Martha Solomon. *Anna Howard Shaw, Suffrage Orator and Social Reformer.* New York: Greenwood Press, 1991.

Livermore, Mary A. *The Story of My Life*. Hartford, CN: A. D. Worthington & Co. Publishers, 1897.

Lockwood, Charlotte. *Church on Main Street, A History of the First United Methodist Church,Jackson, Michigan.* Book One, 1831-1943. Jackson, MI: Citizen Job Printing House for the First United Methodist Church, 1947.

MacLaren, Gay. *Morally We Roll Along*. Boston: Little, Brown, and Co., 1938.

Macmillan, Dr. Margaret Burnham. *The Methodist Church in Michigan: The Nineteenth Century.* Grand Rapids, MI: The Michigan Area Methodist Historical Society and William B. Eerdmans Publishing Company, 1967.

MacNaughton, Dr. A. Douglas. *The Methodist Church in Michigan: The Twentieth Century.*Grand Rapids: The Michigan Area United Methodist Church Historical Society and William B. Eerdmans Publishing Co., 1976.

Majeske, Daniel H. "Obituary." *Cleveland Plain Dealer*. Cleveland: Archives of the Musical, Arts Association and the Cleveland Orchestra, November 29, 1993.

Manhattan Project. Internet: www.me.utexas.edu/~uer/manhattan

Marin, Helen. Interview with Mary Jane Doerr. *Graphic Resorter*. August 28, 1980.

Marshall, Thomas R. *Recollections of Thomas R. Marshall.* Indianapolis: Bobbs-Merrill Co., 1925.

Marx, Leon. Letter to Mary Jane Doerr from Chicago Symphony Orchestra: Rosenthal Archives. Chicago, IL: March 2, 1999.

Massie, Larry B. *On the Road to Michigan's Past.* Allegan Forest, MI: The Priscilla Press, 1995.

Matthews, Linda Jones. Letter to Mary Jane Doerr, November, 1997.

Mattingly, Carol. "Woman-Tempered Rhetoric: Public Presentation and the WCTU." *Rhetoric Review*, Vol.14, No. 1, Fall, 1995.

Mauch, Doris Hunter. Interview with Mary Jane Doerr. Bay View, MI: August 30, 2000.

Maw, Blanche Blynn. comp. *A History of the Michigan State Federation of Women's Clubs 1895-1953.* Ann Arbor: Ann Arbor Press for the Michigan State Federation of Women's Clubs, 1953.

Maxwell, Jeffrey Scott. *The Complete Chautauquan.* Internet: http://members.aol.com/AlphaChautauquan/movement.html March 22, 2004.

McClarran, Harry S. *A Flying Fish, A History of the Independent Chautauqua Assembly Movement.* Unpublished. Archives of the Chautauqua Institutions, NY: August 1, 1994.

McCullough, David. "Chautauqua and Its Place in American Culture." Chautauqua, NY: Speech, August 9, 1993.

McCutchan. Robert Guy. "Obituary." Greencastle, IN: Archives and Special Collections, Roy O. West Library. July 2, 1999.

*Memories of Jane Cunningham Croly "Jennie June."* New York City: The Knickerbocker Press for the Woman's Press Club of New York City, 1904.

Mendelson, Anne. *Stand Facing the Stove*. New York: Henry Holt and Co., 1996.

Merritt, Elizabeth S. Telephone Interview with Mary Jane Doerr from National Trust for Historic Preservation. Washington, D. C., January 10, 2005.

Meyer, Edith Patterson. *Not Charity, But Justice: The Story of Jacob A. Riis*. New York: Vanguard Press, 1974.

Mierzwa, Timothy F. "Ancient Copper Mining." *Great Lakes Trader*. Williamston, MI: April, 2007.

Millar, Valerie Jane. *The Organizational Entry and Socialization of Women in Educational Leadership Positions: A Case Study*. Ph.D. Thesis, Eastern Michigan University, 2000.

Modisett, Franklin, ed. *The Credo of the Commoner, William Jennings Bryan.* Los Angeles: Occidental College, 1968.

Morley, Margaret Warner. *A Song of Life*. Chicago: A. C. McClurg and Co. for the Bay View Reading Circle, 1897.

Morris-Crowther, Jayne. "Municipal Housekeeping: The Political Activities of the Detroit Federation of Women's Clubs in the 1920s." *The Michigan Historical Review*. Vol. 30, No.1, Spring, 2004.

Morrison, Theodore. *Chautauqua.* Chicago, IL: The University of Chicago Press, 1974.

Murdock, Angus (1964). *Boom Copper: The Story of the First U.S. Mining Boom*. Calumet, MI: Roy W. Drier and Louis G. Koepel, 1964.

"Native of Latvia Comes Here as Methodist Minister." *Circulation-Member of Audit Bureau of Circulation*: January 6, 1949.

Neithercut, Edward. Interview with Mary Jane Doerr. Bay View: July 12, 2003.

Nichols, Dr. Will. Interview with Mary Jane Doerr. Alma, MI: April 22, 1999.

Noffsinger, John S. *Correspondence Schools, Lyceums, Chautauquas.* New York: The MacMillan Co., 1926.

Noll, Mark A. *A History of Christianity in the United States and Canada*. Grand Rapids: William B. Eerdmans Publishing Co., 1992.

Obituaries of Charles Henry Adams, C. C. Case, and William Kilgore Breckenridge, Oberlin, OH: Oberlin College Archives, March 19, 1999.

Obituaries of Mrs. Margaret Custer Calhoun. Mrs. David Reed, and Mrs. Anna Gibson Yates, Monroe, MI: Monroe County Historical Commission.

Obituary of W.E.N. Hunter, *History of City of Detroit*. Detroit: S.T. Clarke Publishing Co. 1922, Vol. III. 870.

Orchard, Hugh A. *Fifty Years of Chautauqua.* Cedar Rapids, IA: 1923.

Otis, Philo Adams. *The Chicago Symphony Orchestra.* Chicago: Clayton F. Summy Co.1924.

Pailthorp, Hon. Charles J. "Speech to Petoskey Kiwanis Club." History Museum. Petoskey: July, 1932.

Palmer, Kathy. E-mail to Mary Jane Doerr concerning Traverse City Central Methodist Church. February 7, 2005.

Panney, Mildred F. Place. Telephone Interview with Mary Jane Doerr, Grand Rapids, MI:September 10, 2004.

Parmele, Mary Platt. *Germany.* Flint, MI: Bay View Reading Circle, 1897.

Parry, Emma Louise. *Life Among the Germans*. Flint, MI: Bay View Reading Circle, 1897.

Parish, Julia R. *The Poems and Written Addresses of Mary T. Lathrap*. Michigan: Woman's Christian Temperance Union of Michigan, 1895.

Pegolotti, James. "Howard Barlow and The Rise and Fall of Classical Music on Commercial Radio." *Connecticut Review.* Vol. XVII, No.1. New Haven: Connecticut State University. Spring 1995.

People's Church, East Lansing, MI: http://kevinforsyth.net/ELMI/peoples.htm

Perry, Belle McArthur. *Lucinda Hinsdale Stone*. Detroit, MI: The Blinn Publishing Company, 1902.

*Petoskey Evening News.* Petoskey, MI: Churchill and E. R. Goldsmith, 1902-1952.

*Petoskey News-Review.* Petoskey, MI: Petoskey Evening News Association, 1952-present.

*Petoskey City Record.* Petoskey, MI: James Buckley and George A. Mosher, 1887-1911.

Pierce, Willard. Interviews with Mary Jane Doerr. Sarasota, FL: November 14 and 21, 1998.

Pilcher, Elijah. *Elijah Pilcher Memoirs.* Burton Historical Collection, Detroit Public Library, 1885.

Pilcher, Elijah. *Protestantism in Michigan*. Detroit: R.D.S. Tyler & Co., Publishers, 1878.

Pitezel, Reverend John H. *Lights and Shades of Missionary Life.* Cincinnati: Western Book Concern, 1857.

Plunkett-Powell, Karen. *Remembering Woolworth's.* New York: St. Martin's Press, 1999.

Pond, Major James. *Diary*. July 2, 1895. Used by Courtesy of David Eicher.

Prescott, William Ray. *The Fathers Still Speak, A History of Michigan Methodism*. Michigan: Michigan Printing Service, 1941.

Rajala, Nancy. E-mails to Mary Jane Doerr concerning John M. Hall, April 29, 2004.

Reed, Seth. Letter to the Michigan Conference of the Methodist Church, 1923.

Reed, Seth. *The Story of My Life*. Cincinnati, OH: Jennings & Graham, 1914.

Resnick, Felix. Interview with Mary Jane Doerr. Huntington Woods, MI: December, 1998.

Rieser, Andrew D. *The Chautauqua Moment: Protestants, Progressives, and the Culture of Modern Liberalism*. New York: Columbia University Press, 2003.

Riis, Jacob A. *How the Other Half Lives*. New York: Penquin Books, 1997 edition.

Rombauer, Irma S. *The Joy of Cooking*. St. Louis: A. C. Clayton Printing Co., 1931.

Root, Margaret Cool. *Faces of Immortality.* Ann Arbor, MI: Kelsey Museum of Archaeology, The University of Michigan, 1979.

Root, Margaret Cool. Email and Telephone Interview with Mary Jane Doerr. Ann Arbor: July 19, 2001.

Royal Oak Methodist Episcopal Church, MI: http://www.michmarkers.com/startup.asp?startpage=L1739.htm

Ryan, Scott. "The Rational Temper: Brand Blanshard and What Objectivists Can Learn From Him." http://www.monadnock.net/essays/blanshard.html.

Rybczynski, Witold (1999). *A Clearing in the Distance*. New York, NY: Charles Scribner's Sons, 1999.

Sandburg, Carl. *Ever the Winds of Chance*. Urbana and Chicago: University of Illinois Press, 1983.

Sanford, John. Interview with Mary Jane Doerr. Bay View: July, 1999.

Sanford, Marcelline Hemingway. *At the Hemingways'.* Moscow, ID: University of Idaho Press, 1998.

Sanford, Sterling. *As I Remember Bay View*. unpublished: undated. Used by permission.

Sanford, Sterling, Letters to Bob Marshall. December 2, 1974; January 20, 1975. Copies given to Mary Jane Doerr for publication.

Sanford, Sterling. Letter to Mary Jane Doer and Jane Park Doerr. January 30, 1985.

Sanford, Sterling. Interview with Mary Jane Doerr and Jane Park Doerr. Grosse Pointe Farms: MI, December 15, 1984.

Scarrow, Dr. David. Interview with Mary Jane Doerr. Bay View: August 7, 2000.

Schimpke, Albert J. Photograph Series 88142 Aa2, Ann Arbor: Bentley Historical Library of U-M.

Schlipp, Paul Arthur. *The Philosophy of Brand Blanshard*. La Salle, IL: Open Court, 1980.

Schloff, Carolyn. Interview with Mary Jane Doerr. Bay View, MI: Aug. 4, 2002.

Schloff, Dr. Charles E. *A Pictorial History of Bay View.* Petoskey, MI: Published by Author. Mitchell Graphics, Inc. 2000.

Schultz, James R. *The Romance of Small-Town Chautuauquas*. Columbia, MO. University of Missouri Press, 2002.

Schwarz, Boris. *Great Masters of the Violin*. New York: Simon and Schuster, 1983.

Schwarz, Richard W. Ph.D. *John Harvey Kellogg, M.D.* Berrien Springs, MI: Andrews University Press, 1970.

Schurr, Cathleen. "Chautauqua: Yesterday and Today." *American History*, July/ August, 1992.

Shaw, Dr. Anna Howard. *The Story of a Pioneer*. New York:

Harper & Brothers Publishers, 1915.

Shearer, Thomas. *Telephone Interview with Mary Jane Doerr.* June 12, 2000.

Shepard, O. L. *The Story of Lakeside,* Lakeside, OH: The Lakeside Association, 1923.

Shier, Dr. William H. "Bay View History," *Golden Jubilee*. Bay View: Published by the Bay View Camp ground Association, 1925.

Ship's Log of the *Nokomis* and the *Simokon.* (1924-1955). Used by permission of Harry Begley.

Smith, Karen Manners. *New Paths to Power: American Women 1890-1920*. Oxford: Oxford University Press, 1994.

Smith, Max. Interview with Mary Jane Doerr. Bay View, MI: August 17, 2001.

Smith, Roy. "Fricis Timbers - Faithful." *The Christian Advocate.* July 18, 1946.

Smith, Stafford and Janice. Interview with Mary Jane Doerr. Petoskey, MI, July 15, 2000.

Smith, Stafford and Janice. *Stafford's Cookbook, 40 Years of Recipes from the Bay View Inn.* Petoskey, MI: Published by the authors. 2001.

Solms, Gertrude. Interview with Mary Jane Doerr. Petoskey, MI: May, 1999.

Spong, Bishop John Shelby. *A New Christianity for a New World: Why Traditional Faith is Dying and How a New Faith is Being Born*. New York: Harper Collins, 2001.

Sullivan, Ernest. Interview with Mary Jane Doerr, August 26, 1999.

Sullivan, John. Telephone Interview with Mary Jane Doerr. June 23, 2004.

Taussig, Walter. Telephone Interview with Mary Jane Doerr. New York: November 19, 1998.

*The 50 Most Significant Structures in Michigan.* Detroit, MI: Michigan Society of Architects, 1980.

*The Gods of Egypt.* Ann Arbor, MI: Kelsey Museum of Archaeology, The University of Michigan, 1977.

Tyler, Helen E. *Where Prayer and Purpose Meet: The WCTU Story, 1874-1949.* Evanston, IL: The Signal Press, 1949.

Ullrich, Donna. "The Bay View Magazine." *The Graphic.* Petoskey, MI: August 13, 1989.

Ross, Reverend E. United Methodist Church of Jackson. Interview with Mary Jane Doerr and Suzanne Ternan, Jackson, MI: October, 2004.

U.S. Department of Transportation, Federal Highway Administration, and Michigan Department of Transportation. *US-31 Petoskey Area Improvement Study, SUPPLEMENTAL DRAFT ENVIRONMENTAL IMPACT STATEMENT, Section 4(f)/6(f) Evaluation*. August, 2001.

Vaulis, Chris. Telephone Interview with Mary Jane Doerr. Bay View, MI: July, 2001.

Vincent, Leon H. *John Heyl Vincent, Biographical Sketch.* New York: Macmillan, 1925.

Vogelsberg, Don and Jaunita. Interview with Mary Jane Doerr. Bay View, MI: June 4, 2002.

Voorheis, Mary Ann. "In Tranquil Refuge: The Story of Harbor Point." *Harbor Light*: Aug. 12, 1971. Reprinted by Northern Country Publishing Corporation: Harbor Springs, MI.

Voss, Edward G. "Charles W. Fallass, Pioneer Michigan Botanist." *The Asa Gray Bulletin.* N. S. Vol. III., No.1. Spring, 1955. Ann Arbor, MI: The Gray Memorial Botanical Association.

Weeks, John. *Beneath the Beeches*. Bay View, MI: Bay View Association, 2000.

Weiss, Ellen. "Bay View, Michigan: Camp Meeting and Chautauqua." Chicago: *The Midwest in American Architecture.* University of Illinois Press, 1991.

Weiss, Ellen. *City in the Woods: The Life and Design of an American Camp Meeting on Martha's Vineyard.* New York: Oxford University Press, 1987.

Wesley United Methodist Church, Aurora, Illinois: http://glgm-umc.org/wesleyumcaurora/welcome.htm

Wheeler, Clark S. *Bay View.* Bay View, MI: Bay View Association of the Methodist Church, 1950.

*Who's Who in America*. 38th edition, Vol.1, Chicago, IL: Marquis Who's Who, Inc., 1974-75.

Withey, Henry F. and Elsie Rathburn Withey. Biographical Dictionary of American Architects (Deceased). Los Angles, CA: New Age Publishing Co., 1956.

Wiebe, Robert H. *The Search for Order: 1877-1920*. New York: Hill & Wang, 1967.

Willard, Frances E. *Women and Temperance.* Hartford, CT: Park Publishing Co., 1883.

Willard, Frances E. and Livermore, Mary A. *A Woman of the Century: LeadingAmerican Women*. Buffalo, NY: Charles Wells Moulton, 1893.

Willison, Keith, Interview with Mary Jane Doerr, Bay View, MI: August, 1999.

Witten, Sally Sue. *Lakeside's Women of Distinction.* Lakeside, OH: Published by Sally Sue Witten, 1996.

Woman's Home Companion. *The Woman's Book*. New York: The Crowell Publishing Co., 1907.

Zala, Edward. Interview with Mary Jane Doerr concerning Hugo Gottesmann. Ft. Wayne, IN: January, 1996.

Zuleski, Jim. E-mails to Mary Jane Doerr concerning Samuel O. Knapp. December 21, 2004.

# Index

**E**



**G**

## S



## T

**U**



**V**



**W**



**Y**



**Z**

*This postcard was mailed from Bay View on September 6, 1922, to the Gibson family in East Lansing. By then the Assembly had evolved from its strictly Methodist origins to attract patrons who might attend the interdenominational People's Church in East Lansing. The People's Church, incidently, had been designed by Detroit architect W.E.N. Hunter who also designed Bay View's John M. Hall Auditorium and the Recreation Hall. The popular pastor of the People's Church, Dr. N.A. McCune, also delivered sermons at the Petoskey Methodist Church.* (Courtesy of Larry Massie)